This Book Is a Comp... Study Guide to the Online Course.

http://www.nachi.org/radon-measurement-service-provider-online-course.htm

+ Amazon Wishlist   Read Now   Timezones   More   Other Bookmarks

MEMBERSHIP BENEFITS   STANDARDS & POLICIES   INSPECTOR EDUCATION   INSPECTION NEWS   MEMBERS ONLY   Search

find an inspector

Inspection News
Latest Inspection News
Inspection Success Strategies
Inspection Forum
Inspection Articles
Inspection Events
InterNACHI Blog

InterNACHI Membership
Membership Benefits
Membership Application
Renew Your Membership

Inspection Standards
Residential Standards of Practice
Commercial Standards of Practice
Code of Ethics

Inspection Education
Inspection Courses
Continuing Education Policy
Online Inspector Examination
Glossary of Inspection Terms
NACHI.TV Inspection Videos
Inspection Graphics

InterNACHI Inspectors
Find An Inspector
Featured Inspectors

Advanced Radon Measurement Service Provider Course

InterNACHI Members: Take the free, online *Advanced Radon Measurement Service Provider* course now (free to InterNACHI members)

The course is free to all InterNACHI members.

Upon successful completion of this course, the student shall be able to:

- describe the physics of radon;
- describe the health effects of breathing radon;
- follow protocols in non-real estate transactions;
- develop and follow a quality assurance plan and implement quality control procedures;
- properly use active devices;
- install effective mitigation systems in new homes;
- install materials and follow procedures to build radon-resistant homes;

- list the ways radon enters a home;
- describe the testing procedures for radon;
- follow protocols in real estate transactions;
- list different ways to approach radon mitigation in homes;
- properly use passive devices;
- inspect radon mitigation system; and
- abide by a Code of Ethics.

Take the online course at **www.nachi.org/radon-measurement-service-provider-online-course**

How to Perform Radon Inspections

The purpose of this publication is to teach the student how to perform radon measurements. It is based on the work of hundreds of scientists and radon experts, InterNACHI-certified home inspectors, InterNACHI, the U.S. Environmental Protection Agency (EPA), the World Health Organization (WHO), and the American Association of Radon Scientists and Technologists (AARST). This publication is a useful tool as a portable guide for inspectors on the job. It also serves as a study aid for InterNACHI's online Advanced Radon Measurement Service Provider course and exam.

To order additional training books, visit www.InspectorOutlet.com

Authors:

Ben Gromicko, Director of Education, International Association of Certified Home Inspectors

Nick Gromicko, Founder, International Association of Certified Home Inspectors

Graphics:

Lisaira Vega, Levi Nelson, Erica Saurey & Chris Krowiak

Editor:

Kate Tarasenko / Crimea River, LLC

Layout & Design:

Jessica Langer

www.NACHI.org

Table of Contents

Introduction

The risks to human health posed by ionizing radiation are well known. Radon gas is by far the most important source of ionizing radiation among gases of natural origin. Radon (Rn-222) is a noble gas formed from radium (Ra-226), which is a decay product of uranium (U-238). Uranium and radium occur naturally in soils and rocks. Other decay products of uranium include the isotopes thoron (Rn-220) and actinon (Rn-219). Radon gas, which has a half-life of 3.8 days, emanates from rocks and soils and tends to concentrate in enclosed spaces, such as underground mines or houses. It is a major contributor to the ionizing radiation dose received by the general population.

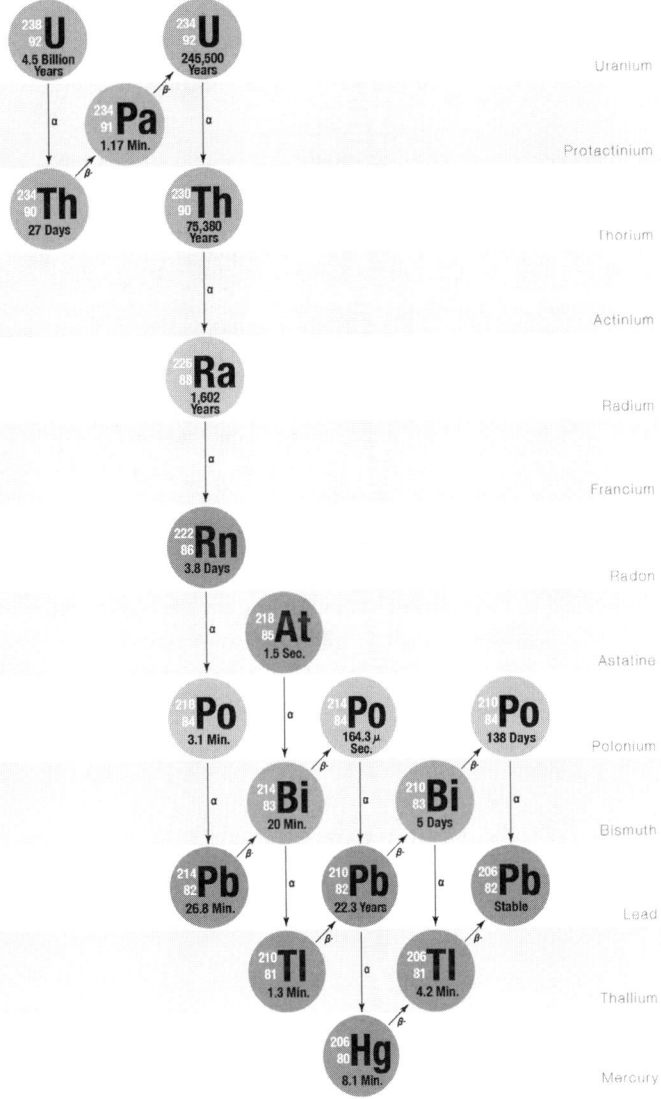

When radon gas is inhaled, densely ionizing alpha particles emitted by the deposited short-lived decay products of radon (Po-218 and Po-214) can interact with biological tissue in the lungs, leading to DNA damage. Cancer generally requires the occurrence of at least one mutation, and proliferation of intermediate cells that have sustained some degree of DNA damage can greatly increase the pool of cells available for the development of cancer. Since even a single alpha particle can cause major genetic damage to a cell, it is possible that radon-related DNA damage can occur at any level of exposure. Therefore, it is unlikely that there is a threshold concentration below which radon does not have the potential to cause lung cancer.

The health effects of radon, most notably lung cancer, have been investigated for several decades. Initially, investigations focused on underground miners exposed to high concentrations of radon in their occupational environment. However, in the early 1980s, several surveys of radon concentrations in homes and other buildings were carried out, and the results of these surveys, together with risk estimates based on the studies of mine workers, provided indirect evidence that radon may be an important cause of lung cancer in the general population. Recently, efforts to directly investigate the association between indoor radon and lung cancer have provided convincing evidence of increased lung cancer risk causally associated with radon, even at levels commonly found in buildings. Risk assessments for radon in both mines and residential settings have provided clear insights into the health risks due to radon. Radon is now recognized as the second-leading cause of lung cancer after smoking in the general population. The understanding of radon sources and radon transport mechanisms has evolved over several decades. In the 1950s, high concentrations of radon were observed in domestic and drinking water from drilled wells. Initially, concern about radon in water focused on health effects from ingesting the water. Later, it was determined that the primary health risk of radon in water was from the inhalation of radon released indoors. By the mid-1970s, emanation of radon from building materials was found to be a problem in some areas due to the use of alum shale with enhanced levels of radium.

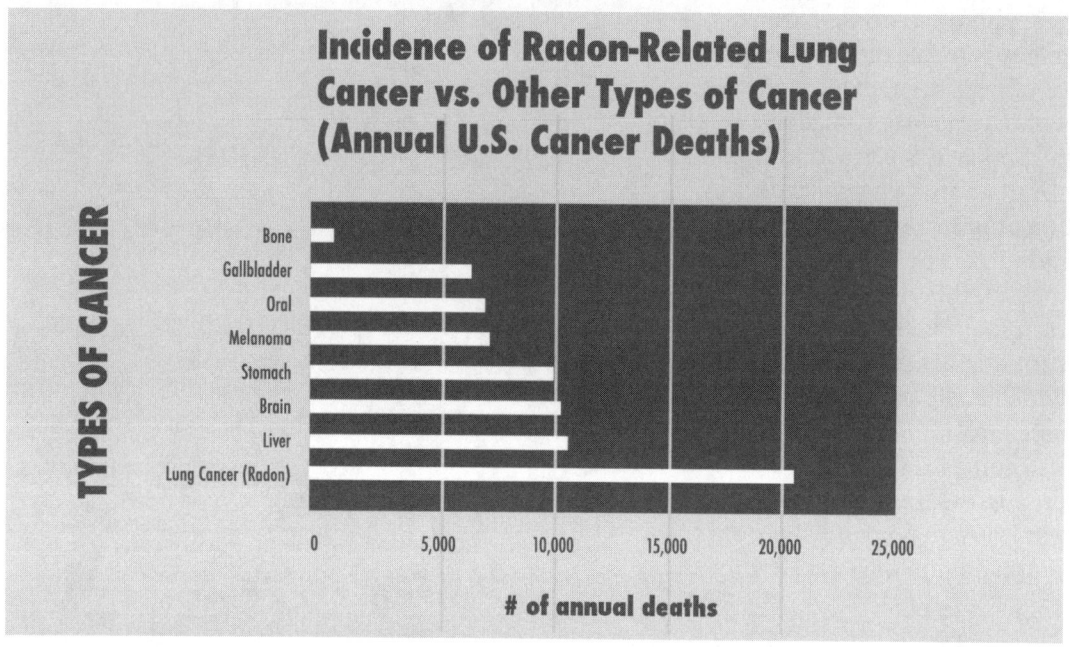

By 1978, houses were identified in which the indoor radon concentrations were not associated with well water transport or emanation from building materials. Soil gas infiltration became recognized as the most important source of indoor radon. Other sources, including building materials and well water, are less important in most circumstances.

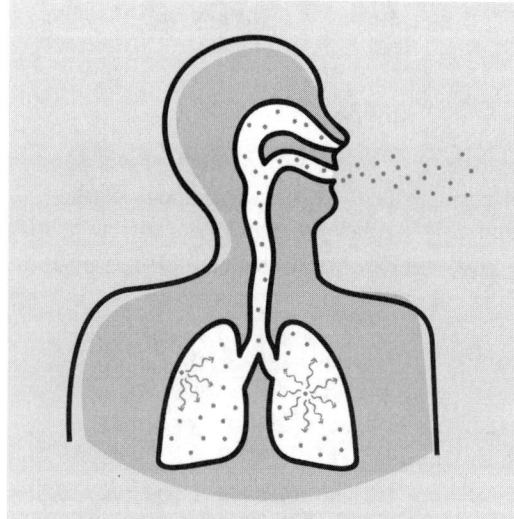

Epidemiological evidence indicates that indoor radon is responsible for a substantial number of lung cancers in the general population. The distribution of indoor radon in most countries is best represented by a log-normal distribution, with the majority of radon concentrations occurring in the lower range. As a result, most radon-induced lung cancers are thought to occur following exposure to low and moderate radon concentrations. There is now a remarkable coherence between the risk estimates developed from epidemiological studies of miners and residential case-control radon studies. While the miner studies provide a strong basis for evaluating risks from radon exposure and for investigating the effects of modifiers to the dose-response relation, the results of the recent pooled residential studies provide a direct method of estimating risks to people at home without the need for extrapolation from the miner studies.

Radon has little practical use. Some medical treatments have employed radon in small sealed glass tubes, called seeds, that are specially manufactured to contain the exact amount of radioactivity needed for the application. Radon spas are used extensively in Russia and Central Europe to treat a number of conditions.

What Is Radon?

Radon is a gas produced by the radioactive decay of the element radium. Radioactive decay is a natural, spontaneous process in which an atom of one element decays or breaks down to form another element by losing atomic particles (protons, neutrons, or electrons). When solid radium decays to form radon gas, it loses two protons and two neutrons. These two protons and two neutrons are called an alpha particle, which is a type of radiation. Elements that produce radiation are referred to as radioactive. Radon itself is radioactive because it also decays, losing an alpha particle and forming the element polonium.

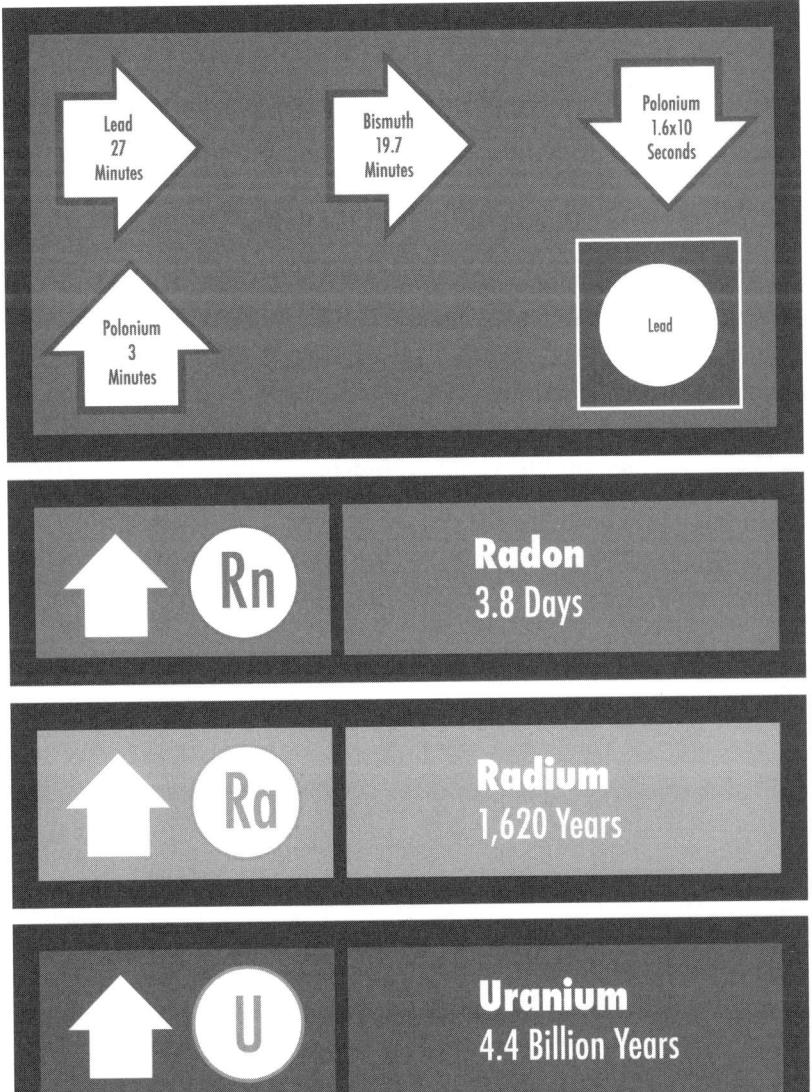

Elements that are naturally radioactive include uranium, thorium, carbon and potassium, as well as radon and radium. Uranium is the first element in a long chain of decay that produces radium and radon. Uranium is referred to as the "parent" element, and radium and radon are called "daughters" or "progeny." Radium and radon also form daughter elements as they decay. The progeny of radon are called radon decay products, or RDPs.

The decay of each radioactive element occurs at a very specific rate. How fast an element decays is measured in terms of the element's "half-life," or the amount of time for one-half of a given amount of the element to decay. Uranium has a half-life of 4.4 billion years, so a 4.4-billion-year-old rock has only half of the uranium with which it started. The half-life of radon is only 3.8 days.

If a jar were filled with radon, only half of the radon would be left after 3.8 days. But the newly made daughter products of radon (or RDPs) would also be in the jar, including polonium, bismuth, and lead. Polonium is also radioactive. It is this element which is produced by radon in the air and in people's lungs that can hurt lung tissue and cause lung cancer.

Radioactivity is commonly measured in picocuries (pCi).

Because the level of radioactivity is directly related to the number and type of radioactive atoms present, radon and all other radioactive atoms are measured in picocuries. For instance, a house having 4 picocuries of radon per liter of air (4 pCi/L) has about eight or nine atoms of radon decaying every minute in every liter of air inside the house. A 1,000-square-foot house with 4 pCi/L of radon has nearly 2 million radon atoms decaying inside it every minute.

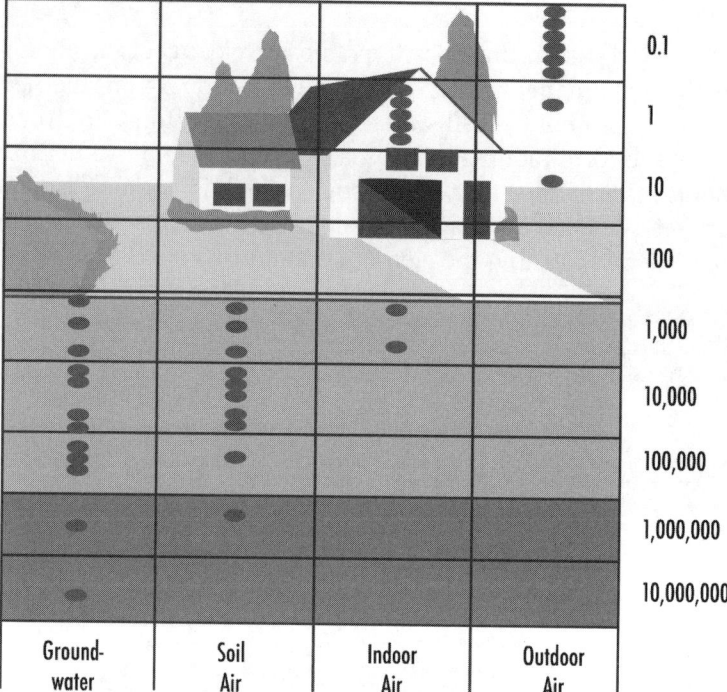

| | Ground- water | Soil Air | Indoor Air | Outdoor Air |

Radon levels in outdoor air, indoor air, soil air, and groundwater can be very different. Outdoor air ranges from less than 0.1 pCi/L to about 30 pCi/L, but it probably averages about 0.2 pCi/L. Radon in indoor air ranges from less than 1 pCi/L to about 3,000 pCi/L, but it probably averages between 1 and 2 pCi/L. Radon in soil air (the air that occupies the pores in soil) ranges from 20 or 30 pCi/L to more than 100,000 pCi/L; most soils in the United States contain between 200 and 2,000 pCi of radon per liter of soil air. The amount of radon dissolved in groundwater ranges from about 100 to nearly 3 million pCi/L.

Natural Radiation Exposure

Since the beginning of time, all living creatures have been exposed to radiation. We live in a radioactive world. There are many natural sources of radiation that have been present since the Earth was formed. In the last century, we have added somewhat to this natural background radiation with artificial sources. However, the naturally occurring sources contribute about four to five times more radiation than human-made sources.

The three major sources of naturally occurring radiation are:

- **cosmic** radiation;
- sources in the Earth's crust, also referred to as **terrestrial** radiation; and
- sources in the human body, also referred to as **internal** sources.

Cosmic

The Earth and all living things on it are constantly bombarded by radiation from space, similar to a steady drizzle of rain. Charged particles from the sun and stars interact with Earth's atmosphere and magnetic field to produce a shower of radiation, typically beta and gamma radiation. The dose from cosmic radiation varies in different parts of the world due to differences in elevation and to the effects of the Earth's magnetic field. Cosmic radiation comes from the sun and outer space, consisting of positively charged particles, as well as gamma radiation. At sea level, the average cosmic radiation dose is about 26 millirems (mrem) per year. At higher elevations, the amount of atmosphere shielding cosmic rays decreases and, thus, the dose increases. The average dose in the United States is approximately 28 mrem per year.

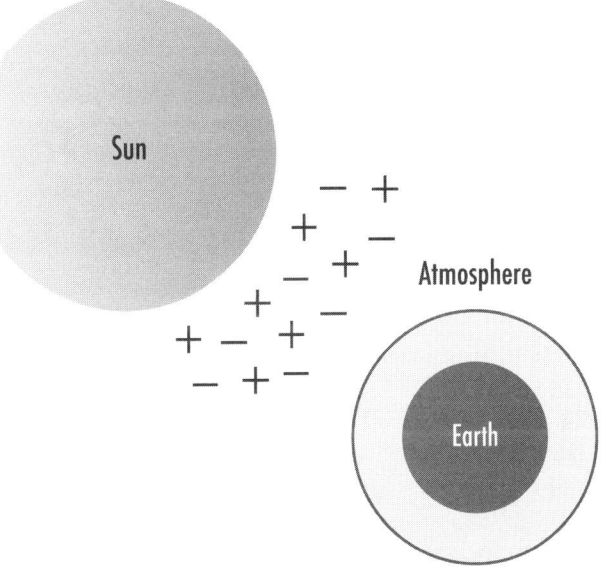

Terrestrial

Radioactive material is also found throughout nature. It is in the soil, water and vegetation. Low levels of uranium, thorium, and their decay products are found everywhere. This is called terrestrial radiation. Some of these materials are ingested with food and water, while others, such as radon, are inhaled. The dose from terrestrial sources also varies in different parts of the world. Locations with higher concentrations of uranium and thorium in their soil have higher dose levels.

The major isotopes of concern for terrestrial radiation are uranium and its decay products, such as thorium, radium and radon.

There are natural sources of radiation in the ground, rocks, building materials, and potable water supplies. Radon gas is a current health concern. This gas results from the decay of natural uranium in soil. Radon emits alpha radiation and rises from the soil under houses, and it can build up in homes, particularly well-insulated homes. In the United States, the average effective whole-body dose of radon is about 200 mrem per year, while the lungs receive approximately 2,000 mrem per year.

Internal

In addition to cosmic and terrestrial sources, all humans are born with naturally occurring radionuclides, such as potassium-40, carbon-14, lead-210, and other isotopes. The variation in dose from one person to another is not as great as the variation in dose from cosmic and terrestrial sources. The average annual "dose" from internal radioactive material is about 40 mrem.

Ionizing Radiation Exposure to the Public

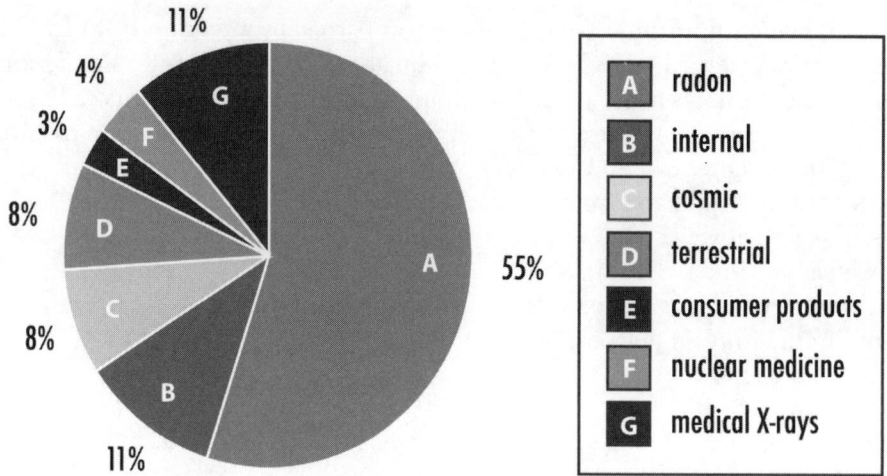

This chart shows that of the total annual dose of about 360 millirems, natural sources of radiation account for about 82% of all public exposure, while man-made sources account for the remaining 18%.

Definitions

- **accuracy:** the degree of agreement of a measurement (X) with an accepted reference or true value (T); usually expressed as the difference between the two values (X – T), or the difference as a percentage of the reference or true value (100[X – T]/T), and sometimes expressed as a ratio (X/T).

- **active radon/radon decay product (RDP) measurement device:** a radon or radon decay product measurement system that uses a sampling device, detector, and measurement system integrated as a complete unit or as separate but portable components. Active devices include continuous radon monitors, continuous working-level monitors, and grab-radon gas and grab working-level measurement systems, but do not include devices such as electret ion chamber devices, activated carbon or other adsorbent systems, or alpha track devices.

- **alpha particle:** two neutrons and two protons bound as a single particle emitted from the nucleus of certain radioactive isotopes in the process of decay.

- **background instrument (analysis system or laboratory) count rate:** the nuclear counting rate obtained on a given instrument with a background counting sample. Typical instrument background measurements are:

  - unexposed carbon, for activated carbon measurement systems;

  - a scintillation vial containing scintillant and a sample known to contain no radioactivity, for scintillation counters; and

  - background measurements made with continuous radon monitors exposed only to radon-free air (aged air or nitrogen).

- **background field measurements (blanks):** measurements made by analyzing unexposed (closed) detectors that accompanied exposed detectors to the field. The purpose of field background measurements is to assess any exposure to the detector caused by radon exposure other than from the concentration in the environment to be measured. Results of background field measurements are subtracted from the actual field measurements before calculating the reported concentration. Background levels may be due to electronic noise of the analysis system, leakage of radon into the detector, detector response to gamma radiation, or other causes.

- **background radiation:** radiation arising from radioactive material other than that under testing. Background radiation due to cosmic rays and natural radioactivity are always present; background radiation may also be due to the presence of radioactive substances in building materials.

- **Becquerel, becquerel (Bq):** the International System of Units (SI) definition of activity. 1 Bq = 1 nuclear disintegration per second.

- **calibrate:** to determine the response or reading of an instrument relative to a series of known values over the range of the instrument; results are used to develop correction or calibration factors.

- **check source:** a radioactive source, not necessarily calibrated, which is used to confirm the continuing satisfactory operation of an instrument.

- **client:** the individual or parties who hire(s) the radon tester.

- **closed-house/building conditions:** During any short-term test, closed-house conditions should be maintained as much as possible while the test is in progress. In tests lasting fewer than four days, closed-house conditions should be maintained for at least 12 hours before starting the test, as well as for the duration of the test. While closed-house conditions are not required before starting tests lasting between four and 90 days, they should be maintained as much as possible.

- **coefficient of variation (CV or COV), relative standard deviation (RSD):** a measure of precision calculated as the standard deviation of a set of values divided by the average, and usually multiplied by 100 to be expressed as a percentage:

  CV = RSD = / x 100 for a sample

  CV' = RSD' = / x 100 for a population

  Also see **relative percent difference**.

- **Curie, curie (Ci):** a standard measurement for radioactivity, specifically, the rate of decay for a gram of radium at 37 billion decays per second; a unit of radioactivity equal to 3.7×10^{10} disintegrations per second.

- **duplicate measurements:** two measurements made concurrently and in the same location, or side by side; used to evaluate the precision of the measurement method.

- **efficiency or intrinsic detector:** the relationship between the number of events recorded (counts, voltage lost, tracks) and the number of radioactive particles incident on the sensitive element of the detector per unit time. Efficiencies for radon detectors are commonly expressed in terms of the calibration factor, which is the number of events (counts) per time (hour or minute) per radon concentration (pCi/L). Methods with high efficiencies will exhibit more counts (signal) per unit time in response to a given radon level than will a method with a low efficiency.

- **equilibrium ratio (for radon):** equilibrium ratio = WL(100)/(pCi/L). At complete equilibrium (i.e., at an equilibrium ratio of 1), 1 WL of RDPs would be present at the radon concentration of 100 pCi/L. The ratio is never 1 in a house; due to ventilation and plate-out, the RDPs never reach equilibrium in a residential environment. A commonly assumed equilibrium ratio is 0.5 (i.e., the decay products are halfway toward equilibrium), in which case 1 WL would correspond to 200 pCi/L. However, equilibrium ratios vary with time and location, and ratios of 0.3 to 0.7 are commonly observed.

- **equilibrium equivalent concentration (EEC):** the radon concentration in equilibrium with its short-lived progeny that has the same potential alpha energy per unit volume as the environment being measured (also see **working level**).

- **exposure time:** the length of time a specific mail-in device must be in contact with radon or radon decay products to get an accurate radon measurement; also called **exposure period**, **exposure parameters**, and **duration of exposure**.

- **gamma radiation:** short-wavelength electromagnetic radiation of nuclear origin with an energy between 10 keV and 9 MeV.

- **integrating device:** a device that measures a single average concentration value over a period of time; also called a **time-integrating device**.

- **lower limit of detection (LLD):** the smallest amount of sample activity that will yield a net count for which there is confidence at a predetermined level that activity is present. For example, for a 5% probability of concluding falsely that activity is present, the LLD is approximately equal to 4.65 times the standard deviation of the background counts (assuming large numbers of counts for which Gaussian statistics can be used).

- **lowest level suitable for occupancy:** the lowest level currently lived in, or a lower level not currently used (such as a basement), that a prospective buyer could use for living space without renovations. This includes a basement that could be used regularly (for example, a recreation room, bedroom, den or playroom).

- **lowest lived-in level:** the lowest level or floor of a home that is used regularly (for example, a recreation room, bedroom, den or playroom).

- **passive radon/radon decay product (RDP) measurement device:** a radon or radon decay product measurement system in which the sampling device, detector, and measurement system do not function as a complete, integrated unit. Passive devices include electret ion chamber devices, activated carbon or other adsorbent systems, or alpha track devices, but do not include continuous radon/RDP monitors, or grab-radon/RDP measurement systems.

- **picocurie, picoCurie (pCi):** one pCi is one-trillionth of a curie, 0.037 disintegrations per second, or 2.22 disintegrations per minute.

- **picocurie per liter (pCi/L):** a unit of radioactivity corresponding to an average of one decay every 27 seconds in a volume of 1 liter, or 0.037 decays per second per liter of air or water. 1 pCi/L = 37 becquerels per cubic meter (Bq/m^3).

- **precision (or precision error):** a measure of mutual agreement among individual measurements of the same property, usually under prescribed and similar conditions, most desirably expressed in terms of the standard deviation, but which can be expressed in terms of the variance, pooled estimate of variance, range, relative percent difference, or other statistics.

- **quality assurance:** a complete program designed to produce results that are valid, scientifically defensible, and of known precision, bias, and accuracy; includes planning, documentation, and quality control activities.

- **quality control:** the system of activities to ensure a quality product, including measurements made to ensure and monitor data quality; includes: calibrations; duplicate, blank and spiked measurements; inter-laboratory comparisons; and audits.

- **radon (Rn):** a colorless, odorless, naturally occurring, radioactive, inert, gaseous element formed by radioactive decay of radium (Ra) atoms. Its atomic number is 86. Although other isotopes of radon occur in nature, radon occurring in indoor air is primarily Rn-222.

- **radon chamber:** an airtight enclosure in which operators can induce and control different levels of radon gas and radon decay products. Volume is such that samples can be taken without affecting the levels of either radon or its decay products within the chamber.

- **relative percent difference (RPD):** a measure of precision, calculated by:

$$RPD = (|X_1 - X_2|)/X_{avg} \times 100$$

where:

X_1 = concentration observed with the first detector or equipment;

X_2 = concentration observed with the second detector, equipment or absolute value;

$|X_1 - X_2|$ = absolute value of the difference between X_1 and X_2; and

X_{avg} = average concentration = $((X_1 + X_2) / 2)$

The relative percent difference (RPD) and coefficient of variation (CV) provide a measure of precision, but they are not equal. Below are examples of duplicate radon results, and the corresponding values of relative percent difference and coefficient of variation:

Rn1 (PCi/L)	Rn2 (PCi/L)	RPD (%)	COV (%)
8	9	12	8
13	15	14	10

Rn1 (PCi/L)	Rn2 (PCi/L)	RPD (%)	COV (%)
17	20	16	11
26	30	14	10
7.5	10	29	20

Note that the RPD divided by the square root of 2 = CV

Also see **coefficient of variation (CV).**

- **relative standard deviation:** see **coefficient of variation.**

- **sensitivity:** the ability of a radon or WL measurement method to produce reliable measurements at low concentrations. This ability is dependent upon the variability of the background signal (counts not due to radon or WL exposure) that the method records, as well as its efficiency. Methods with stable background rates and high efficiencies will be able to produce reliable measurements at lower concentrations than methods with variable background rates and low efficiencies. Sensitivity can be expressed in terms of the lower limit of detection or minimum detectable activity.

- **signal-to-noise ratio:** for radon and WL detectors, this term expresses the proportion of the number of counts due to exposure to radon or WP (signal) to the number of counts due to background (noise). Measurement methods with high signal-to-noise ratios will produce more counts due to radon or WL exposure (signal) in proportion to the background counts (noise) than will methods with low signal-to-noise ratios. A method with a high signal-to-noise ratio is more likely to exhibit pronounced sensitivity (i.e., be able to produce reliable measurements at low concentrations).

- **spiked measurements, or known exposure measurements:** quality control measurements in which the detector or instrument is exposed to a known concentration and submitted for analysis; used to evaluate accuracy.

- **standard deviation:** a measure of the scatter of several sample values around their average. For a sample, the standard deviation (s) is the positive square root of the sample variance:

$$s = \frac{\sqrt{\sum_{i-1}^{n} (x_i - X_{ave})^2}}{\sqrt{n-1}}$$

For a finite population, the standard deviation (s) is:

$$\sigma = \frac{\sqrt{\sum_{i-1}^{N} (x_i - \mu)^2}}{\sqrt{N}}$$

where μ is the true arithmetic mean of the population, and N is the number of values in the population. The property of the standard deviation that makes it most practically meaningful is that it is in the same units as the observed variable X. For example, the upper 95% probability limit on differences between two values is 2.77 times the sample standard deviation.

- **standard operating procedure (SOP):** a written document that details an operation, analysis or action whose mechanisms are prescribed thoroughly, and which is commonly accepted as the method for performing certain routine or repetitive tasks.

- **statistical control chart** or **Shewhart control chart:** a graphical chart with statistical control limits and plotted values (for some applications, in chronological order) of some measured parameter for a series of samples. Use of the charts provides a visual display of the pattern of the data, enabling the early detection of time trends and shifts in level. For maximum usefulness in control, such charts should be plotted in a timely manner (i.e., as soon as the data are available).

- **statistical control chart limits:** the limits on control charts that have been derived by statistical analysis and are used as criteria for action, or for judging whether a set of data does or does not indicate lack of control. On a means control chart, the warning level may be two standard deviations above and below the mean, and the control limit may be three standard deviations above and below the mean.

- *Systeme Internationale* **(SI):** the International System of Units, as defined by the Conference of Weights and Measures in 1960.

- **test interference:** the altering of test conditions prior to or during the measurement in order to change the radon or radon decay product concentrations, or the altering of the performance of the measurement equipment.

- **time-integrated measurement:** a measurement conducted over a specific time period (e.g., from two days to a year or more) producing results representative of the average value for that period.

- **uncertainty:** the estimated bounds of the deviation from the mean value, expressed generally as a percentage of the mean value, taken ordinarily as the sum of: (1) the random errors (errors of precision) at the 95%-confidence level; and (2) the estimated upper bound of the systematic error (errors of accuracy).

- **working level (WL):** any combination of short-lived radon decay products in 1 liter of air that will result in the ultimate emission of 1.3×10^5 MeV of potential alpha energy. This number was chosen because it is approximately the alpha energy released from the decay products in equilibrium with 100 pCi of Rn-222. Exposures are measured in working-level months (WLM).

- **working-level months (WLM):** (working level x hours or exposure)/(170 hours/working month). In SI units, 1 WLM = 6×10^5 Bq-h/m³ (EEC).

Abbreviations and Acronyms

AC: activated charcoal adsorption

AT: alpha track detection (ATD)

Bq: Becquerel

CR: continuous radon monitoring

CW: continuous working-level monitoring

EL: electret ion chamber—long-term

EML: U.S. Department of Energy Environmental Measurements Laboratory

EPA: U.S. Environmental Protection Agency

ER: equilibrium ratio

ES: electret ion chamber—short-term

eV: electron volt

GB: grab radon pump/collapsible bag

GC: grab radon activated charcoal

GS: grab radon scintillation cell

GW: grab working level

L: liter

LLD: lower limit of detection (see Glossary)

LS: charcoal liquid scintillation

m^3: cubic meter

MeV: mega-electron volt

MV: measured value

NCRP: National Council on Radiation Protection and Measurements

ORIA: U.S. EPA Office of Radiation and Indoor Air (formerly ORP)

PB: pump collapsible bag

pCi/L: picocuries per liter

QA: quality assurance (see Glossary)

QAP: quality assurance plan

QC: quality control (see Glossary)

RH: relative humidity

Rn: radon

RP: radon progeny integrating sampling unit (also RPISU)

RPD: relative percent difference (see Glossary)

RPP: Radon Proficiency Program

RV: reference value, used as the known or "true" value

SC: evacuated scintillation cell (three-day integrating)

SOP: standard operating procedure

T: temperature

TLD: thermoluminescent dosimeter

UT: unfiltered track detection

WL: working level

What Is an Atom?

To be able to understand radon, radiation and radioactivity, we need to understand the language of atomic structure. Let's learn about the physics of radon, starting with the atom.

Atoms are the extremely small particles of which we and everything around us are made.

Democritus was a pre-Socratic Greek materialist philosopher in the 5th century B.C. Known as "The Laughing Philosopher," Democritus believed that all matter is made up of various imperishable, indivisible elements, which he called *atoma* or "indivisible units," from which we get the English word "atom." Democritus theorized that the shape of an object's atoms determine that object's physical characteristics.

An atom is the smallest building block of matter. Atoms are made of neutrons, protons and electrons. If one atom were the size of the Houston Astrodome, its nucleus would be roughly the size of a pea.

Dmitri Ivanovich Mendeleev (1834–1907) was a Russian chemist and inventor. He is credited as being the creator of the first version of the Periodic Table of Elements. Using the table, he predicted the properties of elements yet to be discovered.

There are 92 naturally occurring elements. Scientists have created many others, bringing the total number of known elements to more than 100. Atoms are the smallest units of an element that behave the same way, chemically, as the element itself does.

When Mendeleev began grouping elements, he took note of the law of chemical periodicity, which states, "The properties of the elements are periodic functions of atomic number." Scientists use the periodic table to find out important information about various elements. The periodic table orders all known elements according to their similarities, categorizing elements by groups and periods.

Each element is ordered by its atomic number. The atomic number is determined by the number of protons per atom. In an atom with a neutral charge, the number of electrons equals the number of protons. The periodic table represents neutral atoms. The atomic number for a given element is located above the element's symbol.

Beneath the atomic number is the atomic mass number. Atomic mass is measured in atomic mass units, where 1 amu = (1/12) mass of carbon measured in grams. The atomic mass number is equal to the number of protons, plus its neutrons. This number is found beneath the element's symbol.

When two chemicals react with each other, the reaction takes place between individual atoms at the atomic level. The processes that cause materials to be radioactive (to emit particles and energy) also occur at the atomic level.

Atomic Structure

In the early 20th century, Ernest Rutherford, a New Zealand scientist working in England, and the Danish scientist Niels Bohr developed a theory about the structure of an atom that describes an atom as looking very much like our solar system.

At the center of every atom is a nucleus, which is comparable to the Sun in our solar system. Electrons move around the nucleus in orbits, similar to the way planets move around the Sun. While scientists now know that atomic structure is more complex, the Rutherford-Bohr model is still a useful approximation to begin understanding atomic structure.

A **nucleus** contains protons and neutrons; together, these are called nucleons.

A **neutron** has no electrical charge and, like a proton, is about 1,800 times as heavy as an electron.

A **proton** is a positively charged particle. All atoms of an element (radioactive and non-radioactive) have the same number of protons.

Protons and neutrons in the nucleus, and the forces between them, affect an atom's radioactive properties.

The particles that orbit the nucleus as a cloud are called **electrons**. They are negatively charged, and they balance the positive electrical charge of the protons in the nucleus.

Interactions with electrons in the outer orbits affect an atom's chemical properties.

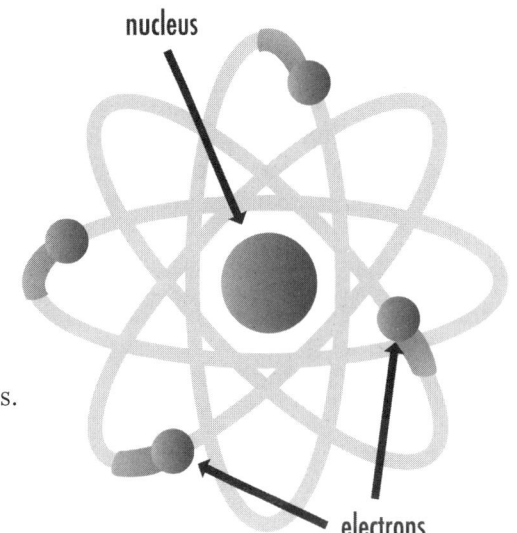

Why Are Some Atoms Radioactive?

The balance of the forces in the nucleus of an atom determines whether a nucleus is stable or unstable (radioactive).

Atoms found in nature are either stable or unstable. An atom is stable if the forces among the particles that make up the nucleus are balanced. An atom is unstable or radioactive if these forces are unbalanced, or if the nucleus has an excess of internal energy. Unstable atoms are called radionuclides. The instability of a radionuclide's nucleus may result from an excess of either neutrons or protons. An unstable nucleus will continually vibrate and contort and, sooner or later, attempt to reach stability by some combination of means, such as:

- ejecting neutrons and protons;
- converting a neutron to a proton (or vice versa) with the ejection of a beta particle or positron; or
- releasing additional energy by photon or gamma-ray emission.

Can unstable atoms become stable?

Yes. As the unstable nucleus disintegrates, it emits radiation, and the radionuclide is transformed into different nuclides. This process is called radioactive decay. It will continue until the forces in the nucleus

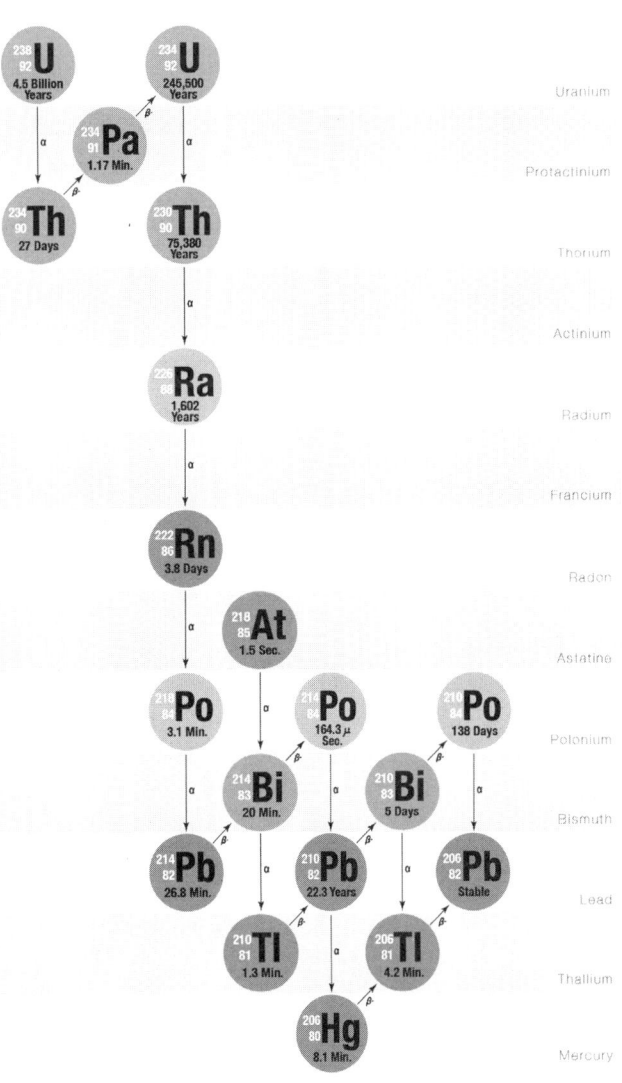

are balanced. For example, as a radionuclide decays, it will become a different isotope of the same element if the number of neutrons changes. It may become a different element altogether if the number of protons changes.

Often, when a radionuclide decays, the decay product (the new nuclide) is also radioactive. This is true for most naturally occurring radioactive materials, and also for some fission products. In order to become stable, these materials must go through many steps, becoming a series of different nuclides, and giving off energy as particles or rays at each step. The series of transformations that a given radionuclide will undergo, as well as the kind of radiation it emits, are characteristic of the radionuclide. This is called a decay chain.

How long do radionuclides stay radioactive?

It depends on the kind of radioactive material. The rate of decay is one of the characteristics of radionuclides. Scientists talk about this rate as a radionuclide's radioactive half-life. It is the time required for the disintegration of one-half of the radioactive atoms that are present when measurement starts. It does not represent a fixed number of atoms that disintegrate but, rather, a fraction. For any given radionuclide, the half-life remains constant.

What's the difference between radiation and radioactivity?

Radiation is the energy that is released as particles or rays during radioactive decay.

Radioactivity is the property of an atom that describes spontaneous changes in its nucleus that create a different nuclide. These changes usually happen as emissions of alpha or beta particles, and often of gamma rays.

The emission of particles or energy by a nucleus is referred to as a disintegration. The number of disintegrations per unit time, or the rate of emission, is called the activity of a sample. Since each disintegration transforms the atom into a new nuclide, "transformation" is often substituted for "disintegration" when talking about radioactive decay and activity.

Activity is expressed in becquerels or curies, with curies being the original unit and which is used more commonly in the U.S. One becquerel equals one transformation per second. One curie equals 37 billion disintegrations per second, but was originally defined as the number of disintegrations of one gram of pure radium per second.

Is all ionizing radiation the same?

No. An ion is an atom (or a group of atoms) that has acquired a net electric charge by gaining or losing one or more electrons. Ionizing radiation is high-energy radiation that is capable of transforming the substances through which it passes into ions. It can be in the form of alpha or beta particles or gamma rays (photons), and each form behaves differently. The kind of radiation given off by a nucleus depends on the nature of the imbalance in the nuclear forces.

Pioneers in Radioactivity

Marie Curie (1867–1934) and her husband Pierre Curie (1859–1906) are perhaps two of the most famous scientists known for their contributions to the study of radioactivity. Pierre was born in Paris and Marie in Poland. They both studied at the Sorbonne. They investigated the properties of uranium and thorium, and, soon after, discovered polonium. Pierre pursued the study of magnetism acting at high temperatures. Marie continued her research in chemistry and physics, and is the only person ever to receive Nobel Prizes in both disciplines. The "curie," named for her, is the unit of measurement now used in radiation research.

Antoine Henri Becquerel (1852–1908) was a French physicist and Nobel laureate who, along with Marie and Pierre Curie, was responsible for the discovery of radioactivity. Later, Becquerel demonstrated that the radiation emitted by uranium shared certain characteristics with X-rays but, unlike X-rays, that radiation could be deflected by a magnetic field and, therefore, must consist of charged particles. The becquerel is also a unit of measurement in radiation studies.

The Curies combined their efforts with Henri Becquerel. In 1903, they were all awarded the Nobel Prize in physics.

Non-Ionizing and Ionizing

Radiation has a wide range of energies that form the electromagnetic spectrum (illustrated below). The spectrum has two major divisions: non-ionizing radiation and ionizing radiation.

Radiation that has enough energy to move around atoms in a molecule or cause them to vibrate, but not enough to remove electrons, is referred to as non-ionizing radiation. Examples of this kind of radiation include visible light and microwaves.

Radiation that falls within the ionizing radiation range has enough energy to remove tightly bound electrons from atoms, thus creating ions. This is the type of radiation that people usually think of as radiation. We take advantage of its properties to generate electric power, to kill cancer cells, and in many manufacturing processes.

The energy of the radiation shown on the spectrum below increases from left to right as the frequency rises.

Types of Radiation in the Electromagnetic Spectrum

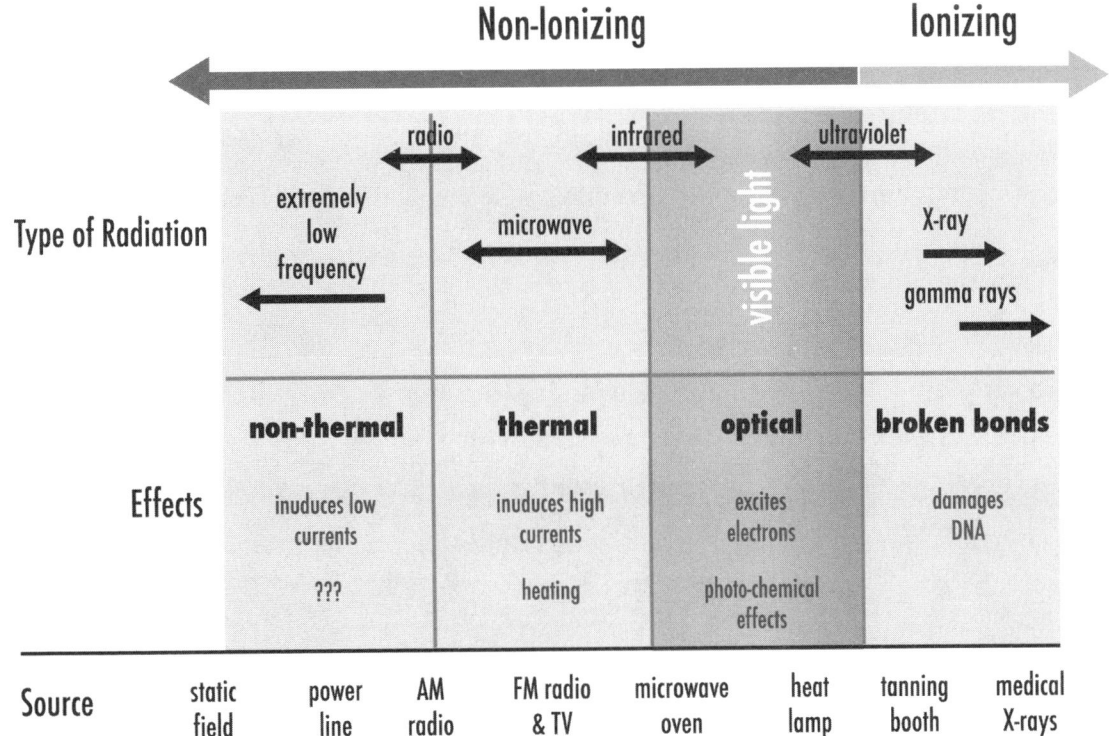

Non-Ionizing Radiation

We take advantage of the properties of non-ionizing radiation for common tasks, including:

- microwave radiation, telecommunications, and heating food;
- infrared radiation and infrared lamps to keep food warm in restaurants; and
- radio-wave broadcasting.

Non-ionizing radiation ranges from extremely low-frequency radiation, through the audible, microwave, and visible portions of the spectrum into the ultraviolet range.

Extremely low-frequency radiation has very long wavelengths (on the order of a million meters or more) and frequencies in the range of 100 hertz (cycles per second) or less. Radio frequencies have wavelengths of between 1 and 100 meters and frequencies in the range of 1 million to 100 million hertz. Microwaves that we use to heat food have wavelengths that are about 1/100th of a meter and have frequencies of about 2.5 billion hertz.

Ionizing Radiation

Higher-frequency ultraviolet radiation begins to have enough energy to break chemical bonds. X-ray and gamma ray radiation, which are at the upper end of magnetic radiation, have very high frequencies (in the range of 100 billion billion hertz) and very short wavelengths of about 1 picometer (1 trillionth of a meter). Radiation in this range has extremely high energy. It has enough energy to strip off electrons, or, in the case of very high-energy radiation, break up the nucleus of atoms.

Ionization is the process in which a charged portion of a molecule (usually an electron) is given enough energy to break away from the atom. This process results in the formation of two charged particles or ions: the molecule with a net positive charge, and the free electron with a negative charge.

Each ionization releases approximately 33 electron volts (eV) of energy. Material surrounding the atom absorbs the energy. Compared to other types of radiation that may be absorbed, ionizing radiation deposits a large amount of energy into a small area. In fact, the 33 eV from one ionization is more than enough energy to disrupt the chemical bond between two carbon atoms. All ionizing radiation is capable, directly or indirectly, of removing electrons from most molecules.

Alpha Particles

There are three main kinds of ionizing radiation:

- **alpha particles**, which include two protons and two neutrons;
- **beta particles**, which are essentially high-speed electrons; and
- **gamma rays and X-rays**, which are pure energy (photons).

The most interesting is alpha particles because they can be stopped by a sheet of paper where they release their energy. Let's learn more about alpha particles in relation to radon.

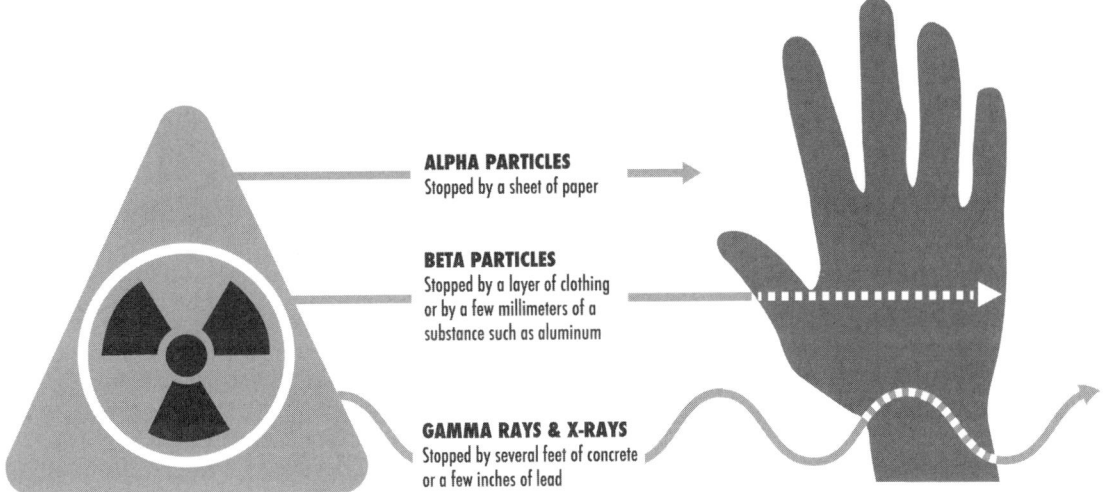

Alpha particles are energetic, positively charged particles consisting of two protons and two neutrons. They are commonly emitted in the radioactive decay of the heaviest radioactive elements, such as uranium-238, radium-226, and polonium-210. Even though they are highly energetic, the high mass of alpha particles means they move slowly through the air.

The effects on human health from alpha particles depend primarily upon the method of exposure. External exposure (for example, by touch) is of far less concern than internal exposure because alpha particles lack the energy to penetrate the outer layer of skin or even a sheet of paper.

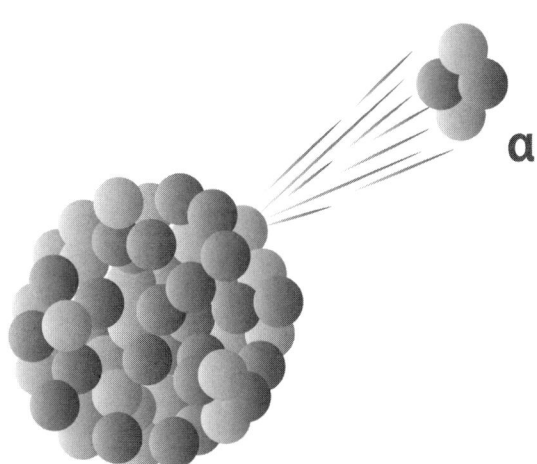

However, radionuclides that emit alpha particles internally can be very harmful. If alpha emitters are inhaled, ingested (swallowed), or absorbed into the bloodstream (through a cut in the skin, for example), sensitive living tissue can be exposed to alpha radiation.

Alpha decay is a type of radioactive decay in which alpha particles are released from the nuclei of atoms. The atomic nucleus emits an alpha particle (two protons and two neutrons bound together into a particle), and then transforms (or decays) into an atom with a mass number that is 4 less, and with an atomic number that is 2 less.

Example: uranium-238 (U-238) ➔ *thorium-234 + helium-4*

Because of their relatively large mass, +2 charge, and relatively low velocity, alpha particles are very likely to interact with other atoms and lose their energy, so their forward motion is effectively stopped within a few centimeters of air. Being relatively heavy and positively charged, alpha particles tend to have a very short "mean free path" (i.e., the average distance a particle travels between collisions with other particles), and they quickly lose kinetic energy within a short distance from their source. This results in several MeV (million electronvolts) being deposited in a relatively small volume of material. This increases the chance of cellular damage in cases of internal contamination.

In general, external alpha radiation is not harmful, since alpha particles are effectively shielded by a few centimeters of air, a piece of paper, or the thin layer of dead skin cells. Alpha particles are low in penetrating power. Even touching an alpha source is usually not harmful, though many alpha sources are also accompanied by beta-emitting radon daughters, and alpha emission is also accompanied by gamma-photon emission. If substances emitting alpha particles are ingested, inhaled, injected, or introduced through the skin, then it could result in a measurable dose of harmful radiation.

Who discovered alpha particles?

English scientist Ernest Rutherford discovered alpha particles in 1899 while working with uranium. Rutherford's studies contributed to our understanding of the atom and its nucleus through the Rutherford-Bohr planetary model of the atom.

Alpha Emitter	Atomic Number
americium-241	95
plutonium-236	94
uranium-238	92
thorium-232	90
radium-226	88
radon-222	86
polonium-210	84

Alpha particles (symbol α) are a type of ionizing radiation ejected by the nuclei of some unstable atoms. They are large subatomic fragments consisting of two protons and two neutrons.

What are the properties of an alpha particle?

An alpha particle is identical to a helium nucleus having two protons and two neutrons. It is a relatively heavy, high-energy particle, with a positive charge of +2 from its two protons. Alpha particles have a velocity in air of approximately 1/20 the speed of light, depending on the individual particle's energy.

What are the conditions that lead to alpha particle emission?

When the ratio of neutrons to protons in the nucleus is too low, certain atoms restore the balance by emitting alpha particles. For example, polonium-210 has 126 neutrons and 84 protons, at a ratio of 1.50 to 1. Following radioactive decay by the emission of an alpha particle, the ratio becomes 124 neutrons to 82 protons, or 1.51 to 1.

Alpha-emitting atoms tend to be very large atoms (i.e., they have high atomic numbers). With some exceptions, naturally occurring alpha emitters have atomic numbers of at least 82 (the element lead).

What happens to atoms during alpha emission?

The nucleus is initially in an unstable energy state. An internal change takes place in the unstable nucleus, and an alpha particle is ejected, leaving a decay product. The atom has then lost two protons along with two neutrons.

The loss of an alpha particle actually changes the atom to a different element because the number of protons determines the element. As an example, polonium-210 is an alpha emitter. During radioactive decay, it loses two protons and becomes an atom of lead-206, which is stable (non-radioactive).

What uses do alpha emitters have?

The positive charge of alpha particles is useful in some industrial processes:

- Radium-226 may be used to treat cancer by inserting tiny amounts of radium into the tumorous mass.
- Polonium-210 serves as a static eliminator in paper mills and other industries. The alpha particles, due to their positive charge, attract loose electrons, thus reducing static charge.
- Some smoke detectors use the alpha emissions from americium-241 to help create an electrical current. The alpha particles strike air molecules within a chamber, knocking electrons loose. The resulting positively charged ions and negatively charged electrons create a current as they flow between positively and negatively charged plates within the chamber. When smoke particles enter the device, they attach to and interrupt the flow of charged particles, breaking the current and setting off the alarm.

Exposure to Alpha Emitters

How do alpha emitters get into the environment?

Most alpha emitters occur naturally in the environment. For example, alpha particles are given off by uranium-238, radium-226, and other members of the uranium decay series. These are present in varying amounts in nearly all rocks, soils and water.

The opportunity for environmental and human exposure increases greatly when soils and rock formations are disturbed by the extraction of minerals.

Uranium mining wastes (uranium mill tailings) have high concentrations of uranium and radium. Once brought to the surface, they could become airborne or enter surface water as runoff.

Mining and current methods for processing phosphate ore for fertilizer generate large piles or "stacks" of phosphogypsum, in which naturally occurring radium is concentrated.

How do alpha particles change in the environment?

Alpha particles don't get very far in the environment. Once emitted, they travel relatively slowly (at approximately 1/20 the speed of light) due to their electric charge and large mass. They lose energy rapidly in air, usually expending it within a few centimeters. Because alpha particles are not radioactive, once they have lost their energy, they pick up free electrons and become helium.

Alpha particles also cannot penetrate most matter they encounter. Even a piece of paper or the dead outer layer of human skin is sufficient to stop them.

Health Effects

The most important information to know about alpha particles is how they affect our health.

How can alpha particles affect people's health?

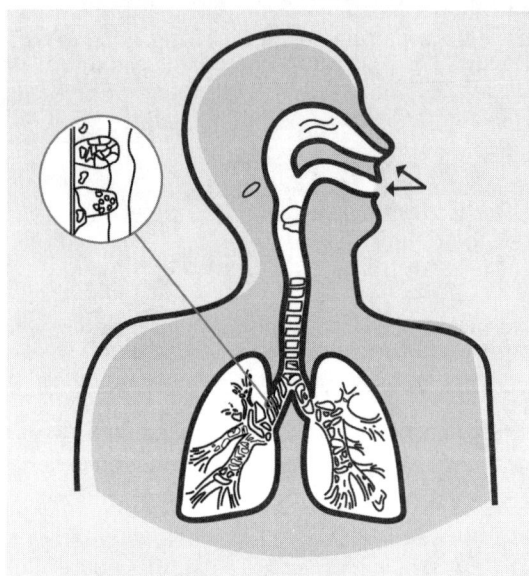

The health effects of alpha particles depend heavily upon how exposure takes place. External exposure (external to the body) is of far less concern than internal exposure because alpha particles lack the energy to penetrate the outer dead layer of skin.

However, if alpha emitters have been inhaled, ingested (swallowed), or absorbed into the bloodstream, sensitive living tissue can be exposed to alpha radiation. The resulting biological damage increases the risk of cancer; in particular, alpha radiation is known to cause lung cancer in humans when alpha emitters are inhaled.

The greatest exposure to alpha radiation for most people comes from the inhalation of radon and its decay products, several of which also emit potent alpha radiation.

Ionizing radiation causes cell damage that can lead to lung cancer.

Is there a medical test to determine exposure to alpha particles?

There are tests that can detect the presence of alpha-emitting radionuclides in the body following an internal contamination event. However, they require special equipment, and testing is generally done by specialized laboratories and facilities or hospitals.

Protecting People from Alpha Particles

How do I know if I'm near alpha emitters and alpha particles?

You must have specialized equipment to detect alpha radiation. Generally, this equipment is expensive and requires an expert to operate it. The one alpha-emitting radionuclide that you can easily measure yourself is radon. Inexpensive home test kits are available from hardware and even grocery stores.

People can easily protect themselves from external exposure to alpha radiation, since alpha particles are unable to penetrate the outer dead layers of skin or clothing. However, tissue that is not protected by the outer layer of dead cells, such as the eyes or open wounds, must be carefully protected.

The exposure pathways of concern are inhalation or ingestion of alpha emitters, which continue to emit alpha particles. Alpha-emitting radionuclides taken into the body release alpha particles directly to sensitive living tissues. As their high energy transfers directly to tissue, it causes damage that may lead to cancer.

The most significant way people come in contact with alpha emitters is in their home, school, or place of business. Radon is a heavy gas and tends to collect in low-lying areas, such as basements. Testing for radon in the home and taking any corrective action necessary is the most effective way to protect yourself and your family from alpha emitters.

What is the government doing to protect people from exposure to alpha emitters and alpha particles?

The U.S. Congress passes laws that authorize the EPA and other federal agencies to protect public health and the environment from radionuclides, including alpha emitters. The EPA has issued a variety of regulations that limit the release of radionuclides into the environment.

Beta Particles

Beta particles are subatomic particles ejected from the nucleus of some radioactive atoms. They are equivalent to electrons. The difference is that beta particles originate in the nucleus, and electrons originate outside the nucleus.

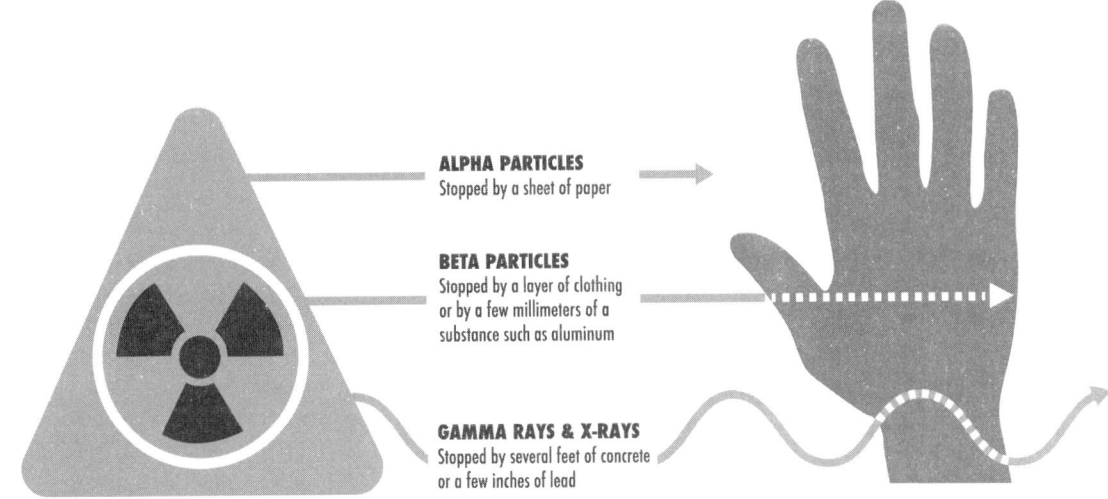

ALPHA PARTICLES
Stopped by a sheet of paper

BETA PARTICLES
Stopped by a layer of clothing or by a few millimeters of a substance such as aluminum

GAMMA RAYS & X-RAYS
Stopped by several feet of concrete or a few inches of lead

Who discovered beta particles?

Henri Becquerel is credited with the discovery of beta particles. In 1900, he showed that beta particles were identical to electrons, which had recently been discovered by Joseph John Thompson.

What are the properties of beta particles?

Beta particles have an electrical charge of -1. They have a mass of 549 millionths of one atomic mass unit, or AMU, which is about 1/2,000 of the mass of a proton or neutron. The speed of individual beta particles depends on how much energy they have, and varies over a wide range. It is their excess energy, in the form of speed, that causes harm to living cells. When transferred, this energy can break chemical bonds and form ions.

What conditions lead to beta particle emission?

Beta particle emission occurs when the ratio of neutrons to protons in the nucleus is too high. In this case, an excess neutron transforms into a proton and an electron. The proton stays in the nucleus and the electron is ejected energetically.

This process decreases the number of neutrons by one and increases the number of protons by one. Since the number of protons in the nucleus of an atom determines the element, the conversion of a neutron to a proton actually changes the radionuclide to a different element.

Gamma ray emission often accompanies the emission of a beta particle. When the beta particle ejection doesn't rid the nucleus of the extra energy, the nucleus releases the remaining excess energy in the form of a gamma photon.

The decay of technetium-99, which has too many neutrons to be stable, is an example of beta decay. A neutron in the nucleus converts to a proton and a beta particle. The nucleus ejects the beta particle and some gamma radiation. The new atom retains the same mass number, but the number of protons increases to 44. The atom is now a ruthenium atom.

Other examples of beta emitters are phosphorous-32, tritium (H-3), carbon-14, strontium-90, and lead-210.

Which radionuclides are beta emitters?

There are many beta emitters, including:

- tritium;
- cobalt-60;
- strontium-90;
- technetium-99;
- iodine-129 and -131; and
- cesium-137

Beta Particles in the Environment

How do we use beta emitters?

Beta emitters have many uses, especially in medical diagnosis, imaging and treatment.

- Iodine-131 is used to treat thyroid disorders, such as cancer and Graves' Disease, which is a type of hyperthyroidism.
- Phosphorus-32 is used in molecular biology and genetics research.
- Strontium-90 is used as a radioactive tracer in medical and agricultural studies.
- Tritium is used for life science and drug metabolism studies to ensure the safety of potential new drugs. It is also used for luminous aircraft and commercial exit signs, and for luminous dials, gauges and wristwatches.
- Carbon-14 is a very reliable tool for dating organic matter up to 30,000 years old.
- Beta emitters are also used in a variety of industrial instruments, such as industrial thickness gauges, which use their weak penetrating power to measure very thin materials.

What happens to beta particles in the environment?

Beta particles travel several feet in open air and are easily stopped by solid materials. When a beta particle has lost its energy, it is like any other loose electron. Whether in the outdoor environment or in the body, these electrons are then picked up by a positive ion.

How are people exposed to beta particles?

There are both natural and man-made beta-emitting radionuclides. Potassium-40 and carbon-14 are weak beta emitters that are found naturally in our bodies. Some decay products of radon emit beta particles, but its alpha-emitting decay products pose a much greater health risk.

Beta emitters that eject energetic particles can pose a significant health concern. Their use requires special consideration of both the benefits and the potential harmful effects.

- Key beta emitters used in medical imaging, diagnostic and treatment procedures are phosphorus-32, and iodine-131. People who have taken radioactive iodine will emit beta particles. They must follow strict procedures to protect family members from exposure.
- Radioactive iodine may enter the environment during a nuclear reactor accident and find its way into the food chain.
- Industrial gauges and instruments containing concentrated beta-emitting radiation sources can be lost, stolen or abandoned. If these instruments then enter the scrap-metal market, or someone finds one, the sources they contain can expose people to beta emitters.

At one time, strontium-90 was the major man-made beta emitter in the environment. Fallout from atmospheric nuclear testing from the 1950s to the early 1970s spread strontium-90 worldwide. However, most of the strontium-90 from these tests has now decayed away.

Testing also released large amounts of cesium-137 into the environment. Although cesium-137 emits beta radiation, its gamma radiation is of greater concern. Some cesium-137 from fallout remains in the environment, but most of it has decayed as well.

Does the way a person is exposed to beta particles matter?

Yes. Direct exposure to beta particles is a hazard because emissions from strong sources can redden or even burn the skin. However, emissions from inhaled or ingested beta particle emitters are the greatest concern. Beta particles released directly to living tissue can cause damage at the molecular level, which can disrupt cell function. Because they are much smaller and have less charge than alpha particles, beta particles generally travel further into tissues. As a result, the cellular damage is more dispersed.

Health Effects of Beta Particles

How can beta particles affect people's health?

Beta radiation can cause both acute and chronic health effects. Acute exposures are uncommon. Contact with a strong beta source from an abandoned industrial instrument is one way that acute exposure could occur. Chronic effects are much more common.

Chronic effects result from fairly low-level exposures over a long period of time. They develop relatively slowly (five to 30 years). The main chronic health effect from radiation is cancer. When taken internally, beta emitters can cause tissue damage and increase the risk of cancer. The risk of cancer increases as the dose is increased.

Some beta emitters, such as carbon-14, distribute widely throughout the body. Others accumulate in specific organs and cause chronic exposures.

- Iodine-131 concentrates heavily in the thyroid gland. It increases the risk of thyroid cancer and other disorders.
- Strontium-90 accumulates in bone and teeth.

Is there a medical test to determine exposure to beta particles?

There are tests that can detect the presence of beta-emitting radionuclides in the body; however, special equipment is required, and testing is generally done by specialized laboratories and facilities, or such testing is associated with a specific medical procedure in a hospital.

Protecting People from Beta Particles

How do I know if I'm near beta emitters and beta particles?

You cannot tell if you are being exposed to beta radiation. You cannot see or feel radiation hitting your body. Specialized equipment is required to determine if you are near a beta radiation source. However, you should be familiar with the radiation warning symbols, such as the trefoil, which indicate that radioactivity is present. You can protect yourself by avoiding devices with that symbol, and not entering areas where that symbol or others are posted.

What is the government doing to protect people from exposure to beta emitters and beta particles?

The U.S. Congress passes laws that authorize the EPA and other federal agencies to protect public health and the environment from radionuclides, including beta emitters. The EPA has issued a variety of regulations that limit the release of radionuclides to the environment.

How do I protect myself from beta particles?

While it is very unlikely, you may encounter an industrial instrument or device containing a radioactive source. Every year, hundreds of devices containing radiation sources are lost or stolen, or otherwise drop out of the system used for tracking them. For example, a factory that has gone out of business may contain one or more such devices. As the building structure is being dismantled, these forgotten devices are often considered scrap metal, and someone may think they have value and try to sell them. You should avoid these devices. They may bear the radiation warning symbol, a trefoil. They may also bear identifying information, such as "Nuclear Regulatory Commission," or the name of a radionuclide. If you find a device you think may be radioactive, promptly call your state's radiation control office, or the hotline for reporting unwanted radioactive material at 1-800-999-7879.

Beta particles are high-energy, high-speed electrons or positrons emitted by certain types of radioactive nuclei, such as potassium-40. The beta particles are the electrons arising from the conversion of a neutron to a proton and electron, and are released by two other short-lived RDPs (radon decay products). Beta particles are emitted from the nucleus during radioactive decay. The beta particles emitted are a form of ionizing radiation also known as beta rays. The production of beta particles is termed beta decay. An unstable atomic nucleus with an excess of neutrons may undergo beta decay.

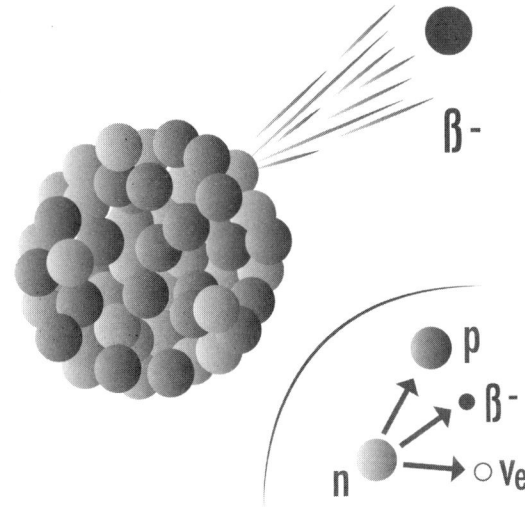

Beta particles have a higher capacity to penetrate than alpha particles do, but they are less damaging over equal distances. They can travel far in the air but can be slowed down or stopped by a layer of clothing, or by a few millimeters of a substance such as aluminum. Humans are exposed to beta particles from both fabricated and natural radiation sources, such as tritium, carbon-14, and strontium-90.

Beta particles cannot be stopped by a sheet of paper. Some beta particles can be stopped by human skin, but others need a thicker shield (like wood) to stop them. Some beta particles are capable of penetrating the skin and causing radiation damage in the form of skin burns. However, as with alpha emitters, beta emitters are most hazardous when they are inhaled or ingested. For example, if ingested, some radionuclides that emit beta particles might be absorbed into the bones.

Gamma Rays and X-Rays

A gamma ray is a packet of electromagnetic energy photons. Gamma photons are the most energetic photons in the electromagnetic spectrum. Gamma rays (gamma photons) are emitted from the nucleus of some unstable (radioactive) atoms.

The Basics

Who discovered gamma radiation?

French physicist Henri Becquerel is credited with discovering gamma radiation. In 1896, he discovered that uranium minerals could expose a photographic plate through a piece of heavy opaque paper. German physicist Wilhelm Röntgen had recently discovered X-rays, and Becquerel reasoned that uranium emitted some invisible light similar to X-rays. He called it metallic phosphorescence.

In reality, Becquerel had found gamma radiation being emitted by radium-226. Radium-226 is part of the uranium decay chain and commonly occurs with uranium.

What are the properties of gamma radiation?

Gamma radiation is very high-energy ionizing radiation. Gamma photons have about 10,000 times as much energy as the photons in the visible range of the electromagnetic spectrum.

Gamma photons have no mass and no electrical charge they are pure electromagnetic energy.

Because of their high energy, gamma photons travel at the speed of light and can cover hundreds to thousands of meters in the air before expending their energy. They can pass through many kinds of materials, including human tissue. Very dense materials, such as lead, are commonly used as shielding to slow or stop gamma photons.

Their wavelengths are so short that they must be measured in nanometers, or billionths of a meter. They range from 3/100 to 3/1,000 of a nanometer.

What is the difference between gamma rays and X-rays?

Gamma rays and X-rays, like visible, infrared, and ultraviolet light, are part of the electromagnetic spectrum. While gamma rays and X-rays pose the same kind of hazard, they differ in their origin. Gamma rays originate in the nucleus. X-rays originate in the electron fields surrounding the nucleus or are machine-produced.

What conditions lead to gamma ray emission?

Gamma radiation emission occurs when the nucleus of a radioactive atom has too much energy. It often follows the emission of a beta particle.

What happens during gamma ray emission?

Cesium-137 provides an example of radioactive decay by gamma radiation, or when a neutron transforms to a proton and a beta particle. The additional proton changes the atom to barium-137. The nucleus ejects the beta particle. However, the nucleus still has too much energy and ejects a gamma photon (gamma radiation) to become more stable.

How do we use gamma emitters?

Gamma-emitting radionuclides are the most widely used radiation sources. The penetrating power of gamma photons has many applications. However, while gamma rays penetrate many materials, they do not make them radioactive. The three most useful radionuclides by far are cobalt-60, cesium-137, and technetium-99m.

The uses of cesium-137 include:

- for cancer treatment;
- to measure and control the flow of liquids in numerous industrial processes;
- to investigate subterranean strata in oil wells;
- to measure the soil density at construction sites; and
- to ensure the proper fill level for packages of food, drugs, and other products.

The uses of cobalt-60 include:

- to sterilize medical equipment in hospitals;
- to pasteurize certain foods and spices;
- to treat cancer; and
- to gauge the thickness of metal in steel mills.

Technetium-99m (or TC-99m) is the most widely used radioactive isotope for diagnostic studies. It is a shorter half-life precursor of technetium-99. Different chemical forms are used for brain, bone, liver, spleen and kidney imaging, and also for blood flow studies.

In manufacturing, gamma radiation from cobalt-60 or cesium-137 can improve the physical characteristics of materials. For example, exposure to gamma radiation improves the durability of some wood and plastic composites. Treated materials can be used for flooring in high-traffic areas of department stores, airports and hotels because they resist abrasion and ensure low maintenance.

Industrial radiography is another process that uses gamma radiation for the inspection of metal parts and welds for defects. A sealed radiation source, usually iridium-192 or cobalt-60, beams gamma radiation at the part. Any gamma radiation passing through a crack or incomplete weld exposes special photographic, or radiographic, film. The process is similar to taking an X-ray of a broken arm. Manufacturers use radiography to inspect jet engine turbine blades.

How does gamma radiation change in the environment?

Gamma rays travel at the speed of light and exist only as long as they have energy. Once their energy is spent, whether in air or in solid materials, they cease to exist. The same is true for X-rays.

Exposure to Gamma Radiation

How are people exposed to gamma radiation?

Most people's primary source of gamma exposure is from naturally occurring radionuclides, particularly potassium-40, which is found in soil and water, as well as meats and high-potassium foods, such as bananas. Radium is also a source of gamma exposure. However, the increasing use of nuclear medicine (for bone, thyroid and lung scans) contributes an increasing proportion of the total for many people. Also, some man-made radionuclides that have been released to the environment emit gamma rays.

Most of the exposure to gamma rays and X-rays is direct external exposure. Gamma rays and X-rays can easily travel great distances through air and penetrate several centimeters in tissue. Most have enough energy to pass through the body, exposing all organs. X-ray exposure of the public is almost always in the controlled environment of dental and medical procedures.

Although they are generally classified as an external hazard, gamma-emitting radionuclides can also be inhaled or ingested with water or food and cause exposures to organs inside the body. Depending on the radionuclide, they may be retained in tissue, or expelled via the urine or feces.

Does the way a person is exposed to gamma rays or X-rays matter?

Both direct (external) and internal exposure to gamma rays and X-rays can be concerning. Gamma rays can travel much farther than alpha or beta particles and have enough energy to pass entirely through the body, potentially exposing all the organs. Huge portions of gamma radiation largely pass through the body without interacting with tissue, as the body is mostly empty space at the atomic level, and gamma rays are incredibly small in size. X-rays behave in a similar way but have slightly lower energy. By contrast, alpha and beta particles inside the body lose all their energy by colliding with tissue and causing damage.

Gamma rays can ionize atoms in tissue directly, or cause what are known as secondary ionizations. Ionizations are caused when energy is transferred from gamma rays to atomic particles, such as electrons, which are essentially the same as beta particles. These energized particles then interact with tissue to form ions through secondary ionizations. Because gamma rays are photons and thus interact less frequently with matter than alpha and beta particles, they are more penetrating, and the damage they cause can occur much farther into tissue—that is, farther from the source of radiation.

Health Effects of Gamma Radiation

How can gamma radiation affect people's health?

Because of the gamma ray's penetrating power and ability to travel great distances, it is considered the primary hazard to the general population during most radiological emergencies. In fact, when the term "radiation sickness" is used to describe the effects of large exposures in short time periods, the most severe damage almost certainly results from gamma radiation.

Protecting People from Gamma Radiation

How do I know if I'm near gamma emitters and gamma radiation?

You need specialized equipment to detect gamma radiation. You cannot see or feel radiation hitting your body. However, you should be familiar with radiation warning symbols. You can protect yourself by avoiding devices with this symbol, and not entering areas where the symbol is posted.

How do I protect myself from X-ray and gamma radiation?

Your exposure to X-rays is almost entirely from dental and medical X-rays, including mammograms. The best way to protect yourself from excessive radiation from X-rays is to make sure the technician performing the procedure has the proper qualifications, and to simply ask questions. You might inquire about the necessity of having an X-ray, or receive assurance the X-ray machine has been inspected recently and that it is properly calibrated. You should be aware of steps that can be taken to prevent exposure to other parts of your body (for example, through the use of a lead apron).

It is possible that you may encounter an industrial instrument or device containing a gamma radiation source. Every year, hundreds of devices containing radiation sources are lost, stolen, or otherwise enter the general public by mistake. For example, a factory that has gone out of business may contain one or more such devices. As the building structure is being dismantled, these forgotten devices are often considered scrap metal, and someone may think they have value and try to sell them. These devices should be avoided. You may recognize them by the radiation symbol, which means the device is radioactive. You should also look for identifying information, such as "Nuclear Regulatory Commission," or the name of a radionuclide. Sometimes the radioactive markings may be covered over and not visible.

Gamma Rays

Like visible light and X-rays, gamma rays are weightless packets or bundles of energy called photons. Gamma rays often accompany the emission of alpha or beta particles from a nucleus. They have neither a charge nor a mass and have the strongest penetrating force. Gamma rays will penetrate paper, skin, wood, and other substances. Several feet of concrete or a few inches of lead may be required to stop gamma rays.

One source of gamma rays in the environment is naturally occurring potassium-40. Fabricated sources include cobalt-60 and cesium-137. Gamma rays are a radiation hazard for humans. While gamma rays can easily pass completely through the body, a fraction of them will always be absorbed by human tissue and remain there. Gamma radiation can cause severe damage to internal organs. However, the amount of gamma rays emitted by radon and its RDPs is not nearly as damaging to the lungs as alpha particles.

X-Rays

X-rays are high-energy photons produced by the interaction of charged particles with matter. X-rays and gamma rays have essentially the same properties, but they differ in origin. X-rays are produced either from a change in the electron structure of an atom, or they are produced by machines. X-rays are emitted from processes occurring outside the nucleus, while gamma rays originate inside the nucleus. X-rays also are generally lower in energy and, therefore, less penetrating than gamma rays. A few millimeters of lead can stop X-rays.

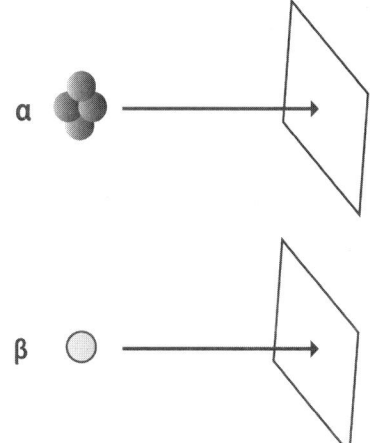

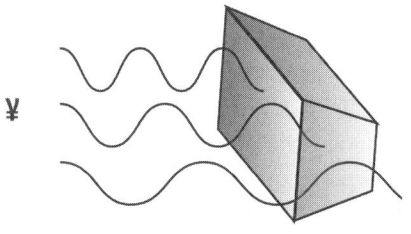

Literally thousands of X-ray machines are used daily in medicine and industry for examinations, inspections, and process controls. Because of their many uses, X-rays are the single largest source of fabricated radiation exposure.

Summary of the Characteristics of Radioactive Matter

- Alpha particle: massive size; charge of +2e; slow speed.
- Beta particle: very small size; charge of -1e; high speed.
- Gamma ray: no mass; no charge; travels at the speed of light.

Where Does Radon Come From?

Radon-222 is the decay product of radium-226. Radon-222 and its parent, radium-226, are part of the long decay chain for uranium-238. Since uranium is essentially ubiquitous in the Earth's crust, radium-226 and radon-222 are present in almost all rock, soil and water.

Who Discovered Radon?

The German chemist Friedrich E. Dorn discovered radon-222 in 1900 and called it "radium emanation." However, a scarcer isotope, radon-220, was actually observed first in 1899 by the British scientist R.B. Owens and the New Zealand scientist Ernest Rutherford. The medical community in the U.S. became aware of the possible extent of a radon problem in 1984. That year, a nuclear plant worker in Pennsylvania discovered radioactivity on his clothing while exiting his place of work through the radiation detectors. The source of the radiation was determined to be radon decay products on his clothing originating from his home.

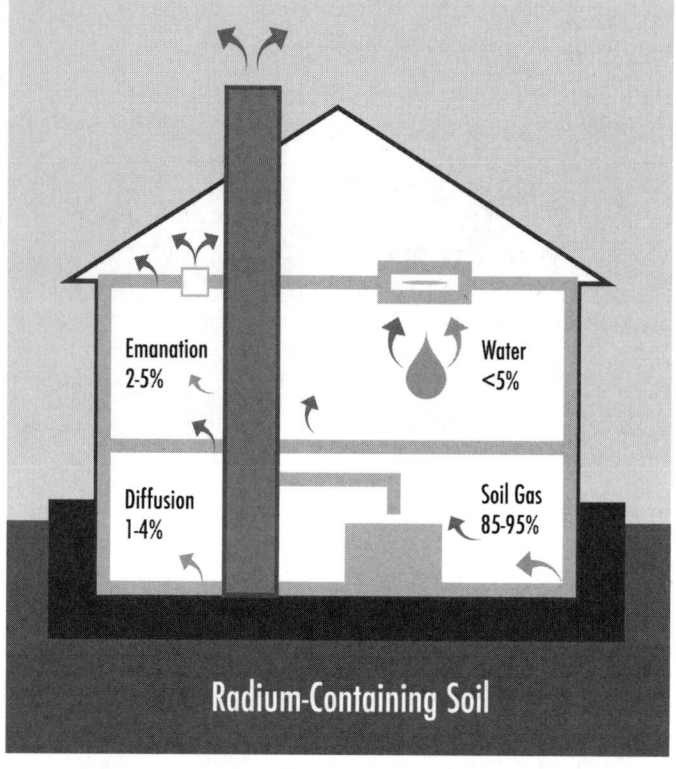

Let's learn more about radon decay products by first learning about uranium.

Uranium

Uranium (chemical symbol U) is a naturally occurring radioactive element, having the atomic number 92. Uranium is commonly found in very small amounts in rocks, soil, water, plants and animals, including humans. Uranium is weakly radioactive and contributes to low levels of natural background radiation in the environment.

Who discovered uranium?

The use of uranium in its natural oxide form dates back to at least 79 A.D. when it was used to add color to ceramic glazes. The German chemist Martin Klaproth is credited with discovering uranium in samples of the mineral pitchblende in 1789. It was first isolated as a metal in 1841 by Eugene-Melchior Peligot. Uranium was discovered to be radioactive in 1896 by French physicist Henri Becquerel. Through his work with uranium metals, he was the first to discover the process of radioactivity.

Where does uranium come from?

Uranium is a naturally occurring element found at low levels in virtually all rock, soil and water.

Significant concentrations of uranium occur in phosphate rock deposits, as well as some minerals, such as uraninite in uranium-rich ores. Because uranium has such a long radioactive half-life (4.47 x 109 years for U-238), the total amount of it on Earth stays almost the same.

What are the properties of uranium?

When refined, uranium is a silvery white, weakly radioactive metal. Uranium metal has a very high density, 65% more dense than lead. Uranium in ores can be extracted and chemically converted into uranium dioxide or other chemical forms usable in industry. Uranium found naturally has three different isotopes: U-238, U-235, and U-234. Other isotopes can be synthesized. All uranium isotopes are radioactive. The table to follow shows the percentage of natural abundance of each natural uranium isotope, and their respective half-lives.

Relative Abundance of Uranium Isotopes			
Isotope	U-238	U-235	U-234
Natural Abundance (%)	99.27	0.72	0.0055
Half-Life (in years)	4.47 billion	700 million	246,000

Uranium isotopes can be separated to increase the concentration of one isotope relative to another. This process is called enrichment. The enriched fraction has increased U-235. Uranium-235 is better for nuclear power reactors and for making nuclear weapons. The process produces huge quantities of uranium that are depleted in U-235, but are almost pure U-238, called depleted uranium, or DU.

What is uranium used for?

Uranium metal is very dense and heavy. When it is depleted (DU), uranium is used by the military as shielding to protect tanks, and also in parts of bullets and missiles. The military also uses enriched uranium to power nuclear-propelled ships and submarines, and in nuclear weapons. Fuel used for naval reactors is typically highly enriched in U-235 (although the exact values are classified information). In nuclear weapons, uranium is also highly enriched, usually over 90% (again, the exact values are classified information).

The main use of uranium in the civilian sector is to fuel commercial nuclear power plants, where fuel is typically enriched in U-235 to 2-3%. Depleted uranium is used in helicopters and airplanes as counterweights on certain wing parts. Other uses include ceramic glazes, for which small amounts of natural uranium (i.e., not having gone through the enrichment process) may be added for color. Some lighting fixtures utilize uranium, as do some photographic chemicals. Phosphate fertilizers often contain high amounts of natural uranium because the mineral material from which they are made is typically high in uranium. Also, people who collect rocks and minerals may have specimens of uranium minerals in their collection, such as pitchblende, uraninite, autunite, uranophane and coffinite.

Exposure to Uranium

How does uranium get into the environment?

Uranium is present naturally in virtually all soil, rock and water. Uranium in soil and rocks is distributed throughout the environment by wind, rain, and geologic processes. Rocks weather and break down to form soil, and soil can be washed by water and blown by wind, moving uranium into streams and lakes, and ultimately settling out and re-forming as rock. Uranium can also be removed and concentrated by people through mining and refining. These processes produce wastes, such as mill tailings, that may be introduced back into the environment by wind and water if they are not properly controlled. Manufacturing of nuclear fuel and other human activities also release uranium into the environment.

How does uranium change in the environment?

All uranium isotopes are radioactive. The three natural uranium isotopes found in the environment (U-234, U-235 and U-238) undergo radioactive decay by emission of an alpha particle accompanied by weak gamma radiation. The dominant isotope, U-238, forms a long series of decay products that includes the key radionuclides radium-226 and radon-222. The decay process continues until a stable, non-radioactive decay product is formed. The release of radiation during the decay process raises health concerns.

How are people exposed to uranium?

A person can be exposed to uranium by inhaling dust in air, or ingesting water and food. The general population is exposed to uranium primarily through food and water. The average daily intake of uranium from food ranges from 0.07 to 1.1 micrograms (µg) per day. The amount of uranium in air is usually very small. People who live near federal government facilities that made or tested nuclear weapons, or facilities that mine or process uranium ore or enrich uranium for reactor fuel may have increased exposure to uranium.

How does uranium get into the body?

Uranium can enter the body when it is inhaled or swallowed. Under rare circumstances, it may enter through cuts in the skin. Uranium does not absorb through the skin, and alpha particles released by uranium cannot penetrate the skin, so uranium that is outside the body is much less harmful than it would be if it where inhaled or swallowed. When uranium gets inside the body, it can lead to cancer or kidney damage.

What does uranium do once it gets into the body?

About 99% of the uranium ingested via food or water will leave a person's body in the feces, and the remainder will enter the bloodstream. Most of this absorbed uranium will be removed by the kidneys and excreted in the urine within a few days. A small amount of the uranium in the bloodstream will deposit in a person's bones, where it will remain for years.

Health Effects of Uranium

How can uranium affect people's health?

Intakes of uranium exceeding EPA standards can lead to increased cancer risk, liver damage, or both. Long-term chronic intakes of uranium isotopes in food, water, or air can lead to internal irradiation and/or chemical toxicity.

Is there a medical test to determine exposure to uranium?

Tests are available to measure the amount of uranium in a urine or stool sample. Hospitals do not perform these tests routinely. These tests are useful if a person is exposed to a large amount of uranium because most uranium leaves the body in the feces within a few days after ingestion. Uranium can be found in the urine for up to several months after exposure. However, the amount of uranium in the urine and feces does not always accurately show the level of uranium to which a person may have been exposed. Since uranium is known to cause kidney damage, special urine tests are often used to determine whether kidney damage has occurred.

Protecting People from Uranium

How do I know if I'm near uranium?

You need specialized equipment and training to detect uranium in the environment.

What can I do to protect myself from uranium?

Most people are not exposed to dangerous levels of uranium. However, people who live near uranium mining areas, government weapons facilities, or certain industrial facilities may have increased exposure to uranium, especially if their water is from a private well. Analytical laboratories can test water for uranium content. Occasionally, household wares may be found with uranium in them, such as some older ceramic dishes and plates whose glazes contain uranium. These generally do not pose serious health risks but should nevertheless be retired from regular use as a prudent measure. A radiation counter is required to confirm if ceramics contain uranium.

What is the EPA doing about uranium?

The EPA standards under the Clean Air Act limit uranium in the air. The maximum dose for an individual from uranium in the air is 10 millirems (mrem). The cleanup of contaminated sites to be released for public use must meet the EPA's risk-based criteria for soil and groundwater. The EPA's site cleanup standards limit a person's increased chance of developing cancer to between 1 in 10,000 to 1 in 1,000,000 from residual uranium on the ground. Site-specific factors, cost, and community concerns are weighed when establishing the actual cleanup value.

Uranium in drinking water is covered under the Safe Drinking Water Act. This law establishes maximum contaminant levels, or MCLs, for radionuclides and other contaminants in drinking water. The uranium limit is 30 µg/L (micrograms per liter) in drinking water.

Uranium Decay Chain

Now, let's learn about what happens when uranium undergoes radioactive decays and energy is emitted in the transformation.

Most naturally occurring radioactive materials and many fission products undergo radioactive decay through a series of transformations (loss of particles or electromagnetic energy from an unstable nucleus), rather than in a single step. Until the last step, these radionuclides emit energy or particles with each transformation and become another radionuclide. Man-made elements, which are all unstable and heavier than uranium, undergo decay in this way. This decay chain, or decay series, ends in a stable nuclide.

Uranium-238 Decay Chain

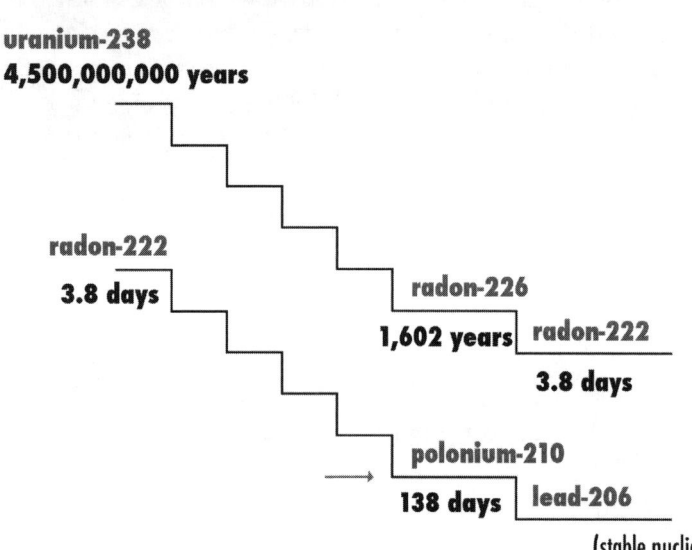

For example, uranium-238 decays through a series of steps to become a stable form of lead. Each step in the illustration at left indicates a different nuclide. Only a few of the steps are labeled, and the numbers below each label indicate the length of the particular radionuclide's half-life. Uranium-238 has the longest half-life of 4.5 billion years, and radon-222 has the shortest, being 3.8 days. The last radionuclide in the chain, polonium-210, transforms into lead-210 and, eventually, into the stable nuclide lead-206.

The radioactive decay chain for radon begins with uranium. Uranium decays to produce radium, which then decays into radon. Radon then decays into other RDPs (or radon decay products), which are also radioactive.

RDPs are different from actual radon is a few ways:

- They are the source of cell damage in the lungs.
- They are short-lived products (less than 30 minutes), but the most significant.
- They have static electrical charges.
- They are chemically reactive.
- They are solid particles, rather than gases, that act like invisible aerosols in the air.
- They are classified as heavy metals.

All of these characteristics make the decay products capable of easily attaching themselves to solid objects, such as dust, smoke, walls, floors, clothing, and more. If the RDPs attach to surfaces, they are no longer floating in the air and are said to "plate out." If they attach to ducts or smoke particles, they can be carried into the lungs where they can cause lung cancer. And this is the important thing to remember: RDPs can be easily inhaled.

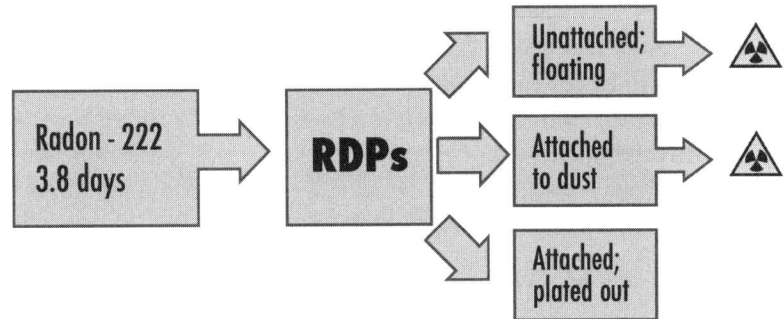

The Importance of Radionuclide Decay Chains

Radionuclide decay chains are important in planning for the management and disposal of radioactive materials and waste and for site cleanup. As radioactive decay progresses, the concentration of the original radionuclides decreases, while the concentration of their decay products increases, and then decreases as they undergo transformation.

Ingrowth

The increasing concentration of decay products and activity is called ingrowth. The illustration below shows ingrowth when the decay product is stable and the original radionuclide is replaced. In this situation, the activity decreases with the decay of the original radionuclide.

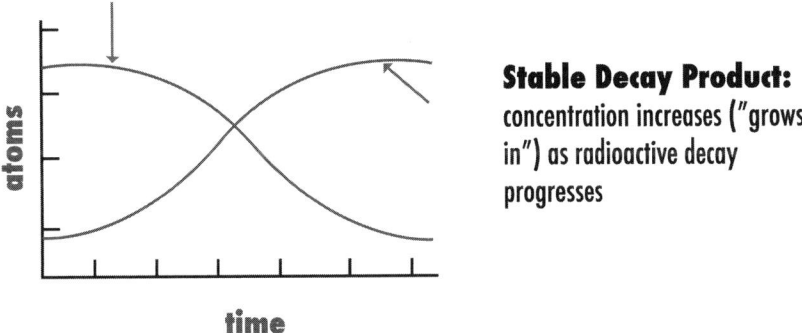

If the decay products are not stable, their decay contributes to the total activity and makes planning for radiation protection more complex.

In the case of a radioactive waste repository, the mix of radionuclides in the waste will change over time. The amount of radiation being released can actually rise over time as successive radioactive decay products undergo decay. The radiation protection standards set for a repository must take into account varying levels of radioactivity as successive iterations of radionuclide ingrowth take place, even though the process continues over thousands of years.

How do scientists know how much radioactivity there will be?

The pattern of ingrowth varies according to the relative length of the half-lives of the original radionuclide and its decay products. Under certain conditions, decay products undergo transformation at the same rate that they are produced. When this occurs, radioactive equilibrium is said to exist. Whether equilibrium occurs depends on the relative lengths of the half-lives of radionuclides and their decay products.

Using equations that account for half-lives, the rate of ingrowth, whether equilibrium occurs, the original amount of radionuclide, and the steps in its decay chain, scientists can estimate the amount of activity that will be present at various points.

Radon Ingrowth During Uranium Decay

The importance of understanding decay chains is illustrated by the ingrowth of radon-222 during the decay of uranium-238. Uranium was distributed widely in the Earth's crust as it formed. Given the age of the Earth, uranium's slowly progressing decay chain now commonly produces radon-222.

Radon is radioactive and has several characteristics that magnify its health effects:

- Radon is a gas. It can seep through soil and the cracks in rocks and into the air. It can seep through the foundations of homes (particularly basements), and accumulate into fairly high concentrations.
- Radon decay emits alpha particles, which is the radiation that presents the greatest hazard to lung tissue.
- Radon's very short half-life of 3.8 days means that it emits alpha particles at a high rate.

During exposure assessments, pay close attention to the potential for radon generation. In designing cleanup standards for uranium mill tailings sites, the EPA targeted radium-226, which decays to radon-222, rather than targeting radon-222 alone. Radium-226 continues to generate radon-222 during its much longer half-life.

Radon and Uranium Miners

A higher-than-expected level of lung disease in uranium miners helped call attention to the effects of radon-222. The miners worked long hours in enclosed spaces, surrounded by uranium ore and radon that seeped out of the rock. Health workers expected to see health problems in the miners that would reflect direct exposure to radiation. Instead, the predominant health problems were lung cancer and other lung diseases.

At first, the health workers suspected the dust itself. They knew that high concentrations of small particles, such as coal dust, asbestos, and cotton fibers, could damage workers' lungs. However, close examination of the uranium-238 decay chain identified radon-222 as the most likely culprit.

This led to regulations in two areas:

1. improved ventilation in uranium mines; and
2. limits on the amount of radon ventilated from the mines to the ambient air.

Radon Half-Life

The half-life of radon is the time period that radon and its decay products (RDPs) have to be dispersed into the environment. A few radon decay products have short half-lives, but if they are inhaled, they can cause radiation damage to the lungs.

The rate of radioactive decay is characteristic of each radionuclide. Scientists talk about this rate as a radionuclide's radioactive half-life. It is the time required for the disintegration of one-half of the radioactive atoms that are present when measurement starts. It does not represent a fixed number of atoms that disintegrate, but only a fraction.

For example, if there are 100 atoms of a radionuclide that has a half-life of one minute, there will be one-half that number, or 50 atoms, of the original radionuclide left one minute later. After the second minute, there will be 25 atoms of the original radionuclide left. The fact that this simple example points to the existence of 12.5 radioactive atoms after three minutes illustrates that a half-life is intended to be used for the very large number of atoms that are found in even small samples of radioactive materials. So, 100 atoms aren't going to give off much radiation.

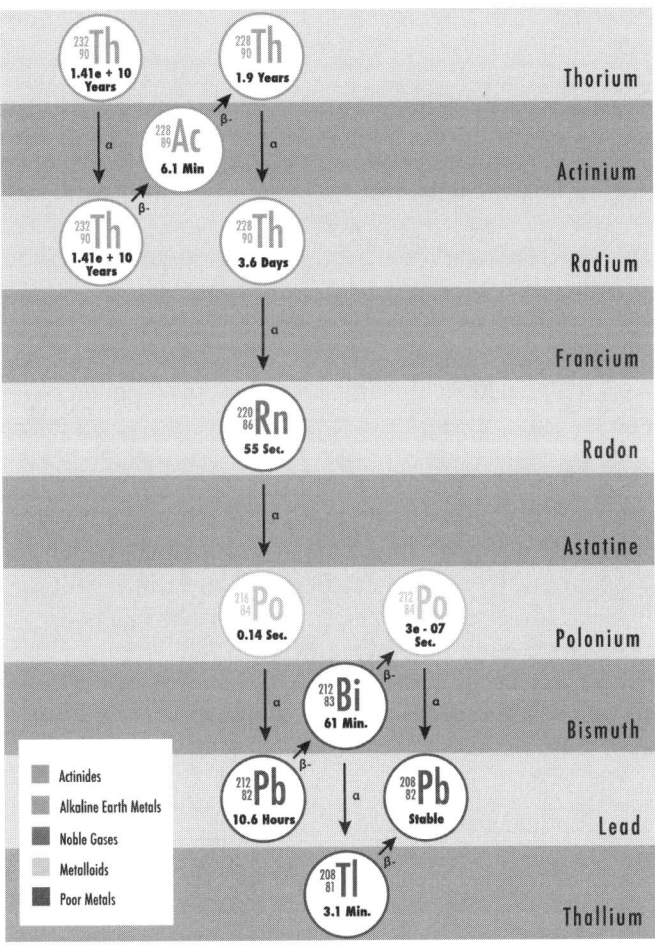

The half-life refers to how quickly the radioactivity from a radionuclide will decrease. Its number of curies tells how active it is now.

Each radioactive element in the radon decay chain has a different half-life. Half-life is the time required for half of the atoms of the element to decay. It is not the time for all of the atoms to decay. If you have an amount of radon with a half-life of 3.8 days, by the end of 3.8 days, you will have half as much. Another 3.8 days later, you will have half that amount, and so on. Usually, by the time 10 half-lives have passed, there is very little left.

It is important to understand the half-life process because it is this time period that radon and its decay products have to be dispersed into the environment. A period of 3.8 days is long enough for radon to move through several feet of soil. The first few radon decay products have short half-lives, but if they are inhaled, they can cause radiation damage to the inner lining of the lungs before they can be exhaled.

Radon gas, like carbon-14 gas, is naturally occurring in our environment. It forms during the decay of uranium-238, an element with a fairly interesting decay sequence.

The graphic above shows the radioactive decay chain of uranium. The shaded circles are the decay products of radon gas. These radon decay products (RDPs) release high-energy alpha particles, which can be very harmful to people.

Radon has no stable isotopes. However, 36 radioactive isotopes have been characterized, with their atomic masses ranging from 193 to 228. The most stable isotope is Rn-222, which is a decay product of Ra-226, a decay product of U-238. A trace amount of the highly unstable isotope Rn-218 is also among the daughters of Rn-222.

There are three other radon isotopes that have a half-life of over an hour: Rn-211, Rn-210 and Rn-224. The Rn-220 isotope is a natural decay product of the most stable thorium isotope (Th-232), and is commonly referred to as thoron. It has a half-life of 55.6 seconds and also emits alpha radiation. Similarly, Rn-219 is derived from the most stable isotope of actinium (Ac-227)—named actinon—and is an alpha emitter with a half-life of 3.96 seconds. No radon isotopes occur significantly in the neptunium (Np-237) decay series, though a trace amount of the extremely unstable isotope Rn-217 is produced.

Rn-222 belongs to the radium and uranium-238 decay chain, and has a half-life of 3.8235 days. Its four first products (excluding marginal decay schemes) are very short-lived, meaning that the corresponding disintegrations are indicative of the initial radon distribution. Its decay goes through the following sequence:

- Rn-222, 3.8 days, alpha decaying to...

- Po-218, 3.10 minutes, alpha decaying to...

- Pb-214, 26.8 minutes, beta decaying to...

- Bi-214, 19.9 minutes, beta decaying to...

- Po-214, 0.1643 milliseconds, alpha decaying to...

- Pb-210, which has a much longer half-life of 22.3 years, beta decaying to...

- Bi-210, 5.013 days, beta decaying to...

- Po-210, 138.376 days, alpha decaying to...

- PB-206, which is stable.

The radon equilibrium factor is the ratio between the activity of all short-period radon progenies (which are responsible for most of radon's biological effects), and the activity that would be at equilibrium with the radon parent.

If a closed volume is constantly supplied with radon, the concentration of short-lived isotopes will increase until an equilibrium is reached where the rate of decay of each decay product will equal that of the radon itself. The equilibrium factor is 1 when both activities are equal, meaning that the decay products have stayed close to the radon parent long enough for equilibrium to be reached (within a couple of hours). Under these conditions, each additional pCi/L of radon will increase exposure by 0.01 WL (see explanation of WL to follow). These conditions are not always met. In many homes, the equilibrium fraction is typically 40%; that is, there will be 0.004 WL of progeny for each pCi/L of radon in air. Pb-210 takes much longer—decades—to come into equilibrium with radon, but if the environment permits accumulation of dust over extended periods of time, Pb-210 and its decay products may contribute to the overall radiation levels, as well.

Because of their electrostatic charge, radon progenies adhere to surfaces and dust particles, whereas gaseous radon does not. Attachment removes them from the air, usually causing the equilibrium factor in the atmosphere to be less than 1. The equilibrium factor is also lowered by air circulation or air filtration devices, and is increased by airborne dust particles, including cigarette smoke. In high concentrations, airborne radon isotopes contribute significantly to human health risk.

Curies, Equations, and Equilibrium Ratio

Since small amounts of material contain very large numbers of atoms, small samples can have a very large number of atoms disintegrating at the same time. It didn't take radiation scientists very long to decide that working with activities in the billions-of-disintegrations-per-second range was too clumsy. To make measuring the activity more convenient, they developed a new unit, the curie, named in honor of Marie Curie, a pioneer in the study of radioactive materials. Radioactive materials are measured in curies. A picocurie is one-millionth of a millionth (or a trillionth) of a curie.

How big is a curie?

A curie is defined as 37 billion disintegrations per second. The curie was originally a comparison of the activity of a sample to the activity of 1 gram of radium. When more accurate techniques measured a slightly different activity for radium, the reference to radium was dropped. A radioactive sample that has an activity of 74 billion disintegrations per second has a measured activity of 2 curies.

Are there smaller and larger units of activity?

The curie, abbreviated Ci, is a very large unit for some purposes, and a very small unit for others. Scientists use the following fractions or multiples of a curie, as well:

- Picocuries (pCi) are 1 million-millionth of a curie (1×10^{-12} Ci). Picocuries are used in measuring the typically small amounts of radioactivity that are present in air and water.

- Megacuries (MCi) are 1 million curies (1×10^{6} Ci) and are used in measuring the very large amounts of radioactivity released from nuclear weapons, for example.

- Other fractions, such as:
  - a millicurie (1/1,000 Ci = mCi), and
  - a nanocurie (1 billionth of a curie = nCi) are used as needed.

Terms and More Equations

- A curie (Ci) is a standard measurement for radioactivity—specifically, the rate of decay for a gram of radium = 37 billion decays per second. A unit of radioactivity equal to 3.7×10^{10} disintegrations per second.

- A picocurie (pCi) measures the rate of the radioactive decay of radon. One pCi is one trillionth of a curie, 0.037 disintegrations per second, or 2.22 disintegrations per minute.

- A picocurie per liter (pCi/L) is a unit of radioactivity corresponding to an average of one decay every 27 seconds in a volume of 1 liter, or 0.037 decays per second per liter of air or water. So, 1 pCi/L = 37 becquerels per cubic meter (Bq/m^3).

- A becquerel (Bq) is defined by the SI or International System of Units in terms of its activity: 1 Bq = 1 disintegration per second. One picocurie per liter of radon is the same as 37 bequerels per cubic meter.

The amount of radon in the air is measured in picocuries per liter of air (pCi/L), which is the number of radioactive disintegrations per minute in a liter of air. A pCi/L is 2.22 disintegrations per minute for each liter. If a gallon container held air with 4 pCi/L, there would be about 4 quarts per gallon multiplied by 4 pCi/L multiplied by 2.22 disintegrations per minute, or about 35.2 disintegrations per minute of radon atoms in the container.

Test results are sometimes expressed in working levels (WL), rather than in picocuries per liter (pCi/L), using this formula: 4 pCi/L = 0.016 WL.

Radon decay products are measured in working levels (WL). Any combination of short-lived radon decay products in 1 liter of air will result in the ultimate emission of 1.3×10^5 MeV (million electron volts) of potential alpha energy. This number was chosen because it represents the approximate amount of alpha energy released from the decay products in equilibrium with 100 pCi of Rn-222. One working level is the concentration of short-lived RDPs produced from 1 liter of air containing 100 pCi of radon.

The average indoor radon level is 1.3 pCi/L.

The average outdoor radon level is 0.4 pCi/L.

The EPA's action level for radon is 4 pCi/L. The EPA's action level for radon is 0.02 WL.

Equilibrium Ratio (ER)

There is a relationship between decay product concentration and radon gas concentration. Radon is said to be at "secular equilibrium" with its decay products when the radioactive activity of radon and its decay products are the same.

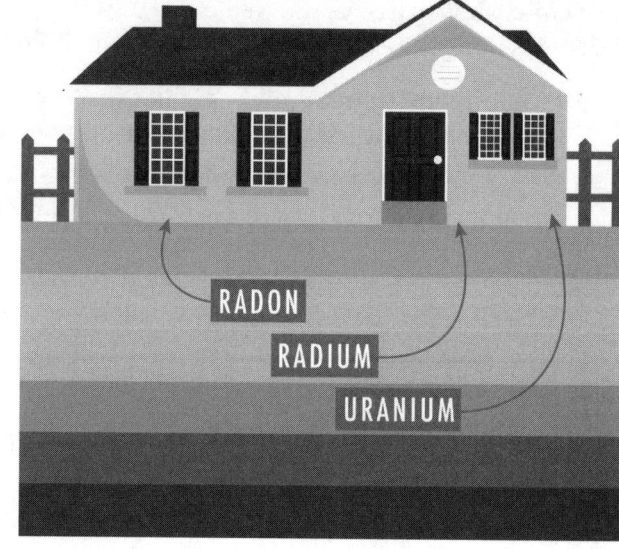

The equilibrium ratio for radon is expressed this way: equilibrium ratio = (WL x 100) ÷ (pCi/L). At complete equilibrium (i.e., at an equilibrium ratio of 1), 1 WL of RDPs is present when the radon concentration is 100 pCi/L. But due to ventilation and plate-out, the RDPs never reach equilibrium in a residential environment, so the ratio is never 1 inside a house. The commonly assumed equilibrium ratio is 0.5 (i.e., the decay products are halfway toward equilibrium), in which case 1 WL would correspond to 200 pCi/L. However, equilibrium ratios vary with time and location, and ratios of 0.3 to 0.7 are common.

RDPs

Atoms of radioactive radon gas decay by the emission of alpha particles and transform into polonium-218 and, in turn, transform into polonium-214 by a successive alpha emission.

Daughters

In the air of the average room, both radon and the two radioactive isotopes of polonium are present (214 and 218) and are often referred to as radon progeny or radon decay products (RDPs). These may stay free or may attach to room aerosol (such as dust or smoke). It is these radon progeny that get deposited in airways and cause the primary risk of inhalation. Radon gas itself does not pose much risk.

Action Level

Based on the actual risk observed in uranium miners, the EPA has set the action level limit at 0.02 WL. Because radon daughter products can get deposited in ventilation systems and on other surfaces, they do not reach equilibrium with radon. Based on some experimental data from typical homes, the EPA assumes that the equilibrium ratio is 50%. The action level limit of 0.02 WL corresponds to the derived radon concentration of 4 pCi/L when the equilibrium ratio is 50%.

There are two methods for characterizing radon: either measure radon gas concentration, or measure radon progeny concentration. The EPA's action level limit is 4 pCi/L for radon gas, and 0.02 WL for radon progeny. These measurements are equivalent to each other only when the equilibrium ratio is 50%. Both measurements are acceptable, as long as EPA-listed devices and methods are used. (These are also now listed as NEHA or NRSB.)

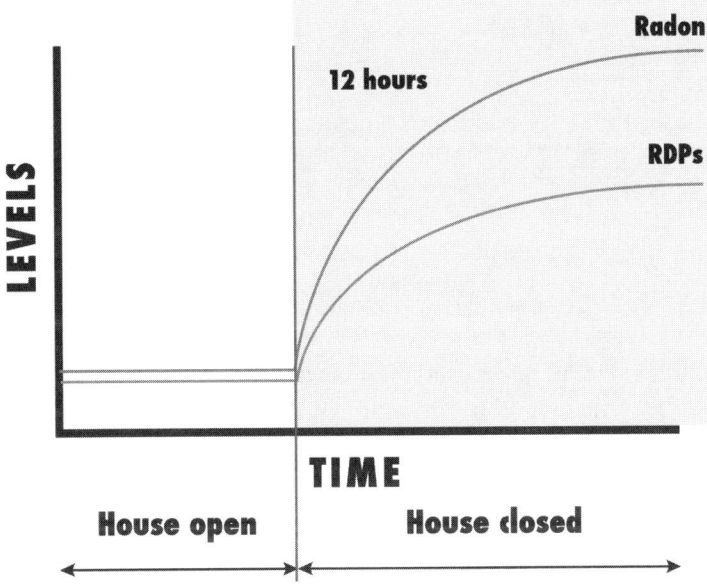

Once radon enters a home, it begins to form decay products. Some activities inside the home may affect the equilibrium. Air filtering would remove some of the decay products, but not the radon because it is an inert gas. Air leakage might allow some of the RDPs to escape. RDPs might cling to or plate out on walls, floors, and other surfaces. All of these factors can prevent the RDPs from reaching the maximum concentration. They will eventually reach a final concentration, which is a balance of the amount of RDPs that are produced and are lost through plate-out and ventilation. It is this balance that is referred to as the equilibrium ratio. In a home, it typically takes about 12 hours for this equilibrium to be achieved, after the doors and windows have been closed.

Assumption

In order to relate the measurement of radon to an equivalent amount of radon decay products, it is necessary to assume a ratio of the amount of radon decay products that are produced and available for inhalation from the amount of radon in the air. That's what the equilibrium ratio or ER is.

ER can be calculated as:

Equilibrium Ratio = Working Level x 100 ÷ Radon Concentration, or ER = (WL x 100) ÷ Rn

For example, if the radon concentration is 75 pCi/L, and the decay product concentration is 0.3 WL, the equilibrium ratio would be calculated as follows:

ER = (0.3) x (100) ÷ 75 = 0.4

This assumption (the equilibrium ratio) came about from extensive research and statistics available when radon in homes and buildings was starting to be investigated. The assumption of 50%, which is used today, is based on residential structures with average air recirculation rates, with a typical range of suspended radon decay products between 30% and 70%.

This assumed equilibrium rate of 50% equates to 0.02 WL measurements, which is the EPA's established action level. So,

radon = WL x 100 ÷ 0.5

and

4 (radon) = 0.02 (radon decay products) x 100 ÷ 0.5 (assumed equilibrium ratio).

ER ≠ 1

Again, an equilibrium ratio of 1 will likely not occur in any house because ventilation removes both radon and RDPs. RDPs have an electrostatic charge and will plate out by clinging to walls, floors, furniture, and other solid objects. This reduces the RDP concentration without affecting the radon concentration. And it takes a while for radon entering the house to produce RDPs. As a result, the ER will always be less than 1.

The equation ER = (WL x 100) ÷ Rn can be arranged to calculate the desired expression:

$$\text{ER} = (\text{WL} \times 100) \div \text{Rn} \qquad \text{or} \qquad \text{WL} = (\text{Rn} \times \text{ER}) \div 100 \qquad \text{or} \qquad \text{Rn} = (\text{WL} \times 100) \div \text{ER}$$

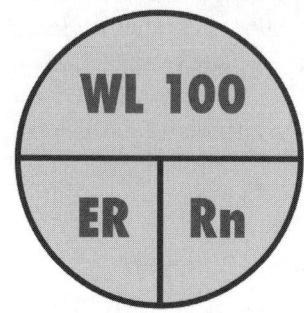

If the radon level is measured at 4 pCi/L and the working levels are measured at 0.02 WL, then the equilibrium ratio (ER) is equal to 0.02 x 100 ÷ 4 = 0.5, or 50%.

Unattached particles (which are solid, electrically charged particles) can be inhaled and become lodged in the lungs. When they stick to objects such as dust, smoke and pollen, RDPs can still present a health hazard if the object is small enough to float in the air. Remember that if they plate out on a wall, they are not a hazard.

If air is being circulated by fans, a lot of the RDPs can plate out on the walls, floors, furniture, and other solid objects. Working levels can be lowered by using fans. The radon concentration will stay the same, but the ER will be lower. The ER is also lower after a house has been ventilated with

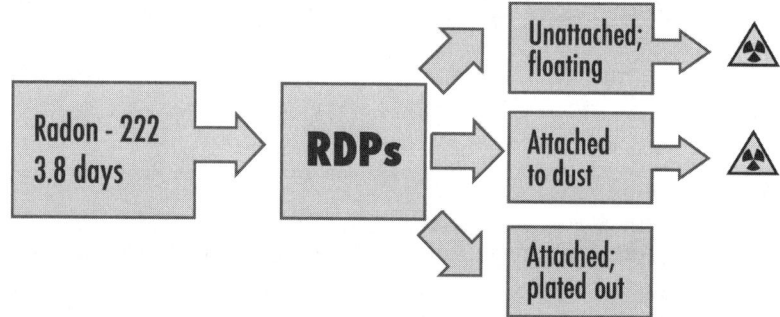

outdoor air. The soil gas entering a house has very low decay products because RDPs will plate out in the soil. Therefore, if a house is ventilated and then closed up, it takes several hours for the decay products to return to an expected equilibrium of radon concentration.

Factors Affecting the Equilibrium Ratio

Increased air movement causes more of the hazardous RDPs to adhere to fixed objects, and they do not detach once in they make contact with an object. This decreases the amount of radon decay products available for inhalation, and also decreases the equilibrium ratio.

For instance, in buildings with large air flows or HEPA filters, the percentage of airborne radon decay products can be considerably lower than in a building without them.

If the indoor air is relatively stable, with little air movement that would remove RDPs, then the ER will likely be high, since there will be more decay products in the air. If there is a high-efficiency, whole-house air filtering system that is operating with a high degree of air movement, then a low ER would be expected.

Summary

Radon-222:

- is a gas;
- is odorless;
- is tasteless;
- is invisible;
- mixes with air;
- is chemically inert (or non-reactive);
- is found everywhere;
- decays by alpha particle emission; and
- has a half-life of 3.8 days.

Radon Decay Products, or RDPs:

- are solids, called daughters or progeny;
- are chemically active;
- are electrically charged;
- can attach to air particles and cling to surfaces;
- have a ratio of progeny-to-radon gas ranging from 0.3 to 0.7 ER (equilibrium ratio), averaging 0.5 ER;
- are short-lived (from 0.2 milliseconds to 26.8 minutes); and
- include polonium-218, 214 and 210, which are alpha particle emitters, and these alpha particle emissions can cause physical cellular damage, such as lung cancer.

Quiz #1

1. _____ are the extremely small particles of which we and everything around us are made.

   ☐ Particles

   ☐ Radon

   ☐ Ions

   ☐ Atoms

2. If one atom were the size of the Houston Astrodome, its nucleus would be roughly the size of a(n) _____.

   ☐ airplane

   ☐ pea

   ☐ building

   ☐ submarine

3. T/F: The balance of the forces in the nucleus of an atom determines whether a nucleus is stable or unstable (radioactive).

   ☐ True

   ☐ False

4. As an unstable nucleus emits radiation as it disintegrates, the radionuclide transforms to different nuclides, and this process is called _____.

   ☐ radon gas mitigation

   ☐ radio transmission

   ☐ radioactive decay

   ☐ radioactive development

5. A _____ refers to the series of transformations that a given radionuclide will undergo, as well as the kind of radiation it emits, which are characteristic of the radionuclide.

   ☐ radon mitigation

   ☐ decay chain

   ☐ radiation

   ☐ radon curies

6. Radioactive half-life is the time required for the disintegration of _____ of the radioactive atoms that are present when measurement starts.

   ☐ one-half

   ☐ one and one-half

   ☐ one-fourth

   ☐ one-third

7. _____ is the energy that is released as particles or rays during radioactive decay.

    ☐ Ioning

    ☐ Disintegration

    ☐ Atomizing

    ☐ Radiation

8. _____ is the property of an atom that describes spontaneous changes in its nucleus that create a different nuclide, and these changes usually happen as emissions of alpha or beta particles, and often gamma rays.

    ☐ Radioactivity

    ☐ Atomic weight

    ☐ Decay chain

    ☐ Gaseous emission

9. Radiation that falls within the _____ range has enough energy to remove tightly bound electrons from atoms, thus creating ions, and this is the type of radiation that people usually think of as radiation.

    ☐ ionizing radiation

    ☐ non-ionizing radiation

10. _____ particles include two protons and two neutrons.

    ☐ Alpha

    ☐ Beta

    ☐ Gamma

11. We're really concerned with the _____ particles because they can be stopped by a sheet of paper where they release their energy.

    ☐ gamma

    ☐ alpha

    ☐ beta

    ☐ X-ray

12. T/F: Radon is a light gas and tends to collect in the upper areas of houses, such as attics.

    ☐ True

    ☐ False

13. Some decay products of radon emit beta particles, but its alpha-emitting decay products pose a much _____ health risk.

    ☐ greater

    ☐ lesser

14. _____ photons can pass through many kinds of materials, including human tissue.

☐ Beta
☐ Gamma
☐ Alpha

15. Most naturally occurring radioactive materials and many fission products undergo radioactive decay through a series of _____, which is a loss of particles or electromagnetic energy from an unstable nucleus, rather than in a single step.

☐ reflections
☐ growth spurts
☐ transformations
☐ misinterpretations

16. _____ are the source of cell damage in the lungs.

☐ Radon elements
☐ RDPs
☐ Radium elements
☐ Uranium materials

17. T/F: Radon gas tastes like sulfur.

☐ True
☐ False

18. T/F: If RDPs plate out on a wall, they are a hazard.

☐ True
☐ False

19. If the radon concentration is 75 pCi/L, and the decay product concentration is 0.3 WL, the equilibrium ratio would be calculated as follows: ER = (0.3) x (100) ÷ 75 = _____.

☐ 2.22
☐ 4.0
☐ 30.75
☐ 0.4

20. T/F: The action level limit of 0.02 WL corresponds to the derived radon concentration of 4 pCi/L when the equilibrium ratio is 50%.

☐ True
☐ False

21. The average indoor radon level is _____ pCi/L.

    ☐ 1.3
    ☐ 4.0
    ☐ 100.3
    ☐ 2.22

22. If a gallon container held air with 4 pCi/L, there would be about 4 quarts per gallon multiplied by 4 pCi/L multiplied by 2.22 disintegrations per minute, or about _____ disintegrations per minute of radon atoms in the container.

    ☐ 35.2
    ☐ 70.4
    ☐ 8.88
    ☐ 4.0

23. If there are 100 atoms of a radionuclide that has a half-life of one minute, there will be one-half that number, or _____ atoms of the original radionuclide left one minute later.

    ☐ 25
    ☐ 200
    ☐ 50
    ☐ 150

24. T/F: If you have an amount of radon with a half-life of 3.8 days, by the end of 3.8 days, you will have half as much.

    ☐ True
    ☐ False

Answer Key is on page 346.

Health Effects

Introduction to Radon's Health Risks

Radon is a worldwide health risk in homes. Most radon-induced lung cancers occur from low- and medium-dose exposures in people's homes. Radon is the second leading cause of lung cancer, after smoking, in many countries.

- Lung cancer kills thousands of Americans every year. Smoking, radon, and secondhand smoke are the leading causes of lung cancer. Although lung cancer can be treated, the survival rate is one of the lowest among all those with cancer. From the time of diagnosis, between 11 and 15% of those afflicted will live beyond five years, depending upon demographic factors. In many cases, lung cancer can be prevented.

- Smoking is the leading cause of lung cancer. Smoking causes an estimated 159,000 cancer deaths in the U.S. every year (American Cancer Society, 2014). And the rate among women is rising. On January 11, 1964, Dr. Luther L. Terry, then U.S. Surgeon General, issued the first warning on the link between smoking and lung cancer. Lung cancer now surpasses breast cancer as the number one cause of death among women. A smoker who is also exposed to radon has a much higher risk of lung cancer.

- Radon is the number one cause of lung cancer among non-smokers, according to EPA estimates. Overall, radon is the second leading cause of lung cancer. Radon is responsible for about 20,000 lung cancer deaths every year. About 2,900 of these deaths occur among people who have never smoked. On January 13, 2005, Dr. Richard H. Carmona, the U.S. Surgeon General, issued a national health advisory on radon.

- Secondhand smoke is the third leading cause of lung cancer and is responsible for an estimated 3,000 lung cancer deaths every year. Smoking affects non-smokers by exposing them to secondhand smoke. Exposure to secondhand smoke can have serious consequences for children's health, including asthma attacks, effects on the respiratory tract (e.g., bronchitis, pneumonia), and possibly ear infections.

The following websites provide a wide range of comprehensive information about lung cancer and its prevention and treatment:

- American Cancer Society: **www.cancer.org**
- American Lung Association: **www.lung.org**
- National Cancer Institute: **www.cancer.gov**
- Vanderbilt-Ingram Cancer Center: **www.vicc.org**
- Memorial Sloan-Kettering Cancer Center: **www.mskcc.org**

Studies Find Direct Evidence Linking Radon in Homes to Lung Cancer

Studies conducted in 2005 showed definitive evidence of an association between residential radon exposure and lung cancer. Two studies, a North American study and a European study, both combined data from several previous residential studies. These two studies go a step beyond earlier findings. They confirm the radon health risks predicted by occupational studies of underground miners who breathed radon for years. Early in the debate about radon-related risks, some researchers questioned whether occupational studies could be used to calculate risks from exposure to radon in the home environment. "These findings effectively end any doubts about the risks to Americans of having radon in their homes," said Tom Kelly, former director of the EPA's Indoor Environments Division. "We know that radon is a carcinogen. This research confirms that breathing low levels of radon can lead to lung cancer."

The WHO's International Radon Project

In 2009, the World Health Organization (WHO) said that radon causes up to 15% of lung cancers worldwide. In an effort to reduce the rate of lung cancer around the world, the WHO launched an international radon project to help countries increase awareness, collect data, and encourage action to reduce radon-related risks. The U.S. EPA is one of several government agencies and countries supporting this initiative and was encouraged by the WHO's attention to this important public health issue. "Radon poses an easily reducible health risk to populations all over the world, but has not, up to now, received widespread attention," said Dr. Michael Repacholi, coordinator of the WHO's Radiation and Environmental Health Unit. He went on to say, "Radon in our homes is the main source of exposure to ionizing radiation, and accounts for 50% of the public's exposure to naturally occurring sources of radiation in many countries."

The U.S. Surgeon General's National Health Advisory on Radon

On January 13, 2005, then-U.S. Surgeon General Richard H. Carmona issued a health advisory warning Americans about the health risk from exposure to radon in indoor air. He urged Americans to test their homes to find out how much radon they might be breathing in. Dr. Carmona also stressed the need to remedy the problem as soon as possible when the radon level is 4 pCi/L or more, noting that more than 20,000 Americans die of radon-related lung cancer each year.

Radon-Related Lung Cancer Deaths Compared to Other Selected Cancers

The following graphic compares EPA estimates of the annual radon-related lung cancer deaths to other selected cancers.

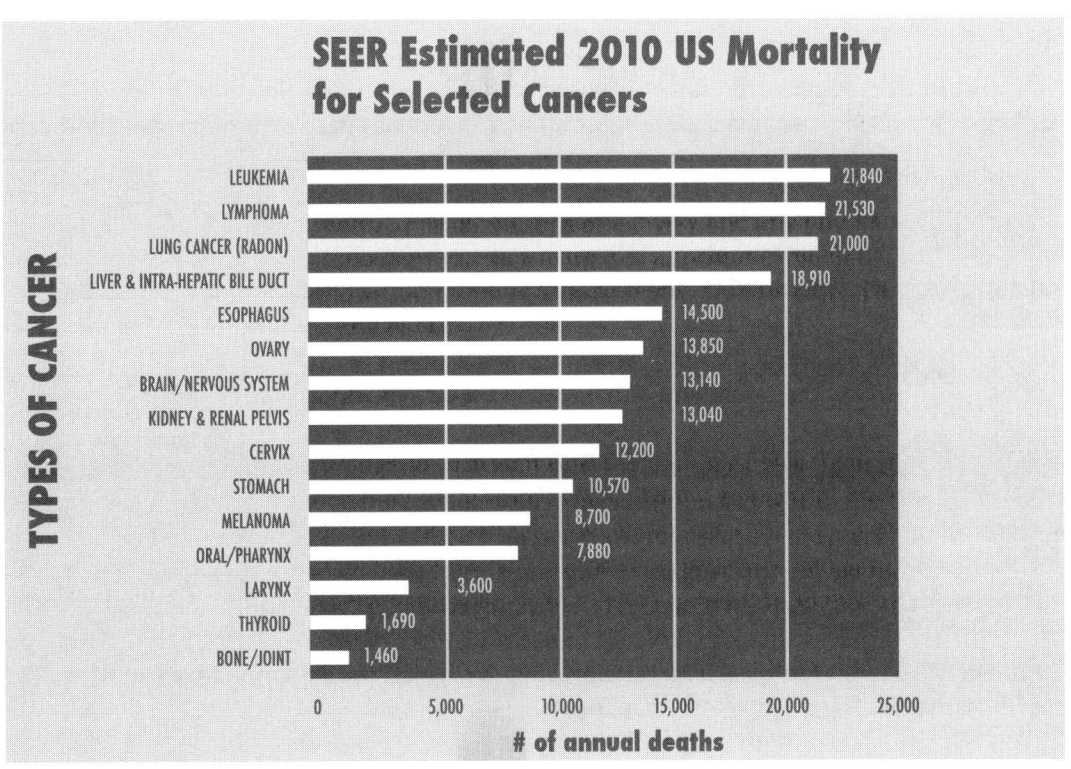

How does radon induce cancer?

If inhaled, radon decay products (polonium-218 and polonium-214 in solid form), unattached or attached to the surface of aerosols, dusts and smoke particles, become deeply lodged in the lungs where they can radiate and penetrate the cells of mucous membranes, bronchi, and other pulmonary tissues. The ionizing radiation energy affecting the bronchial epithelial cells is believed to initiate the process of carcinogenesis. Although radon-related lung cancers are mainly seen in the upper airways, radon increases the incidence of all histological types of lung cancer, including small-cell carcinoma, Aden carcinoma, and squamous cell carcinoma. Lung cancer due to inhalation of radon decay products constitutes the only known risk associated with radon. In studies done on miners, variables such as age, duration of exposure, time since initiation of exposure, and especially the use of tobacco have been found to influence individual risk. In fact, the use of tobacco multiplies the risk of radon-induced lung cancer enormously.

What is the evidence?

More is known about the health risk of radon exposure to humans than about most other human carcinogens. This knowledge is based on extensive epidemiological studies of thousands of underground miners carried out over more than 50 years worldwide, including on miners in the United States and Canada. In addition to the data on miners, experimental exposures on laboratory animals confirm that radon and its decay products can cause lung cancer.

Human Studies and Animal Studies

Research on lung cancer mortality in miners exposed to radon progeny is substantial and consistent. Studies of thousands of miners, some with follow-up periods of 30 years or more, have been conducted in metal, fluorspar, shale, and uranium mines in the United States, Canada, Australia, China and Europe. These studies have consistently shown an increase in the occurrence of lung cancer with exposure to radon decay products, despite differences in study populations and methodologies.

The miner studies detailed the following findings:

- At equal cumulative exposures, low exposures in the range of the EPA's 4 pCi/L action level over longer periods produced a greater risk of lung cancer than high exposures over short periods.

- Increased lung cancer risk with radon exposure has been observed even after controlling for, or in the absence of, other exposure risks, such as asbestos, silica, diesel fumes, arsenic, chromium, nickel, and ore dust.

- Non-smoking miners exposed to radon were observed to have an increased risk of lung cancer.

Animal experiments conducted by the U.S. Department of Energy's Office of Energy Research, as well as those conducted in France, have confirmed the carcinogenicity of radon, and have provided insight into the nature of the exposure-response relationship, as well as the modifying effects of the exposure rates.

To date, these animal studies have produced several relevant findings for humans:

- Health effects observed in animals exposed to radon and radon decay products include lung carcinomas, pulmonary fibrosis, emphysema, and a shortening of lifespan.

- The incidence of respiratory tract tumors grew with an increase in cumulative exposure coupled with a decrease in rate of exposure.

- Increased incidence of respiratory tract tumors was observed in rats at cumulative exposures as low as 20 WLM.

- Exposure to ore dust or diesel fumes simultaneously with radon did not increase the incidence of lung tumors above that produced by radon progeny exposures alone.

- Lifetime lung-tumor risk coefficients that have been observed in animals are similar to the lifetime lung-cancer risk coefficients observed in human studies.

- In a study of rats exposed to radon progeny and uranium ore dust simultaneously, it was observed that the risk of lung cancer was elevated at exposure levels similar to those found in homes. The risk decreased in proportion to the decrease in exposure to radon progeny.

In 1988, a panel of experts convened by the WHO's International Agency for Research on Cancer unanimously agreed that there is sufficient evidence to conclude that radon causes cancer in humans and laboratory animals. Scientific committees assembled by the National Academy of Sciences (NAS), the International Commission on Radiological Protection (ICRP), and the National Council on Radiation Protection and Measurement (NCRP) also have reviewed the available data and agree that radon exposure causes human lung cancer.

Recognizing that radon is a significant public health risk, scientific and professional organizations, such as the American Medical Association, the American Lung Association, and the National Medical Association, have developed programs to reduce the health risks of radon. The National Institute for Occupational Safety and Health (NIOSH) reviewed the epidemiological data and recommended that the annual radon progeny exposure limit for the mining industry be lowered.

Is occupational exposure to radon comparable to residential exposure?

Because questions have been raised about the appropriateness of using the epidemiological studies of underground miners as a basis for estimating the risk that radon poses to the general population, the EPA commissioned the NAS to investigate the difference between underground miners and members of the general public in the doses they receive per unit-exposure due to inhaled radon progeny.

The NAS report, published in 1991, concluded that it is reasonable to extrapolate from the miner data to a residential situation, but that the effective doses per unit of exposure for people in their homes are approximately 30% less than for the miners. In its analysis, the NAS considered variables such as the amount and types of dust to which the radon decay particles would attach, the breathing rates of working miners compared to that of people at home, and the presence of women and children in the homes.

The EPA has adjusted its residential risk estimates accordingly. The result is still considerable. The EPA now estimates that, annually, approximately 20,000 lung cancer deaths in the U.S. are due to residential radon exposures. As more data are gathered, the risk estimates may be adjusted further. Enough statistical evidence exists now, however, to state with certainty that each year in the United States, thousands of deaths due to preventable lung cancer are attributable to indoor residential exposure to radon.

More information is needed to answer important questions about radon's effect on women and children—two groups not included in the occupational studies. Although children have been reported to be at greater risk than adults for developing certain types of cancer from radiation, there is no current or conclusive evidence that radon exposure puts children at a greater risk. Some studies on miners and on animals indicate that, for the same total exposure, a lower exposure over a longer period is more hazardous than brief, high exposures. These findings increase concerns about residential radon exposures. Epidemiological control studies are underway in the U.S. and in Europe, the pooled results of which should enhance the understanding of the risk of residential exposure to radon.

What about smoking and radon exposure?

Some people ask whether the lung cancer deaths attributed to radon exposure actually may be the result of smoking. A 1989 study by researchers from NIOSH, the Centers for Disease Control (CDC), the Harvard School of Public Health, and the University of California at Davis demonstrated a greatly increased risk of lung cancer in non-smoking uranium miners exposed to high radon concentrations. Compared to typical non-smoking populations, these miners had nine to 12 times the risk of developing lung cancer.

Evidence from some of the epidemiological studies of American underground uranium miners indicates that radon exposure and smoking may have a synergistic relationship. Either smoking or radon exposure can independently increase the risk of lung cancer; however, exposure to both greatly enhances that risk.

Radon Risk for Smokers			
Radon Level	If 1,000 people who smoke were exposed to this level over a lifetime...	The risk of cancer from radon exposure compares to...	What to do: Stop smoking and...
20 pCi/L	about 260 of them would get lung cancer.	250 times the risk of drowning.	mitigate the exposure level.
10 pCi/L	about 150 of them would get lung cancer.	200 times the risk of dying in a home fire.	mitigate the exposure level.
8 pCi/L	about 120 of them would get lung cancer.	30 times the risk of dying in a fall.	mitigate the exposure level.
4 pCi/L	about 62 of them would get lung cancer.	5 times the risk of dying in a car crash.	mitigate the exposure level.
2 pCi/L	about 32 of them would get lung cancer.	6 times the risk of dying from poison.	consider mitigation if the level is between 2 and 4 pCi/L.
1.3 pCi/L	about 20 of them would get lung cancer.	(average outdoor radon level)	understand that reducing Rn levels below 2 pCi/L is difficult.

Radon Risk for Smokers			
Radon Level	If 1,000 people who smoke were exposed to this level over a lifetime...	The risk of cancer from radon exposure compares to...	What to do: Stop smoking and...
0.4 pCi/L	——————— ——	(average outdoor radon level)	understand that reducing Rn levels below 2 pCi/L is difficult.

Radon Risk for People Who Have Never Smoked			
Radon Level	If 1,000 people who have never smoked were exposed to this level over a lifetime...	The risk of cancer from radon exposure compares to...	What to do:
20 pCi/L	about 36 of them would get lung cancer.	35 times the risk of drowning.	mitigate the exposure level.
10 pCi/L	about 18 of them would get lung cancer.	20 times the risk of dying in a fall.	mitigate the exposure level.
8 pCi/L	about 15 of them would get lung cancer.	4 times the risk of dying in a fall.	mitigate the exposure level.
4 pCi/L	about 7 of them would get lung cancer.	the same risk of dying in a car crash.	mitigate the exposure level.
2 pCi/L	about 4 of them would get lung cancer.	the same risk as dying from poison.	consider mitigation if the level is between 2 and 4 pCi/L.
1.3 pCi/L	about 2 of them would get lung cancer.	(average indoor radon level)	understand that reducing Rn levels below 2 pCi/L is difficult.

Radon Risk for People Who Have Never Smoked			
Radon Level	If 1,000 people who have never smoked were exposed to this level over a lifetime...	The risk of cancer from radon exposure compares to...	What to do:
0.4 pCi/L	———————— ————	(average indoor radon level)	understand that reducing Rn levels below 2 pCi/L is difficult.

Your chances of getting lung cancer from radon depend mostly on:

- how much radon is in your home;
- the amount of time you spend in your home; and
- whether you are a smoker, or have ever smoked.

Health Effects of Radon

Epidemiological studies confirm that radon in homes increases the risk of lung cancer in the general population. Other health effects of radon have not been consistently demonstrated. The proportion of all lung cancers linked to radon is estimated to be between 3% and 14%, depending on the average radon concentration in the country and on the method of calculation. Radon is the second leading cause of lung cancer, after smoking, in many countries. Radon is much more likely to cause lung cancer in people who smoke, or who have smoked in the past, than in lifelong non-smokers. However, it is the primary cause of lung cancer among people who have never smoked.

There is no known threshold concentration below which radon exposure presents no risk. Even low concentrations of radon can result in a small increase in the risk of lung cancer. The majority of radon-induced lung cancers are caused by low and moderate radon concentrations rather than by high radon concentrations because, in general, fewer people are exposed to high indoor radon concentrations.

This section discusses the current knowledge on the health risks from radon, including lung cancer and other potential health effects. It also gives estimates of radon concentrations in various countries, and summarizes recent estimates of the burden of radon-induced lung cancer. Radon is the largest natural source of human exposure to ionizing radiation in most countries. In the general population, most exposure occurs indoors, especially in small buildings such as houses, although there are some groups for whom occupational exposure presents a greater risk.

Evidence of increased mortality from respiratory disease among certain groups of underground miners in central Europe dates back to the 16th century, but it was not until the 19th century that it was realized that the disease was, in fact, lung cancer. Radon was first suspected as the primary cause of these cancers in radon-exposed miners in the 20th century, and its causal role in lung cancer became firmly established in the 1950s. Studies of underground miners exposed occupationally to radon, usually at high concentrations, have consistently demonstrated an increased risk of lung cancer for both smokers and non-smokers. Based primarily on this evidence, radon was classified as a human carcinogen by the International Agency for Research on Cancer in 1988.

Since the 1980s, several studies have directly examined the relationship between indoor radon and lung cancer in the general population. Individually, these studies are generally too small either to rule out a material risk or to provide clear evidence that a material risk exists. Therefore, the investigators of the major studies in Europe, North America and China brought their data together and re-analyzed it centrally. These three pooled analyses present very similar pictures of the risks of lung cancer from residential exposure to radon. Together, they provide overwhelming evidence that radon is causing a substantial number of lung cancers in the general population, and they provide a direct estimate of the magnitude of the risk. They also suggest that an increased risk of lung cancer cannot be excluded even below 200 Bq/m³, which is the radon concentration at which action is currently advocated in many countries.

Lung Cancer Risks in Radon-Exposed Miners

Lung cancer rates in radon-exposed miners have generally been studied using a cohort design in which all men employed in a mine during a particular time period are identified. The men are then followed up over time, regardless of whether they remain employed in the mine, and the vital status of each man is established at the end of the follow-up period. For those who have died, the date and cause of death is ascertained and the death rate from lung cancer is calculated, both overall and after subdivision by factors such as age, calendar period, and cumulative exposure to radon. In these studies, exposure to radon was usually estimated retrospectively, and in many of the studies, the quality of the exposure assessment was low, particularly in the early years of mining, when the exposures were highest and no radon measurements were performed. In studies of radon-exposed miners, radon progeny concentrations are generally expressed in terms of working levels (WL). Remember that the working level is defined as any combination of the short-lived progeny in 1 liter of air that results in the ultimate release of 1.3×10^5 MeV of potential alpha particle energy. The cumulative exposure of an individual to this concentration over a working month of 170 hours (or twice this concentration over half as long, etc.) is defined as a working-level month (WLM).

A review of the major studies of underground miners exposed to radon that were available in the 1990s was carried out by the Committee on the Biological Effects of Ionizing Radiation (BEIR). Eleven cohort studies were considered, including a total of 60,000 miners in Europe, North America, Asia and Australia, among whom 2,600 deaths from lung cancer had occurred. Eight of these studies were of uranium miners, and the remainder were of miners of tin, fluorspar, or iron. Lung cancer rates generally increased with increasing cumulative radon exposure, but in one study, the rate increased at moderate cumulative exposures and then decreased again at high cumulative exposures. After exclusion of cumulative exposures above 3,200 WLM in this study, the lung cancer rate increased approximately linearly with increasing cumulative radon exposure in all 11 studies, although the size of the increase per unit increase in exposure varied by more than a factor of 10 between the studies, and this variation was much greater than could be explained by chance. Despite the substantial variation in the magnitude of the risk that was suggested by the different studies, the BEIR VI committee carried out a number of analyses considering pooled data from all 11 studies, giving different weights to the different studies. One such analysis estimated that the average increase in the lung cancer death rate per WLM in the 11 studies combined was 0.44% (with a 95% confidence interval of 0.20-1.00%). The percentage increase in the lung cancer death rate per WLM varied with time since exposure, with the highest percentage increase in risk in the period five to 14 years after exposure. It also varied with the age that the person concerned had reached, with higher percentage increases in risk at younger ages. Another finding of the study was that miners exposed at relatively low radon concentrations had a larger percentage increase in lung cancer death rate per WLM than miners exposed at higher radon concentrations. In order to summarize the risks seen in the studies of radon-exposed miners and to make projections about the likely risks in other radon-exposed populations, the BEIR VI committee developed a number of models. For illustration, the exposure-age-concentration model is summarized below.

BEIR VI[a] Committee: German[b] uranium miners		
ERR/WLM in baseline category[c] (%)		
ß	7.68	1.35
Time since exposure		
$\Theta_{5\text{-}14}$	1.00	1.00
$\Theta_{15\text{-}24}$	0.78	1.52
Θ_{25+}	0.51	0.76
Attained age (years)		
$\phi_{<55}$	1.00	1.00
$\phi_{55\text{-}64}$	0.57	0.80
$\phi_{65\text{-}74}$	0.29	0.66
ϕ_{75+}	0.09	0.49
Radon concentration (WL)		
$\gamma_{<0.5}$	1.00	1.00
$\gamma_{0.5\text{-}1.0}$	0.49	0.52
$\gamma_{1.0\text{-}3.0}$	0.37	0.36
$\gamma_{3.0\text{-}5.0}$	0.32	0.31
$\gamma_{5.0\text{-}15.0}$	0.17	0.25
$\gamma_{15.0+}$	0.11	0.12
a. Source: BEIR VI (1999)		
b. Source: Grosche et al. (2006)		
c. i.e. 5-14 years since exposure, attained age <55 years, and concentration <0.5 WL		

Table 1. Patterns of radon-related lung cancer in miners in the studies considered by the BEIR VI Committee and the study of German uranium miners.

Since the publication of this report, further follow-up has been conducted for the Czech study of radon-exposed miners and for the French study. Several papers giving further analyses of some other groups have been published. In addition, cohorts of radon-exposed coal miners in Poland and Brazil have been established, as well as a large cohort of uranium miners in the former German Democratic Republic.

The German cohort includes a total of 59,001 men who had been employed by the Wismut Company in East Germany. By the time of the first mortality follow-up, a total of 2,388 lung cancer deaths had occurred. The German cohort is of particular interest, as it is nearly as large as all the 11 cohorts available to the BEIR VI Committee combined. In addition, the miners were all from the same geographical area and had the same social background, and the entire cohort was subject to the same follow-up procedure and the same system of exposure assessment. In this study, the average increase in lung cancer death rate per WLM was 0.21% (with a 95% confidence interval at 0.18-0.24%), just over half that seen in the BEIR VI analysis. When an exposure-age concentration model similar to that used by the BEIR VI Committee was fitted to the German cohort, the highest percentage increase in the death rate per WLM was during the period 15 to 24 years after exposure, compared to five to 15 years in the BEIR VI model. The percentage increases were lower at older ages, as in the BEIR VI model, although the age gradient was less steep. In both studies, the percentage increase in death rate per unit exposure decreased with increasing radon concentration, with exposures at 15+ WL carrying about one-tenth the risk of those at <0.5 WL.

For some of the miner studies available to the BEIR VI Committee, information on smoking was available. In these studies, the lung cancer death rate increased by 0.53% per WLM on average (with a 95% confidence interval at 0.20-1.38%), similar to the average percentage increase for all 11 studies considered by the BEIR VI Committee. When the analysis was carried out separately for never-smokers (i.e. lifelong non-smokers) and for ever-smokers (i.e. current and ex-smokers combined), the lung cancer death rate increased by 1.02% per WLM (with a 95% confidence interval at 0.15-7.18%) for the never-smokers, and 0.48% per WLM (with a 95% confidence interval at 0.18-1.27%) for the ever-smokers. Thus, the percentage increase in lung cancer risk per WLM was larger in the never-smokers than in the ever-smokers, but the difference was not statistically significant.

Information on smoking habits is not generally available in the German cohort study. However, a case-control study of lung cancer among former employees of a German uranium mining company diagnosed at certain clinics during the 1990s has been carried out. This study also found that the percentage increase in the lung cancer death rate per WLM was larger in never-smokers than in ex-smokers, and larger in ex-smokers than in current smokers, with current smokers: 0.05% (with a 95% confidence interval at 0.001-0.14%); ex-smokers: 0.10% (with a 95% confidence interval at 0.03-0.23%); and never-smokers: 0.20% (with a 95% confidence interval at 0.07-0.48%).

Whether or not the true percentage increase in the lung cancer death rate per WLM differs between never-smokers and ever-smokers, it should be noted that the absolute increase in death rate per WLM will be much higher for current smokers than for never-smokers. This is due to the fact that for a given radon concentration, smokers have much higher lung cancer rates than never-smokers. For ex-smokers, the absolute increase per WLM will lie between those for current and for never-smokers, depending on factors, such as the duration of smoking, the number of cigarettes per day smoked before quitting, and the time since smoking cessation.

Lung Cancer Risks in the General Population from Indoor Radon

The magnitude of lung cancer risk seen in underground miners exposed to radon strongly suggests that radon may be a cause of lung cancer in the general population due to the exposure that occurs inside houses and other buildings. The conditions of exposure in mines and indoors differ appreciably, and the smoking-related risks in the miners that have been studied differ from the smoking-related risks in the general populations of today. Other determinants of lung cancer risk differ between exposure in mines and indoors. For example, many of the miners were exposed to other lung carcinogens, such as arsenic, in addition to radon. All of these differences mean that there is substantial uncertainty in extrapolating from the miner studies to obtain a quantitative assessment of the risk of lung cancer from radon in the home.

Much of the uncertainty associated with quantitative extrapolation from the studies of miners can be avoided by directly studying the association between indoor radon and risk of lung cancer. In such studies, radon exposures are usually expressed as the average concentration of radon gas per cubic meter of air to which an individual has been exposed at home over the previous few decades, and the unit is becquerel per cubic meter (Bq/m^3), where 1 Bq corresponds to one disintegration per second. Indoor radon concentrations in an individual house are usually subject to systematic diurnal and seasonal variation, and the annual average radon concentration is also usually subject to substantial random year-to-year variation related to numerous factors (e.g., weather patterns and occupant behavior, such as window opening).

Initial attempts to study the risk of lung cancer from indoor radon included a number of geographical correlation studies (sometimes known as ecological studies), which examined the correlation between average radon concentrations and average lung cancer rates in different geographical areas. However, the usefulness of such studies is severely limited since they cannot control adequately for other determinants of lung cancer risk, such as cigarette smoking, which causes a much larger number of lung cancers than radon in most populations. Therefore, ecological studies often provide biased and misleading estimates of the radon-related risk. Further details and some illustrations of the biases that can occur are presented elsewhere.

A more appropriate way to examine the association between lung cancer and residential radon exposure is a case-control study, in which a predetermined number of individuals who have developed lung cancer are identified, together with a predetermined number of control individuals who have not developed the disease but who are otherwise representative of the population from which the cases of lung cancer were drawn. In these studies, the controls are usually matched to the cases by age and sex. Detailed residential histories must then be obtained for each individual in the study, as well as detailed information on smoking histories and other factors that determine each person's risk of developing lung cancer. In order to estimate the average radon concentration to which each individual in the study has been exposed over the previous few decades, measurements of the radon concentration need to be made both in their present home and, if the individual has moved in the last few decades, in other homes where the individual has lived. Once this is done, the radon concentrations can be compared between individuals who have developed lung cancer and the control individuals. Special statistical methods have been developed to account for variations in the other factors that influence the risk of developing lung cancer so that, in effect, comparisons are made only between individuals who have similar smoking histories and also similar values for other factors that determine the risk of lung cancer. Using such methods, the relationship between the risk of lung cancer and the average indoor radon concentration over the previous few decades can be estimated.

At least 40 case-control studies of indoor radon and lung cancer have now been conducted. Individually, most of these studies have not been large enough to either rule out an increased risk or provide clear evidence that an increased risk existed. Therefore, in order to combine the information from more than one study, a number of authors have considered the published results from several studies to obtain a pooled estimate. These systematic reviews of published papers have all concluded that the radon-related risk of lung cancer, as published in the individual studies, varies appreciably from one study to another. However, the methodology used to analyze the various studies differs considerably from study to study, notably in the extent to which the differing smoking-related risks of lung cancer for different individuals have been taken into account, and in the quantification of the radon exposure histories of each individual. Such divergences may well lead to differences between the risk estimates in the individual studies and cannot be eliminated without access to basic data for each individual involved in the studies.

In order to compare the findings of the different case-control studies of radon and lung cancer appropriately, and to ensure that the different smoking-related risks for different individuals are fully taken into account, it is necessary to assemble the component data on radon concentration, smoking history, and other relevant factors for each individual in each of the original studies, and to collate the data in a uniform way. When this has been done, parallel analyses of the different studies can be carried out, and the findings from the individual studies can be compared. Then, if the data from the different studies are consistent, they can be combined, and an estimate of the risk of radon-related lung cancer can be derived based on all of the studies included. Three analyses collating and comparing the individual information from a number of component studies have now been carried out, including 13 European studies, seven North American studies, and two Chinese studies. All three analyses concluded that it was appropriate to derive a pooled estimate of the risk of lung cancer from radon in the home from the component studies. A summary of the findings of these pooled analyses appears in Table 2 and further details are presented below.

The European Pooling Study

The European pooling study included data from all 13 European studies of residential radon and lung cancer that satisfied selected inclusion criteria. These criteria required studies to be of a certain size (a minimum of 150 people with lung cancer, and 150 control individuals without lung cancer, drawn from the same population), and that detailed smoking histories for each individual were available. In terms of exposure, radon measurements in homes where the individual had lived during the past 15 years or more were required. In total, over 7,000 lung cancer cases and more than 14,000 controls were entered into the pooled analysis. The study considered the effect on lung cancer risk of exposures to radon during the 30-year period ending five years prior to the diagnosis of lung cancer, or prior to a comparable reference date for control individuals. The available radon measurements covered a mean of 23 years, and, where necessary, were adjusted for seasonal variation so that each measurement was representative of the radon concentration in a home over an entire year. For homes where no radon measurements could be obtained (e.g., the house had been demolished), the concentration was estimated indirectly as the mean of all the radon measurements in the residences of control-group members in the relevant study area. To obtain the measured radon concentration for each individual, a time-weighted average of the radon concentrations in all the homes occupied over the past five to 34 years was calculated, with weights proportional to the length of time that the individual had lived in each of them.

	Number of studies included	Number of lung cancers	Number of controls	Exposure Window (years)[a]	Percentage increase in risk of lung cancer per 100 Bq/m³ increase in radon concentration	
					Based on measured radon	Based on long-term average radon[b]
Pooled analyses of studies of indoor radon in the home						
European (Darby et al., 2005, 2006)	13	7,148	14,208	5-35	8 (3, 16)	16 (5, 31)
North American (Krewski et al., 2005, 2006)	7	3,662	4,966	5-30	11 (0, 28)	—

	Number of studies included	Number of lung cancers	Number of controls	Exposure Window (years)[a]	Percentage increase in risk of lung cancer per 100 Bq/m³ increase in radon concentration	
					Based on measured radon	Based on long-term average radon[b]
Chinese (Lubin et al., 2004)	2	1,050	1,995	5-30	13 (1, 36)	—
Weighted average of above results of pooling studies					10	~20[c]
Studies of radon-exposed miners[d, e]						
BEIR VI analysis (BEIR VI 1999; Lubin et al., 1997)	11	2,787		5-35	• All miners: 5 • Miners exposed to <50 WLM only: 14 • Miners exposed to <50 WLM and at <0.5 WL only: 30	
German uranium miners study (Grosche et al., 2006)	1	2,388		5-35	• All miners: 3 • Miners with low exposures incurred at low-dose rates: 18[f]	
French and Czech uranium miners (Tomasek et al., 2008)	2	574		5+ 5-35	• All miners (mean exposure rate 4.5 WLM/year): 32	

a. i.e., considering radon concentrations during the period starting 35 years before and ending five years before the date of diagnosis for cases of lung cancer, or a comparable date for controls

b. i.e., adjusting for a year-to-year random variability in indoor radon concentration

c. informal estimate indicating the likely effect of removing the bias induced by random year-to-year variation in radon concentration

d. Risks per WLM have been converted to risks per 100 Bq/m³ by assuming that 1 Bq/m³ at equilibrium is equivalent to 0.00027 WL, that the "equilibrium factor" in dwellings is 0.40, that subjects spend 70% of the time at home, that there are 365.25 x 24 / 170 = 51.6 'Working Months' in one year, and that the ratio of the dose to lung cells for exposures in homes to that for similar exposures in mines (sometimes referred to as the K-factor) is unity.

e. Only one study has specifically addressed the effect of measurement error in the estimates of radon-related lung cancer risk in miners (Stram et al., 1999). It concluded that for miners exposed at concentrations below 15 WL, measurement error was of little consequence.

f. informal estimate obtained by multiplying the estimate for all miners in the German cohort by 6 (i.e., the ratio of the estimates for all miners and for miners exposed)

Table 2 (previous page). Summary of risks of lung cancer from indoor radon based on international pooling studies that have combined individual data from a number of case-control studies and on studies of radon-exposed miners

After detailed allowance for the different lung cancer risks due to the varying smoking histories for individuals, the variation between the proportionate increase in risk per unit increase in radon concentration in the European studies was no larger than expected from random variation. It was therefore appropriate to pool the data. When this was done, a clear positive association between radon and lung cancer emerged. The risk of lung cancer increased by 8% per 100 Bq/m³ increase in measured radon concentration (with a 95% confidence interval at 3-16%). The estimated percentage increase in lung cancer rate for each unit increase in residential radon concentration did not vary according to the age or sex of the individual more than would be expected by chance, nor did it vary (on this proportionate scale) more than would be expected by chance according to his or her smoking history.

European pooling study[a]		North American pooling study[b]	
	% risk increase (95% CI)		% risk increase (95%CI)
Sex			
Men	11 (4, 21)	Men	3 (-4, 24)
Women	3 (-4, 14)	Women	19 (2, 46)
p for heterogeneity	0.19		
Age at disease occurrence (years)			
<55	<0 (<0, 20)	<60	2 (<0, 35)
55-64	14 (3, 31)	60-64	80 (13, 257)
65+	7 (1, 16)	65-69	2 (-5, 28)
		70-74	33 (1, 102)
		75+	-2 (-10, 30)
p for trend	0.98		
Smoking status			
Current cigarette smoker	7 (-1, 22)	Never smoked cigarettes	10 (-9, 42)
Ex-smoker	8 (0, 21)		
Lifelong non-smoker	11 (0, 28)	Current or ex-cigarette smoker	10 (-2, 33)
Other	8 (-3, 56)		
p for heterogeneity	0.92		
Overall			
Based on measured radon	8 (3, 16)	Based on measured radon	11 (0, 28)
Sources: a. Darby et al. (2005, 2006), b. Krewski et al. (2005, 2006)			
CI = confidence interval, p-values less than 0.05 denote statistical significance			

Table 3. Risk increase of radon-related lung cancer per 100 Bq/m³ of measured indoor radon concentration based on the results of the European and North American pooling studies

In the European pooling study, the exposure-response relationship appeared to be approximately linear, with no evidence for a threshold below which there was no risk. In particular, the results were incompatible with a threshold above 150 Bq/m³ (i.e., 150 Bq/m³ was the 95% upper confidence limit for any threshold). Furthermore, the investigators found a statistically significant association between radon concentration and lung cancer even when the analysis was restricted to people in homes with measured radon concentrations below 200 Bq/m³. The risk of lung cancer was 20% higher (with a 95% confidence interval at 3-30%) for those individuals with measured radon concentrations 100-199 Bq/m³ (mean: 136 Bq/m³) when compared to those with measured radon concentrations under 100 Bq/m³ (mean: 52 Bq/m³).

As mentioned above, there is substantial year-to-year random variation in the average annual radon concentration in a home depending on, for example, variation in the weather. Therefore, if the risk of lung cancer due to radon from the case-control studies is estimated based only on the measured radon concentrations and without taking this variation into account, then the risk is likely to be underestimated. Therefore, in the European pooling study, the analysis was repeated using long-term average radon concentration (i.e., taking into account the random year-to-year variability in measured radon concentration). The final estimated risk coefficient, based on the long-term average radon concentration, was 16% per 100 Bq/m³ (with a 95% confidence interval at 5-31%). Once again, on this proportionate scale, the risk did not vary more than would be expected by chance with age, sex, or according to the smoking status of the individual, and the dose-response relationship was approximately linear, as demonstrated in Figure 1.

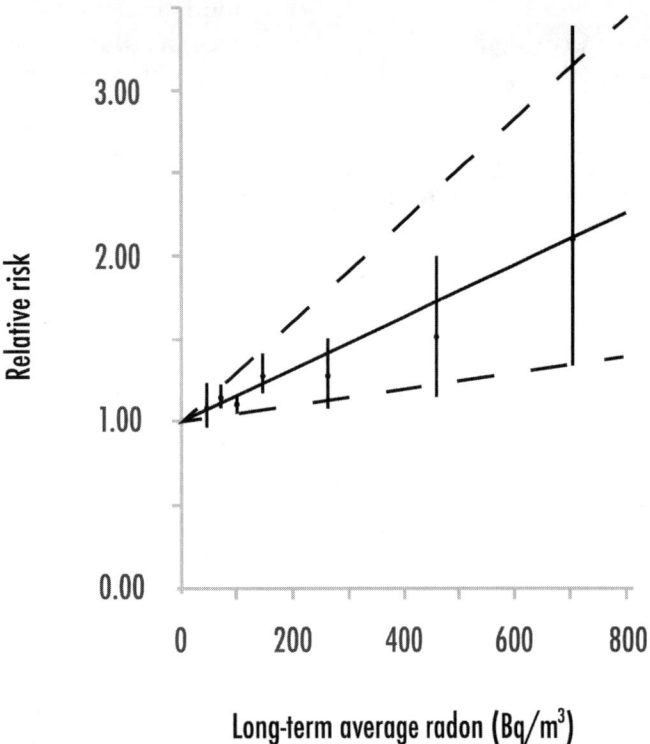

Figure 1. Relative risk of lung cancer versus long-term average residential radon concentration in the European pooling study

The North American Pooling Study

The North American pooling study involved 3,662 cases and 4,966 controls from seven studies in the U.S. and Canada. The methodology was similar to that used for the European study. As with the European study, the radon-related risk in the component studies was found to be consistent, once the data for individual subjects had been collated. When data from all seven studies were combined, the risk of lung cancer increased by 11% per 100 Bq/m³ increase in measured radon concentration (with a 95% confidence interval at 0-28%). When the analyses were restricted to the subsets of data with greater exposure accuracy, the lung cancer risk estimates increased. For example, for individuals who lived in only one or two houses in the period five to 30 years prior to recruitment, with at least 20 years covered by dosimetry, the investigators reported an increase of 18% (with a 95% confidence interval at 2-43%) per 100 Bq/m³. The estimated percentage increase in lung cancer rate for each unit increase in measured residential radon concentration did not vary according to the age or sex of the individual more than would be expected by chance, nor did it vary more than would be expected by chance according to his or her smoking history.

As with the European pooling study, the results of the North American pooling study were consistent with a linear dose-response relationship with no threshold. However, unlike the European pooling study, no formal adjustments for variations in yearly residential radon concentrations have been performed so far. When further analyses become available, a direct comparison between the findings of the North American and European pooled studies after accounting for year-to-year variations in indoor radon concentration will be feasible.

The Chinese Pooling Study

Lubin and colleagues analyzed 1,050 cases and 1,996 controls from two studies in two areas: Gansu and Shenyang. For the pooled data, the risk per 100 Bq/m³ measured radon concentration increased by 13% (with a 95% confidence interval at 1-36%). This effect was chiefly due to the data from the much larger Gansu study, although the results of the two component studies were compatible with each other. As with the European and North American pooling studies, the results were consistent with a linear dose-response relationship with no threshold.

Overall Evidence on the Risk of Lung Cancer from Residential Radon

The three pooling studies present a very similar picture of the risk of lung cancer from residential exposure to radon. There is overwhelming evidence that radon acts as a cause of lung cancer in the general population at concentrations found in ordinary homes. In particular, in all three pooling studies, there was no evidence that the proportionate increase in risk per unit increase in radon concentration varied with the age, sex, or smoking habits of the study subjects more than would be expected by chance. In addition, the dose-response relationship appeared to be linear, with no evidence of a threshold, and there was substantial evidence of a risk increase even below 200 Bq/m³, the concentration at which action is currently advocated in many countries.

The three major pooling studies reported increased risks of lung cancer based on a measured radon concentration of 8% (with a 95% confidence interval at 3-16%), 11% (0-28%) and 13% (1-36%) per 100 Bq/m³ increase in measured radon concentration. As these three estimates are statistically compatible with each other, a weighted average, with weights proportional to their variances, can be calculated. This gives a joint estimate from the three pooling studies, based on measured radon concentrations, of 10% per 100 Bq/m³.

As described above, estimates based on measured radon concentration are likely to underestimate the true risks associated with residential radon due to the year-to-year random variation in radon concentrations in a home. The only pooling study to date that has carried out a detailed analysis of the risks of residential radon based on a long-term average, as opposed to measured radon concentrations, is the European one. In this study, the risk estimate based on long-term average concentrations was twice the risk estimate based on measured radon concentrations. Data from repeated radon measurements made in separate years in the same home in China show a similar year-to-year variation as in the European studies, while data from the United States also suggest considerable year-to-year random variation. If it is assumed that the effect of adjusting for year-to-year random variation in the three pooling studies combined is the same as in the European study, then a joint risk estimate from the three pooling studies, based on long-term radon concentrations, would be around 20% per 100 Bq/m³.

Other potential sources of radon exposure misclassification include detector measurement error, spatial radon variations within a home, missing data from previously occupied homes that are currently inaccessible, failure to link radon concentrations with subject mobility, and measuring radon gas concentration as a surrogate for radon progeny exposure. It is generally difficult to assess the impact of these potential exposure measurement errors. However, if the misclassification does not differ systematically between cases and controls, the observed results tend to be biased towards zero (i.e., the true effect is underestimated). In fact, empirical models with improved retrospective radon exposure estimates were more likely to detect an association between residential radon exposure and lung cancer.

A number of other factors have not been included in the formal analyses for the majority of indoor radon studies. In particular, there are frequently errors in the assignment of individuals to smoking categories and, in some countries, there may have been systematic changes in the radon concentrations over the last few decades due to increased energy efficiency and the introduction of air conditioning. The overall effect of these factors may indicate that the true effect of radon may be somewhat higher than the estimated risk in the residential radon studies, even after correction for year-to-year random variation in measured radon concentrations.

Direct comparison of the risks of lung cancer in studies of indoor radon with risks based on studies of radon-exposed miners is complicated. The generally higher exposures and also the inverse exposure-rate effect in the miners' data contribute to this. Summary risk estimates from miners' studies are somewhat lower than from residential radon studies. For example, when all the miners included in the BEIR VI analysis are considered, the estimated risk is approximately 5% per 100 Bq/m^3, with somewhat lower estimates for the large German study. For the BEIR VI study, an additional analysis including only miners with cumulative exposures below 50 WLM (i.e., the exposure that would be received from living in a house with a radon concentration of around 400 Bq/m^3 for 30 years) has been carried out and suggests an increase of 14% per 100 Bq/m^3, while a further analysis considering only miners with cumulative exposures below 50 WLM and exposed only at <0.5 WL (i.e., <~2,000 Bq/m^3) suggests an increase in risk of 30% per 100 Bq/m^3. Similarly, results from an analysis of French and Czech cohorts that are restricted to workers with low exposure rates, an exposure window of five to 34 years, and a comparatively high precision of exposure assessment indicate a risk increase on the order of 32% per 100 Bq/m^3.

In summary, there is good agreement between the estimates of radon-related risk based on the studies of indoor radon and the studies of underground miners with relatively low cumulative exposures accumulated at low concentrations.

Radon and Diseases Other Than Lung Cancer

When an individual spends time in an atmosphere that contains radon and its decay products, the part of the body that receives the highest dose of ionizing radiation is the bronchial epithelium, although the extrathoracic airways and the skin may also receive appreciable doses. In addition, other organs, including the kidneys and the bone marrow, may receive low doses. If an individual drinks water in which radon is dissolved, the stomach will also be exposed.

The evidence for radon-related increases in mortality from cancers other than lung cancer has been examined in the same studies of radon-exposed miners that were included in the BEIR VI analyses, and no strong evidence was found that radon was causing cancers other than lung cancer. However, further investigations are focusing on this issue. For example, a recent case-cohort study evaluating the incidence of leukemia, lymphoma, and multiple myeloma in Czech uranium miners found a positive association between radon exposure and leukemia, including chronic lymphocytic leukemia. The relationship between radon exposure and cardiovascular disease has been examined in a number of cohorts of radon-exposed miners, but none has found evidence that radon is causing heart disease. A case-control study of stomach cancer in an area where there were high concentrations of natural uranium and other radionuclides in drinking water gave no indication of an increased risk.

About 20 ecological studies of exposure to radon in the general population and leukemia either in children or adults have been carried out. Several of these, including a recent methodologically advanced study by Smith et al., have found associations between indoor radon concentration and the risk of leukemia (including chronic lymphocytic leukemia in the Smith study) at the geographic level. An ecological study performed in Norway showed an association between multiple sclerosis and indoor radon concentration. Generally, these associations has been confirmed in a high-quality case-control or cohort study, either in radon-exposed miners or in the general population, although several such studies have been carried out. As with the studies of radon exposure and lung cancer, these ecological studies are prone to a number of biases. Therefore, they are likely to give misleading answers and should not be taken as evidence that radon is acting as a cause of these diseases.

Burden of Lung Cancer Caused by Indoor Radon

From the evidence presented here, it is clear that exposure to radon is a well-established cause of lung cancer in the general population. In any particular country, the proportion of lung cancers occurring each year that are radon-induced will be determined chiefly by the indoor radon concentrations in that country. Surveys have been carried out to determine the distribution of residential radon concentrations in most of the 30-member countries of the Organization for Economic Cooperation and Development (OECD). The worldwide average indoor radon concentration has been estimated at 39 Bq/m^3.

Country	Arithmetic mean	Indoor Radon Levels [Bq/m^3]	
		Geometric mean	Geometric standard deviation
OECD countries			
Australia	11	8	2.1
Austria	99	15	NA
Belgium	48	38	2
Canada	28	11	3.9
Czech Republic	140	44	2.1
Denmark	59	39	2.2
Finland	120	84	2.1
France	89	53	2.0
Germany	49	37	2.0
Greece	55	44	2.4
Hungary	82	62	2.1
Iceland	10	NA	NA
Ireland	89	57	2.4
Italy	70	52	2.1
Japan	16	13	1.8
Luxembourg	110	70	2
Mexico	140	90	NA
Netherlands	23	18	1.6
New Zealand	22	20	NA
Norway	89	40	NA
Poland	49	31	2.3

Country	Arithmetic mean	Indoor Radon Levels [Bq/m³]	
		Geometric mean	Geometric standard deviation
Portugal	62	45	2.2
Republic of Korea	53	43	1.8
Slovakia	87	NA	NA
Spain	90	46	2.9
Sweden	108	56	NA
Switzerland	78	51	1.8
United Kingdom	20	14	3.2
USA	46	25	3.1
Worlwide average	39		
Sources: WHO (2007), UNSCEAR (2000), Billon et al. (2005) and Menzler et al. (2008)			

Table 4. Indoor radon concentrations in OECD countries

Detailed calculations of the numbers of radon-induced lung cancers attributable to radon exposure have been previously published for a number of countries. The calculations are based on the estimated concentrations of indoor radon from the surveys together with the indirect estimates of risk provided either by the studies of miners in the BEIR VI analysis or by the direct evidence provided by the European pooling studies.

In most populations, lung cancer rates are much higher in current cigarette smokers than in lifelong non-smokers. The proportionate increase in the risk of lung cancer per unit increase in indoor radon concentration is similar in lifelong non-smokers and cigarette smokers in studies of residential radon. Furthermore, in the miner studies for which smoking information is available, the proportionate increase in the risk of lung cancer per unit increase in indoor radon concentration is also similar. It follows that the majority of radon-induced lung cancers are caused jointly by radon and smoking, in the sense that lung cancer would not have occurred if either the individual had not smoked cigarettes or had not been exposed to radon.

Country	Mean indoor radon [Bq/m³]	Risk estimate used in calculation	Percentage of lung cancer attributed to radon	Estimated number of deaths attributed to radon-induced lung cancer each year
Canada (Brand et al., 2005)	28	BEIR VI	7.8	1,400
Germany (Menzier et al., 2008)	49	European Pooling Study[a]	5	1,896
Switzerland (Menzier et al., 2008)	78	European Pooling Study[a]	8.3	231
United Kingdom (AGIR 2009)	21	European Pooling Study[a]	3.3	1,089
		BEIR VI	6	2,005

Country	Mean indoor radon [Bq/m³]	Risk estimate used in calculation	Percentage of lung cancer attributed to radon	Estimated number of deaths attributed to radon-induced lung cancer each year
France (Catelinois et al., 2006)	89	European Pooling Study[a]	5	1,234
		BEIR VI	12	2,913
United States (BEIR VI, 1999)	46	BEIR VI	10-14	15,400-21,800
a. with adjustment for year-to-year variation in indoor radon concentrations				

Table 5. Estimates of the proportion of lung cancer attributable to radon in selected countries

At an individual level, the risk of radon-induced lung cancer following exposure to a given radon concentration is much higher among current cigarette smokers than among lifelong non-smokers. This has been illustrated by the pooled analysis of European residential radon studies. For lifelong non-smokers, it was estimated that living in a home with an indoor radon concentration of 0, 100 or 800 Bq/m³ was associated with a risk of lung cancer death (at the age of 75) of 4, 5 or 10 in 1,000, respectively. However, for a cigarette smoker, each of these risks would be substantially greater, namely 100, 120 and 220 in 1,000. For those having stopped smoking, the radon-related risks are substantially lower than for those who continue to smoke, but they remain considerably higher than the risks for lifelong non-smokers.

Radon Causes Lung Cancer

Most of the radon gas that you inhale is also exhaled. However, some of radon's decay products attach to dusts and aerosols in the air and are then readily deposited in the lungs. Some of these are cleared by the lung's natural defense system and swallowed or coughed out. Those particles that are retained for long enough release radiation, damaging surrounding lung tissues. Small amounts of radon decay products in the lung are absorbed into the blood.

Most of the radon ingested in water is excreted within hours. There is some risk from drinking water with elevated radon because radioactive decay can occur within the body where tissues, such as the stomach lining, would be exposed. However, alpha particles emitted by radon and its decay product in water prior to drinking quickly lose their energy and are taken up by other compounds in water, and do not themselves pose a health concern.

Why is radon the public health risk that it is?

The EPA estimates that radon is responsible for about 20,000 lung cancer deaths each year in the United States. Exposure to radon is the second leading cause of lung cancer after smoking. Radon is an odorless, tasteless and invisible gas produced by the decay of naturally occurring uranium in soil and groundwater. Radon is a form of ionizing radiation and a proven carcinogen. Lung cancer is the only known effect on human health from exposure to airborne radon. Thus far, there is no conclusive evidence that children are at greater risk of lung cancer than adults.

Radon is found in outdoor air and in the indoor air of buildings of all kinds. The EPA recommends that the problem be addressed if a home's radon level is 4 pCi/L (picocuries per liter) or more. Because there is no known safe level of exposure to radon, the EPA also recommends that the problem be addressed for homes with radon levels between 2 pCi/L and 4 pCi/L. The average radon concentration in the indoor air of the average American home is about 1.3 pCi/L. The EPA bases its estimate of 20,000 radon-related lung cancers a year on this number. The average concentration of radon in outdoor air is 0.4 pCi/L, or one-tenth of the EPA's recommended 4 pCi/L action level.

For smokers, the risk of lung cancer is significant due to the synergistic effects of radon and smoking. For this at-risk population, about 62 people out of a 1,000 will die of lung cancer, compared to about seven people in 1,000 who have never smoked. Put another way, a person who has never smoked and is exposed to 1.3 pCi/L has a 2-in-1,000 chance of dying from lung cancer, while a smoker has a 20-in-1,000 chance. The risk to smokers compared to those who have never smoked is six times greater.

The radon health risk is underscored by the fact that, in 1988, the U.S. Congress added Title III on Indoor Radon Abatement to the Toxic Substances Control Act. It codified and funded the EPA's then-fledgling radon program. That same year, the Surgeon General issued a warning about radon, urging Americans to test their homes and to reduce the radon level, when necessary.

Unfortunately, many Americans presume that because the action level is 4 pCi/L, a radon level of less than that is considered safe. This perception is all too common in the residential real estate market. In managing any risk, we should be concerned with the greatest risk. For most Americans, their greatest exposure to radon is inside their homes, especially in rooms that are below grade (such as basements), as well as in rooms that are in contact with the ground, and the rooms directly above them.

Genetic Damage Caused by Radon

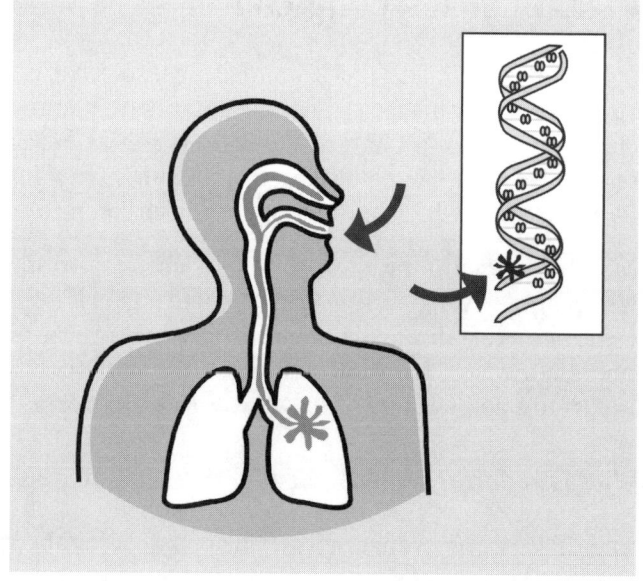

Most of the epithelial cellular damage is not caused by breathing in radon gas itself, which is removed from the lungs during exhalation, but by radon's short-lived decay products (i.e., half-life measured in minutes or less). When inhaled, these decay products may be deposited in the airways of the lungs. The radon decay products (RDPs) subsequently emit alpha particles as they decay further. The total amount of energy emitted by the progeny is several hundred times that produced in the initial decay of radon. The increased risk of lung cancer from radon results primarily from these alpha particles irradiating lung tissue. When an alpha particle passes through a cell's nucleus, the person's DNA is likely to be damaged. More specifically, available data indicate that alpha particle penetration of the cell's nucleus may cause genomic changes, most typically in the form of point mutations and transformations.

Since alpha particles are more massive and more highly charged than other types of ionizing radiation, they are more damaging to living tissue. As previously described, alpha radiation is able to travel only extremely short distances in the body. Thus, alpha radiation from the decay of radon progeny in the lungs cannot reach cells in any other organs, so it is likely that lung cancer is the only major cancer hazard posed by radon.

By breaking the electron bonds that hold molecules together, radiation can damage human DNA, the inherited compound that controls the structure and function of cells. Radiation may damage DNA directly by displacing electrons from the DNA molecule, or indirectly by changing the structure of other molecules in the cell, which may then interact with the DNA. The latter mechanism will be described in more detail later. When one of these events occurs, a cell can be destroyed quickly, or its growth or function may be altered through a change (mutation) that may not be evident for several years.

An alpha particle emitted from radon daughter decay is in the form of a high-energy helium ion, known in scientific notation as He2+. These helium particles traverse a cell's nucleus in a linear pattern and deposit energy via linear energy transfer, or LET. This refers to the energy transferred per unit of path traveled by the ionizing particle. Since alpha particles travel short distances and are slow compared to beta and gamma particles, their efficiency in transferring energy and affecting genomic change is very high, as is their LET quantity. Once deposited, this energy causes DNA alterations, cell-cycle stress, and occasional cell death. Epithelial cellular changes caused by the alpha particle emission from a single radon daughter can be seen with a microscope.

Risk Assessment Facts

The EPA's indoor radon program promotes voluntary public actions to reduce the risks from indoor radon. The EPA and the U.S. Surgeon General recommend that people perform a simple home test using kits that are now widely available in stores. If high levels of radon are confirmed, it is recommended that those high levels be mitigated or reduced using straightforward techniques.

The EPA recently completed an updated assessment of their estimates of lung cancer risks from indoor radon based on the NAS's 1999 report on radon, "The Biological Effects of Ionizing Radiation (BEIR) VI." This report is the most comprehensive review of scientific data gathered on radon, and builds on and updates their previous findings. The NAS concluded that homeowners should still test and, if necessary, mitigate their exposure to elevated radon levels in their homes.

To review: Radon is a naturally occurring radioactive gas that is colorless, odorless, and tasteless. It is naturally produced from the radioactive decay of uranium present in soil, rock, and groundwater. It emits ionizing radiation during its radioactive decay, changing into several radioactive isotopes known as radon decay products or RDPs.

Radon gets into the indoor air primarily from soil under building structures. Radon is a known human lung carcinogen and is the largest source of radiation exposure and risk to the general public. Most inhaled radon is rapidly exhaled, but the inhaled decay products readily deposit in the lung tissue where they irradiate sensitive cells in the airways, increasing the risk of lung cancer.

The NAS BEIR VI Report confirmed the EPA's long-held position that radon is the second-leading cause of lung cancer and a serious public health problem. The NAS estimates that radon causes about 20,000 lung cancer deaths each year. The report found that even very small exposures to radon can result in lung cancer. They concluded that no evidence exists that shows a threshold of exposure below which radon levels are harmless. The report also found that many smokers exposed to radon face a substantially greater risk of getting lung cancer compared to those who have never smoked. This is because of the synergistic relationship between radon and cigarette smoking.

Quiz #2

1. T/F: Radon is a worldwide health risk in homes.

    ☐ True

    ☐ False

2. Radon is the _____ leading cause of lung cancer after smoking in many countries.

    ☐ second

    ☐ first

    ☐ third

3. T/F: The World Health Organization (WHO) says that radon causes up to 15% of lung cancers worldwide.

    ☐ True

    ☐ False

4. T/F: There exists a known threshold concentration below which radon exposure presents no risk.

    ☐ True

    ☐ False

5. Most of the radon ingested in water is excreted within _____.

    ☐ weeks

    ☐ days

    ☐ hours

6. T/F: The EPA also recommends that the problem be addressed for homes with radon levels between 2 pCi/L and 4 pCi/L.

    ☐ True

    ☐ False

7. T/F: Since alpha particles are more massive and more highly charged than other types of ionizing radiation, they are more damaging to living tissue.

    ☐ True

    ☐ False

8. T/F: By breaking the electron bonds that hold molecules together, radiation can damage human DNA, the inherited compound that controls the structure and function of cells.

    ☐ True

    ☐ False

9. T/F: Radon is a known human lung carcinogen and is the largest source of radiation exposure and risk to the general public.

☐ True

☐ False

Answer Key is on page 347.

Radon Entry

Exposure to Radon

Radon-222 is the radioactive decay product of radium-226, which is found at low concentrations in almost all rock and soil. Radon is generated in rock and soil, and it creeps through cracks or spaces between particles up to the outside air. Although outdoor concentrations of radon are typically low (about 0.4 pCi/L of air), it can seep into buildings through foundation cracks or openings and build up to much higher concentrations indoors, if the sources are large enough.

The average indoor radon concentration is about 1.3 pCi/L of air. It is not uncommon, though, for indoor radon levels to be found in the range of 5–50 pCi/L, and they have been found as high as 2,000 pCi/L. The concentration of radon measured in a house depends on many factors, including the design of the house, local geology and soil conditions, and the weather. Radon's decay products are all metallic solids, and when radon decay occurs in air, the decay products can cling to aerosols and dust, which makes them available for inhalation into the lungs.

Radon dissolves easily in water. In areas of the country that have high radium content in soils and rocks, local groundwater may contain high concentrations of radon. For example, underlying rock, such as granite and phosphate rock, typically has increased uranium and radium and, therefore, increased radon. While radon dissolves easily in water, it also easily escapes from water when exposed to the atmosphere, especially if it is stirred or agitated. Consequently, radon concentrations are very low in rivers and lakes but could still be high in water pumped from the ground. Some natural springs that were once considered healthful, such as those in Hot Springs, Arkansas, contain radon.

Radon Entry into a House

Common Radon Entry Points

All homes have some type of radon entry pathway. There are four main factors that permit radon to seep into homes:

1. Uranium is present in the soil nearly everywhere in the United States.

2. The soil is permeable enough to allow radon to migrate into a home through the slab, basement or crawlspace.

3. There are pathways for radon to enter the basement, such as small holes, cracks, plumbing penetrations, and sump pumps.

4. A difference in air pressure between the basement or crawlspace and the surrounding soil draws radon into the home.

Radon enters through:

1. cracks in otherwise solid floors;
2. gaps in suspended floors;
3. cracks in walls;
4. cavities inside walls;
5. gaps around service pipes;
6. construction joints; and
7. the water supply.

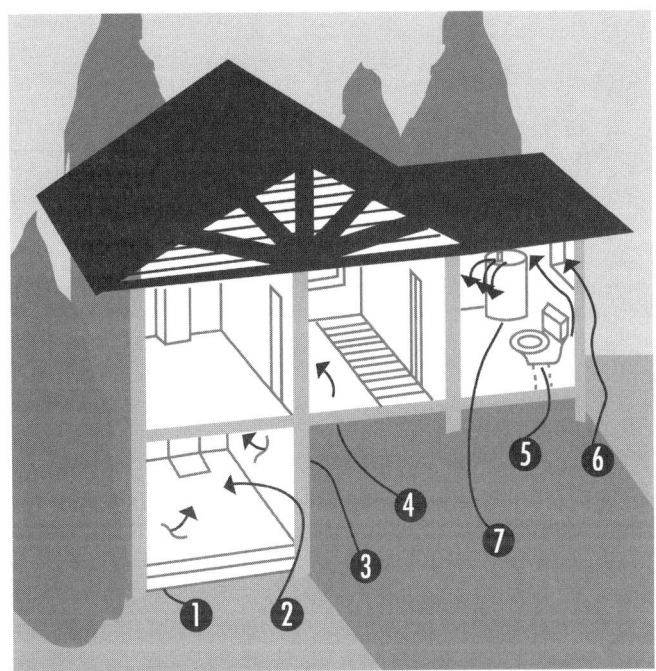

How does air pressure affect radon entry?

The air pressure in a house is generally lower than in the surrounding air and soil, particularly at the basement and foundation levels. This difference in pressure causes a house to act like a vacuum, drawing in air containing radon (as well as other soil gases) through cracks in the foundation and other openings. Some of the replacement air comes from the underlying soil and can also contain radon.

One reason this pressure difference occurs is because exhaust fans remove air from inside the house. When this air is exhausted, outside air enters the house to replace it. Another cause of a pressure difference is that warm air rises and will leak from openings in the upper portion of the house when temperatures are higher indoors than outdoors. This condition, known as stack effect, causes unconditioned replacement air to enter the lower portion of the house.

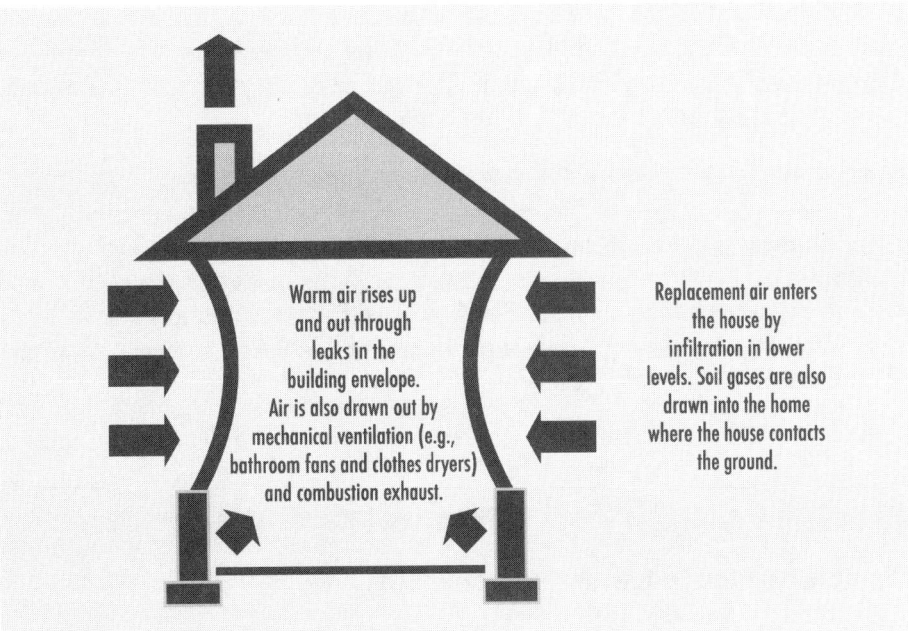

Warm air rises up and out through leaks in the building envelope. Air is also drawn out by mechanical ventilation (e.g., bathroom fans and clothes dryers) and combustion exhaust.

Replacement air enters the house by infiltration in lower levels. Soil gases are also drawn into the home where the house contacts the ground.

Does foundation type affect radon entry?

Because radon can literally be sucked into a home, any home can potentially have a radon problem. All conventional house construction types have been found to have radon levels exceeding the action level of 4 pCi/L.

Basement

Radon can enter through floor-to-wall joints, control joints, and cracks in the slab.

Crawlspace

The vacuums that exist within a home are exerted in the crawlspaces, causing radon and other gases to enter the home from the area below. Even with crawlspace vents, a slight vacuum is still exerted in the crawlspace. Measurements of homes with crawlspaces have shown elevated radon levels.

Slab-on-Grade

Radon can enter a home regardless of whether it has a basement. Slabs built on grade can have just as many openings to allow radon to enter as do basements.

Manufactured Homes

Unless these structures are set up on piers without any skirting placed around them, interior vacuums can cause radon to enter these types of homes as well.

Can radon be kept out by sealing all of the cracks?

Sealing large cracks and openings is important when sealing a home, both in the lower portion of the home to reduce radon entry points, and in the upper portion of the home to reduce stack effect. However, field research has shown that attempting to seal all of the openings in a foundation is both impractical and ineffective as a stand-alone technique. Radon can enter through very small cracks and openings, and these can be too small to locate and effectively seal. Even if all cracks could be sealed during construction, which would be costly, building settlement may cause new cracks to occur. Therefore, sealing large cracks and openings is one of the key components of radon-resistant construction, but it's not the only technique that should be employed.

The following are some radon-resistant construction techniques.

1. Install a sub-slab or sub-membrane depressurization system.

The objective of these systems is to create a vacuum beneath the foundation that is greater in strength than the vacuum imposed on the soil by the house itself. The soil gases that are collected beneath the home are piped to a safe location to be vented directly outdoors.

Usually, a 4-inch layer of clean, coarse gravel is used beneath the slab to allow the soil gas to move freely underneath the house. Other options include installing a loop of perforated pipe or a soil-gas collection mat (also known as drainage mat or soil-gas matting).

2. Use mechanical barriers to prevent soil-gas entry.

Plastic sheeting, foundation sealing, and caulking can serve as barriers to the entry of radon and other soil gases (as well as moisture). Polyethylene sheeting should be placed on top of the gas-permeable layer to help prevent the soil gas from entering the home. The sheeting also keeps concrete from clogging the gas-permeable layer when the slab is poured.

Sealing and caulking help reduce stack effect, and thus reduce the negative pressure in the lower levels of the home. Also, sealing and caulking the rest of the building envelope reduce the stack effect in the home.

3. Install air-distribution systems so that soil air is not mined.

Simply adding the vent pipe and junction box is extremely effective for reducing radon, and it's so cost-effective that even Habitat for Humanity, which relies on donations and grants for its funding, has been adding these features in many of its homes. An electrical junction box is wired in case an electric venting fan is needed later to activate the home's radon mitigation system.

A 3- or 4-inch PVC or other gas-tight pipe (commonly used for plumbing) should be installed and run from the gas-permeable layer through the house and roof to safely vent radon and other soil gases above the house. Although some builders use 3-inch pipe, field results have indicated that passive systems tend to function better with 4-inch pipe.

Air-handling units and all ducts in basements, especially in crawlspaces, should be sealed to prevent air and radon from being drawn into the system. Seamless ducts are preferred for runs through crawlspaces and beneath slabs. Any seams and joints in ducts should be sealed.

What pulls the soil gas through the pipe?

If the pipe is routed through a warm space (such as an interior wall or the furnace flue chase, following local fire codes), the stack effect can create a natural draft in the pipe. Because this method requires no mechanical devices, it is considered a passive soil-depressurization system.

If further reduction is necessary to bring radon levels in a home below the action level of 4 pCi/L, an in-line fan can be installed in the pipe to activate the system. The system is then considered an active soil-depressurization system. The future installation of the fan can be made easier with a little planning during construction.

Radon gas is approximately seven times heavier than air. It is a noble gas with no chemical affinity, but it is influenced by air movements and pressure. In a house with forced-air heating and cooling, radon gas can be easily distributed throughout the entire dwelling. When radon gas is discharged via a radon mitigation system above the roof, the radon concentration depletes dramatically with distance from the point of discharge. In fact, the radon gas concentration approaches background levels at 3 to 4 feet from the discharge point. The EPA disallowed ground-level discharge of radon primarily because of the potential for re-entrainment of the gas into the house, and because of the possibility of children being exposed to high radon levels. The concentration of radon gas at the discharge point can be tens of thousands of picocuries per minute.

Daily Variations Inside a House

Indoor radon levels depend upon a number of variables and can fluctuate significantly from day to day. Short-term tests (particularly tests between two to five days) may, in some cases, reflect an unusual peak in the radon concentration, thus indicating a need for remedial action that may not actually be necessary.

Pressure and temperature differentials, weather conditions such as wind and rain, and the operation of mechanical equipment all contribute to fluctuating levels of radon inside a house. During cold-weather seasons with closed-house conditions, elevated radon levels can be found in the lowest level of the house.

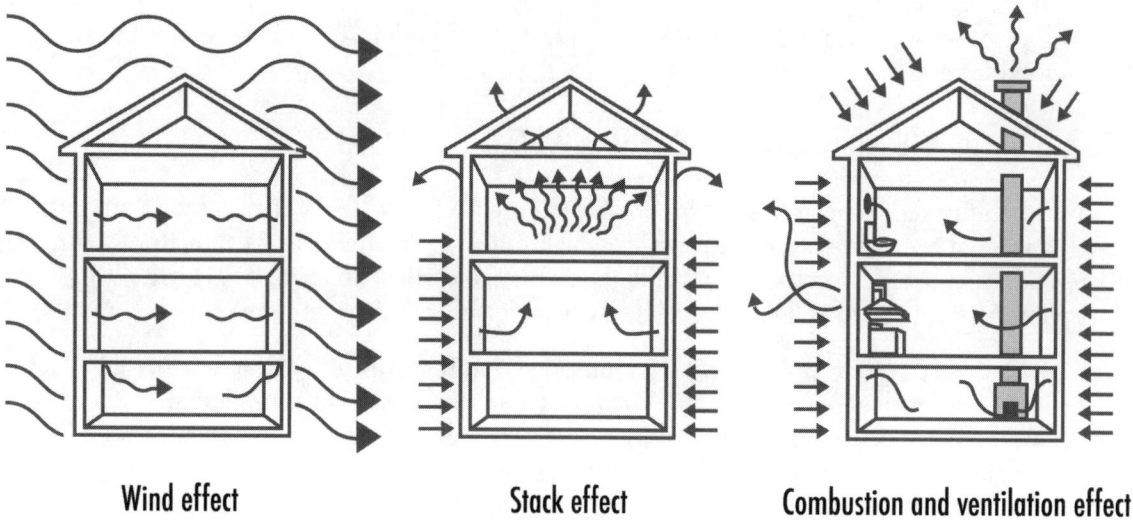

Wind effect   Stack effect   Combustion and ventilation effect

Air pressure inside a home is usually lower than air pressure in the soil around the home's foundation. Because of this difference in pressure, the house acts like a vacuum, drawing radon in through foundation cracks and other openings.

Radon entry by air pressure from below grade is the main way radon enters a house. When air exits a house, air pressure differentials between the indoors and outdoors are created.

Wind-induced pressure differentials acting on a structure's shell may affect both radon entry into the structure, and indoor radon displacement that exits the structure, depending on the wind speed, direction, frequency, wave span, and the structure's features. Wind blowing directly toward the side of a structure may cause an increase in pressure at the structure's wall in order to conserve the change in momentum initiated by the change of wind velocity from the free-stream area to almost zero at the wall side.

The most significant convective component of radon transport from the sub-structure area into the interior, and from the interior to the outdoors, is due to the pressure-driven air-flow processes. Mechanisms that generate air-pressure gradients depend on environmental and indoor operational factors. The environmental factors that induce pressure differences include temperature differences, wind, meteorological conditions, and atmospheric pressure changes. The indoor operational factors can be divided into human- and non-human-induced indoor operational factors. The non-human factors result from mechanically induced pressurization or depressurization of the indoor environment by household appliances, as well as by heating, ventilation, and air-conditioning (HVAC) systems. Human-induced indoor operational factors are characterized by effects such as the opening of windows and doors.

Evaporative or Swamp Coolers

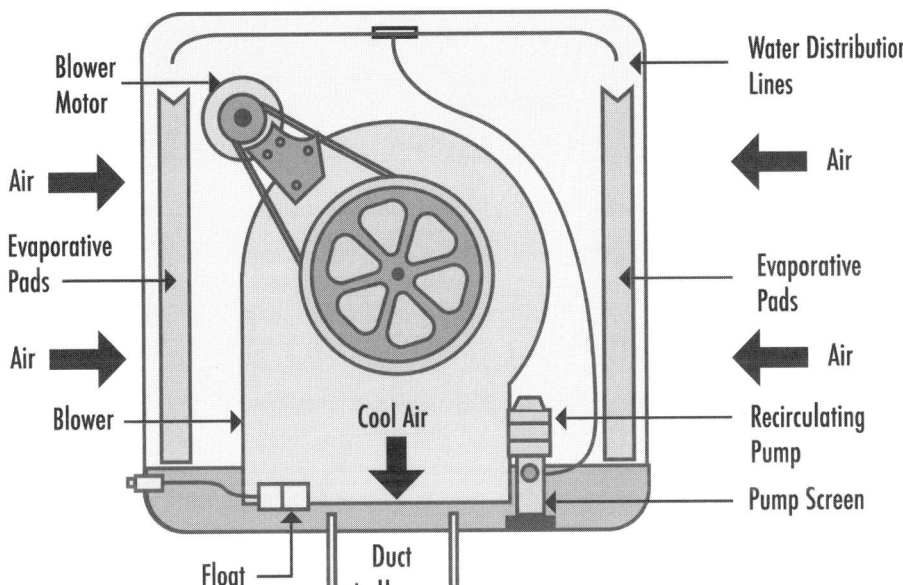

Evaporative or swamp coolers can affect indoor radon levels. A swamp cooler brings air into the house using a blower fan. The cooler pressurizes the building's interior with positive pressure. This lowers the indoor radon level. Evaporative coolers should not be operated during short-term radon measurements.

Radon Potential

One can get an idea as to how great a concern radon may be in a house by learning about the geology of the surrounding site, along with the area's radon potential. If a house is in an area with a high potential for radon, then chances are that the house may have an indoor radon problem. However, the way a house is built can increase the risk, so even in areas of low radon potential, some houses can have unhealthy radon levels.

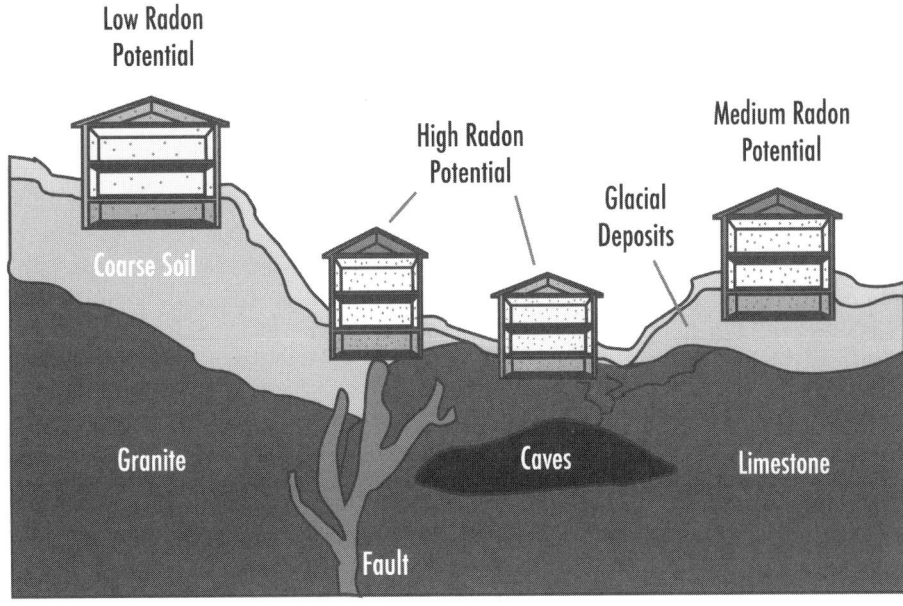

Knowing the types of rock and soil at a site helps a geologist determine its radon potential.

Scientists evaluate the radon potential of an area and create a "radon potential" map by using a variety of data. The data include the uranium or radium content of the soil and underlying rocks, and the permeability and moisture content of the soil. Other related sources of information, such as geologic maps, maps of surface radioactivity, and soil maps, are used.

Another type of information that scientists use to determine the radon potential of an area is radon measurements of local soil air. Existing indoor radon data for homes are also useful. The data are the most direct information available about indoor radon potential, even though the houses that have been sampled may not be typical for the area, and information for the exact locations of measured houses is seldom available to the public.

Sources of Information on Radon Potential

Soil Surveys

The U.S. Department of Agriculture's Natural Resources Conservation Service (formerly the U.S. Soil Conservation Service), in cooperation with state and county extension offices, prepares and publishes soil surveys. Other soil data from surficial (or near-surface) geologic and engineering maps are prepared and published by geoscience agencies. Many published soil surveys are available in local libraries. Modern soil surveys include information on the physical properties and permeability data for the mapped soils at varying depths. In older soil reports, no permeability data are given, and soil names and statements regarding internal drainage must be used to estimate permeability.

Extracting Radon from the Ground

backfill

15"
0.4 m

39"
1.0 m

passive measuring device

natural soil   sample enters here

Indoor Radon Data

State health departments, local agencies of environmental protection, and county and municipal health departments and districts often have data on indoor radon, which they make available to the public in summary form.

Geologic Maps

A geologic map shows the types of rocks and geologic structures in a specific area. Because different types of rocks have different amounts of uranium, a geologic map can tell a geologist the general level of uranium or radium they can expect to find in the rocks and soils in the area. Such maps are especially important in showing where rocks with high levels of uranium occur.

Because radon that enters buildings usually comes from several feet of the earth's top-most surface, knowing the radon levels of the surficial materials is important. Surficial geologic and engineering maps show and describe these surface materials for many regions of the United States. These maps are useful for understanding the physical properties of the materials at the surface, such as permeability, but are generally not as useful for determining what the uranium concentrations in the surface materials might be.

Local geologic maps are often available at:

- the U.S. Geological Survey;
- U.S. Army Corps of Engineers;
- state geological agencies;
- colleges and universities, and their libraries;
- public libraries; and
- county assessors' offices.

Radioactivity Maps

Radioactivity maps give an indication of the uranium levels of surface materials. The most common type of radioactivity map is an aero-radioactivity map, which is based on radioactivity measurements taken by aircraft flying at low altitude using instruments that measure the radioactive energy being emitted from the ground.

There is a strong correlation between areas identified on aero-radioactivity maps as having high levels of surface uranium and areas for which high levels of indoor radon have been reported. In some parts of the country, swamps and marshes are abundant and, in many of these areas, the soils at the surface are full of water, which blocks the radiation of energy. The average amount of radiated energy detected for these areas is lower than it would be if the soils were dry. The uranium content of the soils and the radon potential are likely to be underestimated in these areas.

A large amount of aero-radioactivity data was collected as part of a U.S. Department of Energy program to evaluate the uranium resources of the United States. Most of the energy detected during these flights was from rocks and soils within 800 feet of flight lines that were spaced 1 to 6 miles apart. Many major metropolitan areas were not covered by the survey because of flight restrictions. Therefore, only a small part of the entire surface of the United States was measured. The data from this survey, however, give a good indication of the background uranium concentration of soils and rocks underlying most of the United States.

The digital data from the survey were processed by the U.S. Geological Survey to produce a map showing the uranium content of surface materials in the contiguous United States (the lower 48 states). The smallest data point on the map covers an area of about 1.6 square miles, limiting the amount of detail that can be seen. It is possible to tell how parts of a region, a state, or even a county vary in surface uranium concentration, but it's impossible to tell how the presence of uranium varies from neighborhood to neighborhood or from house to house. The U.S. Geological Survey and state geological agencies prepare and publish radioactivity maps.

Soil-Air Radon Data

Scientists also measure radon in soil air. Data on this give direct evidence about soil radon, but extensive numbers are not commonly available. The two basic methods for measuring the radon concentration of soil air are the same as those used to measure radon in buildings. Both methods measure the alpha particles produced by the decay of the radon in the air.

One method involves burying a passive device (such as a charcoal canister or an alpha track detector, in the soil) and leaving it open to the soil air. This method allows long-term measurements, but the devices can be strongly affected by soil moisture. In the other method, a sample of soil air is collected from a probe driven into the ground, and the radon in the sample is measured by using electronic equipment. This method provides data quickly, but these short-term measurements may vary greatly due to daily, weekly, and even seasonal changes in soil and atmospheric conditions that are averaged out during long-term measurements.

Soil-air methods require specialized equipment because soil-air data are sensitive to many conditions and factors, such as the depth of measurement. Radon levels differ widely in the top 2 to 3 feet of soil because of variations in soil moisture and the amount of radon that escapes into the atmosphere. Taking measurements at 3 feet or deeper avoids many of the problems related to near-surface conditions, but this may be difficult in some soils.

Indoor Radon Data

Indoor radon has been measured in many houses, schools, and commercial buildings across the United States. For the most part, these measurements have been made by homeowners using passive detection devices. Radon concentrations in some homes and businesses are measured by private companies as part of real estate transactions. Many local, state and federal agencies measure radon in buildings for which they are responsible.

Most indoor radon measurements are confidential transactions between homeowners and measurement vendors. The data from these private measurements are not generally available to the public. When they are available, the data are usually given as summaries by state, county or ZIP code. Nonetheless, these summaries are useful in determining which areas of the counties, states, or entire regions of the United States seem likely to have elevated indoor radon levels.

By careful examination and correlation, scientists can evaluate the effects of varying geology and soils on actual readings of indoor radon. The indoor radon information can be used as an additional aid to create a radon potential map, or it can be used as a way of expressing the radon potential of areas mapped by the geologist. However, differences in house construction can also contribute to variations in the indoor radon levels.

Radon Potential Maps

Scientists create radon potential maps by combining a variety of data, such as the locations of rocks containing high levels of uranium, locations of fractures, aero-radioactivity data, soil data on permeability and radon content, and indoor radon data. Not all of these types of data are available for every area, and radon potential maps for different areas may vary if they are based on different types of data.

Evaluating Radon Potential

Again, by knowing something about the geology and soils of the area, scientists can evaluate the radon potential for the rocks and soils of housing sites and areas of interest.

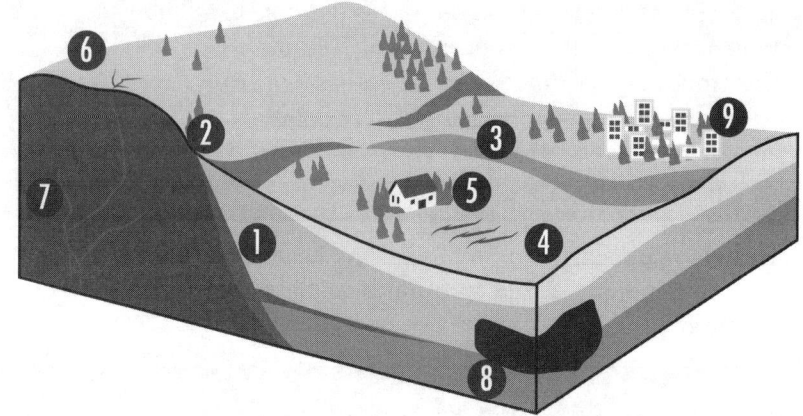

These factors can increase the probability that an area will have above-average areas of radon:

1. Uranium-rich rocks occur in the area.
2. Highly permeable soils are present.
3. Soils are well drained or dry most of the time.
4. Soils form deep cracks during dry times of the year.
5. The site is located on a hill or slope.
6. The soils are thin, and bedrock is close to the surface.
7. Underlying rocks are fractured.
8. The underlying rock contains limestone caverns.
9. High levels of indoor radon have been reported in the neighborhood or county.

Geology of Radon

The geology of radon helps explain why radon levels can vary so greatly between indoor air, outdoor air, soil air, groundwater, and even in different homes in the same area.

Why do some houses have high levels of indoor radon while nearby houses do not?

The reasons lie primarily in the geology of radon—the factors that govern the occurrence of uranium, the formation of radon, and the movement of radon, soil gas, and groundwater. Studies of the geology of radon include research into how uranium and radon sources are distributed in rocks and soils, how radon forms in rocks and soils, and how radon moves. Studying how radon enters buildings from the soil and through the water system is also an important part of understanding the geology of radon.

Uranium: The Source

To understand the geology of radon—where it forms, how it forms, and how it moves—we have to start with its ultimate source: uranium. All rocks contain some uranium, although most contain just a small amount, between 1 and 3 parts per million (ppm). In general, the uranium content of a sample of soil will be about the same as the uranium content of the rock from which the soil was derived.

The bright yellow mineral tyuyamunite is one of the most common uranium-ore minerals.

Some types of rocks have a higher-than-average uranium content. They include light-colored volcanic rocks, granites, dark shale, sedimentary rocks that contain phosphate, and metamorphic rocks derived from these rocks. These rocks and their soils may contain as much as 100 ppm of uranium. Layers of these rocks underlie various regions in the United States.

There are three major classifications of rocks: igneous; sedimentary; and metamorphic.

The higher the uranium level is in an area, the greater the chances are that houses in the area have high levels of indoor radon. But some houses in areas with lots of uranium in the soil have low levels of indoor radon, and other houses on uranium-poor soils have high levels of indoor radon. Clearly, the amount of radon in a house is affected by factors in addition to the mere presence of uranium in the underlying soil.

Radon's Formation

Just as uranium is present in all rocks and soils, so, too, are radon and radium because they are daughter products formed by the radioactive decay of uranium.

Each atom of radium decays by ejecting from its nucleus an alpha particle composed of two neutrons and two protons. As the alpha particle is ejected, the newly formed radon atom recoils in the opposite direction, just as a high-powered rifle recoils when a bullet is fired. Alpha recoil is the most important factor affecting the release of radon from mineral grains.

Newly Formed Radon Nucleus

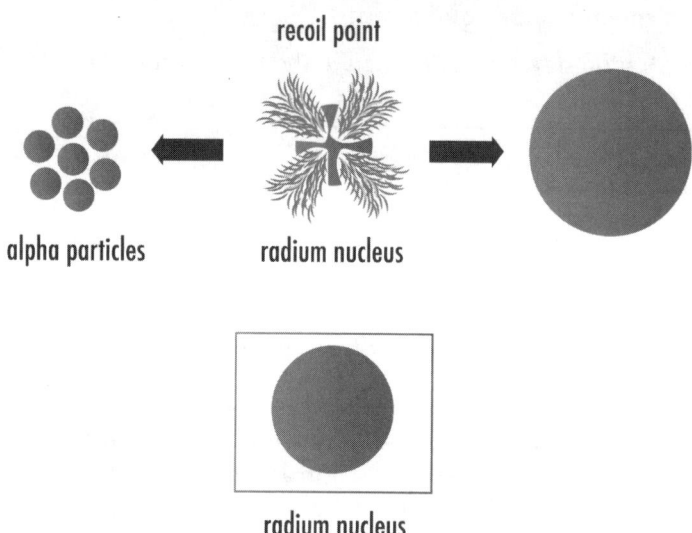

A radium atom decays into radon by releasing an alpha particle, containing two neutrons and two protons, from its nucleus.

The location of the radium atom in the mineral grain (how close it is to the surface of the grain) and the direction of the recoil of the radon atom (whether it is toward the surface or toward the interior of the grain) determine whether or not the newly formed radon atom enters the pore space between mineral grains. If a radium atom is deep within a big grain, then, regardless of the direction of recoil, it will not free the radon from the grain, and the radon atom will remain embedded in the mineral. Even when a radium atom is near the surface of a grain, the recoil will send the radon atom deeper into the mineral if the direction of recoil is toward the grain's core. However, the recoil of some radon atoms near the surface of a grain is directed toward the grain's surface. When this happens, the newly formed radon leaves the mineral and enters the pore space between the grains or the fractures in the rocks.

The recoil of the radon atom is quite strong. Often, newly formed radon atoms enter the pore space, cross all the way through the pore space, and become embedded in nearby mineral grains. If water is present in the pore space, however, the moving radon atom slows very quickly and is more likely to stay in the pore space.

Radon Within Mineral Grains

● Radium atom before it decays
○ Newly formed radon atom

Most of the radon produced within a mineral grain remains embedded in the grain. Only about 10 to 50% escapes to enter the pore space. If the pore space is dry, the radon can remain there more easily. The radon atom may shoot across the pore and embed in another grain where it cannot move.

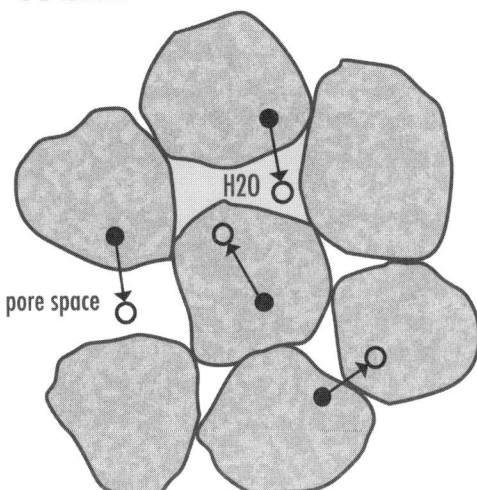

For most soils, only 10 to 50% of the radon produced actually escapes from the mineral grains and enters the pores. Most soils in the United States contain between 0.33 to 1 pCi of radium per gram of mineral matter, and between 200 to 2,000 pCi of radon per liter of soil air.

Radon's Movement

Because radon is a gas, it has much greater mobility than uranium and radium, which are fixed in the solid matter of rocks and soils. Radon can more easily leave the rocks and soils by escaping into fractures and openings in rocks and into the pore spaces between grains of soil.

The ease and efficiency with which radon moves in the pore space or fracture affect just how much radon enters a house. If radon is able to move easily in the pore space, then it can travel a great distance before it decays, and it is more likely to collect in high concentrations inside a building.

The method and speed of radon's movement through soils are controlled by the amount of water present in the pore space (the soil's moisture content), the percentage of pore space in the soil (the porosity of the soil), and the interconnectedness of the pore spaces that determines the soil's ability to transmit water and air (called soil permeability).

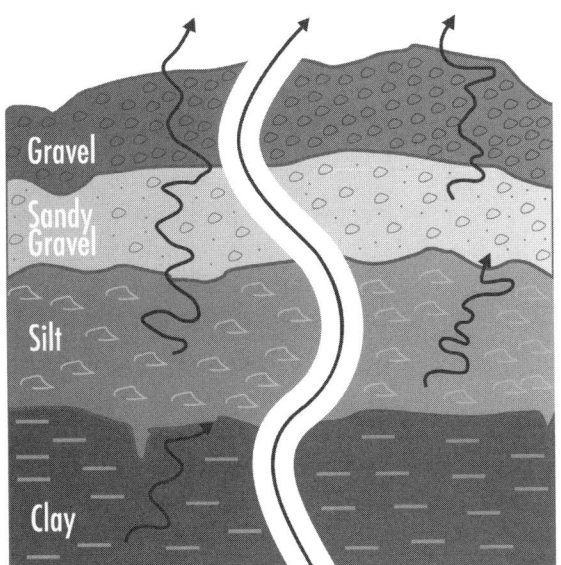

Radon can move through cracks in rocks and through pore spaces in soils.

Radon moves more rapidly through permeable soils (such as coarse sand and gravel) than through impermeable soils (such as clay). Fractures in any soil or rock allow radon to move more quickly.

Some radon atoms remain trapped in the soil and decay to form lead; other atoms escape quickly into the air.

Radon in water moves more slowly than radon in air. The distance that radon moves before most of it decays is less than 1 inch in water-saturated rocks and soils, but it can move more than 6 feet, and sometimes tens of feet, through dry rocks and soils. Because water also tends to flow more slowly through soil pores and rock fractures than does air, radon travels shorter distances through wet soils than through dry soils before it decays.

For these reasons, homes in areas with drier, highly permeable soils and bedrock— such as hill slopes, mouths and bottoms of canyons, coarse glacial deposits, and fractured or cavernous bedrock —may have high levels of indoor radon. Even if the radon content of the air in the soil or fracture is within the "normal" range (200 to 2,000 pCi/L), the permeability of these areas permits radon-bearing air to move greater distances before it decays, and thus contributes to high indoor radon.

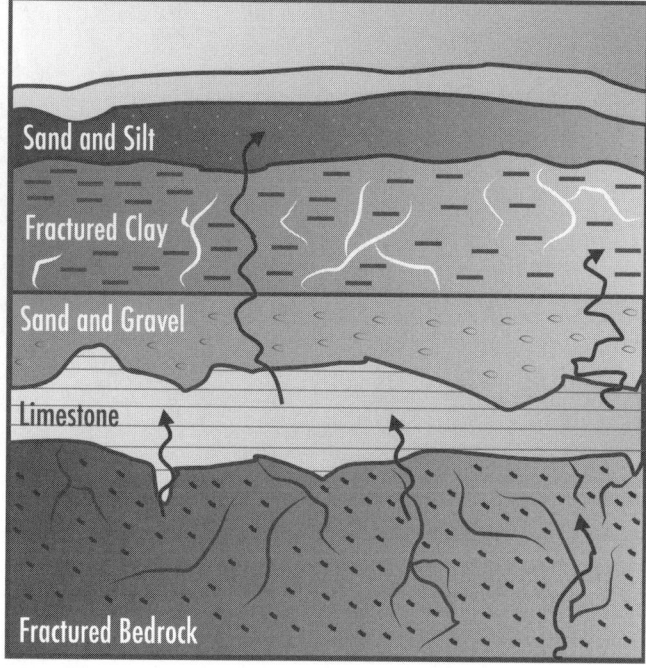

Radon Entry into Buildings

Radon moving through soil pore spaces and rock fractures near the surface of the earth usually escapes into the atmosphere.

Where a house is present, however, soil air often flows toward its foundation for three reasons:

1. differences in air pressure between the soil and the house;

2. the presence of openings in the house's foundation; and

3. increases in permeability around the basement (if one is present).

In constructing a house with a basement, a hole is dug, footings are set, and coarse gravel is usually laid down as a base for the basement slab. Then, once the basement walls have been built, the gap between the basement walls and the ground outside is filled with material that often is more permeable than the original ground. This filled gap is called a disturbed zone.

Radon moves from the surrounding soil into the disturbed zone and the gravel bed underneath. The backfill material in the disturbed zone is commonly made up of rocks and soil from the foundation site. These also generate and release radon. The amount of radon in the disturbed zone and gravel bed depends on the amount of uranium present in the rock at the site, the type and permeability of soil surrounding the disturbed zone and underneath the gravel bed, and the soil's moisture content.

The air pressure in the ground around most houses is often greater than the air pressure inside the house. Thus, air tends to move from the disturbed zone and gravel bed into the house through openings in the house's foundation. All house foundations have openings, such as cracks, utility entries, seams between foundation materials, and uncovered soil in crawlspaces and basements.

Most houses draw less than 1% of their indoor air from the soil; the remainder comes from outdoor air, which is generally quite low in radon. However, houses with low indoor air pressures, poorly sealed foundations, and several entry points for soil air may draw as much as 20% of their indoor air from the soil. Even if the soil air has only moderate levels of radon, the levels inside the house may be very high.

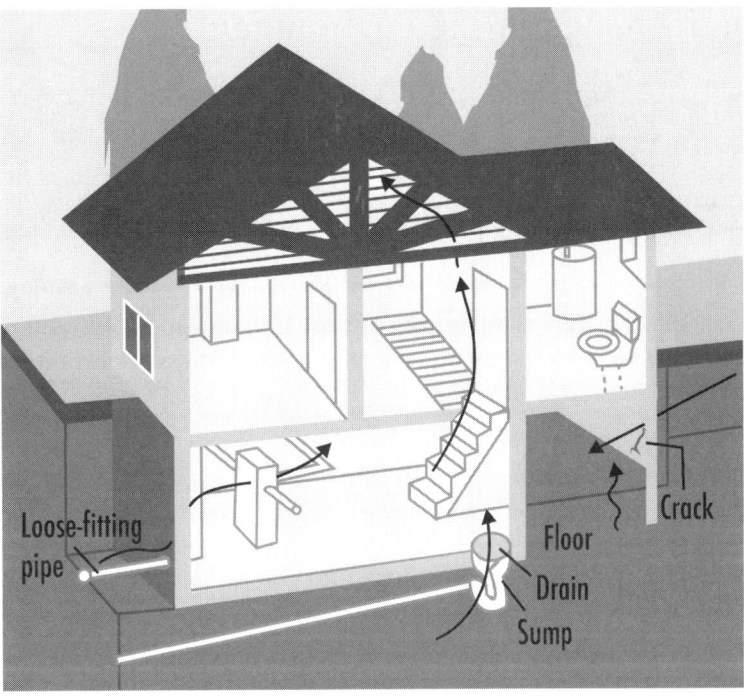

Radon in Water

Radon can also enter the home through its water system. Water from rivers and reservoirs usually contains very little radon because it escapes into the air, so homes that rely on surface water usually do not have a radon problem from the water. In big cities, water processing in large municipal systems aerates the water, which allows radon to escape, and also delays the use of water until most of the remaining radon has decayed.

In many areas of the country, however, groundwater is used as the main water supply for homes and communities. These small public water works and private domestic wells often have closed systems and short transit times that do not remove radon from the water or permit it to decay. This radon escapes from the water to the indoor air as people take showers, wash clothes, do the dishes, and use water in general. A rule of thumb for estimating the contribution of radon from domestic water to the indoor level of airborne radon is that water with 10,000 pCi/L of radon contributes about 1 pCi/L to the level of radon in the indoor air.

The areas most likely to have problems with radon in groundwater are areas that have high levels of uranium in the underlying rocks. For example, granites in various parts of the United States are sources of high levels of radon in groundwater that is given off to private water supplies.

In areas where the main water supply is from private wells and small public water works, radon in groundwater can add radon to the indoor air.

Radon escapes from water when it's agitated.

How Does Radon Change in the Environment?

Because radon is a chemically inert (unreactive) gas, it can move easily through rock and soil and arrive at the surface. The half-life of radon-222 is 3.8 days. As it undergoes radioactive decay, radon-222 releases alpha radiation and changes to polonium-218, a short-lived radioactive solid. After several more transformations (loss of particles or electromagnetic radiation from the nucleus), the series ends at lead-206, which is stable.

Radon dissolves in water, and easily leaves water that is exposed to the atmosphere, especially if the water is agitated. Consequently, radon levels are very low in rivers and lakes, but water drawn from underground can have elevated radon concentrations. Radon that decays in water leaves only solid decay products, which will remain in the water as they decay to stable lead.

How Are People Exposed to Radon?

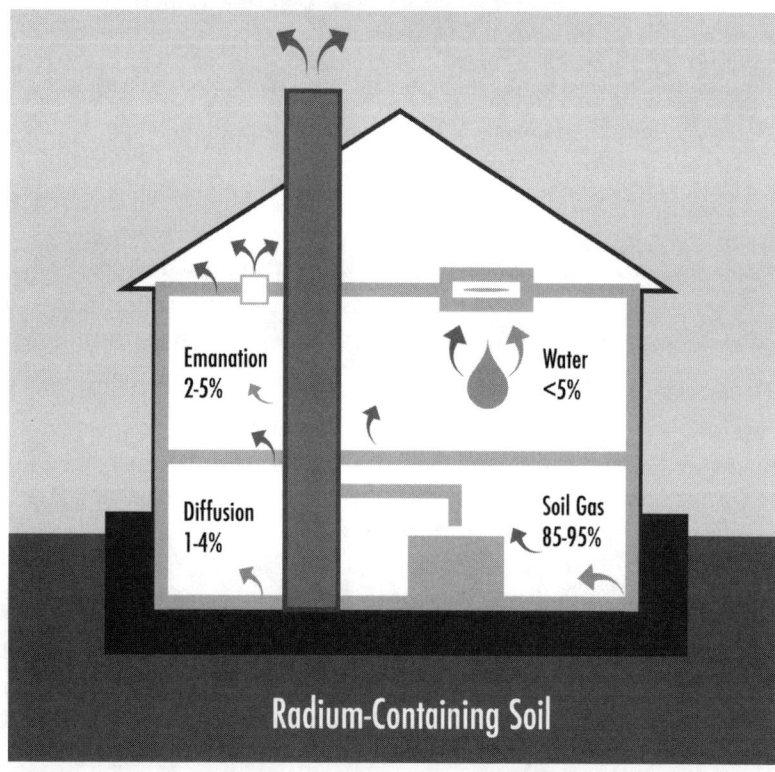

Emanation
2-5%

Water
<5%

Diffusion
1-4%

Soil Gas
85-95%

Radium-Containing Soil

Most of the public's exposure to natural radiation comes from radon, which can be found in homes, schools and office buildings. The illustration shows the sources of radon that can accumulate in buildings.

Most radon in homes comes from radon in the soil that seeps into homes through cracks in the foundation or slab. The amount of radon in the soil varies widely and depends on the chemical makeup of the soil. There can be large house-to-house differences in soil radon concentrations. The only way to know is to test.

Radon is also found in the water in homes, particularly in homes that have their own private wells rather than those that rely on municipal water supplies. When the water is agitated, as when showering or washing dishes, radon escapes into the air. However, radon from water in the home generally contributes only a small proportion (less than 5%) of the total radon in indoor air in most housing. Municipal water systems hold and treat water, which helps to release radon, so levels are very low by the time the water reaches our homes. But people who have private wells, particularly in areas having high radium soil content, may be exposed to higher levels of radon.

The EPA estimates that the national average indoor radon level in homes is about 1.3 pCi/L of air. They also estimate that about one in 15 homes nationwide has levels at or above the level of 4 pCi/L, the level at which it recommends taking action to reduce concentrations. Levels greater than 2,000 pCi/L of air have been measured in some homes. The only way to know if there is radon in a home is to test for it.

How Does Radon Get into the Body?

People may ingest trace amounts of radon with food and water. However, inhalation is the main route of entry into the body for radon and its decay products. Radon decay products may attach to particulates and aerosols in the air we breathe (for example, through cooking oil vapors). When they are inhaled, some of these particles are retained in the lungs. Radon decay products also cling to tobacco leaves (which are sticky) during the growing season, and enter the lungs when the tobacco is smoked. Smoke in indoor environments is also very effective at picking up radon decay products from the air and making them available for inhalation. It is likely that radon decay products contribute significantly to the risk of lung cancer from cigarette smoke.

How Can Radon Affect Your Health?

Almost all risk from radon comes from breathing air containing radon and its decay products. The health risk from ingesting radon is much smaller than the risk from inhaling radon and its decay products.

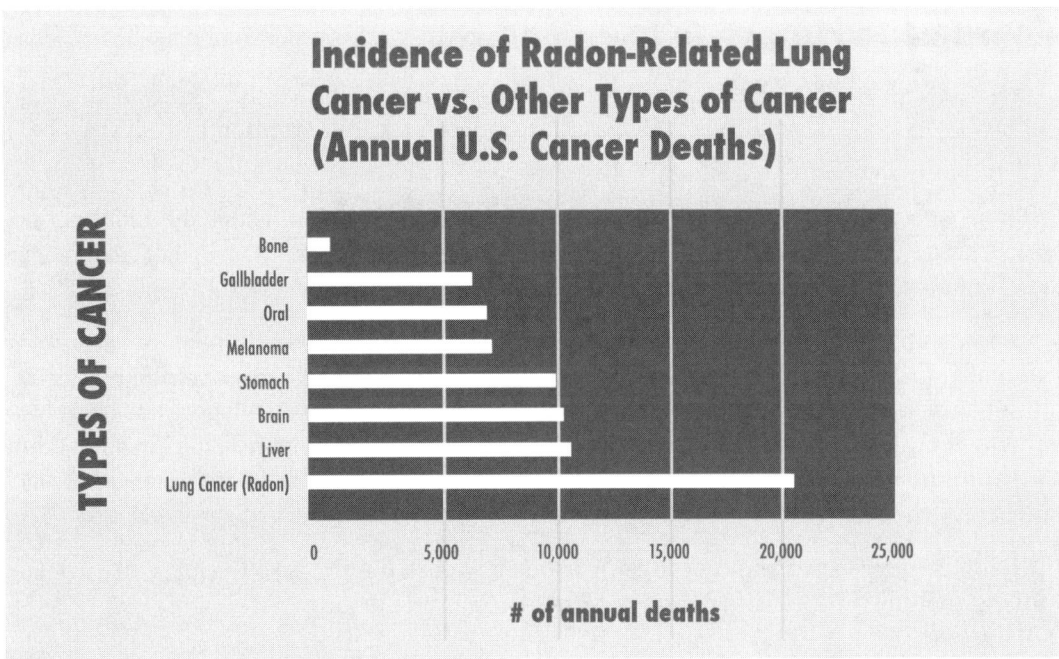

When radon is inhaled, the alpha particles from its radioactive decay directly strike sensitive lung tissue, causing damage that can lead to lung cancer. However, since radon is a gas, most of it is exhaled. The radiation dose comes largely from radon's decay products. These enter the lungs on dust particles that lodge in the airways of the lungs. These radionuclides decay quickly, exposing lung tissue to damage and producing other radionuclides that continue damaging the lung tissue.

There is no safe level of radon; any exposure poses some risk of cancer. The National Academy of Sciences (NAS) studied and described the causes of lung cancer in two 1999 reports. They concluded that radon in indoor air is the second leading cause of lung cancer in the U.S. after cigarette smoking.

The NAS estimated that 15,000 to 22,000 Americans die every year from radon-related lung cancer. When people who smoke are exposed to radon as well, the risk of developing lung cancer is significantly higher than the risk from smoking alone.

The NAS also estimated that radon in drinking water causes an additional 180 cancer deaths per year. However, almost 90% of those deaths were from lung cancer caused by inhaling radon released to the indoor air from water. Only about 10% of the deaths were from cancers of internal organs, mostly the stomach, caused by ingesting radon in water.

Medical Tests to Determine Exposure

Several decay products can be detected in urine, blood, and lung and bone tissue. However, these tests are not generally available through typical medical facilities. Also, they cannot be used to determine accurate exposure levels, since most radon decay products deliver their dose and decay within a few hours.

The best way to assess exposure to radon is by measuring concentrations of radon (or radon decay products) in the air in homes.

For Consumers: Protect Yourself and Family

You cannot see, feel, smell, or taste radon. Testing the home is the only way to know if there is a risk from radon. The EPA and the Surgeon General recommend testing for radon in all homes below the third floor.

The first step is to test your home for radon and have it fixed if it is at or above the EPA's action level of 4 picocuries per liter. You may want to take action if the levels are in the range of 2-4 picocuries per liter. Generally, levels can be brought below 2 pCi/L fairly simply.

The best method for reducing radon in your home will depend on how radon enters your home and the design of your home. For example, sealing cracks in floors and walls may help to reduce radon, but it is not sufficient. There are also systems that remove radon from crawlspaces or from beneath the concrete floor or basement slab that are effective at keeping radon from entering your home. These systems are simple and don't require major changes to your home. Other methods may be necessary.

Radon testing is inexpensive and easy to do. Various low-cost, do-it-yourself test kits are available in retail outlets and online. A trained contractor can also conduct testing.

Homeowners who have private wells should test their well water to ensure that its radon levels meet the EPA's proposed standard.

Read *InterNACHI's Citizen's Guide to Radon* online at **www.nachi.org/citizens-guide-to-radon**

What Is the EPA Doing About Radon?

The EPA has established a voluntary program to promote radon awareness, testing and reduction. The program sets an action level of 4 picocuries per liter (pCi/L) of air for indoor radon. The action level is not the maximum safe level for radon in the home. However, the lower the level of radon, the better. Generally, levels can be brought below 2 pCi/L fairly simply.

In addition to working with homeowners, the EPA is working with home builders and building-code organizations. The goals are to help newly constructed homes be more radon-resistant and to encourage radon testing when existing homes are sold.

For More Info

- Radon-Resistant New Construction: **http://www.epa.gov/radon/rrnc/**
  This webpage provides information on radon-resistant homes.

- Radon and Real Estate: **http://www.epa.gov/radon/realestate.html**
  You will find a number of tools and resources use by the real estate community that the EPA and its radon partners have developed.

The 1988 Indoor Radon Abatement Act authorizes the EPA to provide grants to states to support testing and reducing radon in homes. With various non-governmental and public health organizations, the EPA promotes awareness and reduction of indoor radon. Partners include the American Lung Association, the National Environmental Health Association, the International Association of Certified Home Inspectors, and others.

The EPA has also proposed a standard for the maximum amount of radon that may be found in drinking water from community water systems that use groundwater.

Quiz #3

1. T/F: Radon-222 is the radioactive decay product of radium-226, which is found at low concentrations in almost all rock and soil.

    ☐ True
    ☐ False

2. T/F: All homes have some type of radon-entry pathway.

    ☐ True
    ☐ False

3. A difference in _____ between the basement or crawlspace and the surrounding soil draws radon into the home.

    ☐ square footage
    ☐ indoor air quality
    ☐ water pressure
    ☐ air pressure
    ☐ height

4. T/F: Field research has shown that attempting to seal all of the openings in a foundation is both impractical and ineffective as a stand-alone technique.

    ☐ True
    ☐ False

5. The objective of a sub-slab or sub-membrane depressurization system is to create a _____ beneath the foundation, which is greater in strength than the vacuum imposed on the soil by the house itself.

    ☐ vacuum
    ☐ layer of sand
    ☐ high-pressure system
    ☐ impermeable barrier

6. T/F: Radon gas is approximately seven times heavier than air.

    ☐ True
    ☐ False

7. Because radon is a chemically inert (unreactive) gas, it can move _____ through rock and soil to arrive at the surface.

    ☐ with great difficulty
    ☐ easily

8. About one in _____ homes nationwide have levels at or above the level of 4 pCi/L, the level at which the EPA recommends taking action to reduce concentrations.

□ 50

□ 1,000

□ 15

□ two

9. T/F: You can see, feel, smell, and taste radon.

□ True

□ False

Answer Key is on page 348.

General Testing Procedures

General Procedural Recommendations

The following sections outline basic procedural recommendations for anyone involved in the measurement of radon in homes related to both real estate and non-real estate transactions. Let's start with learning about action levels, mitigation, and radon in water.

Action Levels, Mitigation, and Radon in Water

Radon and the EPA

In 1986, the EPA recommended that all homes be tested for radon. In 1987, the National Institute for Occupational Safety and Health (NIOSH) recommended that exposure for underground miners be reduced from 4 WLM to 1 WLM per year. In 1988, the U.S. Congress enacted the Indoor Radon Abatement Act, which set a national goal for the reduction of radon in buildings compared to the ambient level in outdoor air.

As a result, the EPA set an action level of 4 pCi/L for indoor radon. The EPA recommends that if radon is found above 4 pCi/L, those levels should be mitigated. There is still some risk at levels below 4 pCi/L, and the EPA suggests that people may want to mitigate their homes to get them as close to the ambient outdoor level as possible. Outdoor air has an average of approximately 0.4 pCi/L.

Other countries have adopted different action levels. The following chart lists some of these international action levels.

International Comparison of Radon Action Levels		
Country	Existing Dwellings	New Buildings
Canada	11 pCI/L	
Finland	22 pCi/L	5 pCI/L
Germany	8 pCI/L	8 pCI/L
Ireland	5 pCI/L	5 pCI/L
Norway	22 pCI/L	5 pCI/L
Sweden	11 pCI/L	4 pCI/L

International Comparison of Radon Action Levels		
Country	Existing Dwellings	New Buildings
Spain	11 pCI/L	5 pCI/L
Switzerland	5 pCI/L	
United Kingdom	5 pCI/L	5 pCI/L
United States	4 pCI/L	4 pCI/L

Canada

Recent research by Health Canada estimates that 16% of lung cancer deaths among Canadians are attributable to indoor radon exposure, making radon gas the second leading cause of lung cancer after tobacco smoking. Action to reduce the radon level should be taken in a home whenever the average annual radon concentration exceeds 200 Bq/m³, and the radon level should be reduced to a value as low as practicable.

For more information from Health Canada, visit
www.hc-sc.gc.ca/ewh-semt/radiation/radon/index-eng.php

Radon Measurement

Even though the biological effects of radon are caused by RDPs, radon gas itself, rather than RDPs, is usually measured. This is because there are fewer variables in radon measurements, since gas concentration is not affected by circulation or plating-out; therefore, it is easier to make time-weighted measurements of radon gas, and radon gas measurements are a good indicator of RDPs.

There are three basic methods of sampling for radon:

- time-integrated sampling;
- grab sampling; and
- continuous monitoring.

The most common measurement method is time-integrated sampling, where a device is exposed to the radon gas for a measured amount of time. Charcoal canisters and alpha track devices are typical passive devices used in most homes. Charcoal devices are usually left out for two to seven days, then sealed up and sent to a laboratory where they are analyzed. Alpha track devices are usually left out for longer periods, typically three months to one year. Both types are simple and inexpensive to use.

Continuous monitors and grab-sampling usually require expensive, complex electronic equipment. These require constant calibration to maintain accuracy. Professionals and scientists doing research use this type of equipment.

For short-term devices, the following protocols should be followed:

- Closed-house conditions must be maintained throughout the test, and if the test is only two or three days long, the house must be closed up 12 hours before the test starts.

- The test devices must be placed in the lowest occupied level of the home. For real estate measurements, an unfinished basement would be tested.

- The device should not be placed near doors, windows, air currents, sunlight, or heat sources. Areas of high humidity should be avoided. Devices should be placed at least 20 inches off the floor, 4 inches from other objects, 12 inches from walls, and 12 inches from ceilings.

Results of the test, if above 4 pCi/L, should be verified either by deploying a second device in the same location, or by deploying a long-term device.

Radon Mitigation

Mitigation can be accomplished by addressing elevated radon levels via:

- sources of radon in the soil, building material, and/or well water;

- transport mechanisms that drive radon into a building, usually through pressure differentials;

- radon-entry pathways that allow radon inside, usually through cracks or openings in the foundation or through open crawlspaces; and

- the accumulation of radon and RDPs in the building.

Of these, controlling radon transport by pressure-driven entry is the most common mitigation technique employed. This is called active soil depressurization (ASD). This technique creates a suction or area of low pressure beneath the structure that is stronger than the partial vacuum applied to the soil by the building itself.

ASD systems consist of pipes connected to a fan that draws gases from under the building. Radon is captured and vented to the outside before it has a chance to enter the home.

Types of ASD (active soil depressurization) systems include:

- sub-slab depressurization systems;

- drain tile depressurization systems;

- sub-membrane depressurization systems;

- block-wall depressurization systems; and

- a combination of the above methods.

All of these ASD systems require expert installation, additional sealing of openings into the home, and, of course, testing to verify that radon levels have been reduced to below 4 pCi/L. Professional radon mitigators, such as those taking measurements, are also listed by the NEHA and NRSB.

Radon in Water

Soil gas is the largest natural source of radon in homes. However, well water can be a significant factor if dissolved radon at high concentrations is found. It takes high levels of radon in water to result in a significant elevation of radon in air. The EPA uses a rule of thumb of 1:10,000. That is, if 10,000 pCi/L of radon are measured in the water, indoor radon concentrations in air are increased by 1 pCi/L.

Recent studies have indicated that elevated levels of radon in water are not only an inhalation threat, but may be an ingestion hazard as well, increasing the risk of stomach cancer. In 1992, the EPA proposed a maximum contaminant level (MCL) of 300 pCi/L for public water supplies. At this time, this MCL has not been promulgated. There is also an alternate MCL being proposed of 4,000 pCi/L; however, what the water supplier has to do to be eligible to qualify for this has not been established. As a result of these proposed MCLs, radon may become the most commonly treated contaminant in well water. Radon in well water in Colorado, for example, averages well above the proposed MCL.

Treatment for Radon in Water

There are three recognized treatment methods to remove radon from water:

- storage of the water until the radon decays and depletes;

- aeration to strip the radon from the water; and

- the use of granular activated carbon (GAC) filters.

Water storage until the radon decays is somewhat impractical, since it takes 27 days for radon to decay (depleted 99%). For a typical family of four using 300 gallons of water per day, they would need 8,100 gallons of storage. A tank this large is impractical and expensive.

Aeration is the preferred method of treatment for radon in water. As the water is aerated, radon is released and piped outside. This method requires another pump to pressurize the pressure tank, a radon fan, and biological treatment of the aerated water, as it may be contaminated by the air used for aeration.

Granular activated carbon filters remove radon in water by adsorbing the radon onto the carbon. However, gamma radiation results from the RDPs that accumulate in the filter. The filter thus needs to be shielded or remotely located to prevent radiation hazards to the home's occupants.

Short-Term Radon Tests and Measurement Devices

Activated Charcoal Adsorption

Adsorption is a process by which gases or vapors condense to create a thin film. These devices utilize an airtight container filled with activated charcoal and covered with a screen and filter. The detector is opened in the area to be sampled and exposed to the air for a specified period of time. Radon present in the air adsorbs onto the charcoal. At the end of the sampling period, the container is sealed and then sent to a laboratory for analysis using a scintillation detector. Charcoal detectors may be subject to effects from drafts and high humidity. These detectors are normally deployed for measurement periods of two to seven days.

Charcoal Liquid Scintillation

This method is very similar to the activated charcoal detector in that it employs a small vial of activated charcoal for sampling the radon. Following exposure, the vial is sealed and returned to a laboratory for analysis by treating the charcoal with a scintillation fluid, then the fluid is analyzed using a scintillation counter. These detectors are also deployed for periods of two to seven days.

Electret Ion Chamber

This is the same device described for long-term tests. However, variations in the design of the electret allow for a short-term measurement, as well. The short-term electret ion chamber is deployed for two to seven days.

Continuous Radon Monitoring

This device measures radon and produces results in pCi/L. This detection category includes devices that record real-time continuous measurements of radon gas over a series of minutes, and then report the results in hourly increments. Air is either pumped (in active mode) or diffuses (in passive mode) into a counting chamber, which is typically a scintillation cell or ionization chamber. The RDPs are filtered out. Alpha particles are counted from radon (active mode) or radon and its RDPs (passive mode). The result using this type of detector is normally available at the completion of the test in the home or building without additional processing or analysis. These detectors are usually deployed for a minimum of 48 hours.

When an alpha scintillation cell is used, the room air is continuously collected in a scintillation cell, and the RDPs are filtered out. The alpha particles cause the cell's scintillation material coating to release light. The "glows" are then counted by a photo-multiplier tube.

When a pulsed ion chamber is used, the ions are created from the alpha radiation. The ions are detected by the electrometer. The test produces results in short-term averages.

When a solid-state silicon detector is used, the alpha particles from the radon and its RDPs impact a silicon chip. The impacts produce electrical pulses. The pulses are measurable and counted, and the counts are averaged. This test is passive only. It needs a power supply, and it has relatively low efficiency.

Continuous Working-Level Monitoring

These devices record real-time continuous measurement of the radioactive decay products of radon in the air. Radon decay products are sampled by continuously pumping air through a filter. Alpha particles from the decay of products trapped on the filter are counted to determine the concentration of radon decay products in the air sampled. Continuous working-level monitors should be deployed for a minimum of 48 hours.

Specialized Measurement Devices

A number of other specialized measurement methods are available for radon testing. However, they all require a skilled technician and/or specialized analytical equipment to achieve proper sampling results. These requirements tend to make these measurement methods more expensive than those previously described, and thus they are not commonly used for radon testing in homes or public buildings. Instead, these methods find greater application in research work or to evaluate the success of radon reduction efforts. A list of these methods is provided for informational purposes. The methods listed may only be used for short-term measurements.

These devices include:

1. grab radon/activated charcoal;

2. grab radon/pump-collapsible bag;

3. grab radon/scintillation cell;

4. three-day integrating evacuated scintillation cell;

5. pump/collapsible bag (one-day);

6. grab working level; and

7. radon progeny (decay product) integrating sampling unit.

Long-Term Tests and Radon Measurement Devices

There are several radon measurement devices that may be used to test a home or building for radon. These devices fall into two broad categories: those used for long-term measurements having a testing period of three to 12 months; and those designed for short-term measurements having a testing period of less than three months and, more typically, between two and seven days.

Alpha Track Detector

These detectors use a small piece of special plastic or film inside a container with a filter-covered opening. Air being tested diffuses (with a passive detector) or is pumped (with an active detector) through a filter covering a hole in the container. When alpha particles from radon and its decay products strike the detector, they cause damage tracks. At the end of the test period, the container is sealed and returned to a laboratory for reading. The laboratory counts the damage marks (tracks) left by the alpha particles. The radon exposure duration of an alpha track detector is usually one to 12 months.

Alpha track devices are relatively inexpensive. They are convenient to handle and use. They can be distributed by mail. They are small and not cumbersome to set up in a house. They do not need electrical power. They can be used for long-term tests.

Electret Ion Chamber

This device consists of a special plastic canister (the ion chamber) containing an electrostatically charged disk detector or electret. The detector is exposed during the measurement period, allowing radon to diffuse through a filter-covered opening into the chamber. The radon decays. The RDPs release alpha, beta and gamma radiation. The radiation produces ions and electrons. The electrons are attracted to a positively charged electret disk. Ionization resulting from the decay of radon produces a reduction in the charge on the electret. The drop in voltage on the electret is related to the radon concentration. The change in the voltage is used to calculate an average radon concentration for the testing time period.

The detectors may be read in the home using a special analysis device to measure the voltage, or they may be mailed to a laboratory for analysis. The electret voltages are measured before and after deployment. There are two types of chambers. The large chambers are used for short-term measurement tests. The small chambers are used for long-term tests. This type of detector may be deployed for one to 12 months.

Digital Continuous Radon Monitor

This detector plugs into a standard wall outlet, much like a consumer-grade carbon monoxide detector, and continuously monitors for radon. It is a passive device based on an ion chamber. It allows the homeowner to take radon measurements in different areas of the home. After being plugged in for an initial period of 48 hours, the device displays the average radon concentration continuously.

Initial Client Interview

Reasonable efforts should be made to determine whether the home is new and/or occupied, and who will be in charge of the home during the measurement period. Radon testing individuals should inform the client of:

- the appropriate EPA testing recommendations as outlined the 1992 *Citizen's Guide to Radon* (EPA 402-K-92-001; U.S. EPA 1992a), and/or the *Home Buyer's and Seller's Guide to Radon* (EPA 402-R-93-003; U.S. EPA 1993); and
- the types of devices they will be using for that test, as well as EPA documentation indicating that the testing organization is proficient.

Organizations should provide the client with the following information:

- Devices that will be placed by the customer must be accompanied by instructions on how to use the device. These instructions should be consistent with the EPA's Indoor Radon and Radon Decay Product Measurement Device Protocols, and include specific information on the minimum and maximum length of time that the device must be exposed.
- In addition to the measurement results, the organization should provide information on how to mitigate, especially if the results are elevated. The EPA's *Consumer's Guide to Radon Reduction*, or state-required brochures, provide this information. If the Consumer's Guide brochure is used, it should be reproduced in its entirety. The company's name may not be placed on the brochure so as to avoid any suggestion of the EPA's endorsement.

Measurement Recommendations

Selecting a Measurement Approach

The purpose of the measurements, along with budget and time constraints, dictate the protocol used. Measurements for the purpose of assessing the need for mitigation should be made according to the guidance discussed in this section. (The next section outlines options for protocols for measurements made for real estate transactions.) Organizations that provide consultant services, or place or retrieve devices, should review the protocol options and the client's needs, and inform the client of the building and testing period conditions necessary for conducting valid measurements. In some areas, companies may offer different types of radon service agreements. Some agreements allow for a one-time fee that covers both testing and, if needed, radon reduction.

Adherence to the EPA's device protocols outlined in *Indoor Radon and Radon Decay Product Measurement Device Protocols* (EPA 520-402-R-92-004; U.S. EPA 1992c) was a requirement for participation in the EPA's former National Radon Proficiency Program (RPP).

Radon Measurement Duration

Radon levels in a home or building can vary significantly over time. In fact, it is not uncommon to see radon levels in a home change by a factor of two to three over a one-day period. Variations from season to season can be even larger. The highest radon levels are usually observed during the winter months. As a result, a long-term measurement period will give a much better indication of the annual average radon concentration than measurements of shorter duration. Long-term measurements are typically three to 12 months in duration. During this type of measurement, there are no requirements for the occupants to change their lifestyle once the measurement devices have been put in place. A radon test should be performed in a home or public building for a long-term measurement. A minimum of three months is recommended, and 12 months is optimum.

In rare cases, a more rapid indication of the radon concentration may be required. Under such circumstances, a short-term measurement of less than three months (more typically, two to seven days) can be performed. However, short-term measurements should be used with caution. Testing durations of less than two days (48 hours) are never acceptable to determine radon concentrations for purposes of assessing the need for mitigation. Since radon concentrations vary over time, it is strongly recommended that the result of any short-term measurement be confirmed with a follow-up long-term measurement. The follow-up measurement should be made at the same location as the initial measurement. A single short-term measurement does not provide sufficient data upon which to base a decision to mitigate. In such cases, a follow-up measurement is always necessary for mitigation decision-making, regardless of the initial measurement result.

Written Measurement Guidance

Measurement organizations should provide clients with written measurement instructions that clearly explain the responsibilities of the client (and the occupant, if different) during the test period. Written and verbal guidance should be in accordance with the EPA's *Indoor Radon and Radon Decay Product Measurement Device Protocols*. At a minimum, the guidance should include a statement as to whether the device measures radon or radon decay products (RDPs), and a discussion of the units in which all results will be reported.

The results of RDP measurements should be reported in working levels (WL). If the WL value is converted to a radon concentration and is reported to the homeowner, it should be stated that this approximate conversion is based on a 50% equilibrium ratio, unless the actual equilibrium ratio is determined. In addition, the report should indicate that this ratio is typical of the home's environment, but that any indoor environment may have a different and varying relationship between radon and its decay products.

Additionally, the instructions should include:

- a description of closed-building conditions, and a stated requirement that these conditions be maintained 12 hours prior to and during all short-term measurements lasting less than four days and, preferably, for those lasting up to one week;

- directions that the building's heating, ventilating and air-conditioning (HVAC) system and any existing mitigation system should be normally operated 24 hours prior to and during all measurements;

- specific information on the minimum and maximum duration of exposure for the device;

- procedures for placing, retrieving and handling the device, should the client be performing the test, and a written non-interference agreement to be signed and returned by the client confirming that they followed all instructions and did not interfere with the conditions or the measurement device. Instructions should include the problems of introducing unconditioned air into the home or closure of normally accessible areas of the home. In this case, the measurement organization should inform the client that these conditions will invalidate measurement results. The tester should then decline to conduct a measurement until the conditions have been corrected.

A permanent radon-reduction system should be fully operational for at least 24 hours prior to testing to determine the mitigation system's effectiveness. The mitigation system is to be operated normally and continuously during the entire measurement period.

Non-Interference Controls

As previously discussed, the measurement organization should provide clients with a written statement that discusses the importance of proper measurement conditions and of not interfering with the measurement device or building conditions. A non-interference agreement should be signed and returned by the client confirming that they followed all written instructions and did not interfere with the measurement device.

In addition to providing written guidance, organizations that place and retrieve devices should take steps to identify attempts to interfere with the measurement device or building conditions.

The signed non-interference agreement, a description of all non-interference controls employed, and a statement addressing any observed breaches of the non-interference agreement and/or controls should be made part of the measurement documentation for each test.

Measurement Documentation

Measurement organizations should record sufficient information on each measurement in a permanent log to allow for future data comparisons, interpretations, and reports to clients. The EPA recommends that a measurement log be kept with the following information to be maintained for five years (additional method-specific documentation is outlined in the EPA's *Indoor Radon and Radon Decay Product Measurement Device Protocols*):

- a copy of the final report, including the measurement results, and the statement outlining any recommendations concerning re-testing or mitigation provided to the building's occupant or agent;
- the address of the building measured, including ZIP code;
- the exact locations of all measurement devices deployed. It is advisable to diagram the test area, noting the exact location of the detector;
- the exact start and stop dates of the measurement duration (and any times required for analysis);
- a description of the device used, including manufacturer, model, type, and identification or serial number;
- a description of the condition of any permanent vents, such as crawlspace vents or combustion air supply to combustion appliances;
- a description of any variations from or uncertainties about standard measurement procedures, closed-building conditions, or other factors that may affect the measurement result;
- a description of any non-interference controls used, and copies of signed non-interference agreements; and
- a record of any quality control measures associated with the test, such as results of simultaneous or secondary measurements.

Quality Assurance in Radon Testing

Anyone providing measurement services using radon or radon decay product (RDP) measurement devices should establish and maintain a quality assurance program.

These programs should include written procedures for attaining quality assurance objectives, and a system for recording and monitoring the results of the quality assurance measurements, as described below. The EPA offers general guidance on preparing quality assurance plans (QAMS-005/80; U.S. EPA 1980); a standard template prepared by a radon industry group is also available (AARST 1991). The quality assurance program should include the maintenance of control charts and related statistical data, as described by Goldin (Goldin 1984), and by the EPA (EPA 600/9-76-005; U.S. EPA 1984).

All organizations should develop, implement, revise periodically, and maintain a detailed quality assurance plan (QAP) appropriate to each device or method used. (This was a requirement for participation in the EPA's former National Radon Proficiency Program. Specific guidance on the necessary quality control measures for each measurement method is provided in the EPA's *Indoor Radon and Radon Decay Product Measurement Device Protocols*.)

Organizations that do not use continuous monitors or do not analyze detectors also need to write and follow a QAP, and conduct quality control measurements. These include duplicate, blank, and spiked measurements.

Calibration Measurements

Calibration measurements are measurements made in a known radon environment, such as a calibration chamber. Detectors requiring analysis, such as charcoal canisters, alpha track detectors, electret ion chambers, and radon progeny integrating samplers, are exposed in a calibration chamber and then analyzed. Instruments providing immediate results, such as continuous working-level and radon monitors, should be operated in a chamber to establish individual instrument calibration factors.

Calibration measurements must be conducted to determine and verify the conversion factors used to derive the concentration results. These factors are determined normally for a range of concentrations and exposure times, and for a range of other exposure and/or analysis conditions pertinent to the particular device. Determination of these calibration factors is a necessary part of the laboratory analysis and is the responsibility of the analysis laboratory. These calibration measurement procedures, including the frequency of tests and the number of devices to be tested, should be specified in the quality assurance program maintained by manufacturers and analytical laboratories.

Known Exposure Measurements

Known exposure measurements or spiked samples consist of detectors that have been exposed to known concentrations in a radon calibration chamber. These detectors are to be labeled and submitted to the laboratory in the same manner as ordinary samples in order to preclude special processing. The results of these measurements are used to monitor the accuracy of the entire measurement system. Suppliers and analytical laboratories should provide for the blind introduction of spiked samples into their measurement processes, and the monitoring of the results in their quality assurance programs. All organizations providing measurement services with passive devices should conduct spiked measurements at a rate of three per 100 measurements, with a minimum of three per year, and a maximum required of six per month.

Under the EPA's former program, providers of measurements with active devices were required to recalibrate their instruments at least once every 12 months and perform cross-checks with approved devices at least once every six months. Participation in the EPA's former National Radon Proficiency

Program did not satisfy the need for annual calibration, as this program was a performance test and not a calibration procedure.

Background Measurements

Background measurements are required both for continuous monitors and passive detectors that need laboratory analysis. Users of continuous monitors must perform sufficient instrument background measurements to establish a reliable measurement and to check on instrument operation. (For more specific information on how often background measurements should be made, refer to the EPA's *Indoor Radon and Radon Decay Product Measurement Device Protocols*.)

Passive detectors requiring laboratory analysis need one type of background measurement made in the laboratory and another in the field. Suppliers and analysis laboratories should routinely measure the background of a statistically significant number of unexposed detectors from each batch or lot to establish the laboratory background for the batch, as well as the entire measurement system. This laboratory blank value is subtracted by the laboratory from the field sample results reported to the user, and should be made available to the users for quality assurance purposes. In addition to these background measurements, the organization performing the measurements should calculate the lower limit of detection (LLD) for its measurement system, according to the U.S. Department of Energy. The LLD is based on the detector and analysis system's background and can restrict the ability of some measurement systems to measure low concentrations.

Providers of passive detectors should employ field controls, called blanks, equal to approximately 5% of the detectors that are deployed, or 25 each month, whichever is smaller. These controls should be set aside from each detector shipment, kept sealed and in a low-radon environment, labeled in the same manner as the field samples (to preclude special processing), and returned to the analysis laboratory along with each shipment. These field blanks measure the background exposure that may accumulate during shipment and storage, and the results should be monitored and recorded. The recommended action to be taken if the concentrations measured by one or more of the field blanks is significantly greater than the LLD is dependent upon the type of detector used. (More information is available in the EPA's *Indoor Radon and Radon Decay Product Measurement Device Protocols*.)

Duplicate Measurements

Duplicate measurements provide a check on the quality of the measurement result, and allow the user to make an estimate of the relative precision. Large precision errors may be caused by detector manufacture, and/or improper data transcription or handling by suppliers, laboratories or technicians performing placements. Precision error can be an important component of the overall error, so it is essential that all users monitor precision.

Duplicate measurements for both active and passive detectors should be side-by-side measurements made in at least 10% of the total number of measurement locations, or 50 each month, whichever is smaller. The locations selected for duplication should be distributed systematically throughout the entire population of samples. Groups providing measurement services to homeowners can do this by providing two measurements (instead of one) to a random selection of purchasers, with the measurements made side by side. As with spiked samples introduced into the system as blind measurements, the precision of duplicate measurements should be monitored and recorded in the quality assurance records. The analysis of data from duplicates should follow the methodology described in Appendix B. If the precision estimated by the user is not within the precision expected of the measurement method, the problem should be reported to the analysis laboratory and the cause investigated.

Routine Instrument Performance Checks

Proper functioning of analysis equipment and operator usage require that the equipment and measurement system be subject to routine checks. Regular monitoring of equipment and operators is vital to ensure consistently accurate results. Performance checks of analysis equipment include the frequent use of an instrument check source. In addition, important components of the device (such as a pump and pump flow rate, battery, or electronics) should be checked prior to each measurement, with the results noted in a log. Each user should develop methods for regularly monitoring their measurement system, and for recording and reviewing results. Regular monitoring can be daily, or at least prior to each measurement.

Operating Procedures

Organizations performing radon measurements should have a written, device-specific standard operating procedure (SOP) in place for each radon measurement system they use. An SOP must include specific information describing how to operate and/or analyze a particular measurement device. Organizations that analyze devices should develop their own SOP, or adapt manufacturer-developed SOPs for their device(s). Organizations that receive results from a laboratory should have a device-specific SOP for each brand, model and type of device that they use. All SOPs should be consistent with the appropriate protocol outlined in the EPA's *Indoor Radon and Radon Decay Product Measurement Device Protocols*.

Reporting Test Results

Organizations should report radon measurement results to clients within a few weeks of retrieving exposed devices or receiving an exposed device that has been delivered for analysis.

At a minimum, the client report should contain the following information:

- measurement results reported in the units that the device measures. Any measurement results based on radon gas (pCi/L of air) should be stated to no more than one decimal place (e.g., 4.3 pCi/L). Any measurement result based on working levels (WL) of radon decay products should be reported to no more than three decimal places (e.g., 0.033 WL). Any conversions from WL to pCi/L, or from pCi/L to WL, should be presented and explained clearly. If the WL value is converted to a radon concentration, it should be stated in the report to the homeowner that this approximate conversion is based on a 50% equilibrium ratio, unless the actual equilibrium ratio is determined. In addition, the report should indicate that this ratio is typical of the home's environment, but that any indoor environment may have a different and varying relationship between radon and its decay products;

- the dates of the measurement period and address of the building tested;

- a description of the device used, its manufacturer, model and/or type, and the device identification (serial) number(s);

- the name (and any relevant identification numbers) of the organization and individual placing and retrieving the device, and the organization analyzing the device, if they are different;

- a statement concerning any observed tampering or deviations from the required test conditions;

- organizations that offer measurement services with grab-sampling devices should provide clients with written notification stating that grab-sample results can be useful diagnostic tools, but should not be used for deciding whether or not to mitigate; and

- diagnostic measurements should be reported as "for diagnostic purposes only."

Accuracy and Precision

The precision of a radon test is measured by quality control tests called duplicates.

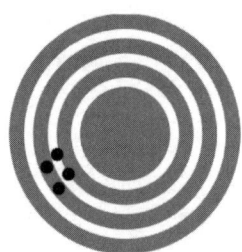

Accuracy is the degree of closeness of a measured or calculated quantity to its actual or true value. Accuracy is closely related to precision, also called reproducibility or repeatability, which is the degree to which further measurements will show similar results. The result of a measurement can be accurate but not precise, precise but not accurate, neither, or both. A measurement is considered valid if it is both accurate and precise.

Accuracy refers to the degree of validity, while precision refers to the degree of reproducibility. The analogy used here to explain the difference between accuracy and precision is this target comparison. In this analogy, repeated measurements are compared to the arrows that are shot at the target. Accuracy describes the closeness of the arrows to the bull's-eye at the target's center. Arrows that strike closer to the bull's-eye are considered more accurate. The closer a system's measurements are to the accepted value, the more accurate the system is considered to be.

To continue the analogy, if a large number of arrows is shot, precision would be determined by the size of the arrows' cluster. (When only one arrow is shot, precision refers to the size of the cluster one would expect if this were repeated many times under the same conditions.) When all the arrows are grouped tightly together, the cluster is considered precise because all the arrows struck close to the same spot, if not necessarily near the bull's-eye. The measurements, therefore, are considered precise, though not necessarily accurate.

Interpretation of Side-by-Side Results

1. Assessment of Precision (Precision Error)

2. Examples of Control Charts for Precision Error

3. Interpretation of Precision Control Charts

1. Assessment of Precision (Precision Error)

Radon and working-level measurements, like all measurements, usually do not produce exactly the same results, even for simultaneous (duplicate) co-located measurements. The objective of performing simultaneous or duplicate measurements is to assess the precision error of the measurement method, or test how well two side-by-side measurements agree. This precision error is the random component of error, as opposed to the calibration error, which is systematic. The precision error, or the degree of disagreement between duplicates, can be composed of many factors. These include the error caused by the random nature of counting radioactive decay, the slight differences between detector construction (for example, small differences in the amount of carbon in activated carbon detectors), and differences in the handling of detectors (for example, differences in accuracy of the weighing process, and variations of analysis among detectors).

It is critical to understand, document and monitor the precision error. This knowledge and documentation will allow the tester to characterize the precision error for clients. Furthermore, the continual monitoring of precision provides a check on every aspect of the measurement system.

There are many ways to quantitatively assess the precision error based on duplicate measurements. First, it is necessary to understand that precision is characterized by a distribution; that is, the side-by-side measurements will exhibit a range of differences. There is some chance that any level of disagreement will be encountered merely due to the statistical fluctuations of counting radioactive decays. The probability of encountering a very large difference between duplicates is smaller than the chance of observing a small difference similar to those that are routinely observed. It is important to recognize that a few high precision errors do not necessarily mean that the measurement system is flawed.

Ideally, the results of duplicates should be assessed in a way that allows for the determination of what level of chance is associated with a particular difference between duplicates. This will allow for the pre-determination of limits for the allowable differences between duplicates before an investigation into the cause of the large differences is made. For example, the warning level, or the level of discrepancy between duplicates that triggers an investigation, may be set at a 5% probability. This level is a difference between duplicates that is so large that, when compared with previous precision errors, should be observed only 5% of the time. A control limit, where further measurements should cease until the problem is corrected, may be set at 1% probability.

A control chart for duplicates for a check source is not as simple as a control chart used to monitor instrument performance. This is because the instrument's response to a check source should be fairly constant over time. Duplicates are performed at various radon concentrations, however, and the total difference between two measurements is expected to increase as radon levels increase.

The use of statistics, such as the relative percent difference (RPD: the difference divided by the mean), or the coefficient of variation (COV: standard deviation divided by the mean), can be used in a control chart for duplicate measurements at radon concentrations where the expected precision error is fairly constant in proportion to the mean (e.g., at levels greater than around 4 pCi/L or 0.02 WL). At lower concentrations—for example, between 2 pCi/L (or 0.01 WL) and 4 pCi/L (or 0.02 WL)—a control chart may be developed by plotting these same statistics; however, the proportion of the precision error to the mean will be greater than that proportion at levels above 4 pCi/L (or 0.02 WL). At concentrations less than about 2 pCi/L (or 0.01 WL), the lower limit of detection may be approached, and the precision error may be so large as to render a control chart not useful.

2. Examples of Control Charts for Precision Error

Before a control chart can be developed, it is necessary to know, from a history of making reliable quality measurements using the exact measurement system (detectors, analysis equipment, and procedures), the level of precision that is routinely encountered when the system is operating well or "in control." It is that in-control precision error that forms the basis of the control chart, and upon which all the subsequent duplicate measurements will be judged. There are two ways of initially determining this in-control level. The preferred method is to perform at least 20 duplicate pairs of measurements at each range of radon concentration for which a control chart is to be prepared. For example, if the tester will assess only precision at concentrations greater than 4 pCi/L (or 0.02 WL), he or she will need at least 20 pairs of measurements at concentrations greater than 4 pCi/L (or 0.02 WL) to assess the in-control level. The average precision error (RPD or CV) should be the in-control level.

The second way to initially set the in-control precision error level is to use a level that has been used by others and that is recognized by the industry and the EPA as a goal for precision (for example, a 10% CV corresponding to a 14% RPD). After at least 20 pairs of measurements are plotted, it will become apparent whether the 10% CV (or 14% RPD) is appropriate for the system. If it is not, a new control chart (using the guidelines to follow) should be prepared so that the warning and control limits are set at the correct probability limits for the testing system.

2.1 Sequential Control Chart Based on Coefficient of Variation

It can be demonstrated that when the expected precision is a constant function of the mean, control limits can be expressed in terms of the CV (CV = S/Xm , where S is the variance or the square of the standard deviation, and Xm is the mean or average of the two measurements). One method for obtaining percentiles for the distribution of the CV is to apply a X-squared (X2) test:

EXAMPLE EQUATION 1: $X^2_{n-1} = B[(n-1)CV_n^2/(n+(n-1)CV_n^2)]$

where $B = n[(1 + (1/CV^2)]$;

CV_n = the observed CV of the nth pair (the pair that is to be evaluated); and

CV = the in-control CV (e.g., 10% at levels greater than 4 pCi/L)

For duplicates, where n = 2, *Example Equation 1* becomes:

EXAMPLE EQUATION 2: $X^2 = [2 + (2/CV^2)][CV_n^2/(2 + CV_n^2)]$

For a value of 0.10 for CV, it further reduces to

EXAMPLE EQUATION 3: $X^2 = 202[CV_n^2/(2 + CV_n^2)]$

Referring to a X^2 chart, we learn that the probability of exceeding a X^2 of 3.84 is only 5%. Inserting this value of 3.84 for X^2 and solving for CV_n produces a CV_n of 0.20. This level of probability forms the warning level shown in Exhibit 2-1. The control limit corresponds to a X^2 of 6.63 and a CV_n of 0.26, where the probability of exceeding those values is only 1%.

This sequential control chart should be used by plotting results from each pair on the Y axis, and noting the date and measurement numbers on the X axis.

2.2 Sequential Control Chart Based on Relative Percent Difference

The relative percent difference, or RPD, is another expression of precision error, and is given as:

EXAMPLE EQUATION 4: RPD = $[100|x_1-x_2|]/[(x_1+x_2)/2]$

For n = 2,

EXAMPLE EQUATION 5: RPD = CV SQRT 2

The control limits for RPD can be obtained simply by multiplying the control limits for CV by the square root of 2, or 1.41. These limits are shown in Exhibit 2-2. This sequential control chart for RPD should be used in the same way as the control chart for CV—that is, with the vertical scale in units of RPD, and the horizontal scale in units of date and measurement numbers.

A control chart using the statistic RPD based on an in-control level of 25% RPD is shown in Exhibit 2-3. The warning level and control limit are set at 50% and 67%, respectively. Use of these limits may be appropriate for measured radon concentrations of less than 4 pCi/L.

Exhibit 2-1:

*Control Chart for Coefficient of Variation (CV) Based on an In-Control Level of 10%
(for duplicates where the average >4 pCi/L or 0.02 WL):*

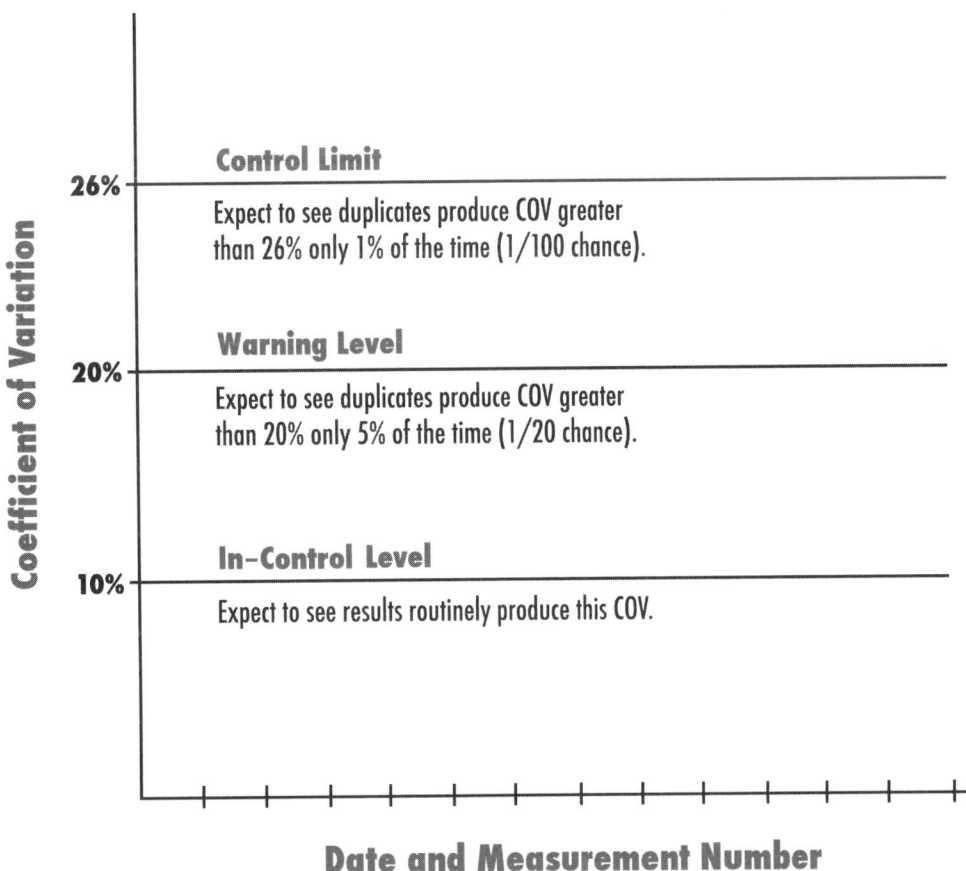

CV or COV = standard deviation of two measurements divided by their average.

Example: Detector A = 5 pCi/L, B=6 pCi/L, CV=13%

If the CV exceeds the control limit, cease measurements until the problem is identified and corrected.

If the CV exceeds the warning level, follow the guidance in #3 and see Exhibit 3-1.

Exhibit 2-2:

Control Chart for Relative Percent Difference (RPD) Based on an In-Control Level of 14% or CV of 10% (for duplicates where average >4 pCi/L or 0.02 WL):

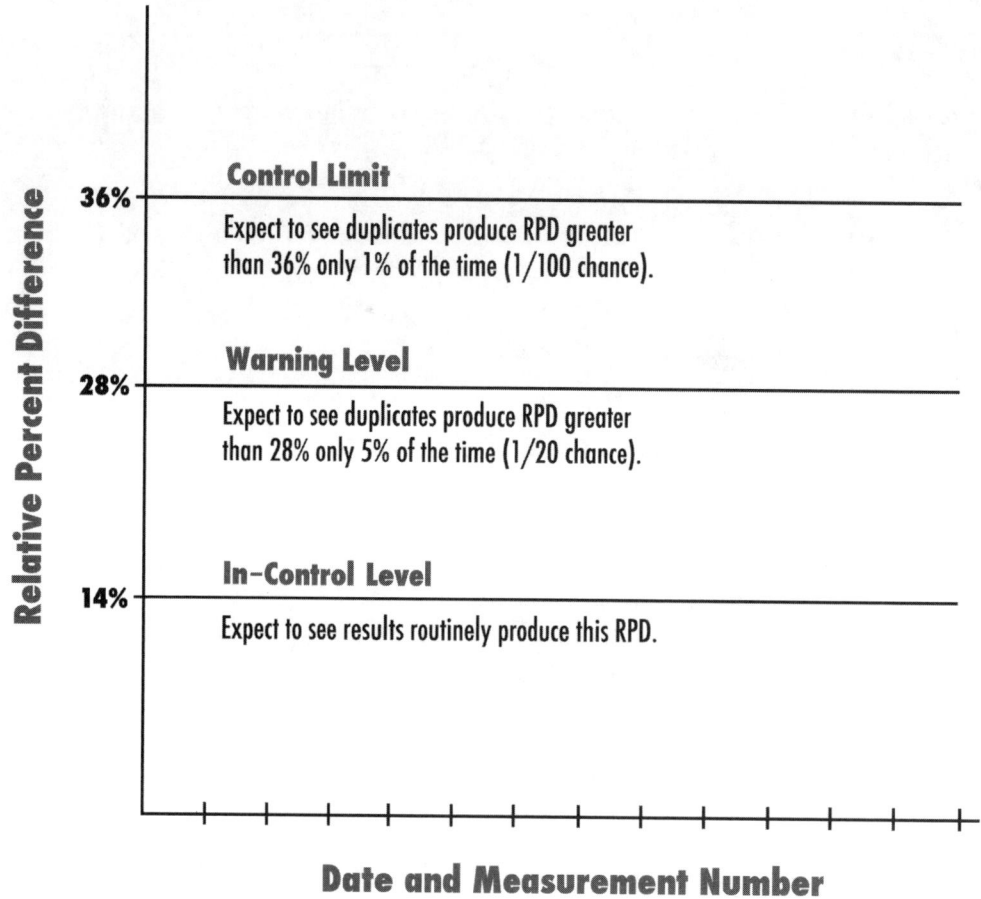

RPD = difference between two measurements divided by their average.

   Example: Detector A = 5 pCi/L, B = 6 pCi/L, RPD = 18%

If the RPD exceeds the control limit, cease measurements until the problem is identified and corrected.

If the RPD exceeds the warning level, follow the guidance in #3 and see Exhibit 3-1.

Exhibit 2-3:

Control Chart* for Relative Percent Difference (RPD) Based on an In-Control Level of 25% = CV of 18% (for duplicates where average <4 pCi/L or 0.02 WL):

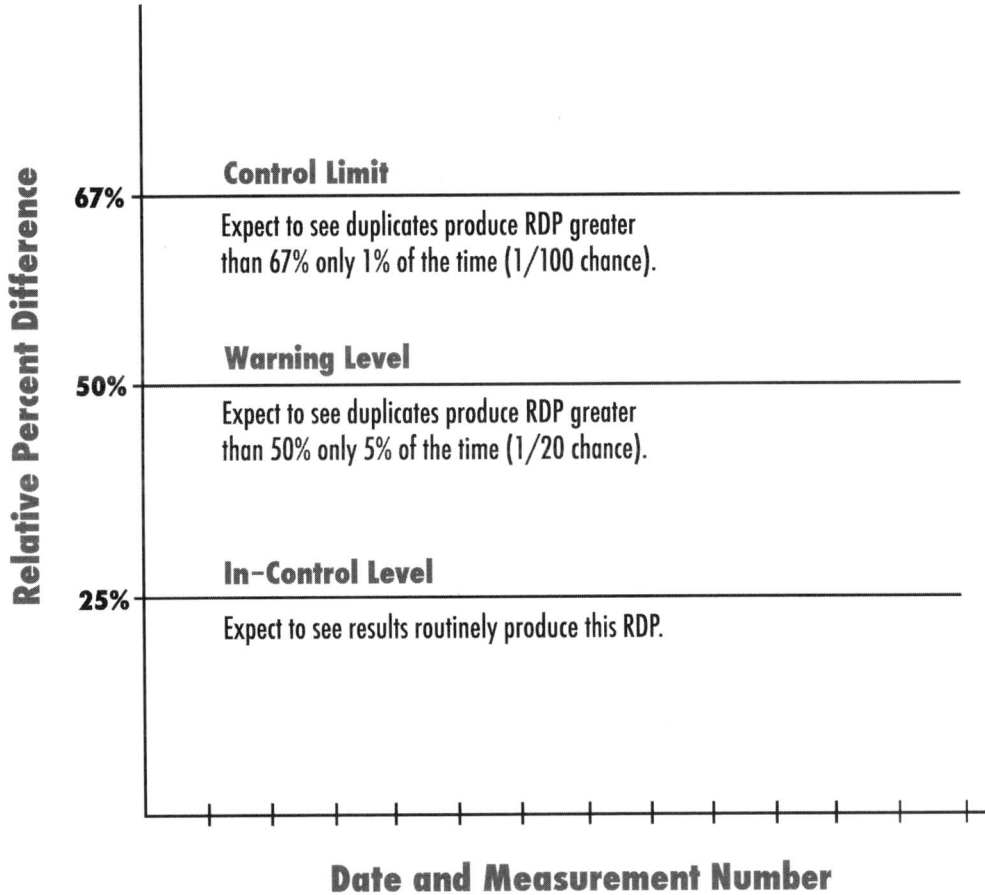

RPD = difference between two measurements divided by their average.

   Example: Detector A = 2 pCi/L, B = 3 pCi/L, RPD = 40%

If the RPD exceeds the control limit, cease measurements until the problem is identified and corrected.

If the RPD exceeds the warning level, follow the guidance in Section #3 and see Exhibit 3-1.

2.3 Range Control Chart

A range control chart can be constructed to evaluate precision using the statistics of the range (difference between two measurements) plotted against the average of the two measurements. The control limits are, again, based on the variability of the measurements, as decided upon from previous results or using an industry standard (e.g., 10%).

In this type of control chart, the limits are expressed in terms of the mean range (Rm) where, for n=2,

> *EXAMPLE EQUATION 6:* $Rm = 1.128\ s(x)$

where s(x) is the standard deviation of a single measurement that reflects counting and other precision errors. The limits can be expressed as follows:

> *EXAMPLE EQUATION 7:* Control limit $= 3.69\ s(x)$

> *EXAMPLE EQUATION 8:* Warning level $= 2.53\ s(x)$

An example range control chart using an assumed s(x) equal to 10% of the mean concentration is shown in Exhibit 2-4. The chart is used by plotting the range versus average concentration as duplicate measurements are analyzed.

Exhibit 2-4:

Range Control Chart to Evaluate Precision Limits Based on s(x) = 0.1xm

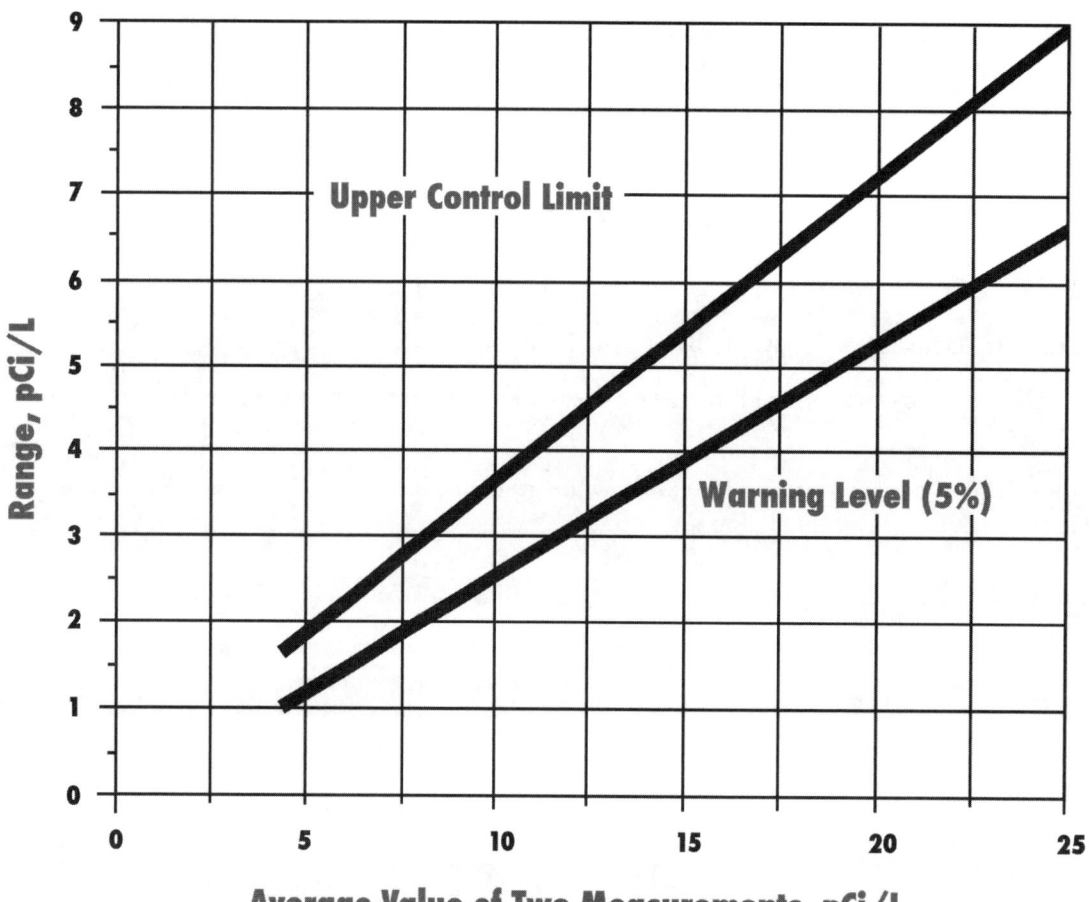

If the results exceed the control limit, cease measurements until the problem is identified and corrected.

If the results exceed the warning level, follow the guidance in Section #3 and see Exhibit 3-1.

3. Interpretation of Precision Control Charts

The control chart should be examined carefully every time a new duplicate result is plotted. If a duplicate result falls outside the control limit, repeat the analyses, if possible. If the repeated analyses also fall outside the control limit, stop taking measurements and identify and correct the problem.

If any measurements fall outside the warning level, use the table in Exhibit 3-1. Refer to the row showing the number of duplicate results outside the warning level. If the total number of duplicate results accumulated in the control chart is contained in Column A, investigate the cause of the high level of precision error, but continue taking measurements. If the total number of duplicate results on the chart is contained in Column B, stop taking measurements until the cause for the high precision error is found, and it is determined that subsequent measurements will not suffer the same high level of precision error.

Note that the example control charts shown are simplifications of actual conditions because they are premised on the assumption that the precision error is a constant fraction of the mean concentration. In fact, the total precision error may best be represented by a different function of the mean concentration—for example, the square root of the concentration. The most accurate control chart can be rendered by a range control chart using the measurement of uncertainty expressed as the standard deviation s(x) expected at the concentrations where measurements are made. If the precision error is not a constant fraction of the mean, the control limits will not appear as straight lines but may exhibit changing slope. However, methods discussed here present a conservative way to monitor, record and evaluate precision error and are very useful for comparing observed precision errors with an industry standard.

Exhibit 3-1:

Number of Duplicate Results Outside the Warning Level	Total Number of Duplicates	
	Investigate, But Continue Operations A	Stop Operations Until Problem Is Corrected B
2	8-19	2-7
3	17-34	8-16
4	29-51	17-28
5	41-67	29-40
6	54-84	41-53
7	67-100	54-66
*Modified from Goldin (Goldin 1984) and based upon cumulation probability tables of the binomial distribution		

Note: Charts and calculations are based on guidance provided in the EPA's *Quality Assurance Handbook for Air Pollution Measurement Systems, Volume I.*

Recommendations for Mitigation

The measurement organization should inform the client that the EPA recommends mitigating exposure for houses with radon levels equal to or greater than 4 pCi/L. Because the EPA has closed its National Radon Proficiency Program, organizations should refer clients to their state radon office for copies of the EPA's *Consumer's Guide to Radon Reduction*, as well as for any requirements for radon service providers, and for the use of EPA Radon Contractor Proficiency (RCP)-listed and/or state-listed mitigation contractors to perform the work.

Homes should also be tested again after they are mitigated to ensure that the radon levels have been reduced. If the occupants' living patterns change and they begin occupying a lower level of their home (such as a basement), the home should be re-tested on that level. In addition, it is a good idea for homes to be re-tested at some point in the future to be sure that mitigated radon levels remain low.

Temporary Risk-Reduction Measures

Contractors should refer the home's occupants and agents to the EPA's *Radon Mitigation Standards* (U.S. EPA 1992d) or the *Consumer's Guide to Radon Reduction* for information on temporary and permanent risk-reduction measures.

If any radon-reduction efforts are identified during the measurement procedures, testers should inform clients that altered conditions during the measurement will invalidate the results, and they should further decline to conduct a measurement until the conditions have been corrected.

Worker Safety

Individuals and organizations should comply with all applicable Occupational Safety and Health Administration (OSHA) standards and guidelines relating to occupational worker exposure, health and safety. Information on worker health and safety contained in EPA or state publications is not considered a substitute for any provisions of the Occupational Safety and Health Act of 1970, or for any standards issued by OSHA.

Quiz #4

1. T/F: The U.S. Environmental Protection Agency (EPA) recommends that all homes be tested for radon.

    ☐ True

    ☐ False

2. T/F: Even though the biological effects of radon are caused by RDPs, radon gas is usually measured, rather than RDPs.

    ☐ True

    ☐ False

3. The most common measurement method is _____, where a device is exposed to the radon gas for a measured amount of time.

    ☐ time-integrated sampling

    ☐ grab-sampling

    ☐ continuous monitoring

    ☐ using a measuring stick

4. For short-term testing devices, _____-house conditions must be maintained during the testing period.

    ☐ open

    ☐ closed

5. Short-term testing devices should be placed at least _____ inches off the floor, 4 inches from other objects, 12 inches from walls, and 12 inches from the ceiling.

    ☐ 48

    ☐ 30

    ☐ 72

    ☐ 20

6. The _____ method is very similar to the activated charcoal detector in that it employs a small vial of activated charcoal for sampling the radon.

    ☐ electret ion chamber

    ☐ charcoal liquid scintillation

    ☐ continuous working-level monitor

    ☐ activated charcoal adsorption

    ☐ continuous radon monitor

7. T/F: Organizations that provide consultant services, or place or retrieve devices, should review the protocol options and the client's needs, and inform the client of the building's and test period conditions necessary for conducting valid measurements.

    ☐ True
    ☐ False

8. All organizations providing measurement services with passive devices should conduct spiked measurements at a rate of _____ per 100 measurements, with a minimum of three per year, and a maximum required of six per month.

    ☐ three
    ☐ 10
    ☐ 50
    ☐ 25

9. _____ measurements for both active and passive detectors should be side-by-side measurements made in at least 10% of the total number of measurement locations, or 50 each month, whichever is smaller.

    ☐ Blanked
    ☐ Duplicate
    ☐ Spiked

10. _____ is the degree of closeness of a measured or calculated quantity to its actual or true value.

    ☐ Precision
    ☐ Accuracy

11. T/F: If the occupants' living patterns change and they begin occupying a lower level of their home (such as a basement), the home should be re-tested on that level.

    ☐ True
    ☐ False

Answer Key is on page 348.

Non-Real Estate Protocols

Introduction

This section of the course covers the following topics:

- Introduction and Summary
- Measurement Location
- Initial Measurements
- Follow-Up Measurements

Radon Measurement Protocols

This section provides technical guidance for measuring radon concentrations in residences. It contains protocols for measuring radon for the purpose of deciding on the need for remedial action.

The guidelines are primarily intended to certify home inspectors who provide radon measurement services.

InterNACHI recognizes that radon concentrations in buildings may vary over time. Furthermore, concentrations at different locations in the same house often vary by a factor of two or more.

InterNACHI recommends that initial measurements be short-term tests performed under closed-building conditions. An initial short-term test, which lasts for two to 90 days, ensures that residents are informed quickly, should a home contain very high radon levels. Long-term tests, which are conducted for longer than 90 days, give a better estimate of the year-round average radon level. The closer the long-term test is to 365 days, the more representative it will be of the home's annual average radon levels.

Method Category	Abbreviations	
	Common	RPP Method
Continuous Radon Monitors	CRM	CR
Alpha Track Detectors	ATD	AT
Electret Ion Chambers Short-Term Long-Term	EIC/EC	ES EL
Activated Charcoal Adsorption Devices (formerly called charcoal canisters)	CC	AC
Charcoal Liquidation Scintillation	CLS	LS

Method Category	Abbreviations	
	Common	RPP Method
Three-Day Integrating Evacuated Scintillation Cells		SC
Pump/Collapsible Bag Devices (24-hour sample)		PB
Grab-Sampling Scintillation Cells Activated Charcoal Pump/Collapsible Bag		GS GC GB
Unfiltered Track Detectors	UTD	UT
Continuous Working-Level Monitors	CWLM	CW
Radon Progeny Integrating Sampling Units	RPISU	RP
Grab Sampling (Working Level)		GW

Citizen's Guide to Radon

The *InterNACHI Citizen's Guide to Radon* (**www.nachi.org/citizens-guide-to-radon**) presents a measurement strategy for assessing radon levels in homes for the purpose of determining the need for remedial action. This measurement strategy is intended to reduce the risk to public health from exposure to radon in the air in homes. The strategy begins with an initial measurement made to determine whether a home may contain radon concentrations sufficient to cause high exposures to its occupants.

InterNACHI recommends that initial measurements be short-term tests placed in the lowest lived-in level of the home, and performed under closed-building conditions. An initial short-term test ensures that residents are informed quickly, should a home contain very high levels of radon. Short-term tests are conducted for between two days to 90 days. Closed-building conditions should be initiated at least 12 hours prior to testing for measurements lasting less than four days, and are recommended prior to tests lasting up to a week.

If the short-term measurement result is equal to or greater than 4 picocuries per liter (pCi/L), or 0.02 working levels (WL), a follow-up measurement is recommended. Follow-up measurements are conducted to confirm that radon levels are high enough to warrant mitigation. If the result of the initial measurement is below 4 pCi/L (or 0.02 WL), a follow-up test is not necessary. However, since radon levels change over time, the homeowner may want to test again sometime in the future, especially if living patterns change and a lower level of the house becomes occupied or used regularly.

There are two types of follow-up measurements that may be conducted, and the choice depends, in part, on the results of the initial test. An initial measurement result of 10 pCi/L (or 0.05 WL) or greater should be followed by a second short-term test under closed-building conditions. If the result of the initial measurement is between 4 pCi/L (or 0.02 WL) and 10 pCi/L (or 0.05 WL), the follow-up test may be made with either a short-term or a long-term method. Long-term tests are conducted for longer than 90 days, as they give a better estimate of the year-round average radon level. The closer the long-term measurement is to 365 days, the more representative it will be of the home's annual average radon levels. On the other hand, short-term tests yield results more quickly and can be used to make mitigation decisions. If the long-term follow-up test result is 4 pCi/L (or 0.02 WL) or higher, the EPA recommends remedial action. If the average of the initial and second short-term results is equal to or greater than 4 pCi/L (or 0.02 WL), radon mitigation is recommended.

These recommendations are summarized in the following illustration:

Perform Initial Short-Term Radon Measurement

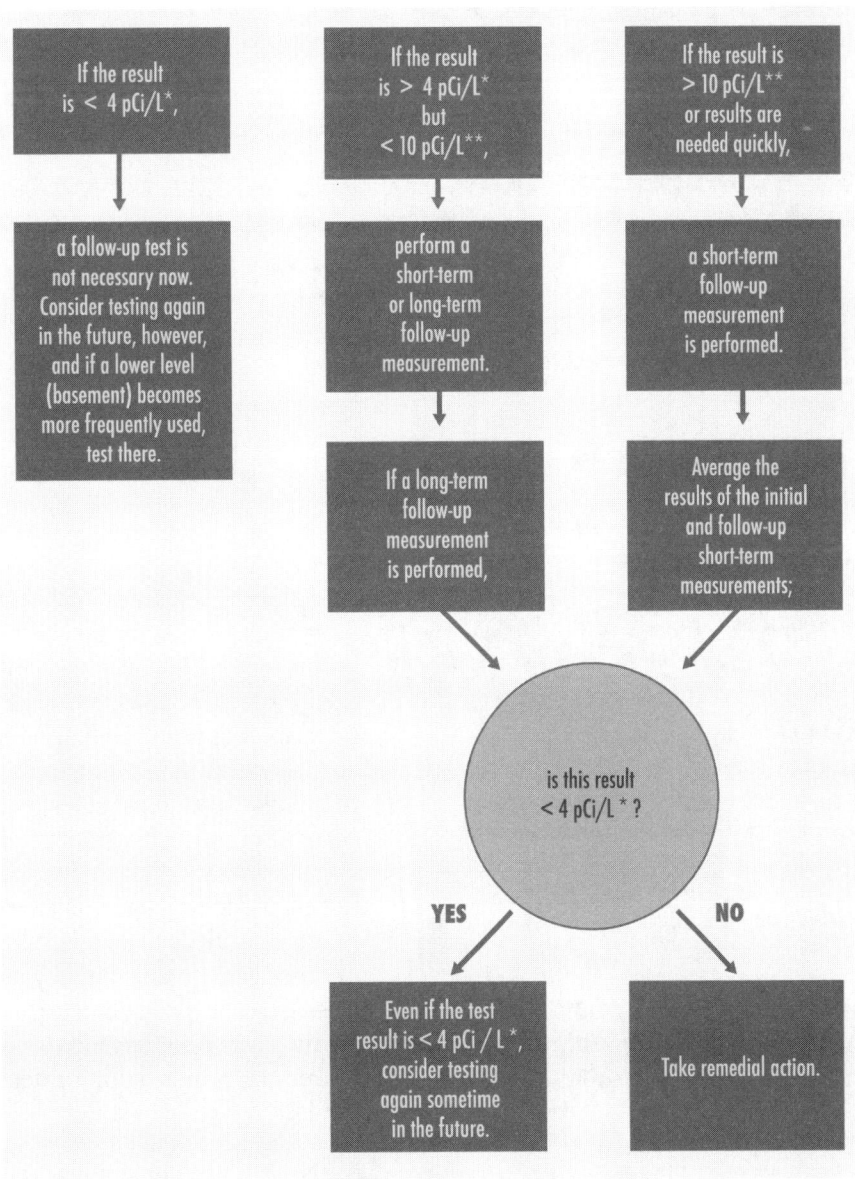

In certain instances, such as may occur when measurements are performed during different seasons or under different weather conditions, the initial and follow-up tests may vary by a considerable amount. Radon levels can vary significantly between seasons, so different values are to be expected. The average of the two short-term test results can be used to determine the need for remedial action.

The testing strategy policies presented here can assist homeowners in deciding on the need for mitigation, with a high level of confidence that their decision is correct.

Measurement Location

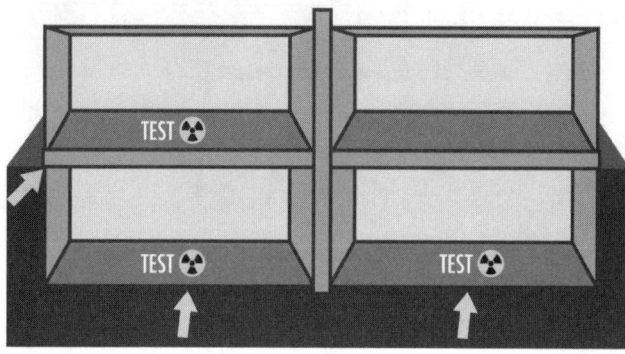

FLOORS & WALLS
(basement or upper area)

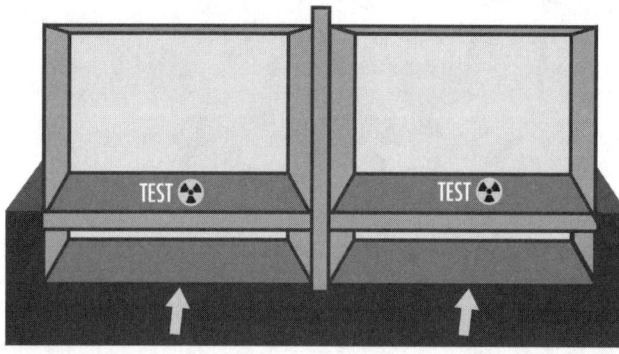

OVER CRAWLSPACES OR GARAGES
(basement or upper area)

FLOORS
(on slab)

Short-term and long-term measurements should be made in the lowest lived-in level of the house. The following criteria should be used to select the location of the detectors within a room on this level.

The measurements should be made in the lowest level that contains a room that is used regularly. Test areas include family rooms, living rooms, dens, play rooms, and bedrooms. A bedroom on the lower level may be a good choice because most people generally spend more time in their bedrooms than in any other room in the house. If there are children in the home, it may be appropriate to measure the radon concentration in their bedrooms or in other areas where they spend a lot of time (such as a play room) that are situated in the lowest level of the home.

In general, measurements should not be made in kitchens, laundry rooms, or bathrooms. The measurements should not be made in a kitchen because of the likelihood that an exhaust fan system exists, as well as the fact that changes in small airborne particles (caused by cooking) might affect the stability of WL measurements. Measurements should not be made in a bathroom because relatively little time is spent in a bathroom, because high humidity may affect the sensitivity of some detectors, and because of the likelihood that the use of a fan may temporarily alter radon or decay product levels.

Although radon in water may be a contributor to the concentration of airborne radon, radon in the indoor air should be measured before any diagnostic water radon measurements are taken. (Diagnostic measurements may be made in the bathroom; however, such diagnostic measurements should not be used to determine the need for mitigation.)

A location should be selected where there is adequate room for the detector and where it will not be disturbed during the measurement period.

The measurement should not be made near drafts caused by heating, ventilating and air-conditioning vents, doors, fans or windows. Locations near heat (such as on appliances), near fireplaces, or in direct sunlight, as well as areas of high humidity should be avoided.

Because some detectors are sensitive to increased air motion, fans should not be operated in the test area. Forced-air heating or cooling systems should not have the fan operating continuously unless it is a permanent setting.

The measurement location should not be within 3 feet of doors, windows, or other potential openings to the outdoors. If there are no doors or windows to the outdoors, the measurement should not be within 1 foot of the exterior wall of the building.

The detector should be at least 20 inches from the floor, and at least 4 inches from other objects. For those detectors that may be suspended, an optimal height is in the general breathing zone, such as 6 to 8 feet from the floor.

Sound judgment is required to determine what space actually constitutes a room. Measurements made in closets, cupboards, sumps, crawlspaces, or nooks within the foundation should not be used for a representative measurement.

Initial Measurements

InterNACHI recommends that a homeowner assessing the need for mitigation should first make a short-term test. Short-term measurements can be simple, produce results quickly, and allow homeowners to make decisions about radon reduction that are cost-effective and protective of human health.

The duration of short-term measurements can range from 48 hours to 90 days, depending upon the method used.

Closed-Building Conditions

Short-term measurements lasting between two and 90 days should be made under closed-building conditions. Closed-building conditions are necessary for short-term measurements in order to stabilize the radon and radon decay product concentrations, and increase the reproducibility of the measurement. Windows on all levels and external doors should be kept closed (except during normal entry and exit) during the measurement period. Normal entry and exit include a brief opening and closing of a door, but—to the extent possible—external doors should not be left open for more than a few minutes. In addition, external-internal air-exchange systems (other than a furnace), such as high-volume, whole-house and window fans, should not be operating. However, attic fans intended to control attic air (and not whole-building temperature or humidity) should continue to operate. Combustion or make-up air supplies must not be closed.

In addition to maintaining closed-building conditions during the measurement, maintaining those conditions for 12 hours prior to the initiation of the measurement is required for measurements lasting less than four days, as well as recommended prior to measurements lasting up to a week. Normal operation of permanently installed energy-recovery ventilators (also known as heat-recovery ventilators or air-to-air heat exchangers) may also continue during closed-building conditions. In houses where permanent radon mitigation systems have been installed, these systems should be functioning during the measurement period.

Closed-building conditions will generally exist as normal living conditions in northern areas of the country when the average daily temperature is low enough so that windows are kept closed. Depending on the geographical area, this can be the period from late fall to early spring. In some houses, the most stable radon levels occur during late fall and early spring, when windows are kept closed but the home heating system (which causes some ventilation and circulation) is not used. Available information about variations of indoor radon levels in a particular area can be used to choose a measurement time when the radon concentrations are most stable.

It may be necessary, however, to make measurements during mild weather when closed-building conditions are not the normal living conditions. It will then be necessary to establish some more rigorous means to ensure that closed-building conditions exist prior to and during the measurements.

Those performing measurements in southern areas that do not experience extended periods of cold weather should evaluate seasonal variations in living conditions, and identify if there are times of the year when closed-building conditions normally exist. Ideally, measurements should be conducted during those times. The closed-building conditions must be verified and maintained more rigorously when they are not the normal living conditions. Air-conditioning systems that recycle interior air can be operated during the closed-building conditions when radon measurements are being made. However, homeowners should be aware that any air-circulation system could alter the radon decay product concentration without significantly changing the radon concentration.

Short-term tests lasting just two or three days should not be conducted during unusually severe storms or periods of unusually high winds. Severe weather will affect the measurement results in several ways. First, high wind will increase the variability of radon concentration because of wind-induced differences in air pressure between the building's interior and its exterior. Second, rapid changes in barometric pressure increase the chance of a large difference in the interior and exterior air pressures, consequently changing the rate of radon influx. Weather predictions available on local news stations can provide sufficient information to determine if these conditions are likely. While unusual variations between radon measurements may be due to weather or other effects, the measurement system should be checked for possible problems.

Interpretation of Initial Results

If the initial measurement result is less than 4 pCi/L (or 0.02 WL), follow-up measurements are typically not necessary. There is a relatively low probability that mitigation is warranted if the result is less than 4 pCi/L (U.S. EPA 400-R-92-011; U.S. EPA 1992g). Even if the measurement result is less than 4 pCi/L, however, a homeowner may want to test again sometime in the future. If the occupants' living patterns change, or if renovations are made to the house and they begin using a lower level as a living area (such as a basement), a new test should be conducted on that level.

The average year-round indoor radon level is estimated to be about 1.3 pCi/L, and about 0.4 pCi/L of radon is normally found in the air outside. The U.S. Congress has set a long-term goal that indoor radon levels be no more than outdoor levels. There is some risk from radon levels below 4 pCi/L, and the EPA recommends that the homeowner consider reducing the radon level if the average of the first and second short-term measurements (or if a long-term follow-up measurement) is between 2 and 4 pCi/L (between 0.01 and 0.02 WL). While it is not yet technologically achievable for all homes to have their radon levels reduced to outdoor levels, the radon levels in some homes today can be reduced to 2 pCi/L or below.

If the result of the short-term measurement is equal to or greater than 4 pCi/L, the homeowner should have a follow-up measurement conducted using a short-term or long-term test.

Follow-Up Measurements

The purpose of a follow-up measurement is to provide the homeowner with enough information to make an informed decision as to whether to mitigate to reduce radon levels. The follow-up measurement, whether it is short-term or long-term, provides an additional piece of information to potentially confirm that radon levels are high enough to warrant mitigation.

There are two major reasons a second measurement is necessary. First and foremost, radon levels fluctuate over time, and a second short-term measurement, when averaged with the first test result, will provide a more representative value for the average radon level during the period of the test. If a long-term follow-up measurement is conducted, that result should provide an even more accurate representative value for the long-term average radon concentration. The second reason for making a follow-up measurement prior to mitigation is that there is a small chance of laboratory or technician error in all measurements, including radon measurements, and a second test will serve as a check on the first test.

A follow-up test is necessary regardless of the initial test result. Homes tested using the protocol described in this section should not be mitigated on the basis of a single short-term test.

Short-Term and Long-Term Follow-Up Testing

Follow-up testing should be conducted in the same location as the first measurement.

A follow-up test can be conducted with either a short-term or long-term measurement device. Long-term tests (longer than 90 days) will produce a reading that is more likely to represent the home's year-round average radon level than a short-term test. However, if the initial test result is high (for example, greater than about 10 pCi/L, or 0.05 WL), or if results are needed quickly, InterNACHI recommends a second short-term test. This will allow the homeowner to obtain information necessary to quickly decide on the need for mitigation. If the result of the initial measurement is not severely elevated (between 4 pCi/L and 10 pCi/L, or between 0.02 WL and 0.05 WL), then either a short-term or long-term test can be conducted.

If the long-term follow-up test result is 4 pCi/L or higher, the EPA recommends remedial action. Likewise, if the average of the initial and second short-term results is equal to or greater than 4 pCi/L, radon mitigation is recommended.

As with the initial short-term test, the second short-term test should be conducted under closed-building conditions. These conditions, however, are not necessary for long-term tests (those lasting longer than 90 days).

Quiz #5

1. T/F: InterNACHI recommends that initial measurements for non-real estate testing be short-term tests performed under closed-building conditions.

     ☐ True
     ☐ False

2. InterNACHI recommends testing devices for initial measurements be placed in the _____ lived-in level of the home.

     ☐ lowest
     ☐ highest

3. If the short-term measurement result is equal to or greater than _____ picocuries per liter (pCi/L), or 0.02 working levels (WL), a follow-up measurement is recommended.

     ☐ 8
     ☐ 4
     ☐ 0.02
     ☐ 12

4. T/F: Circulating fans should be operating in the test area.

     ☐ True
     ☐ False

5. If there are no doors or windows to the outdoors in the immediate testing area, the measurement should not be taken within _____ of the exterior wall of the building.

     ☐ 1 foot
     ☐ 2 feet
     ☐ 3 feet
     ☐ 4 feet

6. Closed-building conditions should be maintained for _____ hours prior to the initiation of measurements lasting less than four days, as well as recommended prior to measurements lasting up to a week.

     ☐ two
     ☐ 48
     ☐ 12
     ☐ five

7. Follow-up testing should be conducted in _____ location as the first measurement.

     ☐ the same
     ☐ a different

8. T/F: If the average of the initial and second short-term results is equal to or greater than 4 pCi/L, radon mitigation is recommended.

☐ True

☐ False

Answer Key is on page 349.

Real Estate Protocols

Home Buyer's and Seller's Guide

The unique nature of a real estate transaction involving multiple parties and financial interests presents radon measurement issues not encountered in non-real estate testing. The EPA's objectives for issuing recommended protocols for radon measurements for real estate transactions are intended to reduce misunderstandings and protect the public health in several ways. First, it seeks to provide home buyers, sellers, real estate agents, and testing organizations with a common basis for understanding the recommended testing procedures. Second, the widespread implementation of these guidelines will produce results that are reliable indicators of the potential need for mitigation. A significant proportion of radon measurements are conducted as part of real estate transactions, and all aspects of these transactions are carefully scrutinized, so specific guidance from the EPA can help ensure trustworthy results. When the results are interpreted properly and the appropriate remedial action is taken, these protocols will assist the buyer and seller in reducing the risk to the home's occupants from radon exposure. The availability of nationally recognized protocols for radon measurements, and for the interpretation of the measurement results, can greatly assist home buyers, sellers, real estate agents, builders, lenders, and radon measurement experts.

The document *InterNACHI's Home Buyer's and Seller's Guide to Radon* (**www.nachi.org/ home-buyers-home-sellers-guide-to-radon**) offers general information on radon and testing protocols for residential applications. It also presents a more technical description of the EPA's recommendations, including discussion of guidelines for the interpretation of measurement results. As with all of the EPA's policies regarding radon measurements, these guidelines have been developed after review and assistance from the radon measurement community and the EPA's Science Advisory Board. Technical information on a variety of radon measurement methods is available in the EPA report titled "Indoor Radon and Radon Decay Product Measurement Device Protocols" (EPA 520-402-R-92-004; EPA 1992c). These and other EPA publications are available at their website and from state and regional EPA offices.

The radon testing guidelines in InterNACHI's *Home Buyer's and Seller's Guide to Radon* have been developed specifically to deal with the time-sensitive nature of home purchases and sales, and the potential for radon device interference. These guidelines are somewhat different from the guidelines in other EPA publications, such as the 1992 *Citizen's Guide to Radon* (EPA 402-K-92-001; U.S. EPA 1992a), which provide radon testing and reduction information for non-real estate situations.

The EPA investigated a variety of options for real estate testing. It recommends testing in advance of putting the house on the market. A long-term test, which is conducted for longer than 90 days, is the most representative indication of the annual average radon concentrations in a home. However, for time-sensitive real estate transactions, the *Home Buyer's Guide* offers three short-term testing options. Short-term tests are conducted from two days to 90 days, depending on the measurement device. Based on extensive quantitative analyses to evaluate the frequency with which long-term and short-term testing results lead to the same mitigation decision, the EPA and its independent Science Advisory Board concluded that short-term tests can be used to assess whether a home should be remediated.

The reliability of each radon measurement made for a real estate transaction, or for any purpose, is highly dependent upon the existence and documentation of an adequate quality assurance program implemented by both the tester and the analysis laboratory. All the parties involved in the real estate transaction depend upon the testers doing their jobs. This includes ensuring that the measurements are valid via the performance of quality control measurements and activities, and detecting measurement interference. The protocols outlined in this section were developed by the EPA for testers and homeowners adhering to the quality assurance practices summarized in Part 4.4, and in the EPA's *Indoor Radon and Radon Decay Product Measurement Device Protocols* (EPA 520-402-R-92-004; U.S. EPA 1992c).

Three options were determined to be satisfactory and are described here. These three options allow for flexibility for the party purchasing the test. Each of these options will produce results that can be used to determine the need for mitigation.

Options 1 and 2 both require the use of two measurements made for similar durations. Both measurements should report their results in units of pCi/L or both in WL. Similar durations mean that the two measurements must be made for a similar time period, with a two-hour grace period. Specific information on measurement methods (listed in the following table) can be found in the EPA's *Indoor Radon and Radon Decay Product Measurement Device Protocols*.

A (pCi/L)	B (WL)
AC: Activated Charcoal Adsorption	RP: Radon Progeny Sampling Unit (RPSU)
AT: Alpha Track Detection	CW: Continuous Working-Level Monitoring
LS: Charcoal Liquid Scintillation	
CR: Continuous Radon Monitoring	
PB: Pump/Collapsible Bag	
SC: Evacuated Scintillation Cell (three-day integrating)	
EL: Electret Ion Chamber: Long-Term	
ES: Electret Ion Chamber: Short-Term	
UT: Unfiltered Track Detection	

Sequential Testing

Sequential tests should be conducted under conditions that are as similar as possible, in the same location, and using similar devices and durations. Both should produce results in the same units (pCi/L or WL). That is, both methods should be from Column A, or both from Column B. Any EPA-recognized method may be used. In addition, the results of the first test should not be reported prior to making the second measurement; both measurements should be reported at the same time in order to discourage tampering that may occur if the first test is known to be greater than 4 pCi/L (or 0.02 WL). Note that measuring with different methods (for example, with AC and ES) may increase the potential for differences or measurement bias between the results. The results of both measurements should be reported, and the average of the two results should be used to determine the need for mitigation. There will be some variation between the two results, which may be caused by the radon levels fluctuating in response to weather or other factors. If the variation is unusually large, it may be due to weather or other effects, but the measurement system should be checked for possible problems.

A (pCi/L)	B (WL)
AC: Activated Charcoal Adsorption	RP: Radon Progeny Sampling Unit (RPSU)
AT: Alpha Track Detection	CW: Continuous Working-Level Monitoring
LS: Charcoal Liquid Scintillation	
CR: Continuous Radon Monitoring	
PB: Pump/Collapsible Bag	
SC: Evacuated Scintillation Cell (three-day integrating)	
EL: Electret Ion Chamber: Long-Term	
ES: Electret Ion Chamber: Short-Term	
UT: Unfiltered Track Detection	

Simultaneous Testing

This option involves the use of two tests conducted simultaneously and side by side, made for similar durations, and producing results in the same units. As with option 1, using different methods for the two measurements (for example, ES and LS) may increase the potential for differences between the two results. The two test results should be averaged to determine the need for remedial action. The collocated devices should be placed 4 inches apart.

Because radon measurements, like any measurements, usually do not produce exactly the same results even for simultaneous testing, there will typically be a difference between the two results. The EPA offers the following guidance to testers for judging when two simultaneous, side-by-side measurements disagree to such an extent that two additional measurements should be performed.

The results of the simultaneous measurements will fall into one of the three categories discussed next.

Two Simultaneous, Side-by-Side Measurements

Both are < 4 pCi/L*	One is > 4 pCi/L* and one is < 4 pCi/L**	Both are < 4 pCi/L*
↓	↓	↓
Use Exhibit B-3, or, is RPD > 67%?	Is the higher result greater than twice the lower result?	Use Exhibit B-2, or, is RPD > 35%?

NO — Provide the individual measurement results and the average value to the client.

YES — Provide the individual measurement results and the average value to the client and investigate the source of error.

NO — Provide the individual measurement results and the average value to the client.

YES — Provide the individual measurement results and the average value to the client. Inform the client of the large discrepancy and re-test.

NO — Provide the individual measurement results and the average value to the client.

YES — Provide the individual measurement results and the average value to the client and investigate the source of error.

Both Measurement Results Less Than 4 pCi/L (or 0.02 WL)

In this case, the average of the two measurements is less than 4 pCi/L (or 0.02 WL), and both measurement results and the average result should be reported to the client.

Both Measurement Results Equal to or Greater Than 4 pCi/L (or 0.02 WL)

In this case, the average of the two results is equal to or greater than 4 pCi/L, or 0.02 WL, and mitigation is recommended. The tester should report both measurement results, as well as the average of the two results.

One Measurement Result Greater Than 4 pCi/L (or 0.02 WL), and One Measurement Result Less Than 4 pCi/L (or 0.02 WL)

This is a special situation in which the average of the results is critical. To assist testers in ensuring that the difference between two measurements is small enough so that clients may have confidence in and understand the results, the EPA offers the following simple guidance.

If the higher result is twice (or more) the lower result, then the two results are not within a factor of two, and a re-test should be conducted.

If the higher result is less than twice the lower result, then the two results are within a factor of two, and a re-test is not necessary. The results of both measurements and the average of the two results should be reported to the client.

Precision Recommendations

Measurements near the lower limit of detection (LLD) for the measurement system often have large and varying precision errors, and it is difficult to assign any sort of probability level to very low results.

Simultaneous measurement results that are equal to 4 pCi/L (or 0.02 WL) or greater should, however, exhibit some agreement. A relative percent difference (defined as the difference divided by the average) greater than 36% should be observed less than 1% of the time. Based upon this, the EPA recommends that any side-by-side simultaneous measurements with results greater than or equal to 4 pCi/L, and which exhibit a relative percent difference greater than 36%, would provide justification for informing the client that the two results do not show agreement. However, since both results are greater than 4 pCi/L, the EPA recommends mitigation in this case. Testers should investigate the source of such an error.

Results between 2 pCi/L and 4 pCi/L (or 0.01 WL and 0.02 WL) should also exhibit some agreement. The level of agreement expected should be based upon the tester's experience with duplicate measurements made with that technique in this range of radon concentrations. A relative percent difference between duplicates greater than 67% should be observed less than 1% of the time. Based on this, the EPA recommends that any side-by-side simultaneous measurements with results less than 4 pCi/L, and which exhibit a relative percent difference greater than 67%, would provide justification for informing the client that the two results do not show agreement, but that both are less than 4 pCi/L and, therefore, mitigation is not recommended. Testers should investigate the source of such an error.

Recommended Language for Informing the Client That a Re-test Is Warranted

If a re-test is warranted, the EPA recommends that the tester inform the client that the EPA provides guidance for how closely two measurements should agree, that the measurements performed fall outside that range, and that a re-test should be conducted.

Single Test Option

This option requires an active continuous monitor (method CR or CW) that has the capability to integrate and record a new result at least every four hours. If the monitor cannot integrate over a period of four hours or less, then an additional (secondary) passive or active measurement device must be used. Shorter integration periods and more frequent data logging afford greater ability to detect unusual variations in radon or radon decay product concentrations. The minimum measurement period is 48 hours. The first four hours of data from a continuous monitor may be discarded or incorporated into the result using system correction factors (EPA 520-402-R-92-004; EPA 1992c). There must be at least 44 continuous hours of usable data to produce a valid average. (The "backing out" of data—i.e., removal of portions embedded in the two days—to account for weather or other phenomena will invalidate the measurement.) The periodic results should be averaged to produce a result that is then reported to the client.

The best way to increase confidence in a radon measurement is to perform a second measurement with another measurement device. The second measurement, which may be made with a passive or active device, can be used simultaneously or sequentially. If the two measurements are performed simultaneously, their results should be evaluated. If the two measurements are performed sequentially, it can be expected that the two results will be different. The difference between sequential tests may be due to radon levels fluctuating in response to weather or other factors.

However, there are other approaches or features that can be used to increase the confidence in a measurement result obtained using a single active monitor testing device. These include the use of the device's self-diagnostic features, and data validation or verification procedures that could be employed before and/or after the measurement. Examples of such approaches are the use of check sources before and after each measurement, and the use of spectrum readouts. These capabilities are examples, and different technologies may be able to perform other similar self-diagnostic or quality assurance checks. Other features that increase the confidence in a single active test include (but are not limited to) the ability to check air flow rates and voltage meters before and after each measurement. Measurement companies should incorporate such controls into their routine instrument performance checks as part of their standard operating procedures.

Additional features that can increase confidence in measurement results are those that detect measurement interference. For example, a continuous monitor that offers a variety of ways to detect tampering may serve to deter—as well as detect—interference with the monitor's operation or with proper closed-building measurement conditions. Potential tampering indicators include the ability of the monitor to record changes in temperature, humidity, and/or movement of the device during the measurement period.

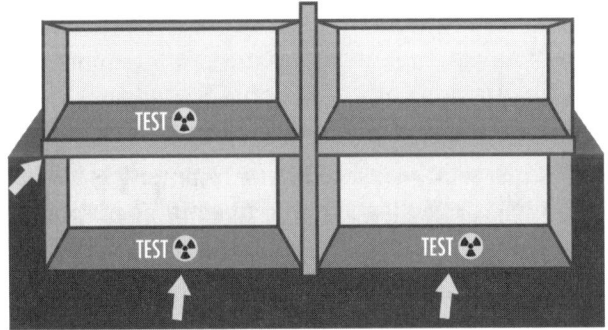

FLOORS & WALLS
(basement or upper area)

Instruments with greater efficiency or sensitivity, or a high signal-to-noise ratio, can achieve results with less uncertainty than instruments with low efficiency, poor sensitivity, or low signal-to-noise ratio. The reliability of any type of equipment, however, needs to be established and documented via a complete quality assurance program. This includes routine instrument performance checks prior to and after each measurement, annual calibrations, semi-annual instrument cross-checks, the performance of duplicate measurements in 10% of the measurement locations, and frequent background and spiked measurements.

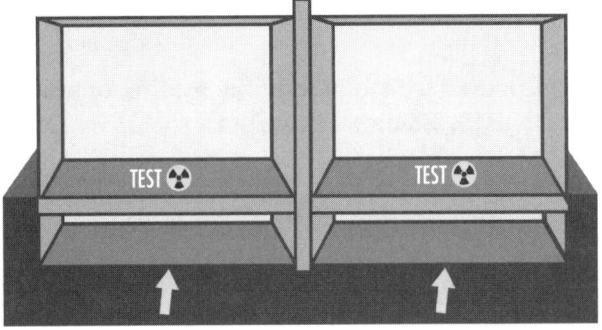

OVER CRAWLSPACES OR GARAGES
(basement or upper area)

Measurement Location

The EPA recommends that measurements made for a real estate transaction be performed in the lowest level of the home that is currently suitable for occupancy.

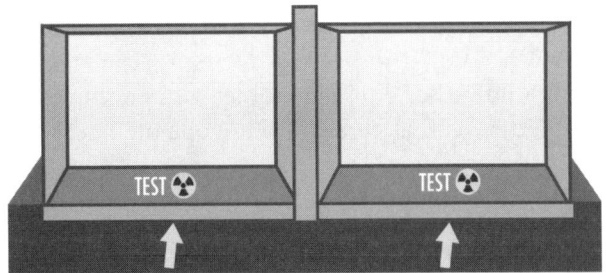

FLOORS
(on slab)

This means the lowest level that is currently lived in, or a lower level that is not currently used, such as a basement, but which a buyer could use for living space without renovations. Measurements should be made in a room that is used regularly, such as a living room, play room, den, or bedroom. This includes a basement that can be used as a recreation room, bedroom, or play room. This provides the buyer with the option of using a lower level of the home as part of the living area with the knowledge that it has been tested for radon.

Measurement Checklist

The EPA presents the following checklist to help ensure that a radon measurement conducted for a real estate transaction is done properly. The seller should be able to confirm that all the items in this checklist have been followed. If the tester cannot confirm this, another test should be conducted.

Before the Radon Test:

- Notify the home's occupants of the importance of proper testing conditions. Give them written instructions or a copy of the EPA's *Home Buyer's and Seller's Guide to Radon*, or an EPA or state-required alternative, and explain the directions carefully.

- The radon measurement equipment used should be listed by some proficiency organization or the state. Follow the manufacturer's instructions that come with the device.

- If a testing professional conducts the test, he or she should be listed with some national or state-listed program. Check with the state radon contact for more information. Under the former National Radon Proficiency Program (RPP), the EPA recommended that photo identification should be provided to the client or homeowner before or at the time of the test, and the contractor's identification number should be clearly visible on the test report.

- The test should include any method(s) to prevent or detect interference with the testing conditions or with the testing device itself.

- Conduct the radon test for a minimum of 48 hours. Some devices must be exposed for longer than the 48-hour minimum.

- Check to see if an active radon reduction system is installed in the house. Before starting a short-term test lasting less than four days, make sure the active system has been operating for at least 24 hours before beginning the test.

- The EPA recommends that short-term radon testing, which lasts for no more than a week, be done under closed-building conditions. Closed-building conditions require keeping all windows closed, keeping doors closed except for normal entry and exit, and not operating fans or other machines that bring in air from outside. Note that fans that are part of a radon-reduction system or small exhaust fans operating for only short periods of time may run during the test.

- When doing short-term testing lasting less than four days, it is important to maintain closed-building conditions for at least 12 hours before the beginning of the test, as well as for the entire testing period. Do not operate fans or other machines that bring in air from the outside.

During the Radon Test:

- Maintain closed-building conditions during the entire time of a short-term test, especially for tests shorter than one week.

- Operate the home's heating and cooling systems normally during the test. For tests lasting less than one week, it is permissible to operate air-conditioning units that recirculate only interior air.

- Do not disturb the testing device at any time during the test.

- If a radon-reduction system is in place, make sure that the system is working properly and will be in operation during the entire radon test.

After the Radon Test:

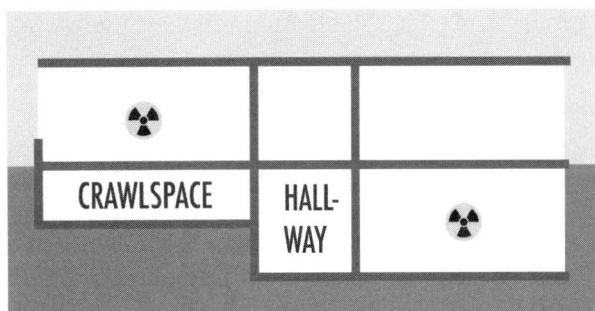

- If a high radon level is confirmed, mitigate the level. The EPA's *Home Buyer's and Seller's Guide to Radon* recommends the next steps that should be taken, such as contacting a qualified radon-reduction contractor to lower the home's radon level.

- The radon tester or homeowner should be able to verify or provide documentation asserting that testing conditions were not violated during the testing period.

Interference-Resistant Testing

The EPA strongly encourages the use of radon testing devices having built-in or associated interference-resistant features.

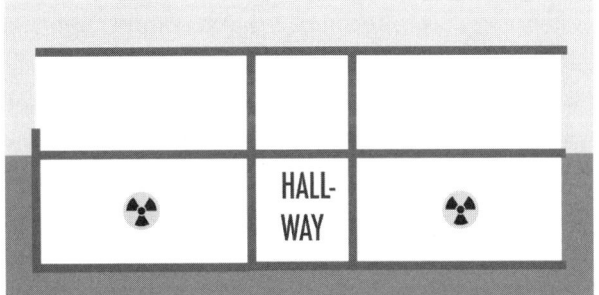

Interference with a radon measurement is defined as the altering of test conditions prior to or during the measurement to either change the radon or RDP concentrations, or to alter the performance of the measurement equipment. The following discussion reviews some of the types of test interferences, and methods of detecting and preventing such interference.

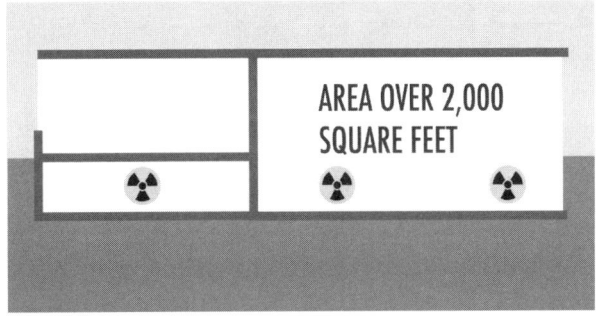

Test interference typically causes measurement results to be lower than if all proper testing conditions were maintained. False low results have been primarily associated with testing during a real estate transaction, although they also happen when the occupants of the dwelling are not properly informed about the necessary testing conditions. Test interference can also inadvertently increase measurement results, although the intent of any interference is to lower the results.

The dwelling's current owner may have an interest in the test results being as low as possible to avoid hindering the sale of the dwelling or incurring the added expense of having to install a mitigation system. The potential for test interference puts the professional radon tester in the position of verifying that the equipment and the required testing conditions were maintained. A measurement result that is below the action guidelines may be suspect if the tester cannot verify that the necessary testing conditions were maintained.

If the tester arrives at a property and finds windows or doors open, or suspects that closed-building conditions were not maintained for 12 hours prior to his or her arrival, then he or she should extend the testing time period to account for this condition.

Influencing the Test Area's Concentration

The primary method of temporarily reducing radon levels is to ventilate the test area with outdoor air. Ventilation will slow down radon entry by reducing negative pressure in the test area and by diluting the reduced radon concentration. Even a small opening of a single window in the test area can have an effect. Ventilating the floors above the test area has significantly less effect, unless the test area is connected with the ventilated room(s) by an operating central air-handling system.

Radon decay product levels are sensitive to air movement. As air movement increases, decay products will plate out on walls and other surfaces, including fans, thereby reducing airborne decay product concentrations. Decay products will be further reduced if the fan also includes a filter. Radon levels are, however, not affected by filtering or air movement.

It is also possible to alter concentrations in a tight room if the heating system is operating in an abnormal fashion. Since this may not be the typical operation of the system, it is, in effect, interfering with normal house conditions.

It is important to recognize that test interference can increase radon or decay product levels, despite an intent to lower the results.

Equipment Interference

The primary method of interfering with testing equipment is to move the detector to an area of low radon concentration. Other types of interference vary in their ability to influence different types of detectors. For example, interfering with the air-sampling mechanisms can maintain the radon concentration at the time of interference, or cause a large decrease in the reported concentration. Similarly, covering a decay product or charcoal detector could cause a large drop in the reported values, while other types of radon detectors would show only a reduced response time to changes in the test area level. In addition, charcoal detectors are sensitive to heat. Some active radon monitors and open-face charcoal canisters are also sensitive to high humidity. Any detector that yields a single result could be turned off or sealed in its container or lid during most of its exposure period.

Preventing Interference

The EPA recommends that a radon measurement conducted for a real estate transaction be performed using tamper-resistant testing techniques. It is more advantageous for the tester and the client to prevent interference than to simply detect it.

Preventing interference can best be accomplished by:

- educating the client about the necessary test conditions;
- including in the standard documentation for each measurement an agreement (signed by the client) listing the necessary test conditions, and the client's agreement not to interfere with the conditions;
- including in such an agreement a statement that any test interference that is detected will be documented in the report, and will nullify the test results;
- informing the client that interference with the test conditions may increase the radon levels; and
- informing the client that the tester is using interference-detecting techniques, and that these

allow the detection and documentation of test interference.

Interference-Resistant Detectors

The following is a partial list of common equipment and measures that can serve to prevent and/or detect test interference. There may be other methods available. Equipment that offers a combination of tamper-detecting features also offers a greater chance of detecting interference.

- The ability to integrate and record frequent radon measurements over short intervals (an hour or less) is an important tamper-detection feature. Continuous (active) monitors that provide frequent measurements can indicate unusual concentration changes that can be indicators of test interference.

- Measuring other parameters may provide additional indicators of test interference, such as a detector tilt-indicator, or a continuous recording of pump-flow rate.

- A motion indicator can also document when the detector is approached or moved.

- A simultaneous, multiple-day, continuous measurement of both radon and decay product concentrations will produce a series of equilibrium-ratio values. These values can be inspected for unusual swings or abnormal levels, possibly indicating interference.

- Measurement of CO_2 levels can indicate changes in the test area's infiltration rate of outdoor air.

- The performance of a grab-radon measurement, a grab-decay product measurement, or both, before and after a longer-term measurement can offer useful information. For example, the initial and final concentrations and equilibrium ratios can be compared for consistency.

- Frequent temperature readings may help to indicate changes in the test area's infiltration rate of outdoor air.

- Humidity (as well as temperature) recordings can be especially helpful in identifying potentially unusual changes in testing conditions that occur during the test period that might not be detected simply through data logging.

- Instruments that do not allow occupants to view preliminary results (via a visible printer or screen) may reduce interference.

- Placement indicators can also reveal whether a detector has been moved or tampered with. The position of the detector should be noted so that, upon retrieval, any handling of the detector can be indicated by a change in its position. A detector may be hung or placed slightly over the edge of its support to discourage covering it. Passive detectors may be hung or suspended in a radon-permeable bag that uses a unique strap and seal to prevent removing or covering it. Cages can be equipped with a movement indicator to deter handling of the cage or the detector inside it.

- Sealing can be a practical and effective method for detecting and discouraging test interference. Non-sealable caulks and/or tapes can be used to verify that a detector has not been altered or moved, and that windows or non-primary exterior doors have not been opened.

Unless the detector has other mechanisms for revealing interference, seals should be placed on the lowest operable windows and non-primary exterior doors, as well as between the detector and its support, and any other components of the detector that could be tampered with. It may be advisable to place a seal on the furnace-control fan switch. It may also be necessary to attach something fragile to the caulk seal that protrudes out to indicate any handling or covering of the detector.

A number of different products or combination of products can be used for tamper seals. For a seal to be effective, it needs, at minimum, the following unique qualities:

1. The seal must adhere readily to a variety of surfaces, and yet be easily removed without marring the surface.

2. It needs to be non-re-sealable or show evidence of disturbance.

3. It must be unique enough to prevent easy duplication.

4. It should be visible enough to discourage tampering.

The tamper-resistance of the seal can be increased by using caulk over the seal edges, or by slicing a large portion of the center of the seal to ensure that it is broken in case of tampering.

Most paper or plastic tapes and caulks have only some of these qualities. There are, however, a number of seals manufactured specifically for radon testing. It would be advisable to use one of these products and follow the manufacturer's installation recommendations. The best caulking to use as a seal is a removable weatherstripping caulk. This type of caulking adheres readily to most surfaces, yet comes off easily without leaving a mark or being re-sealable.

Upon retrieval of the detector, the tester should carefully inspect the following:

• that all closed-building conditions are still being maintained;

• any changes in the detector's placement;

• the condition of all seals; and

• any abnormal variations in any of the measurements made.

Quiz #6

1. T/F: During a real estate test, sequential tests should be conducted under conditions that are as similar as possible, in the same location, and using similar devices and durations.

    ☐ True
    ☐ False

2. T/F: The results of both measurements of a sequential test should be reported, and the average of the two results should be used to determine the need for mitigation.

    ☐ True
    ☐ False

3. When one measurement result is greater than 4 pCi/L and one measurement result is less than 4 pCi/L, then if the higher result is _____ the lower result, then the two results are not within a factor of two, and a re-test should be conducted.

    ☐ 150% greater than
    ☐ twice (or more)
    ☐ equal to

4. Before starting a short-term test lasting less than four days, make sure the active system has been operating for at least _____ before beginning the test.

    ☐ a few minutes
    ☐ 24 hours
    ☐ one week

5. For a real estate test, conduct the radon test for minimum of ____ hours.

    ☐ 24
    ☐ 12
    ☐ 96
    ☐ 48

6. False _____ results have been primarily associated with testing during a real estate transaction, although they also happen when the occupants of the dwelling are not properly informed about the necessary test conditions.

    ☐ high
    ☐ low

7. T/F: Prevention interference can be best accomplished by informing the client that the tester is using interference-detecting techniques.

    ☐ True
    ☐ False

Answer Key is on page 349.

QA and QC

Introduction

This section provides guidance in the areas of quality assurance (QA) and quality control (QC) radon testing programs.

The QA practices described in this report are necessary and expected components of high-quality radon and radon decay product measurements. The specific QC measurements, recordkeeping, and analysis methods outlined here are consistent with routine procedures for radiation measurements and standard practices by federal laboratories and contractors.

The information presented in this section includes recommendations from a variety of organizations involved in the radon measurement industry, including organizations that do not analyze detectors but that deploy devices and provide clients with measurement results. This information is designed to provide a framework of QA practices that can be modified and added to, according to the specific needs of the measurement program.

QA and QC Defined

The International Organization for Standardization (ISO) defines a **quality system** as the organized structure, responsibilities, procedures, processes, and resources needed for implementing quality management. Quality management includes defining roles and responsibilities, planning the level of quality provided to the customer, clearly defining objectives for quality, and defining accountability and reporting. It is implemented at the management level, and focuses not only on systems, policies, criteria, documentation, and procedures, but also on program structure, which includes the delegation of authority and responsibility needed to ensure adequate quality of the product.

Quality assurance (QA) is defined by the American Society of Testing and Materials (ASTM) as all activities required to provide the evidence needed to establish confidence that data provided are of the required precision and accuracy. The EPA similarly defines QA as "an integrated system or program of activities involving planning, quality control, quality assessment, reporting, and quality improvement to ensure that a product or service meets defined standards of quality."

The ASTM defines quality control (QC) as the process through which an organization measures its performance, compares its performance with standards, and acts on any differences. In other words, the intent of QA/QC is to maintain a good quality-measurement program and to ascertain and document the quality. Quality control consists of measurements and associated activities needed to control and assess measurement-program quality, as determined by estimated precision, relative bias, and the lower limit of detection (as well as other factors, such as the rates of data entry errors) on an ongoing basis, and to revise procedures to improve quality, if necessary.

QA/QC must be an integral part of any measurement program. The results of measurements that are not associated with a program to ensure and document their reliability are useless because the validity of each measurement rests upon the QA program. There are many experienced and knowledgeable measurement experts who perform adequate work but who do not have the time or support from management to implement and document QA/QC practices. They may produce accurate results, or they may have incorporated an erroneous calibration factor and not know it. In either case, the lack of adequate documentation makes it impossible for their measurement results to be as incontrovertible as they need to be.

There are benefits to conducting a QA program other than substantiating the adequacy of each measurement result.

First, making some of the types of measurements that are described here will add greatly to an operator's understanding of the methods employed. This will enable organizations to improve their techniques, or to justify results that they would not otherwise understand. For example, it is crucial to know how low a concentration can be reliably measured and the variability that is expected at low concentrations.

Second, a QA/QC program includes procedures for monitoring the performance of equipment, supplies, and operators.

Third, a QA program is often specified as a contractual requirement, and records of a QA/QC program may be critical in the event of a legal dispute.

A credible measurement program cannot exist without QA activities. Measurement companies provide results to clients that may become critical to the sale of property. If the measurement result is questioned, the tester may be liable if QA records do not provide adequate documentation of conformance to recommended practices. Although the costs may be significant and ultimately borne by clients, the substantiated validity of the result is only possible in a program that implements appropriate QA practices.

Elements of a QA Program for Radon

This section briefly describes elements of a program for planning, measuring, and ensuring the quality of radon and/or decay product measurements. Each of these elements is discussed in greater detail elsewhere. This section introduces the activities that should be included in a quality assurance program and system.

Quality Management: Commitment, Quality Assurance Planning, and Quality Objectives

No endeavor will be completely successful without the interest, involvement and commitment of management. The role and responsibilities of management regarding QA, including QA planning and methods of reporting and oversight, should be documented.

Small organizations with limited personnel and resources may have an advantage regarding QA management because one person may be responsible for all company policies. In this case, the commitment of management ensures the commitment of the organization.

QA Documentation

There are many forms of documentation that are important in the planning and implementation of quality control procedures. Most of these can be referenced in the QA Plan (QAP), which is a document that includes specifics on those procedures (chain of custody, quality control measurements, etc.) that are used to ensure that the planned quality is achieved.

Measurement System Calibration

Measurement equipment requires initial and periodic calibrations.

Internal QC and Assessment

There are many quality control measurements that are performed to assess the quality of procured material and equipment, the continued performance of instruments and procedures, estimated errors of imprecision and bias, and contributions of field and laboratory background.

Corrective Action

Corrective action may be necessary as a result of unsatisfactory QC results, client dissatisfaction, audit reports, or for other reasons. The responsibility for taking action and for verifying that the action was successful in correcting the problem should be documented for various personnel and categories of activities. Corrective action for specific occurrences (e.g., quality control results outside of specified numeric bounds, more than a specified rate of data input errors, etc.) should also be documented, along with the time frame for action and the person responsible. Corrective action procedures are the responsibility of the QA officer.

Training

Training is an important quality control issue. The responsibilities, goals, and schedules for training, both in general procedures and in specific QA activities, should be clear and documented.

Responsibilities

An analytical radon measurement service provider performs the analysis or reading of the radon measurement devices. A residential service provider is an individual who offers radon measurement services but relies on an analytical organization for analysis or reading of the measurement device.

Services provided by a residential service provider may include consulting with the homeowner or realtor, packaging, placing and retrieving measurement devices, and preparing and issuing measurement reports (using the values provided by the analytical organization). Over-the-counter retailers of measurement devices are not considered analytical or residential service providers because they merely make the devices available and provide no services to the consumer.

It is possible for an organization to function as an analytical organization and employ individuals to provide residential measurement services. The roles and responsibilities of analytical and residential service providers in terms of quality assurance are described in this section.

ANALYTICAL SERVICE PROVIDERS

Roles

Analytical service providers analyze the detectors or read the monitors and produce the final result that is reported to clients. Any organization or individual that obtains the final results from continuous radon (CR) or working-level monitors (CW), performs grab measurements made with the pump/collapsible bag (GB) method, the grab activated charcoal (GC) method, the scintillation cell (GS) method, or the grab working-level (GW) method is classified as an analytical service provider. An organization or individual who uses an electret reader to obtain results from electret ion chambers (EL or ES) is an analytical service provider. Similarly, the analysis of detectors, such as alpha track detectors (AT), activated charcoal absorbers (AC), charcoal liquid scintillation devices (LS), pump/collapsible bag devices (PB), radon progeny integrated-sampling units (RP), and unfiltered track detectors (UT) classify an organization or individual as an analytical service provider. The RPP listings are device-specific.

Responsibilities of Analytical and Residential Service Providers		
Responsibility	**Analytical Service Provider**	**Residential Service Provider**
Preparing, updating, and implementing a QA plan	X	X
Obtaining copies of the analytical organization's QA plan, including schedules of calibration, and ensuring their adequacy		X
Calibrating analysis equipment as recommended by the manufacturer, or at least once every 12 months, as described in the EPA's *Indoor Radon and Radon Decay Product Measurement Device Protocols*	X	
Conducting laboratory/field background measurements at a rate, recording the results in control charts and other documentation, and using the results to calculate (for analytical service providers) or check against (for residential service providers) the lower limit of detection	X	X (Laboratory background measurements and calculation of LLD are not expected.)
Employing a QA officer who is responsible for conducting audits, monitoring QC data, the oversight and accountability for corrective action, and reporting to management	X	X
Conducting known exposure or cross-check measurements at a rate	X	X
Conducting side-by-side duplicate or comparison measurements at a rate	X	X
Making available the results of laboratory background measurements, the lower limit of detection, and estimates of precision to those service organizations using the analytical service provider	X	

Responsibilities of Analytical and Residential Service Providers		
Responsibility	Analytical Service Provider	Residential Service Provider
Conducting routine instrument performance checks, including battery, electronics, pump flow rates, and the stability of the system using a check source or cell	X	X (for residential service providers using active instruments, as specified by the manufacturer and analytical organization)
Maintaining a documented system to track measurement devices (chain of custody), locations, dates, clients, methods/laboratories, and results	X	X
Conforming to EPA guidelines for conducting measurements, reporting measurement results, and providing information to clients	X	X

Responsibilities

Analytical service providers are responsible for the following activities:

- preparing, updating, and implementing a QA plan;
- ensuring that all equipment is calibrated and re-calibrated according to the schedules described for that method herein, by the manufacturer, or in the EPA's *Indoor Radon and Radon Decay Product Measurement Device Protocols*;
- conducting background measurements (laboratory and field, as appropriate), recording the results in control charts and other relevant documentation, and using the results to calculate the lower limit of detection;
- employing a QA officer who is organizationally independent of the analysis and distribution processes;
- conducting routine and ongoing measurements to assess bias according to EPA recommendations, and recording and analyzing the results;
- conducting routine and ongoing measurements to track precision error, recording the results in control charts and other documentation, and using the results to estimate precision;
- making available the results of background measurements, the lower limit of detection, and estimates of precision error to residential service providers using the analytical organization regularly;
- conducting routine instrument performance checks;
- maintaining a documented system to track measurement devices (chain of custody), locations, dates, clients, methods/laboratories, and results; and

• conforming to EPA guidelines for conducting measurements, reporting measurement results, and providing information to clients.

RESIDENTIAL SERVICE PROVIDERS

Roles

Residential service providers distribute measurement devices to clients and report results but do not analyze the detectors or generate the result that is reported to the client. These individuals may, however, have considerable impact on the measurement process and result. Residential service providers must exercise skill and judgment in assessing measurement conditions, deploying and retrieving devices, and communicating with their clients.

Responsibilities

The QA-related responsibilities of residential service providers are to ensure that their activities do not contribute to any degradation of the measurement quality (such as by excessive storage time or storage in unsuitable environments, improper placement, errors in reporting or recordkeeping, or other factors), and to understand and monitor the performance of their measurement system, which includes their operation, as well as the operation of the analysis laboratory that they are using. There should be clear and open communication between residential service providers and the analysis laboratory they use.

Specific requirements of residential service providers include:

• preparing, updating, and implementing a QA plan;

• reviewing the analytical organization's QA plan;

• conducting field background measurements, as appropriate, and recording the results in control charts and other relevant documentation;

• employing a QA officer;

• conducting routine and ongoing measurements to assess bias, and recording and analyzing the results;

• conducting routine and ongoing measurements to estimate precision error, as feasible, and recording the results in control charts and other documentation;

• conducting routine instrument performance checks according to directions from the analytical service provider;

• maintaining a documented system to track measurement devices (chain of custody), locations, dates, clients, methods/laboratories, and results; and

• conforming to EPA guidelines for conducting measurements, reporting measurement results, and providing information to clients.

Quality Management

Management Commitment and Responsibility

A primary concern of any organization must be the quality of its products and services. In order to meet its objectives, the organization should function so that the technical, administrative and operational factors affecting the quality of its products and services is known and is under control. An effective quality management system should be designed to satisfy customer needs and expectations while serving to protect the organization's interests. Quality management is just as important in small organizations as in large ones. However, small organizations may find that communicating and implementing changes in policy-related procedures are simpler to do than in large organizations because fewer people are involved. In addition, small organizations are often comprised of highly motivated people who are committed to the success of the company. Since small organizations generally consist of people with multiple responsibilities, they are likely to designate their single technical expert as the QA officer. In these cases, it may be helpful to obtain the services of an outside expert to serve as an auditor for several hours each quarter in order to ensure an outside review of procedures.

The responsibility for and commitment to quality in delivered services belongs to the highest level of management. If the organization's management does not provide an environment that supports a QA program and in which concerns and suggestions for improving quality can be raised, the quality of the measurements will suffer. Management should foster a "no-fault" attitude to encourage the identification of quality issues and problems. The terms "continuous improvement" and "quality improvement" refer to a structure and environment in which improvement is considered part of the daily work, and resources are provided for eliminating problems at their source. The quality policy of an organization should be a statement that is realistic, implemented, and documented in the QA plan or other written materials.

QA management is that aspect of the overall management that determines and implements quality policy. The direct and ultimate responsibility for assuring data quality rests with the laboratory or field managers. These people have the primary responsibility for developing QA policies, procedures and criteria, and for delegating QA authority and responsibility. The term "management by fact" refers to the use of quality control data, market data, and other information and their analysis as input to the organization's assessment and improvement.

Accountability is an important part of QA management. Each person in the organization needs to understand the organizational framework in order to understand and be accountable for his/her own QA responsibilities.

The term "quality system" refers to the organization's structure and function relating to managing, overseeing, and improving quality. The system includes documentation (quality assurance plans, procedures, logs, and accountability for their maintenance and review) and procedures for audits and reviews for quality assurance and quality control.

The national standard for quality systems describes elements of quality management. These include:

- management and organization;
- quality system and description;
- personnel qualification(s) and training;
- procurement of items and services;
- documents and records;
- computer hardware and software;
- planning;
- implementation of work processes;
- assessment and response; and
- quality improvement.

These elements are essentially equivalent to the requirements found in other standards, including the ISO 9000 series and ASME NQA-1. These elements of quality management may be described in the QA plan or in a separate quality management plan.

Quality Assurance Officer

The establishment of a QA program requires a QA officer within the organization to supervise and, as appropriate, carry out the monitoring, recordkeeping, statistical techniques, and other functions required to maintain high-quality data. This person may have these duties as a sole responsibility or, in smaller organizations, along with other responsibilities. The QA officer should be assimilated into the organization, reporting to the lowest level at which he/she can be effective and unbiased in objectively serving the needs of the organization. Even organizations consisting of one or two people need to designate the responsibilities of a QA officer to someone involved in the day-to-day operations. In addition, however, an outside expert can be used to review statistical methods, procedures, training, or other QA issues.

The QA officer assists management in interpreting and developing the QA policy for the organization. The QA officer also provides technical support and review, and approves QA products for the top manager.

The QA officer should, at a minimum, be responsible for:

- developing and ensuring the implementation of a QA program, including procedures for chain-of-custody, statistical analyses, and data verification, among others, which will help the organization to meet the authorized standards of quality at minimum cost;

- advising and assisting management in the installation, staffing and supervision of a QA program;

- monitoring QA/QC activities of the laboratory to determine conformance with authorized policies and procedures and with recognized industry practices;

- making appropriate recommendations for correction and improvement of QA/QC activities, as necessary;

- assisting in the development of specifications and acceptance criteria for purchased items and materials;

- seeking out and evaluating current developments and new ideas in the field of QA, and recommending means for their application wherever advisable; and

- advising management in reviewing technology, methods and equipment with respect to their quality assurance applications.

In addition, the organization's QA officer needs to have sufficient authority and responsibility to exercise whatever oversight is necessary to assure that:

- all data-collection activities are covered by appropriate QA planning documentation (such as in the company's official QA plan);

- all routinely used procedures that impact data quality are documented in standard operating procedures (SOPs) that are complete and have been reviewed and approved by both management and the staff responsible for implementing those procedures;

- audits/reviews are performed to assure adherence to approved QAPs and to identify deficiencies in QA/QC systems;

- adequate follow-through actions are implemented in response to audit/review findings; and

- all laboratory, field and/or office personnel involved in data collection have access to any training or QA information needed to be knowledgeable in QA requirements, protocols, and technology.

In implementing these oversight responsibilities, the QA officer should have a reporting relationship with the top managers of the organization to assure that the appropriate laboratory or field managers are aware of their responsibilities for prescribing any needed corrective actions.

For example, the QA officer should be included in regular staff meetings or conference calls, and receive all organization memoranda and bulletins regarding staffing, training, equipment, recordkeeping, and changes in business practice and procedures.

Quality Assurance Training

All personnel involved in any function affecting data quality (detector custody, sample analysis, data reduction, and QA) should receive training in their appointed jobs to contribute to the reporting of complete and high-quality data. The expectations and qualifications for each position should be documented (e.g., as in a job description). The QA officer is responsible for periodic reviews of the requirements for training.

QA Documentation and Reporting

Standard Operating Procedures

Organizations should assure that all work affecting the quality of results (such as handling, storing and analyzing devices) be prescribed in clear and complete written instructions. These work instructions, known as standard operating procedures (SOPs), provide the criteria for performing the work, particularly the analytical and testing functions, and prescribe the chain-of-custody procedures that are necessary to assure that analytical results can be used as evidence. The preparation and maintenance of, and compliance with, SOPs should be monitored by the organization's QA officer. A schedule and the responsibility for reviewing and updating the SOP should be documented as one of the QA officer's responsibilities.

Anyone performing radon measurements should have a written, device-specific SOP in place for each radon measurement system used. An SOP must include specific information describing how to operate and/or analyze a particular measurement device. Organizations that analyze devices should develop their own SOP or adapt manufacturer-developed SOPs for their devices. Organizations that receive results from a laboratory should have a device-specific SOP for each brand, model and type of device that they use. In addition, both analytical and residential service providers need to document their procedures for validating data (including client information) and preparing reports.

Recordkeeping and Chain of Custody

There are sources of error other than errors inherent in the measurement process. Inadequate recordkeeping can lead to errors, such as transposing results from different locations, or misplacing results or detectors. There are computer spreadsheets and other programs available that can be adapted for many uses and large quantities of data. When planning procedures for data entry, the following factors are important.

First, ensure that the proper forms and labels are available and can be easily understood by the homeowner, technician, data entry operator, or whoever must use and read them.

Second, anyone recording data must receive adequate instructions that are documented and updated in the SOP for easy reference.

Third, the data-recording process should be monitored for errors. Many organizations use a double-entry method, wherein each field is entered by two different operators (or entered at two different times by the same operator) and checked automatically by the computer for differences. If this is not feasible, organizations should manually check at least a portion of the day's entries for errors. In general, less involvement of human operators ensures fewer opportunities for error. A very useful tool in large operations is the bar-code system.

Chain-of-custody procedures to track detectors and placement/analysis dates should be established and documented in the SOP. These may be as simple as labeling large boxes or shelves for unexposed detectors ready to be used, detectors ready to be shipped or analyzed, and detector custody sign in-out sheets. Identical printed peel-off sample ID numbers placed on detectors, information sheets, result letters, and shipping containers can help reduce mix-ups. For detector types that need to be analyzed immediately following exposure, a daily check that all detectors received have been shipped and analyzed may be appropriate.

Logbooks are useful tools for maintaining records of QA practices and QC measurements, including calibration results, background measurements results, and any changes in operators, materials or procedures. Logbooks should be bound, and records entered in pen. Every entry should include the name of the person making the entry, and the date. Any relevant printouts or plots should be photocopied and pasted into the logbook. Such a log can serve as an invaluable record, with all relevant information in one place.

The following items should be included in a separate QA logbook for each active instrument or passive method:

- equipment calibration records (for analytical service providers), including:
  - the date of the calibration, and the date that the calibration expires, as appropriate;
  - the facility where the calibration was performed;
  - the procedures used (an SOP or calibration report can be referenced);
  - the results; and
  - changes in calibration factors implemented.
- laboratory background measurements (for analytical service providers), including:
  - the date of the background measurement;
  - the location and type of measurement (e.g., aged air or nitrogen);
  - the procedures used (an SOP can be referenced);
  - the results; and
  - changes in LLD or background values.
- field background measurements (for both analytical and residential service providers), including:
  - the date and location of the field background measurement;
  - the procedures used (appropriate documentation can be referenced);
  - the results; and
  - changes implemented because of the results.

- results of all QC measurements (for both analytical and residential service providers), including:
  - results of comparison measurements (for users of active instruments);
  - results of duplicate measurements; and
  - results of spiked measurements.
- routine instrument performance checks (for analytical and some residential service providers using active devices), including the dates and results of:
  - battery checks and replacement;
  - check source/cell measurements;
  - pump flow-rate measurements; and
  - self-diagnostic checks.

Control charts containing the results of any of these QC measurements may be kept in the QA notebook or posted for easy reference.

Each organization should derive its own system for tracking measurements. Residential service providers may use a logbook or a system of duplicate copies of data sheets to record the information gathered and generated for each measurement.

Information stored for each measurement should include:

- a copy of the final report, including the measurement results, and the statement (or reference to the statement in the SOP) outlining any recommendations concerning re-testing or mitigation provided to the client;
- the address of the building and room numbers to identify the location of the measurement. It may be useful to diagram the test area, noting the exact location of the detector;
- the exact start and stop dates and times of the measurement duration;
- a description of the device used, including its manufacturer, model and/or type, and identification (serial) number;
- a description of the condition of any permanent vents, such as crawlspace vents or a combustion-air supply to combustion appliances;
- the name and RPP identification number of the providers used to analyze devices;
- the name and RPP identification number (or state license number) of the individual who conducted the test;
- a description of any variations from, or uncertainties about, standard measurement procedures, closed-building conditions, or other factors that may affect the measurement result;
- a description of any non-interference controls used, and copies of signed non-interference agreements; and
- a record of any QC measures associated with the test, such as results of simultaneous measurements.

Regardless of the system used, SOPs for tracking the detectors (part of detector custody) should be written, adhered to, and revised as appropriate. All personnel should be trained and should understand the importance of maintaining proper correlation of information with the detector and measurement result.

Computer files should be backed up regularly to ensure against data loss. Retention time and location for different types of records should be specified in the SOP.

Data Validation

Each step in the process between obtaining the original counts, tracks or voltage losses and the final results reported to clients should receive some data validation. In general, a percentage of each phase of the data should be checked. Hand-checking is sufficient if it is done conscientiously (e.g., calculations are performed again on a hand calculator, information is compared field by field, and these procedures are documented). There must be a record noting which files were checked, by whom, the date, and how any errors that were found were resolved. Dates and initials in the records may be sufficient if the procedure used is documented.

QA Audits

States may audit companies as part of state certification. School districts, federal agencies, or private companies may conduct audits of the measurement organizations they are using or are considering using. These audits may be formally specified in a contract, or consist of less formal on-site visits or written requests for QC data and procedures. In any case, all logbooks and QA records should be easily available when not actually in use in the field. Both residential and analytical service providers should maintain records appropriate for their activities in the event of an audit or a request for information.

The focus of QA audits should be on the following topics:

- the existence and adequacy of a written and signed QA plan for all measurement methods and operations;
- the performance of measurements to assess precision, their results, and how frequently they are performed;
- the performance of measurements to assess bias, their results, and how frequently they are performed;
- the performance of background measurements, their results, and how frequently they are performed;
- the proper recording and analysis of QC measurements, including the use of control charts;
- the operating conditions of all equipment;
- the existence of SOPs for each measurement method and operation;
- the records and the person responsible for preventative maintenance on all equipment;
- the existence of a detector tracking (custody) procedure;
- the existence of adequate records for tracking measurement location, condition, operator, etc.;
- an adequate system for data validation, including records, procedures, and corrective action in case of the discovery of errors;
- the conditions under which detectors and equipment are stored (e.g., low humidity, radon concentration);
- documentation of the specific serial numbers of the equipment or counters used in each analysis;
- the backups of all computer files;
- corrective action procedures and how they are implemented; and
- the complete records of any changes in materials or technicians.

For analytical organizations, audits should be conducted on the topics described above, as well as on:

- appropriate client reporting, including use of the LLD as calculated from laboratory background measurements (which may change over time), appropriate use of significant figures, and furnishing clients with relevant information about what their measurement results mean;

- the calibration of the equipment and whether it is done in conformance with the QA plan; and

- the records and results from performance evaluations (federal, state or industry).

Internal audits may be conducted by the QA officer or his/her designee. Audits should be performed by someone not having direct authority or responsibilities in the area(s) being audited. Checklists prepared by the QA officer may be helpful during the audit.

QA Reporting

Periodic reports should be made to management on the results of QC measurements, reviewing any problems that were encountered, along with their solutions (or proposed solutions). These reports should be included in the QA logbooks and be available during audits. At a minimum, there should be one report after every six months of operation.

Quality Control

Quality assurance or QA is an umbrella term that includes many activities designed to ensure the validity of measurements and measure their quality. The measurements that are made for the purpose of assessing and monitoring data quality are called quality control or QC measurements. The QC measurements described here are those that are recommended specifically by the EPA and others for radon measurements. Guidance for QA in radon or related measurements can also be found in documents written by the American National Standards Institute (ANSI), the National Council on Radiation Protection and Measurements (NCRPM), and the American Association of Radon Scientists and Technologists (AARST). Guidance for accreditation of laboratories used by the American Association for Laboratory Accreditation is available, and the recommendations in this section are consistent with that guidance.

Measurements to Monitor Precision Errors

Duplicates are defined as co-located measurements in which side-by-side detectors measure over the same time interval. Replicated measurements, consisting of more than two simultaneous side-by-side measurements, can be used to estimate the precision error of the system, and are especially useful initially and whenever the measurement system is altered. The purpose of making duplicate measurements is to track, over time, the variations that are observed between two identical measurements of the same concentration. A program of performing duplicate or replicated measurements allows the organization to monitor the component of measurement error caused by random differences in devices and/or the measurement process. Some precision error is unavoidable and may be due to the detector manufacture or configuration, inconsistent data transcription, or handling by suppliers, laboratories or technicians performing placements. Since any one of these factors can change suddenly or gradually over time, continual monitoring of precision can serve to check on the continuity of the entire measurement system.

The ideal estimate of precision is that which is inherent in the entire measurement system. This includes random component(s) of error introduced during shipping, distribution, storage, placement, and report generation. Different organizations may be involved in only a portion of this measurement system; for example, some analytical service providers may sell or lease detectors to residential service providers and never or rarely perform actual field measurements.

Each measurement organization—even if they are a residential service provider or an analytical organization that does not perform field measurements—should perform some measurements to estimate precision error. In addition, clear and frequent communication between analytical and residential service providers will help track the quality of the measurements and quickly identify any changes.

Specific recommendations for different types of organizations are described in the following sections.

Duplicate Measurements for Analytical Service Providers Distributing Passive Detectors Directly to Homeowners

Analysis laboratories that sell detectors directly to homeowners can estimate and track the precision inherent in their entire measurement system, including distribution. Duplicate measurements for passive detectors should be side-by-side measurements made in at least 10% of the total number of measurement locations, or 50 pairs each month, whichever is smaller. The locations selected for duplication should be distributed systematically throughout the entire population of samples. Groups selling measurements directly to homeowners can do this by providing two measurements, instead of one, to a random selection of purchasers, with instructions for the measurements to be made side by side.

The measurement locations selected to receive duplicate detectors should be distributed among all measurement locations. In other words, it is not adequate to place all duplicate devices in one basement. Some duplicate measurements must be made in locations that require all the different handling protocols that are routine in the operation, such as mailing to various locations, traveling by car, handling by different technicians, counting by different equipment, and recording by different office personnel. This is the only way to estimate and monitor the average precision error inherent in all the measurements. One way to implement this program is to target every tenth detector or client number to receive a duplicate.

An exception to this rule is when all the systematically selected locations that receive duplicates have radon concentrations less than 4 pCi/L (about 150 Bq/m^3). In this case, a portion of the duplicates should be placed in environments with higher concentrations. This can be accomplished by periodically placing side-by-side devices in an environment with radon concentrations known to be elevated.

Duplicate Measurements for Analytical Organizations Selling Passive Detectors to Residential Service Providers

An analysis laboratory must estimate the precision error inherent in its portion of the measurement operation by analyzing devices that have been exposed to the same radon environment. The QA officer should manage a program to regularly place at least two detectors side by side in the same radon environment. The QA officer should determine the frequency of duplicate measurements, but they should be systematically distributed (e.g., every 20th analysis should be a duplicate) so that the entire range of handling, technicians, background, and other laboratory conditions impact the duplicate analyses just as those conditions impact the normal analyses of detectors. A range of radon concentrations spanning the concentrations usually encountered in the field should be used. In addition, the QA officer is responsible for making these results available to the residential service providers that use the analysis services, and for obtaining the results of duplicates arranged by the residential service provider.

The organization performing analyses should measure duplicate (or replicated) devices at a frequency designed to ensure that a reliable estimate of laboratory analysis precision error is obtained. A rate of at least 25 pairs per month or 5% of the total number of devices analyzed (whichever is smaller) may be sufficient; this rate is for the analysis portion of the measurement system only, and assumes that additional duplicate devices, as exposed by the residential service organizations, will also be processed by the same analysis laboratory.

Duplicate Measurements for Residential Service Providers Using a Passive Detector System

Residential service providers perform activities that may impact the precision of the measurement. These include handling, storage, shipping, deployment, and data transcription. In fact, it is the residential service provider that bears the responsibility of the critical portion of the measurement—exposure—and often the ultimate reporting of the result to the client. Because of this, it is important that residential service providers expose and arrange the analysis of duplicate detectors and track their results. The residential service provider's QA officer should manage a program ensuring that the following guidelines for duplicate devices are met.

Duplicate measurements for passive detectors exposed by residential service providers should be side-by-side measurements made in at least 5% of the total number of measurement locations or 25 pairs each month, whichever is smaller. The locations selected for duplication should be distributed systematically throughout the entire population of measurements. The residential service provider can provide two measurements instead of one to a random selection of purchasers, with the measurements made side by side. Special instructions and detector packaging may be necessary to ensure that the detectors are not separated during exposure.

The measurement locations selected to receive duplicate detectors should be distributed among all measurement locations. In other words, it is not adequate to place all duplicate devices in one basement. Some duplicate measurements must be made in locations that require all the different handling modes that are routine in the operation, such as mailing to various locations, traveling by car, handling by different technicians, and recording by different office personnel. This is the only way to estimate and monitor the average precision error inherent in the measurements. One way to implement this program is to target every twentieth detector or customer number to receive a duplicate.

An exception to this rule is when all the systematically selected locations that receive duplicates have radon concentrations less than 4 pCi/L (about 150 Bq/m^3). In this case, a portion of the duplicates should be placed in environments with higher concentrations.

QA Plans

A quality assurance plan (QAP) is a written document that presents, in specific terms, the policies, organization, objectives, functional activities, and specific QA and QC activities that are designed to achieve the objectives of the project.

The QAP serves three main purposes:

1. First, and most importantly, it is the culmination of the discussion and planning that went into designing the operation to produce results that are of the quality needed.
2. Second, it is an historical record that documents the operation in terms of measurement methods used, calibration standards and frequencies planned, auditing planned, etc.

3. Lastly, a QAP provides management with a document that can be used to assess whether the planned QA activities are being implemented, and to examine the importance of these activities toward the goal of quality data in terms of relative bias, precision error, and other indicators of quality.

There are 16 elements of a QAP that are described in the EPA's guidance for preparing such plans. These elements are described here, along with terminology used by other organizations. These elements should be present in a QAP, and presentation in the order described in this section will facilitate review by the EPA and others (for example, by residential service providers). Exhibit 9-1 describes the elements that are necessary for the QAPs of analytical and residential service providers.

Exhibit 9-1

Required Elements of a Quality Assurance Plan for Analytical and Residential Service Providers		
Element	Analytical	Residential
1. Signature page	Required	Required
2. Table of contents, with revision numbers and dates	Required	Required
3. Description of operations	Required	Required
4. Organization and responsibilities	Required	Required
5. QA objectives for measurement data in terms of precision error and relative bias	Required	Required—obtain this information from the analytical organization
6. Measurement procedures (brief discussion of measurement method, procedures for selecting measurement location, and procedures for recordkeeping and shipping)	Required	Required
7. Detector custody for field and laboratory operations	Required	Required—describing sample custody for the residential organization's operations only
8. Calibration procedures and frequency	Required	Not required
9. Analytical procedures	Required	Not required

Required Elements of a Quality Assurance Plan for Analytical and Residential Service Providers		
Element	Analytical	Residential
10. Data reduction, validation, and reporting	Required	Required—omitting the data reduction conducted by the analytical organization's operations
11. Internal QC checks	Required	Required
12. QA audits	Required	Required—only pertaining to activities relevant to the residential organization's responsibilities
13. Preventative maintenance	Required	Required—only pertaining to equipment used by the residential organization
14. Procedures used to assess precision, relative bias, and lower limit of detection (LLD)	Required	Required—except for the assessment of LLD
15. Corrective action	Required	Required—only pertaining to the residential organization's operations
16. QA reports to management	Required	Required

There is considerable information available on preparing quality assurance plans and quality management plans. A QAP that is written in addition to a separate quality management plan and extensively referenced SOPs may be fairly lean. A QAP that serves as the sole quality document and contains the procedures for many quality control procedures may be lengthy and detailed.

The responsibility for reviewing and updating the QAP lies with the QA officer. As this may require periodic expenditures of time, this task must be supported by management.

Signature Page

The title page of the QAP must include the signatures of the organization's QA officer and their supervisor. Other individuals who are also responsible for the quality of measurements should sign and date the completed QAP, indicating that they have reviewed and approved the plan and consider the plan final.

Table of Contents

The table of contents must include page numbers for each of the elements of the QAP, and the revision number, which signifies the number of times and most current date that each element was revised.

Description of Operations

This part of the QAP should provide a complete description of all the relevant organizational operations, including different measurement methods, distribution activities, on-site visits, and transmittal of results to clients. The description must be sufficiently comprehensive for someone unfamiliar with the operations to understand the numbers and types of measurements made by the organization. Although SOPs may be referenced, the QAP should include a brief description of operations.

Organization and Responsibilities

This part of the QAP usually includes a detailed organization chart showing management structure and lines of communication. The names of all key individuals in charge of every major activity in the project should be included. Phone numbers and/or email addresses should also be provided to facilitate communication between project officials. Both technical and QA/QC functions should be listed.

An important person to identify is the QA officer, and the line of authority for his/her activities. This section should include a description of the regular methods of communication regarding quality assurance issues. Unless a separate quality manual or quality management plan is written, this section should include a statement of commitment to quality (or quality policy) by the organization's management.

Work performed by parties outside the organization should be identified, with a description of management and technical responsibilities for this work.

Quality Assurance Objectives

The quantitative QA objectives should be discussed and presented in this section. In general, objectives for relative bias and precision error should be listed, and other objectives may be listed as well. These may include, for example, numeric objectives relevant to marketing (e.g., measures of customer satisfaction, referrals, etc.) or employee performance (e.g., data entry errors). Analytical service organizations may need to set objectives for the parameters necessary for the calculation of final concentrations (for example, flow rates or weight gains). The objectives for intermediate parameters may be, for example, that flow rate will remain between values x and y; corrective action will be taken and the QA officer notified if values deviate beyond these boundaries.

Precision Error

Precision is defined as the measure of the variability of a process used to make repeated measurements under carefully controlled (identical) conditions. Duplicate measurements provide a check on the quality of the measurement result and allow the user to monitor precision error. Large precision errors may be caused by inconsistencies in the manufacture of the detector, or inconsistent data transcription or handling by suppliers, laboratories, or technicians performing placements.

Precision error can be an important component of the overall error, so it is important that all users monitor precision error.

Because variability is not usually constant at different concentrations, estimates of precision must be made at different concentrations in the range of interest. Precision objectives for several concentrations or ranges should be specified.

The estimate of precision error may be specified in terms of:

    1. relative percentage difference, defined as the absolute value of the difference between two measurements divided by their average;

    2. coefficient of variation, defined as the sample standard deviation of two or more measurements divided by their average;

    3. the range, defined as the difference between the two measurements; or

    4. some other parameter.

The quantitative goals for precision could be specified, for example, as an average relative percentage difference of less than 25% for duplicates, where at least one result is less than 4 pCi/L (150 Bq/m³), and an average relative percentage difference of less than 14% for duplicates, where both results are greater than 4 pCi/L (150 Bq/m³).

Relative Bias

Relative bias is defined as the degree of agreement of a measurement result with an accepted reference or true value. In the case of passive detectors, the reference value is the concentration in the radon calibration facility where the spiked measurements are performed. In the case of active instruments for which bias was assessed with a cross-check, the reference value is that given by the recently calibrated instrument.

Bias may be expressed in terms of relative percent error, or as:

    RPE = [(MV-RV)/RV] 100%, where: RPE = relative percentage error;

    MV = measured value of spiked measurement; and

    RV = reference value.

Note that the definition of relative percentage error is similar to the definition of individual relative error (IRE), except that the numerator of the IRE is the absolute value of the difference, while RPE can have positive or negative values. This formula is identical to the relative bias formula used by the Nuclear Regulatory Commission.

It is advisable to specify ranges over which the relative bias goals are to be met. The quantitative goal for relative bias could be stated, for example, as a RPE of ±15% or less at radon concentrations greater than 4 pCi/L (150 Bq/m³).

Another expression of bias is performance ratio, which can be defined as the measured value divided by the reference value. Note that the difference between percentage bias and performance ratio is 1, so that, for example, if the percentage difference is 0.25, the performance ratio will be 1.25.

This part of the QAP should describe the following:

    • the method by which the radon or radon decay product concentrations are to be measured. A technical person unfamiliar with the method must be able to understand the descriptions of the method used. The RPP handbook contains a brief description of each of the measurement methods currently described by the EPA's *Indoor Radon and Radon Decay Product Measurement Device Protocols*;

- the guidelines used to select the locations for detector deployment, including the procedures for choosing the exact sampling locations;

- measurement conditions, as described in Protocols for *Radon and Radon Decay Product Measurements in Homes*;

- the logbooks or recordkeeping procedures, with a list of the information routinely gathered with each measurement; and

- relevant information about shipping detectors to the laboratory, including the schedule for shipping detectors.

Detector Custody

A complete description of all chain-of-custody procedures, forms, documentation, and the responsibilities of each person is needed to ensure both the technical validity and the legal defensibility of data obtained from all measurements.

The information that is relevant under this part is a description of:

- the names of field operators/technicians;

- how, by whom, and where the records of measurement data are kept, including location, time, and other pertinent parameters;

- examples of labels, custody seals, and field tracking forms; and

- office documentation of procedures for transporting detectors from the field to the laboratory, including identification of the individuals or organizations responsible for transport.

Laboratory Operations

This part of the QAP describes how the detectors are handled by each laboratory facility when they are received after exposure.

The following information should be included:

- the names of laboratory detector custodians responsible for logging in devices or data;

- forms for laboratory detector tracking;

- records of laboratory chain of custody;

- specification of procedures for detector handling, storage, and final disposition; and

- documentation of procedures for disbursement and transfer of detectors within the laboratory and between the analytical and residential service provider.

A residential service provider's QAP must include the identification of the person responsible for the detectors, and a description of the laboratory's detector handling procedures.

Calibration Procedures and Frequency (for Analytical Service Providers Only)

This section of the QAP should include descriptions of the calibration procedures, and the frequency of calibration for each analytical system, instrument, device, and any components (scales, flowmeter, etc.) used to obtain measurement results.

A summary table should be used, whenever possible, to present the following information:

- references to EPA-recognized or other standard methods;
- a complete description of non-standard or modified methods;
- appended instrument-specific calibration SOPs, as needed, to support SOPs that do not include detailed calibration procedures; and/or
- the definition of specific acceptance criteria for all calibration measurements.

The information that needs to be included in this part of the QAP or the appendix of SOPs should be specific; for example: shipment of 20 detectors every six months to the calibration facility (provide the name and address); exposure to humidities and radon levels (specify ranges of values) at the calibration facility; adjustment of calibration curves accordingly; and other information.

Analytical Procedures (for Analytical Service Providers Only)

This part of the QAP should describe the procedures for analyzing the detectors. The laboratory SOPs should be reproduced and appended to the QAP, or referenced and kept available.

Data Reduction, Validation and Reporting

This section of the QAP describes how the organization maintains good data quality throughout data reduction (i.e., calculation of results), transfer, storage, retrieval, and reporting.

The following topics are recommended for discussion:

- For data reduction:
  - the names of the individuals responsible;
  - a summary of data reduction procedures;
  - examples of data sheets;
  - a description of how results from field and laboratory blanks are used in the calculations; and
  - presentation of all calculations (equations) and significant underlying assumptions.
- For data validation:
  - the means by which the data are checked for errors;
  - the names of the individuals responsible; and
  - procedures for determining outliers and flagging data for review by the QA officer or others.
- For data reporting:
  - the names of the individuals responsible; and
  - a flow chart of the data-handling process, covering all data collection, transfer, storage, recovery, and processing steps, and including QC data for both field and laboratory operations.

This section must also describe the procedures and persons responsible for non-routine occurrences, such as when detectors are returned opened or late, or when some other deviation from the planned circumstances has occurred.

Finally, this section of the QAP should describe the procedures for re-checking results that indicate exposures to radon concentrations greater than a specified limit (e.g., 100 pCi/L or about 4,000

Bq/m³), or the limit above which all measurements are re-calculated before being reported as final.

Internal QC measurements must be conducted by both analytical and residential service providers.

The following QC activities should be described:

- use of internal laboratory standards (check sources, canisters, etc.), self-diagnostic tests, and other routine instrument performance checks, their frequency, treatment of results, (e.g., use of means control charts), and plans for corrective action if results fall outside predetermined criteria;

- duplicate or replicated measurements made to estimate precision, their frequency, the criteria by which locations for duplicate measurements will be chosen, the procedures for deploying and documenting duplicates, and the procedures for assessing the need for corrective action;

- comparison measurements in which different types of devices are placed side by side and the results compared.

- known exposure (spiked) measurements made to assess relative bias, the calibration facility where spikes are exposed, their frequency, the range of concentrations to which they will be exposed, the procedures for documenting their results, and the procedures for assessing the need for corrective action (e.g., analysis of results and comparison with predetermined limits); and

- proficiency testing of analysts and operators.

In addition, this part should describe the QA checks on incoming detectors, equipment, and supplies, for both new shipments of detectors and for detectors mailed back after deployment. For example, some fraction of incoming charcoal canisters should be checked for high background rates and package integrity; detectors mailed in after deployment should be checked to ensure that they were sealed properly and that the paperwork was completed correctly. The corrective action to be taken if either of these types of internal QA checks indicate unusual results should be discussed here and referenced in the "Corrective Action" chapter of the QAP.

After the procedures for field and laboratory operations have been developed, an audit must be conducted to ensure that all the procedures work as planned. QA audits are based on the QAP. Therefore, the QAP should be sufficiently detailed to form the basis of a meaningful audit. QA audits can be conducted by the QA officer or an outside expert who will review the written procedures for completeness. All QA audits should be documented in a written report that specifies the nature and findings of the audit. Additional audits are conducted periodically during the operations to check on the accuracy of the reported results.

This section of the QAP should describe the plans for these audits, including who will conduct them, when they will be conducted, and the focus of the audits. The QA officer should conduct an audit after any change in method or procedure, and conduct additional audits at least once every six months.

Preventative Maintenance

This section should include descriptions of the types of preventative maintenance needed for adhering to schedules and for achieving good quality data (for example, mechanical maintenance of laboratory equipment).

The descriptions may include:

- a schedule of important preventative maintenance tasks for the measurement systems, and the person responsible for their implementation;

- a list of critical spare parts; and

- reference to current maintenance contracts and standard maintenance procedures for the measurement systems.

This information may not be relevant for a residential service provider, or may apply only to computer or other non-analysis equipment.

Procedures to Estimate Data Precision, Relative Bias, and Lower Limit of Detection (LLD)

This part of the QAP should describe the processes (including equations and descriptions of calculations, statistical tests, control charts, etc.) by which the:

- duplicate or replicated measurement results will be analyzed to estimate precision, and the limits of acceptability for precision error;

- known exposure (spikes or crosschecks) measurement results will be used to assess and monitor relative bias, and the limits for acceptable levels of relative bias.

- field and laboratory background-measurement results will be used to assess and track the background level and lower limit of detection, as appropriate for that method.

Corrective Action

A corrective action plan is a contingency plan spelled out in "If...then" statements: "If this happens, then we will do the following..." For each critical measurement, the following topics should be presented (in table form, if adequate):

- Trigger points: What pre-specified conditions will automatically require corrective action?

- Personnel: Who initiates, approves, implements, evaluates, and reports corrective action?

- Response: What specific procedures will be followed if the corrective action is needed?

There may be different types of corrective actions that will be required as a result of QC measurement results. This section of the QAP should describe at least three types:

- the corrective action to be taken if results are outside the action limits when plotted on the control charts;

- the corrective action to be taken to correct problems found during audits; and

- the corrective action to be taken when there are deviations from the routine circumstances (for example, detectors not returned within 10 days of exposure, or incoming unused detectors with high backgrounds).

It may be appropriate to describe most types of corrective action in various sections described previously (e.g., corrective action due to an occurrence related to preventive maintenance may be discussed in that section); the section on corrective action should mention that other corrective action procedures are described in other portions of the QAP.

Quality Assurance Reports to Management

The main purpose of this section of the QAP is to:

1. identify the individuals responsible for reporting;

2. describe the form and contents of anticipated reports; and

3. plan the presentation of QA/QC data so that management can monitor data quality effectively.

This section should describe:

- the names and titles of the people who prepare and receive the reports;
- the type of report (written or oral), and their frequency;
- the contents of the various reports, such as:
  - changes in the QAP;
  - a summary of the current QA/QC programs, training, and accomplishments;
  - results of QA audits;
  - significant QA/QC problems, recommended solutions, and results of corrective actions;
  - data quality assessment in terms of precision, relative bias, field and laboratory background, and lower limit of detection (LLD); and
  - limitations on the use of the measurement data.

Analysis and Interpretation of QC

This section contains a review of the methods of calculating and monitoring the various sources of error that can be expected with a radon or radon-decay product measurement system. The total error is comprised of both random and systematic errors.

For the purposes of this discussion, the following terms are defined:

- **error:** the difference between the measurement result and the true value (or best estimate) of the quantity being measured.
- **systematic errors:** those errors that occur consistently (errors caused during calibration that impact all subsequent measurements is a typical example) and cause a consistently high or low bias in the result (note that there may be multiple systematic errors in a measurement system).
- **random errors:** those errors that give rise to a range of results distributed around an average value (a distribution); random errors cause imprecision.
- **precision:** the closeness of agreement between measurement results obtained under prescribed like conditions (e.g., replicated measurements in the same environment).
- **accuracy:** the closeness of agreement between a measurement result (or the average of more than one result) and an accepted reference value. There are two schools of thought on defining the accuracy of a measuring process. One school argues that accuracy should connote the agreement between the long-run average of the measurement results and the reference value, in which case accuracy represents bias or systematic error. In this case, errors of precision are reduced because of the use of a large number of measurements. This definition is in wide use among experimenters.

The other school of thought defines accuracy as the agreement between an individual measurement result and the reference value. In this case, the errors of precision are not reduced, and the total error depends on both precision (random errors) and bias (systematic errors). Because of these different usages, the American Society of Testing and Materials (ASTM) *Standard Practice for Use of the Terms Precision and Bias in ASTM Test Methods* states: "In order to avoid confusion resulting from use of the word 'accuracy,' only the terms 'precision' and 'bias' should be used as descriptors of ASTM test methods."

These guidelines will maintain consistency with ASTM nomenclature and use the terms "precision error" and "bias" (or "relative bias") to describe the components of error.

The combination of both systematic errors and random errors comprise the total error. The estimate of overall uncertainty associated with a measurement result should be comprised of upper bounds of both bias and precision errors.

This section will also discuss the calculation of the lower limit of detection (LLD) and related concepts. The LLD is important to understand, report properly, and place in context of your measurement program.

Routine Instrument Performance Checks

Proper operation of analytical instruments requires that their response to a given radon or decay-product concentration be as consistent as possible from one measurement to the next. This consistency can be checked using a reference source, counting background, and verifying that the results fall within predetermined limits. In addition, proper operation of an energy-sensitive instrument requires that its energy response be constant. Instrument QC, therefore, requires regular measurements of the following responses.

- Instrument check sources are used for monitoring the constancy of response of an instrument. The response characteristics of instrument reference sources should be as similar as possible to those of real measurements, and the response caused in the instrument should be stable (or predictable) over time.

- Energy alignment sources are used to check the overall gain and linearity of spectrometers. The sources should emit radiation of two energies (at least) and, preferably, of a number of energies covering the range for which the spectrometer is set. In some cases, the same source can be used both for instrument checks and energy alignment. Gamma alignment sources can be made by the laboratory. They are also available as Standard Reference Materials from the National Institute of Standards and Technology.

- Internal diagnostics can be performed that evaluate specific components of measurement systems, including voltages, pump flow rates, and other parameters. Some instruments provide pre-programmed self-diagnostic procedures.

Routine instrument performance checks should be conducted following the manufacturer's instructions, whenever the equipment has been significantly handled, whenever the operator requires assurance that the equipment is providing a stable response, and according to a regular schedule (e.g., daily, weekly, prior to sets of measurements or each measurement). The results of the routine instrument performance checks need to be recorded in a log with the date, time, and initials of the person who performed the check. If the check yields numeric results, it should be plotted on a means control chart. The QA officer is responsible for setting up the control chart with limits and guidelines for corrective action and for monitoring the results. The QA officer is accountable for oversight of the investigation and corrective action, when needed.

BACKGROUND MEASUREMENTS

Laboratory Background Measurements for Analytical Service Providers

Laboratory background measurements should be as similar as possible to actual measurements, but without the influence of radon or decay products. Various types of background measurements may be needed, including those for incoming materials, equipment, and unexposed devices. Background measurements for continuous monitors should be made in a glove box or with direct flow into the detector of aged air or nitrogen. Background measurements are a component of the calibration process.

Field Background Measurements for Analytical and Residential Service Providers

The results of field background measurements performed by analytical or residential service providers should be compared with the reported LLD. If the results of the field blanks are consistently and significantly greater than the LLD (more than several blank results in row), the analytical organization should be consulted and the potential for extraneous background be investigated. The analytical organization should be responsible for changing background labels or adjusting results due to changed background.

The results of field background measurements may also be plotted on a means control chart in the manner described in Section A.3.1 to ensure that a change in background levels can be quickly identified.

EVALUATION OF QC DATA

Means Control Chart for Repeated Measurements of Background and Routine Instrument Performance Checks

Control charts are basic tools for evaluating internal QC data. Taylor provides an excellent discussion of a variety of control charts, including those described here. See Taylor's "property" or "X-chart" for the means chart described in this section. A control chart can be used to evaluate the variation of replicated measurements either about a mean value to assess instrument stability (means chart), or among themselves to assess precision error (range chart).

A means control chart consists of measurement results plotted on the Y-axis, and their dates plotted sequentially with time on the X-axis. Limits are plotted as horizontal lines (± three-sigma from the mean), and data falling within these limits indicate that the system is "in control" and operating as it was when the limits were established based on previous data. A control chart may be used for a limited period, such as a month or two months, and then replaced by a new chart.

A standard Shewhart means control chart may be used for making day-to-day checks on whether any repetitive measurement (such as of background or a check source) is "in control" (see later in this section). The control chart shows the mean of the measurements, the warning levels that are two standard deviations above and below the mean, and the control limits that are three standard deviations above and below the mean. An example means control chart is shown in Exhibit A-1; example background control chart data are plotted in Exhibit A-1a.

After data from check sources or background have been gathered for several weeks or months, and well over 20 measurements have been made and plotted, the data can be analyzed in terms of the standard deviation. Lines denoting the mean ± one-, two-, and three-sigma can be plotted. If the system produces results that are consistent, ± one-sigma should contain two-thirds of the points, ± two-sigma should contain 19/20 of the points, and ± three-sigma should contain nearly all of the points. The probability of obtaining value outside the control limits is very low (less than 1%). Note that these limits are two-tailed limits (values near both limits or tails are of interest), as opposed to the limits for duplicates, which are one-tailed. If a value is obtained that is outside the three-sigma control limits, then the count should be repeated. If the repeat value is still outside the three-sigma limit, then measurements should be stopped and the situation evaluated and corrected. If results are outside the warning levels (± two-sigma), measurements can continue while the QA officer evaluates the situation.

As the data are plotted, rule-of-thumb indicators that the measurement system may be "out-of-control" include:

- two successive points outside the two-sigma limits;

- four successive points outside the one-sigma limits; and

- any systematic trends high or low.

A systematic trend includes a series of points in the same direction or successive points all on the same side of the mean, even if all are within the control limits. Note that one does expect to see measurements outside the warning limits, and this does not necessarily mean that the process is out of control. Repeated data falling outside the limits are evidence of loss of control and requires an investigation. If no cause of increased variability or shift can be found, then the control limits should be broadened and a sufficient number of data points gathered so that the QA officer is confident that the new limits are appropriate.

Note that the count rate of radioactive check sources changes with time. If the user is not aware of the pattern of change, it may appear that the instrument is drifting when, in fact, it is not. Instead of plotting total counts in a given period of time, it may be appropriate to plot another parameter, such as counts per disintegration.

Exhibit A-1

Means Control Chart for Background or Check Source Results	
Result	3 sigma control limit
	2 sigma warning level
	average or mean line of results
	2 sigma warning level
	3 sigma control limit

Date.......................................

The results plotted on these charts should be in sequential order by date. At least about 20 in-control measurements should be made before calculating the sample standard deviation of the results. "In-control" means that the operator has confidence that the instruments are operating properly and there is no evidence to suspect that there is anything faulty about the result. The QA officer is responsible for periodically assessing the spread of values on the charts, re-calculating the sample standard deviation based on new results, and determining whether the limits on the charts should be revised.

Exhibit A-1a

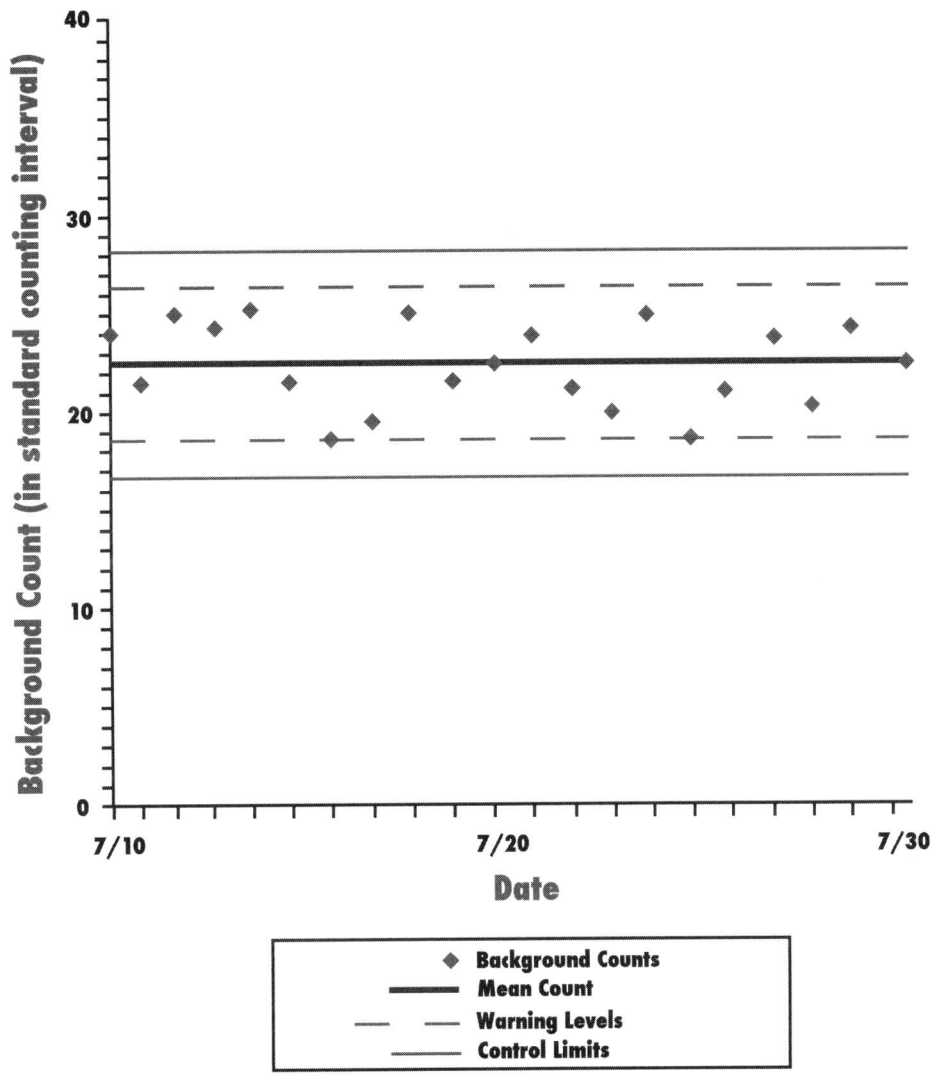

Example Means Control Chart for Background

Example Means Control Chart for Background	
Date	Background Count (in standard counting interval)
7/10/95	24
7/11/95	22
7/12/95	25
7/13/95	24
7/14/95	25

Example Means Control Chart for Background	
Date	**Background Count (in standard counting interval)**
7/15/95	22
7/16/95	19
7/17/95	20
7/18/95	25
7/19/95	22
7/20/95	23
7/21/95	24
7/22/95	22
7/23/95	21
7/24/95	25
7/25/95	19
7/26/95	22
7/27/95	24
7/28/95	21
7/29/95	25
7/30/95	23

Plotted Results	
Mean (average) =	23 counts
Sample standard deviation =	1.95 counts
Upper warning level =	27 counts
Lower warning level =	19 counts
Upper control limit =	29 counts
Lower control limit =	17 counts

A-8

This report presents one strategy for assessing instrument performance and background based on control charts; it involves simple rule-of-thumb concepts and is taken from Taylor. Other more sophisticated criteria for evaluating whether a measurement system is "out-of-control" can also be used.

A.3.2 Means Control Chart to Evaluate Relative Bias from the Results of Known Exposure Measurements

The results of known exposure measurements (spikes for passive methods and crosschecks for active methods) can also be plotted on a means control chart. Bias may be expressed in terms of relative percent error, or as:

RPE = [(MV-RV)/RV] 100%

where RPE = relative percent error;

MV = measured value of the spiked measurement or the instrument being evaluated; and

RV = reference value (chamber or recently calibrated instrument).

Note that the definition of relative percent error is similar to the definition of individual relative error (IRE), as defined in the RPP handbook, except that the numerator of the IRE is the absolute value of the difference, while RPE can have positive or negative values.

The mean line should be set at zero, and the two-sigma and three-sigma limits can be set using:

1) the coefficient of variation among the RPE values from at least 20 spikes or crosschecks,

or, and only until the results of 20 spikes or crosschecks are available,

2) the average standard deviation as determined via duplicate measurements. Note that this ? option is a temporary measure that should be used only at the inception of an operation until the RPE values from valid spikes or cross-checks are available.

It may be appropriate to construct separate control charts for different ranges of radon concentrations; for example, less than and greater than 4 pCi/L (150 Bq/m³) or 10 pCi/L (370 Bq/m³) if the bias changes non-linearly with concentration.

An example means control chart for using data from spikes from a passive system is shown in Exhibit A-2, and a means control chart for plotting the results of cross-checks using an active system is shown in Exhibit A-3. Data from example spiked measurements are plotted on a means control chart in Exhibit A-2a.

A.4 ESTIMATING PRECISION

The precision of a measurement expresses the degree of reproducibility (repeatability) of that measurement. Precision can be expressed in terms of the standard deviation s or, equivalently, by the variance, s^2. The variance of a measured quantity x, denoted by $s^2(x)$, is the combination of two contributing variances, $s_n^2(x)$ and $s_p^2(x)$:

$$s^2(x) = s_n^2(x) + s_p^2(x)$$

$s_n^2(x)$ is the component of the variance associated with signal-to-noise problems and is closely related to the variability of the noise level; $s_p^2(x)$ is the component of the variance associated with procedures and with measurements not affected by noise variability, such as weighing and handling. At low concentrations, sn becomes the major part of the total variance. This assumption is extremely important because it allows the treatment of the counts measured at low concentrations as exhibiting Poisson distribution. The value for sigma may be different at different radon levels, so assess RPE values at different radon concentrations. If appropriate, keep different control charts for different ranges of radon levels.

The objective of performing more than one measurement is to assess the precision error of the measurement method, or how well side-by-side measurements agree. This precision error is the random component of error (as opposed to the calibration error, which is systematic). The precision error, or the degree of disagreement between duplicates, can be composed of many factors. These include the error caused by the random nature of counting radioactive decay, slight differences between detector construction (for example, small differences in the amount of carbon in activated carbon detectors), and differences in the handling of detectors (for example, differences in the errors of the weighing process, and variations of analysis among detectors).

Exibit A-2

Means Control Chart for Spiked Results of Passive Methods (Chart Used to Assess Bias)		
RPE = [(MV-RV)/RV] * 100 MV = measured spiked result RV = reference or chamber value		
RPE	30%	3 sigma control limit
	20%	2 sigma warning level
	-20%	2 sigma warning level
	-30%	3 sigma control level

Run Number or Date ....

The value of sample standard deviation (sigma) of the RPE values should be calculated from the results of at least 20 spiked results (within the same range of radon concentrations). If this number of spikes has not yet been conducted, the sigma may temporarily be assumed to be 10%, and then revised after calculating the sample standard deviation from the actual RPE values of the spiked results. The control limits on the chart should be drawn at 0 + - 3 * sigma, and the warning levels at 0 + -2 * sigma.

The value for sigma may be different at different radon levels, so assess RPE values at different radon concentrations. If appropriate, keep control charts for ranges of radon levels (e.g., 4 - 20 pCi/L or about 150 - 750 Bq/m³).

A-11

Exhibit A-2a

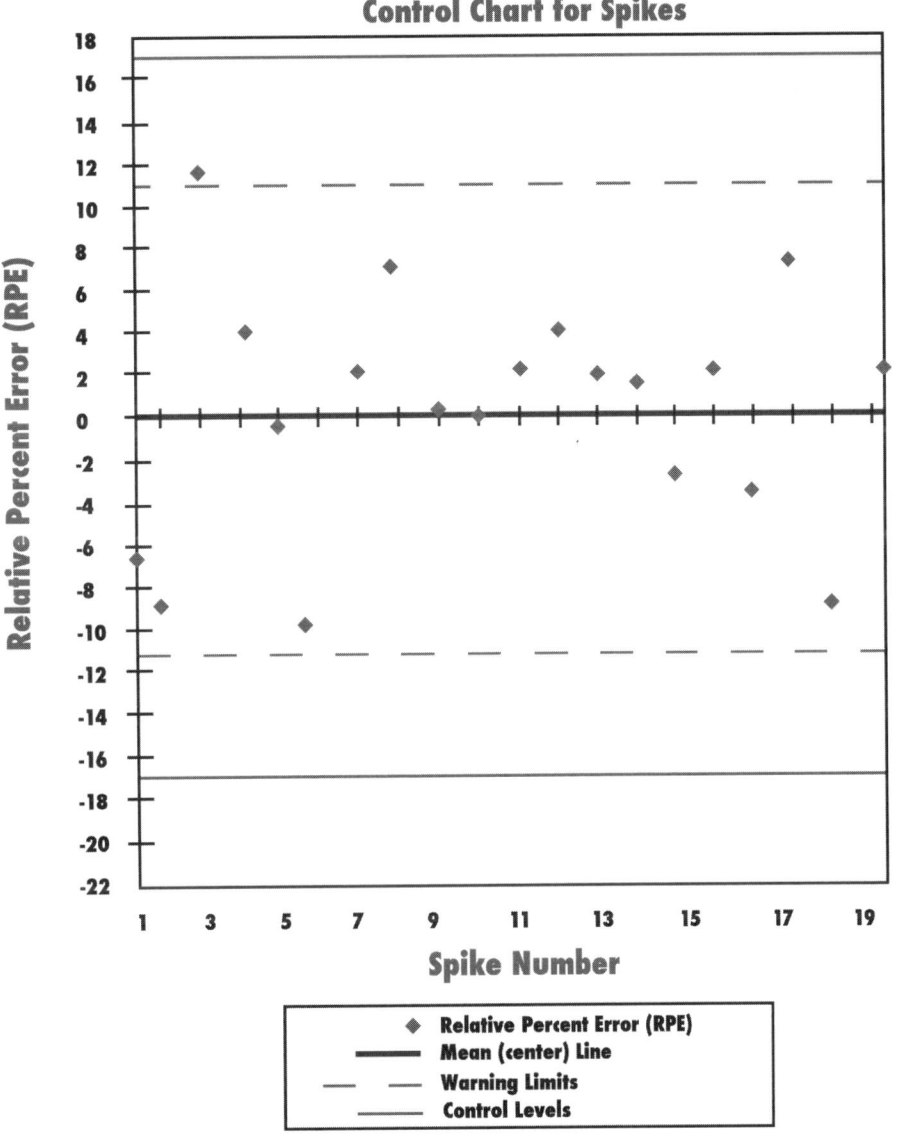

Example Means Control Chart for Relative Bias Based Upon Results of Spikes				
Date	Spike Number	Reference (Chamber) Value	Measured Value (pCi/L)	Relative Percent Error (RPE)
7/14/95	1	25.1	23.5	-6.4
7/14/95	2	25.1	22.9	-8.8
7/14/95	3	25.1	28.0	11.6
7/14/95	4	25.1	26.1	3.9

176

How to Perform Radon Inspections

Example Means Control Chart for Relative Bias Based Upon Results of Spikes				
Date	Spike Number	Reference (Chamber) Value	Measured Value (pCi/L)	Relative Percent Error (RPE)
7/14/95	5	25.1	25.0	-0.4
7/30/95	6	21.6	19.4	-10.2
7/30/95	7	21.6	22.0	1.9
7/30/95	8	21.6	23.1	6.9
7/30/95	9	21.6	21.5	0.0
7/30/95	10	21.6	21.6	0.0
8/13/95	11	32.5	33.1	1.8
8/13/95	12	32.5	34.0	4.6
8/13/95	13	32.5	33.0	1.5
8/13/95	14	32.5	32.9	1.2
8/13/95	15	32.5	31.6	-2.7
8/29/95	16	45.8	46.5	1.5
8/29/95	17	45.8	44.2	-3.5
8/29/95	18	45.8	48.9	6.8
8/29/95	19	45.8	41.8	-8.7
8/29/95	20	45.8	45.0	1.7

Plotted Results	
Mean (Center) Line =	0
Coefficient of Variation of the 20 RPE Values =	5.60%
Warning Limits =	+ 11.2%
Control Levels =	+ 16.8%

Exhibit A-3

Means Control Chart for Cross-Checks Using Active Methods (Chart Used to Assess Bias)		
	RPE = [(MV-RV)/RV] * 100 MV = measured result from instrument to be checked RV = reference value from recently calibrated instrument	
RPE	30%	3 sigma control limit
	20%	2 sigma warning level
	-20%	2 sigma warning level
	-30%	3 sigma control level

Run Number or Date ....

The value of sample standard deviation (sigma) of the RPE values should be calculated from the results of at least about 20 cross-checks (within the same range of radon concentrations). The sample standard deviation of the RPE values is used. If this number of cross-checks has not yet been conducted, the sigma may temporarily be assumed to be 10%, and then revised after calculating the sample standard deviation from the actual RPE values of the cross-check results. The control limits on the chart should be drawn at 0 + - 3 * sigma, and the warning levels at 0 + - 2 * sigma.

It is critical to understand, document, and monitor precision error. This continual monitoring and documentation provides a check on every aspect of the measurement system.

For radiation measurements, counting statistics are often given as the measure of the variability or repeatability of the measurements, primarily because of the ease of calculations. Counting statistics error (i.e., using the square root of the total number of counts as the one-sigma error) is a valid description of the variability of a measurement only when:

- the quantity of nuclide present is so small that the procedure-calibration variability is negligible in contrast with the background variability; and
- all other sources of variability in the background are negligibly small in comparison to counting error (a very rare occurrence).

There is a variety of ways to quantitatively assess the precision error based on duplicate measurements. It is first necessary to understand that precision is characterized by a distribution; that is, side-by-side measurements will exhibit a range of differences. There is some chance that any level of disagreement will be encountered due merely to the statistical fluctuations of counting radioactive decays. The probability of encountering a very large difference between duplicates is smaller than the chance of observing small differences. It's important to recognize that a few duplicate results with high precision errors does not necessarily mean that the measurement system is flawed.

Ideally, the results of duplicates should be assessed in a way that allows for the determination of what level of chance is associated with a particular difference between duplicates. This will allow for the pre-determination of limits for the allowable differences between duplicates as triggers for an investigation into the cause of the large differences. For example, the warning level, or the level of discrepancy between duplicates that triggers an investigation, may be set at 5% probability (or some other level, as desired). At these levels, a difference between duplicates that is so large that, when compared with previous precision errors, it should only be observed (for example) 5% of the time. A control limit, where further measurements should cease until the problem is corrected, may be set at a 1% probability or less. The normal practice is to set control limits corresponding to a three-sigma level, which means that a difference this large would only occur by chance about one-tenth of 1% of the time.

If the data from a particular group of measurements are to be used for a study, and it is desired to attach confidence limits for the precision errors to results, the pooled standard deviation can be calculated for ranges of different radon concentrations. A method of pooling results of duplicate detectors is outlined by the NCRP.

The range ratio is defined as the difference between two measurements divided by the expected difference at that concentration (see the following section). Use of this statistic is recommended because it is normalized to the expected precision at that concentration and, therefore, the same limits can be used for all concentrations. Other statistics, such as the relative percent difference (RPD; difference divided by the mean) or the coefficient of variation (COV; standard deviation divided by the mean), can be used in control charts for duplicate measurements at radon concentrations, where the expected precision error is fairly constant in proportion to the mean (e.g., at levels greater than around 4 pCi/L or 150 Be/m³), and with some upper bound, as determined by duplicate measurements at various concentrations. At lower concentrations, such as between 2 pCi/L (or 80 Bq/m³) and 4 pCi/L (or 150 Bq/m³), a control chart may be developed by plotting these same statistics; however, the proportion of the precision error to the mean will be greater than the proportionate higher concentrations. In either case, the assumption that the precision error is a constant fraction of the mean is a simplification and represents a conservative and convenient way to monitor precision (see Section A.4.2). At concentrations less than about 2 pCi/L, or 80 Bq/m³, the LLD may be approached, and the precision error may be so large as to render a control chart not useful.

A.4.1   Control Charts for Monitoring Precision Error

Before a control chart can be developed, it is necessary to know, from a history of making good quality measurements with the exact measurement system (detectors, analysis equipment, and procedures) that the level of precision that is routinely encountered when the system is operating well or "in control." It is that in-control precision error that forms the basis of the control chart, and upon which all the subsequent duplicate measurements will be judged. There are two ways of initially determining this in-control level. The first and preferable way is to perform at least 20 simultaneous, side-by-side measurements at each range of radon concentrations for which a control chart is to be prepared. For example, if you will only estimate precision at concentrations greater than 4 pCi/L, or 150 Be/m³, you will need at least 20 measurements at concentrations greater than 4 pCi/L, or 150 Be/m³, to assess the in-control level. The average precision error should be the in-control level, and measurements that were suspect should not be included. If using a range ratio control chart (see below), the average range between duplicates exposed to similar concentrations can be used as the in-control level.

The second way to initially set the in-control precision error level is to use a level that has been used by others, and one that is recognized by industry and the EPA as a goal for precision, such as a 10% COV (corresponding to a 14% RPD; see Exhibit A-4). After at least 20 pairs of measurements are plotted, it will become apparent whether the 10% COV (or 14% RPD) is appropriate for your system. If it is not, a new control chart (using the guidelines below) should be prepared so that the warning and control limits are set at appropriate probability limits for your system.

A.4.1.1 Range Ratio Control Chart

A range ratio control chart is an easily understood type of precision control chart that can be very useful when the variability (precision) cannot be simplified as a constant fraction of the mean. The range ratio chart allows all results (greater than the LLD) to be plotted on the same chart, regardless of concentration. This is a sequential chart on which duplicate results are plotted as they are analyzed, with the date and/or other identification on the X-axis. The value that is plotted is the actual difference between duplicates divided by the expected difference at that concentration.

Exhibit A-4
Range (Difference) Between Two Measurements with a 14% Relative Percent Difference (or a 10% Coefficient of Variation)

where Relative Percent Difference (RPD) = [(A-B)/mean] *100

and A = the larger result,
    B = the smaller result, and
mean = the average of the two results

and where Coefficient of Variation (COV) = s/mean

and s = sample standard deviation (see Glossary)

Note that a 14% RPD corresponds to a 10% COV.

Mean	Range (difference), based on 14% RPD
4.3 pCi/L	0.6 pCi/L
4.8	0.7
5.5	0.8
6.1	0.9
7.4	1.0
10.8	1.5
16.2	2.3
21.5	3.0
26.9	3.8

Mean	Range (difference), based on 14% RPD
32.3	4.5
43.0	6.0
53.8	7.5
80.6	11.3
108.0	15.0
215.0	30.0
323.0	45.0
430.0	60.0

Conversion from the traditional U.S. units is not provided for each value here; 1 pCi/L corresponds to 37 Bq/m³; see the Glossary for conversions.

The range ratio, R, is defined as

$$R = Ro/Rc$$

where Ro = the observed range between duplicates, and

Rc = the expected range between duplicates at that concentration.

The center line for this chart would be set at 1, and the upper control limit set at 3.3 (corresponding to about a one-tenth of 1% probability of seeing a range this large), and a warning level of 2.5 (corresponding to about a 2.3% probability of seeing a range this large), or a warning level of 2.2 (corresponding to a 5% probability). An example chart with various limits is shown in Exhibit A-5. Exhibit A-5a presents example duplicate data plotted on a range ratio control chart.

The expected value of the range can be taken from a plot of range versus concentration, as determined from previous measurements at or near that concentration. In the absence of a considerable number of previous measurements, a plot of expected range versus concentration developed from a 10% coefficient of variation can be used (see Exhibit A-4). After about ten in-control measurements have been made near that concentration, the expected range on the plot can be changed.

The probability limits for the range ratios (one-tenth of 1% probability at 3.3, and 5% at 2.2) can be understood using one-tailed statistics, as follows. The difference between two measurements can be termed the range. A frequency plot of the range on the X-axis versus the number of observed duplicates with that range on the Y-axis would show that most duplicates have a value near the mean range, and fewer are out in the tails near zero and the maximum range. The mean range is equal to 1.128 times the standard deviation of a measurement. This can be used to calculate the percentiles for the right-hand tail of the distribution, where large ranges are found. We are not interested in the probabilities in the left tail of the distribution, where the ranges are near zero, and will not include all those small values in the percentiles. Therefore, approximately 50% of the ranges will be between zero, and the mean range, 34%, will be between the mean range and the mean range plus sigma, etc. Only about 0.0013 of the ranges should fall outside the mean range plus three-sigma (sigma of the range).

Exhibit A-5

Control Chart for Duplicates Using the Range Ratio Statistic (to Assess Precision)	
Where the range ratio, R, is defined as: $R = R_o/R_c$; R_o = the observed range between duplicates; and R_c = the expected range between duplicates at that concentration, and the expected range between duplicates is taken from experience, with duplicates near that concentration or, if sufficient data are not yet available, using a plot constructed from the data in Exhibit A-4.	
3.3	99.99% control limit; expect to see a range this great
	only about 0.13% of the time if all is operating in control
2.7	99% control limit; expect to see a range this great
	only about 1% of the time if all is operating in control
2.2	95% warning level; expect to see a range this great
	only about 5% of the time if all is operating in control
1.0	in-control level; range ratio results will routinely be around this level of precision
Date or Sequential Duplicate ID Number	

Exhibit A-5a

Example Range Ratio Control Chart for Tracking Precision						
Date	Dup. No.	A (pCi/L)	8 (pCi/L)	Ro	Re	R=Ro/Re
6/19/95	1	5.5	4.8	0.7	0.7	1.0
6/19/95	2	6.1	5.8	0.3	0.8	0.4
6/22/95	3	6.0	5.2	0.8	0.8	1.0
6/23/95	4	10.2	11.5	1.3	1.5	0.9
6/25/95	5	4.9	5.3	0.4	0.7	0.6
6/25/95	6	4.7	5.8	1.1	0.7	1.6
6/30/95	7	8.5	9.0	0.9	1.3	0.7
7/10/95	8	6.3	7.0	0.7	0.9	0.8
7/14/95	9	10.4	9.0	1.4	1.4	1.0
7/14/95	10	9.8	11.6	1.8	1.5	1.2

Ro = range observed (larger minus smaller result)

Re = range expected at this concentration (initially based on a 14% relative percent difference)

Example Range Ratio Control Chart for Tracking Precision

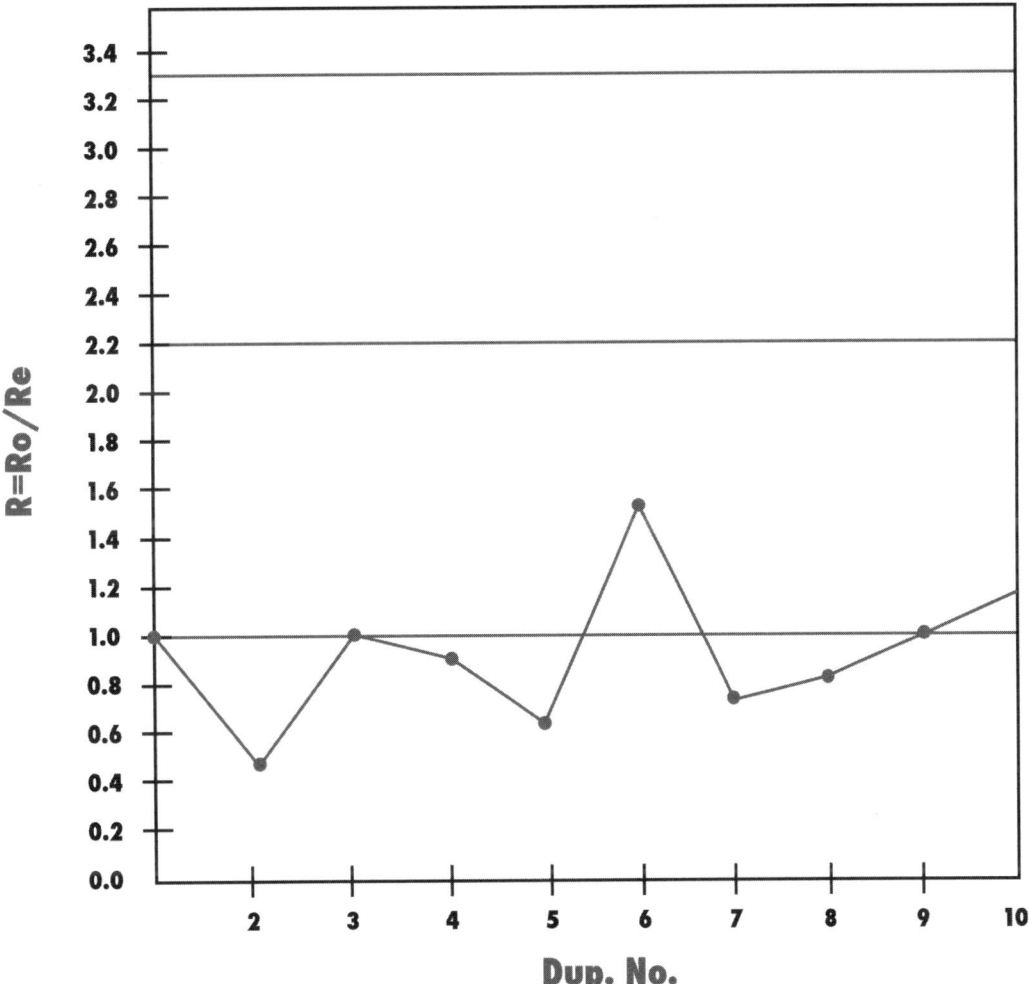

Experience with control charts in the industry has shown that the exact percentages (such as 0.13%) often do not apply, and these percentiles should not be treated as exact numbers. However, the limits are useful as trigger points and reference values.

The probabilistic interpretations of the control chart (e.g., less than 1% of the measurements outside the control limit by chance, and 5% outside the warning limit by chance) will not apply if the expected range is not representative of actual in-control measurements. However, comparing your results with the range given in Exhibit A-4 can serve as a starting point.

A.4.1.2 Sequential Control Chart Based on Coefficient of Variation

An alternate method of plotting the results of duplicates is to use a sequential control chart based on the coefficient of variation.

It can be shown that when the expected precision is a constant function of the mean, control limits can be expressed in terms of the COV (COV = S/Xm, where S is the standard deviation, and Xm is the mean or average of the two measurements). One method for obtaining percentiles for the distribution of the COV is to apply a chi-squared ($X2$) test, where $X2$ can be approximated as follows:

$X^2 = B[(n-1)COV\ 2/(n+(n-1)COV\ 2)]$

Equation 1:

n-1 where: $B = n[1 + (1/COV2)]$;

COVn = the observed COV of the n pair (the pair that is to be evaluated); and

COV = the in-control COV (e.g., 10 percent at levels greater than 4 pCi/L).

For duplicates, where n = 2, Equation 1 becomes $X^2 =$

$[2 + (2/COV2)][COV\ 2/(2 + COV\ 2)]$

Equation 2:

For a value of 0.10 for COV, it further reduces to $X^2 = 202[COV\ 2/(2 + COV\ 2)]$

Referring to an X2 chart, one learns that the probability of exceeding a X2 of 3.84 is only 5%. Inserting this value of 3.84 for X2 and solving for COV, produces a COV of 0.20. This level of probability forms the warning level of 0.20. The control limit corresponds to a X2 of 6.63 and a COVn of 0.26, where the probability of exceeding that value is only about 1%. This sequential control chart should be used by plotting results from each pair on the Y-axis, and noting the date and measurement numbers on the X-axis.

A.4.1.3 Sequential Control Chart Based on Relative Percent Difference

The RPD (or percent difference) is another expression of precision error, and is given by RPD = $[100\backslash x1-x2\backslash]/[(x1+x2)/2]$.

For n=2, RPD = COV f2, the control limits for RPD can be obtained simply by multiplying the control limits for COV by the square root of 2, or 1.41. These limits are 28% and 36%, respectively. This sequential control chart for RPD should be used in the same way as the control chart for COV—that is, with the vertical scale in units of RPD and the horizontal scale in units of date and measurement numbers.

A control chart using the statistic RPD based on an in-control level of 25% RPD can also be constructed. The warning level and control limit are set at 50% and 67%, respectively. Use of these limits maybe appropriate for measured radon concentrations less than 4 pCi/L, or 150 Bq/m³, as determinedly multiple simultaneous measurements at these low concentrations.

A.4.1.4 Range Control Chart

A range control chart, also termed a range performance chart, can be constructed to evaluate precision using the statistics of the range (the difference between two measurements) plotted against the mean of the two measurements. The control limits are again based on the variability of the measurements as decided upon from previous results, or using an industry standard (e.g., 10%).

In this type of control chart, the limits are expressed in terms of the mean range (Rm), where n = 2, Rm = 1.128 s(x), and where s(x) is the standard deviation of a single measurement, which reflects counting and other precision errors. Goldin shows that the limits can be expressed as follows:

- Control limit = 3.69 s(x)
- Warning level = 2.53 s(x)

This type of chart is used by plotting the range versus mean concentration as duplicate measurements are analyzed.

A.4.2 Interpretation of Precision Control Charts

The control chart should be examined carefully every time a new duplicate result is plotted. If a duplicate result falls outside the control limit, repeat the analyses, if possible. If the repeated analyses also fall outside the control limit, stop taking measurements and identify and correct the problem. If any measurements fall outside the warning level, the QA officer is responsible for investigating the system and determining whether corrective action is appropriate.

Note that with the exception of the range ratio control chart, the charts described here are simplifications of actual conditions because they are premised on the assumption that the precision error is a constant fraction of the mean concentration. In fact, the total precision error may best be represented by a different function of the mean concentration—for example, the square root of the concentration. However, methods discussed here present a conservative way to monitor and record measurement error and are useful for comparing observed errors with an industry standard.

A.5 Minimum Detectable Levels

Many terms are now used to express the smallest amount of radioactivity that can be reliably measured. Each term has a specific meaning and is calculated differently. This section reviews some of these terms and the purposes for which they can be used.

These limits are based on counting statistics alone and do not include other errors of precision, including errors caused during manufacture, handling, and analysis. Because of this, the reporting of limits of detection using the following methods must be tempered with the user's knowledge of their system and its capabilities. It is instructional, however, to calculate the lowest detection limit possible based solely on counting statistics, and to know the practical detection limit lies somewhere close to or greater than that level. In addition, it is also useful to review the various terms and their definitions to allow meaningful comparisons among results reportedly different programs.

A.5.1 Lower Limit of Detection (LLD)

The lower limit of detection (LLD) is defined as the smallest amount of sample activity that will yield a net count sufficiently large as to imply its presence. It is based on work by Altshuler and Pasternack, and Currie. It is the quantity that Altshuler and Pasternack called "minimum detectable true activity" and that Currie called the LD, or the a priori detection limit.

The LLD is based on a balance of the risk of false detection of activity not actually present (Type A-25 I error, or false positive) against the risk of missing activity, which is actually present (Type II error, or false negative). Values of a and b represent the probabilities of these errors, respectively.

The derivation of the LLD can be described in the following way. A series of measurements of background made at different times will produce different results. These results will be distributed as a Gaussian frequency distribution, with a spread indicative of the variability of the background. Some laboratories base their LLD only on this frequency distribution—for example, by using two times the standard deviation of the background, and estimating a 95% confidence limit from this value. This method does not take into account the fact that the measurements of true activity (with background subtracted) will also show a frequency distribution. In cases where the radon concentration measured is low, the two distributions will overlap.

The LLD can be approximated by:

$$LLD = (K_a + K_b)(s_o^2 + s_b^2)^{1/2}$$

where

K_a = the value for the upper percentile of the standardized normal variant corresponding to the pre-selected risk for concluding falsely that activity is present (e.g., a value of 1.96 for an upper-tail risk of a = 0.025);

K_b = the corresponding value for the pre-determined degree of confidence for detecting the presence of activity (1 - b); and

s_o and s_b = the standard deviation for the observed (true activity plus background) and background activity, respectively.

If the values of a and b are set at the same level (i.e., if one is willing to take the same risk for concluding falsely that activity is present as for missing the presence of activity), then $K_a = K_b$.

The formula then reduces to:

$$LLD = 2K_a(s_o^2 + s_b^2)^{1/2}$$

If $s_o = s_b$ (i.e., the variability of the observed activity is the same as the variability of the background), then

$$LLD = 2^{3/2}K_a s_b$$

The values of K are given as tables of the normal distribution in statistical texts; some common values are given below.

a	1-b	K	$2^{3/2}K$
0.01	0.9	2.327	6.59
0.02	0.98	2.054	5.81
0.025	0.975	1.960	5.54
0.05	0.95	1.645	4.65
0.10	0.90	1.282	3.63
0.20	0.80	0.842	2.38
0.50	0.50	0.000	0.00

Therefore, for a 95% confidence level for detecting activity when it is present (1-b = 0.95), the LLD is set equal to 4.65 times the standard deviation of the background counts, or LLD = 4.65 s_b, when:

1. the background is relatively stable;

2. the measurement and background counting times are equal; and

3. the distribution of the background counts follows a Gaussian distribution.

This means that with this LLD, one accepts the chance of detecting activity when it is present 95% of the time but missing it 5% of the time. The NRC applies the same definition: "the LLD is defined as the smallest concentration of radioactive material sampled that has a 95% probability of being detected, with only a 5% probability that a blank sample will yield a response interpreted to mean that radioactive material is present. In other words, there is only a 5% chance of concluding that activity is present when it is not, and a 95% chance of correctly concluding that activity is present when it actually is."

The value of K for a 50% chance shows that the LLD is zero if one is willing to accept a 50% chance of detecting activity when it is present. The nature of the LLD should be kept in mind. It is an *a priori* estimate of the quantity of activity that will be detected with a given confidence.

The limitations of the LLD should also be considered. Foremost among these are the assumptions that so = sb and that the variability in the background is entirely Poisson. For example, with a background count rate of 1 cpm and a 50-minute counting time, the LLD is 4.65 (.02)1/2, or 0.66 cpm. The counting rate for a sample plus background is 1.66 cpm, so that its Poisson variance is 1.66/50, or 0.033. Approximating this by the variance of the background counting rate 0.02 introduces an underestimate of 15% in the LLD. This underestimate is larger for a small number of background counts (low background counting rate combined with short counting times), and smaller for a larger number of background counts. This limitation of the LLD is particularly severe in alpha spectrometry, where the total background count in a peak area may be only 1 or 2, even with counting times of several hundred minutes. For such low total counts, the assumption that the Poisson distribution can be approximated by a normal distribution also breaks down.

An alternate and more statistically sophisticated formula accounts for the case when repeated measurements of the blank yield significant variation. This formula adds a term:

$$LLD = 2.71 + 4.65s_b$$

$$LLD = 4.65s_b$$

Note that both formulas apply only for equal blank and sample counting times. For unequal counting times:

$$LLD = [3 + 3.29\ (R_b t_g\ [1 + t_g\ /t_b\ ])^{1/2}]/t_g$$

where R_b = background count rate;

t_b = background count time;

and t_g = gross count time.

Note that the electret ion chamber manufacturer does not calculate the LLD using these formulas, which were developed for radiation counting. Users of electret systems should consult the manufacturer for details of the LLD approximations specific to electret ion chamber systems.

A.5.2 Minimum Significant Measured Activity (MSMA)

Altshuler and Pasternack defined the minimum significant measured activity (MSMA) as the smallest measurement interpreted to demonstrate the presence of activity in the sample. Currie called this quantity LC or the critical level. These terms refer to the evaluation of a gross measurement after it has been made as being significantly greater than background or, equivalently, a net measurement as being greater than zero. The test for this is the conventional statistical test of a difference as being greater than zero.

If expressed in terms of counting rate, the net counting rate r is the difference between the gross observed counting rate ro, and the background counting rate rb.

The variance of r is:

$$s^2(r) = s^2(r_o) + s^2(r_b)$$

$$= (r_o/t_o) + (r_b/t_b)$$

If $t_o = t_b = t$ (i.e., the counting times for the sample and background are equal),

$$s^2(r) = (r_o + r_b)/t$$

If $r_o = r_b$, then $s^2(r) = 2\, r_b/t$.

The net measurement has conventionally been considered to be significantly different from zero at the .05 level if $t > 1.96$. Actually, the one-sided test for which $t_{.05} = 1.65$ is probably more appropriate.

The t statistic is defined as:

$$t = (r_o - r_b)/s(r)$$

For $t = 1.96$, the MSMA is the corresponding difference of counting rates: MSMA = $1.96\, (2r_b/t_b)^{1/2}$ = $2.77\, (r_b/t_b)^{1/2}$.

A.5.3 Use of LLD and MSMA

Both the LLD and the MSMA are useful when each is restricted to its proper sphere. The LLD is a prediction of measurement capability; MSMA is an evaluation of a completed measurement. The LLD should be used when describing a system's measurement capability (e.g., in proposals). The LLD has been used improperly to evaluate a completed measurement. When this is done, there is a gray area between the point where the measurement, as evaluated by MSMA, has not been shown to be different from a background 2.77 s_b, and the LLD, 4.65 s_b. LLD cannot address measurements in this range.

The MSMA has been used also improperly to estimate minimum detectable activity. The MSMA is equal to an LLD with kb = 0. This corresponds to a probability of 0.5 of detection. The MSMA, when used in this way, corresponds to only a 50% chance of detecting activity.

A.5.4 Reporting Low Values

The result obtained in a measurement, which is a sample of the infinite population of possible results, is the best estimate of the mean value of the population. These actual results, whether greater than or less than the LLD, and whether positive, negative, or zero, should be used in averaging. Elimination of results less than the LLD, or of results less than zero, introduces bias into the overall average value.

Measurement organizations need to maintain records of all results as measured, which will include negative values in some cases. However, reporting results less than the LLD or less than zero to most clients will not serve the clients' or the measurement organizations' interests. When appropriate, results less than the LLD should be reported as less than the lower limit of detection, including the LLD, as recently calculated using results of background measurements.

Quiz #7

1. _____ is defined as all activities required to provide the evidence needed to establish confidence that data provided are of the required precision and accuracy.

   ☐ QC or quality control

   ☐ QM or quality management

   ☐ QA or quality assurance

2. The EPA defines _____ as an integrated system or program of activities involving planning, quality control, quality assessment, reporting and quality improvement to ensure that a product or service meets defined standards of quality.

   ☐ QA

   ☐ QM

   ☐ QC

3. T/F: There are many quality-control measurements that are performed to assess the quality of procured material and equipment, the continued performance of instruments and procedures, estimated errors of imprecision and bias, and contributions of field and laboratory background.

   ☐ True

   ☐ False

4. The establishment of a QA program _____ a QA officer within the organization to supervise and, as appropriate, carry out the monitoring, recordkeeping, statistical techniques, and other functions required to maintain high-quality data.

   ☐ requires

   ☐ does not require

5. Organizations should assure that all work affecting quality of results (such as handling, storing, and analyzing devices) be prescribed in clear and complete written instructions, which are known as _____.

   ☐ QA

   ☐ SOPs or standard operating procedures

   ☐ QC

6. The term _____ refers to the process of determining the response of an instrument (or measurement system) to a series of known values over the range of the instrument (or measurement system).

   ☐ assurance

   ☐ calibration

   ☐ qualification

   ☐ duplication

7. _____ refer to errors that occur consistently and cause a consistently high or low bias in the result.

    ☐ Accuracy errors

    ☐ Random errors

    ☐ Systematic errors

    ☐ Precision errors

8. _____ is the closeness of agreement between a measurement result (or the average of more than one result) and an accepted reference value.

    ☐ Randomness

    ☐ Accuracy

    ☐ Precision

Answer Key is on page 350.

Passive Devices

Considerations for Passive and Active Devices

The risk of lung cancer due to exposure to radon and its decay products is of concern to state and federal health officials. There is increased awareness that indoor radon concentrations may pose a significant health threat, and that there are areas in the country where some indoor levels are such that even short-term exposures can cause a significant increase in risk. It is extremely important that homes and other buildings be tested to determine if elevated radon levels are present indoors. However, in the process, the collection of unreliable or misleading data must be avoided.

There are many federal, state, university, and private organizations now performing measurements or planning measurement programs. It is important for these different groups to follow consistent procedures to assure accurate and reproducible measurements, and to enable valid inter-comparison of measurement results from different studies.

The objective of this section is to present information, recommendations, and technological guidance for anyone providing measurement services using 15 radon and radon-decay product measurement methods. The EPA has evaluated these techniques and found them to be satisfactory. However, the agency has not conducted large-scale field tests using the unfiltered track-detection technique, and an interim protocol has been prepared with the assistance of researchers who have field experience with this method. As the EPA and others acquire more experience with this interim technique, the relevant guidelines may be revised.

These protocols provide method-specific technological guidance that can be used as the basis for standard operating procedures. In keeping with good laboratory practices, each radon measurement company should develop its own detailed, instrument-specific procedures that incorporate recommendations found in this and other radon-related EPA protocol and guidance documents. Mere duplication of sections of this information will not constitute an adequate standard operating procedure.

The recommendations contained in this report are similar to those being developed by industry and other groups, including the American Society of Testing and Materials (ASTM) and the American Association of Radon Scientists and Technologists (AARST). This information should be used as guidance; however, one condition of participation in the EPA's National Radon Proficiency Program (RPP) was conformance with these protocols.

General Guidance on Measurement Strategy, Measurement Conditions, Device Location Selection, and Documentation Measurement Strategy

The choice of measurement strategy depends upon the purpose of the radon measurement and the type of building where the measurement is made, such as a home, school or workplace. The EPA's recommendations for measuring radon in various situations are outlined in the second edition of *A Citizen's Guide to Radon*, the EPA's *Home Buyer's and Seller's Guide to Radon*, the *Protocols for Radon and Radon Decay Product Measurements in Homes*, and in *Radon Measurements in Schools*. The following discussion on measurement conditions, device location selection, and documentation apply to measurements made in all types of buildings.

Measurement Conditions

The following conditions should exist prior to and during a measurement period to standardize the measurement conditions as much as possible.

Short-term measurements lasting 90 days or less should be made under closed-building conditions. To the extent reasonable, all windows, outside vents and external doors should be closed (except for normal entrance and exit) for 12 hours prior to and during the measurement period. Normal entrance and exit include opening and closing a door, but an external door should not be left open for more than a few minutes. These conditions are expected to exist as normal living conditions during the winter in northern climates. For this reason, short-term measurements should be made during winter periods whenever possible.

In addition to maintaining closed-building conditions during the measurement, closed-building conditions are required for 12 hours prior to the initiation of the measurement for those lasting less than four days, and are recommended prior to measurements of up to a week.

Internal-external air exchange systems (other than a furnace), such as high-volume attic and window fans, should not be operating during measurements and for at least 12 hours before measurements are initiated. Air-conditioning systems that recycle interior air may continue to operate. Normal operation of permanently installed air-to-air heat exchangers may also continue during closed-building conditions.

In buildings where permanent radon mitigation systems have been installed, these systems should be functioning during the measurement period.

Short-term tests lasting just two or three days should not be conducted if severe storms with high winds (greater than 30 mph) or rapidly changing barometric pressure are predicted during the measurement period. Weather predictions available on local news stations can provide sufficient information to determine if these conditions are likely.

In southern climates, or when measurements must be made during a warm season, the closed-building conditions are satisfied by meeting the criteria listed above. The closed-building conditions must be verified and maintained more rigorously, however, when they are not the normal living conditions.

Measurement Device Location Selection

The following criteria should be applied to select the location of the detector within a room. For further guidance on selecting an appropriate area in a building in which to place the measurement device, refer to the previous sections.

A position should be selected where the detector will not be disturbed during the measurement period and where there is adequate room for the device. The measurement should not be made near drafts caused by heating, ventilating, and air-conditioning vents, doors, fans, or windows. Locations near excessive heat, such as fireplaces or in direct sunlight, and areas of high humidity should be avoided.

The measurement location should not be within 3 feet of windows or other potential openings in the exterior wall. If there are no openings (such as windows) in the exterior wall, then the measurement location should not be within 1 foot of the exterior walls of the building.

The detector should be at least 20 inches from the floor, and at least 4 inches from other objects. For those detectors that may be suspended, an optimal height for placement is in the general breathing zone, such as 6 to 8 feet from the floor. In general, measurements should not be made in kitchens, laundry rooms, closets or bathrooms.

Documentation

The operator of the measurement device must record enough information about the measurement in a permanent log so that data interpretation and comparison can be made.

The results of radon-decay product measurements should be reported in working levels (WL). If the WL value is converted to a radon concentration, which is also reported to the homeowner, it should be stated that this approximate conversion is based on a 50% equilibrium ratio. In addition, the report should indicate that this ratio is typical of the home environment, but any indoor environment (especially in schools and workplaces) may have a different and varying relationship between radon and decay products.

The following list may be applied to each of the measurement methods (however, there may be method-specific documentation requirements that will be mentioned in the applicable protocol):

- the start and stop times and dates of the measurement;
- whether the standardized measurement conditions are satisfied;
- the exact location of the device—on a diagram of the room and building, if possible;
- easily obtained information that may be useful, such as the type of building and heating system, the existence of a crawlspace or basement, the occupants' smoking habits, and the operation of humidifiers, air filters, electrostatic precipitators, and clothes dryers;
- the serial number and manufacturer of the detector, along with the code number or description that uniquely identifies the customer, building, room, and sampling position; and
- the condition (open or closed) of any crawlspace vents.

Quality Assurance

The objective of quality assurance is to ensure that data are scientifically sound and of known precision and accuracy. This section discusses the four general categories of quality control measurements; specific guidance is provided for each method in the relevant section.

Anyone providing measurement services using radon and radon decay-product measurement devices should establish and maintain quality assurance programs. These programs should include written procedures for attaining quality assurance objectives, and a system for recording and monitoring the results of the quality assurance measurements described below. The EPA offers general guidance on preparing quality assurance plans; a draft standard prepared by a radon industry group is also available. The quality assurance program should include the maintenance of control charts and related statistical data, as described by Goldin and the EPA.

Calibration Measurements

Calibration measurements are samples collected or measurements made in a known radon environment, such as a calibration chamber. Detectors requiring analysis (such as charcoal canisters, alpha track detectors, electret ion chambers, and radon progeny integrating samplers) are exposed in a calibration chamber and then analyzed. Instruments providing immediate results, such as continuous working-level and radon monitors, should be operated in a chamber to establish individual instrument calibration factors.

Calibration measurements must be conducted to determine and verify the conversion factors used to derive the concentration results. These factors are determined normally for a range of concentrations and exposure times, and for a range of other exposure and/or analysis conditions pertinent to the particular device. Determination of these calibration factors is a necessary part of the laboratory analysis, and is the responsibility of the analysis laboratory. These calibration measurement procedures, including the frequency of tests and the number of devices to be tested, should be specified in the quality assurance program maintained by manufacturers and analysis laboratories.

Known exposure measurements or spiked samples consist of detectors that have been exposed to known concentrations in a radon calibration chamber. These detectors are labeled and submitted to the laboratory in the same manner as ordinary samples to preclude special processing. The results of these measurements are used to monitor the accuracy of the entire measurement system. Suppliers and analysis laboratories should provide for the blind introduction of spiked samples into their measurement processes, and the monitoring of the results in their quality assurance programs. Providers of passive measurement devices should conduct spiked measurements at a rate of three per 100 measurements, with a minimum of three per year, and a maximum required of six per month. Providers of measurements with active devices are required to re-calibrate their instruments at least once every 12 months. Participation in the EPA's former National Radon Proficiency Program (RPP) did not satisfy the need for annual calibration, as this program was a performance test and not a calibration procedure.

Background Measurements

Background measurements are required for continuous monitors and for passive detectors requiring laboratory analysis. Users of continuous monitors must perform sufficient instrument background measurements to establish a reliable instrument background, and to act as a check on instrument operation.

Passive detectors requiring laboratory analysis require one type of background measurement made in the laboratory and another in the field. Suppliers and analysis laboratories should routinely measure the background of a statistically significant number of unexposed detectors from each batch or lot to establish the laboratory background for the batch and the entire measurement system. This laboratory blank value is subtracted routinely (by the laboratory) from the field sample results reported to the user, and should be made available to the users for quality assurance purposes. In addition to these background measurements, the organization performing the measurements should calculate the lower limit of detection (LLD) for its measurement system. This LLD is based on the detector and analysis system's background and can restrict the ability of some measurement systems to measure low concentrations.

Providers of passive detectors should employ field controls (called blanks) equal to approximately 5% of the detectors that are deployed, or 25 each month, whichever is smaller. These controls should be set aside from each detector shipment, kept sealed and in a low-radon environment, labeled in the same manner as the field samples to preclude special processing, and returned to the analysis laboratory along with each shipment. These field blanks measure the background exposure that may accumulate during shipment and storage, and the results should be monitored and recorded. The recommended action to be taken if the concentrations measured by one or more of the field blanks is significantly greater than the LLD is dependent upon the type of detector and is discussed in the section for each method.

Duplicate (Collocated) Measurements

Duplicate measurements provide a check on the quality of the measurement result and allow the user to make an estimate of the relative precision. Large precision errors may be caused by detector manufacture, or improper data transcription or handling by suppliers, laboratories or technicians performing placements. Precision error can be an important component of the overall error, so it is important that all users monitor precision.

Duplicate measurements should be side-by-side measurements made in at least 10% of the total number of measurement locations, or 50 each month, whichever is smaller. The locations selected for duplication should be distributed systematically throughout the entire population of samples. Groups selling measurements to homeowners can do this by providing two measurements (instead of one) to a random selection of purchasers, with the measurements made side by side. As with spiked samples introduced into the system as blind measurements, the precision of duplicate measurements should be monitored and recorded in the quality assurance records. The analysis of data from duplicates should follow the methodology described by Goldin in part 5.3 of his report, and plotted on range control charts. If the precision estimated by the user is not within the precision expected of the measurement method, the problem should be reported to the analysis laboratory and the cause investigated.

Routine Instrument Performance Checks

Proper functioning of analysis equipment and operator usage require that the equipment and measurement system be subject to routine checks. Regular monitoring of equipment and operators is vital to ensure consistently accurate results. Performance checks of analysis equipment include the frequent use of an instrument check source. In addition, important components of the device (such as a pump, battery and electronics) should be checked regularly, and the results noted in a log. Each user should develop methods for regularly monitoring their measurement system (preferably, daily), and for recording and reviewing results.

The EPA established the National RMP Program (the National Radon Proficiency Program, or RPP) under the Indoor Radon Abatement Act of 1988 to enable participants to demonstrate their proficiency at measuring radon and radon decay product concentrations. One condition of successful participation in the former RPP was that the total error of any individual device (including errors in both precision and accuracy) be within ±25% of the "true" radon or radon decay product concentration at or above 4 pCi/L. For further information on the former RPP and the two private proficiency programs run by the NEHA and the NRSB, visit the EPA's website at **www.epa.gov**.

Continuous Working-Level (CW) Monitors

Protocol for Using Continuous Working-Level (CW) Monitors to Measure Indoor Radon-Decay Product Concentrations

This protocol provides guidance for using continuous working-level (CW) monitors to obtain accurate and reproducible measurements of indoor radon-decay product concentrations. Adherence to this protocol will help ensure uniformity among measurement programs and allow valid inter-comparison of results. Measurements made in accordance with this protocol will produce results representative of closed-building conditions. Measurements made under closed-building conditions have a smaller variability and are more reproducible than measurements made when the building conditions are not controlled. The investigator should also follow guidance provided by the EPA in *Protocols for Radon and Radon Decay Product Measurements in Homes*, or other appropriate EPA measurement guidance documents.

Scope

This protocol covers, in general terms, the sample collection and analysis method, the equipment needed, and the quality control objectives of measurements made with CW. It is not meant to replace an instrument manual but, rather, to provide guidelines to be incorporated into standard operating procedures by anyone providing measurement services. Questions about these guidelines should be directed to the EPA.

Method

The CW method samples the ambient air by filtering airborne particles as the air is drawn through a filter cartridge at a low flow rate of about 0.1 to 1 liter per minute. An alpha detector, such as a diffused-junction or surface-barrier detector, counts the alpha particles produced by the radon decay products as they decay on the filter. The detector is set normally to detect alpha particles with energies between 2 and 8 MeV. The alpha particles emitted from the radon decay products Radium A (Po-218) and Radium C (Po-214) are the significant contributors to the events that are measured by the detector. All CW detectors are capable of measuring individual radon and thoron decay products, while some can be adapted to measure the percentage of thoron decay products. The event count is directly proportional to the number of alpha particles emitted by the radon decay products on the filter. A typical unit contains a microprocessor that stores the number of counts and the elapsed time. The CW detector can be set to record the total counts registered over specified time periods. The unit must be calibrated in a calibration facility to convert the count rate to working-level (WL) values. This may be done initially by the manufacturer, and should be done periodically thereafter by the operator.

Equipment

In addition to the CW detector, the equipment needed includes replacement filters, a readout or programming device (if not part of the detector), an alpha-emitting check source, and an air flow-rate meter.

Pre-Deployment Considerations

The plans of the occupant during the proposed measurement period should be considered before deployment. The CW measurement should not be made if the occupant will be moving during the measurement period. Deployment should be delayed until the new occupant is settled in the house.

The CW detector should not be deployed if the user's schedule prohibits terminating the measurement at the appropriate time.

Pre-Sampling Testing

The CW detector should be tested carefully before and after each measurement in order to:

- verify that a new filter has been installed, and the input parameters and clock are set properly;
- measure the detector's efficiency with a check source, such as Am-241 or Th-230, and ascertain that it compares well with the technical specifications for the unit; and
- verify the operation of the pump.

When feasible, the unit should be checked after every fourth 48-hour measurement or week of operation to measure the background count rate using the procedures that are in the operating manual for the instrument.

In addition, participation in a laboratory inter-comparison program should be conducted initially, at least once every 12 months thereafter, and after equipment repair to verify that the conversion factor used by the microprocessor is accurate. This is done by comparing the unit's response to a known radon-decay product concentration. At this time, the correct operation of the pump also should be verified by measuring the flow rate.

DEPLOYMENT AND OPERATION

Location Selection

A standard criteria must be considered when choosing a measurement device location.

Operation

The CW detector should be programmed to run continuously, recording the periodic integrated WL and, when possible, the total integrated average WL. The sampling period should be 48 hours, with a grace period of two hours (i.e., a sampling period of 46 hours is acceptable if conditions prohibit terminating sampling after exactly 48 hours). The longer the operating time, the smaller the uncertainty associated with using the measurement result to estimate a longer-term average concentration. The integrated average WL over the measurement period should be reported as the measurement result. If results are also reported in pCi/L, it should be stated that this approximate conversion is based on a 50% equilibrium ratio, which is typical of the home environment, and any individual environment may have a different relationship between radon and decay products.

Retrieval of Detectors

When the measurement is terminated, the operator should note the stop date and stop time, and whether the standardized conditions are still in effect.

Documentation

Standard information must be documented so that data interpretation and comparison can be made. In addition, the serial number of the CW detector and calibration factor used should be recorded.

ANALYSIS REQUIREMENTS

Sensitivity

All known commercially available CW detectors are capable of a lower limit of detection (LLD) of 0.01 WL or less.

Precision

Precision should be monitored and recorded using the results of side-by-side measurements. This method can produce duplicate measurements with a coefficient of variation of 10% or less at 0.02 WL or greater. An alternate measure of precision is a relative percent difference, defined as the difference between two duplicate measurements divided by their mean; note that these two measures of precision are not identical quantities. It is important that precision be monitored frequently over a range of radon concentrations, and that a systematic and documented method for evaluating changes in precision be part of the operating procedures.

Quality Assurance

The quality assurance program for a CW system includes four parts:

1. calibration and known exposures;

2. background measurements;

3. duplicate measurements; and

4. routine instrument checks.

The purpose of a quality assurance program is to identify the accuracy and precision of the measurements, and to ensure that the measurements are not influenced by exposure from sources outside the environment to be measured. The quality assurance program should include the maintenance of control charts; general information is also available.

Calibration and Known Exposures

Every CW detector should be calibrated in a radon calibration chamber before being put into service, and after any repairs or modifications. Subsequent re-calibrations should be done once every 12 months, with cross-checks to a recently calibrated instrument at least semi-annually.

Background Measurements

Background count-rate checks must be conducted after at least every 168 hours or fourth 48-hour measurement of operation, and whenever the unit is calibrated. The CW should be purged with clean, aged air or nitrogen, in accordance with the procedures given in the instrument's operating manual. In addition, the background count rate may be monitored more frequently by operating the CW in a low-radon environment.

Duplicate Measurements

When two or more CW detectors are available, the precision of the measurements can be estimated by operating the detectors side by side. The analysis of duplicate results should follow the methodology described by Goldin, Taylor, or the EPA. Whatever procedures are used must be documented prior to beginning measurements. Consistent failure in duplicate agreement may indicate a problem in the measurement process and should be investigated.

Routine Instrument Checks

Checks using an Am-241 or similar energy alpha check source must be performed before and after each measurement. In addition, it is important to regularly check all components of the equipment that affect the result. Pump and flow meters should be checked routinely to ensure the accuracy of volume measurements. This may be performed using a dry-gas meter or other flow measurement device of traceable accuracy.

Alpha Track Detectors (AT or ATD)

Protocol for Using Alpha Track Detectors (AT or ATD) to Measure Indoor Radon Concentrations

Purpose

This protocol provides guidance for using alpha track detectors (AT or ATD) to obtain accurate and reproducible measurements of indoor radon concentrations. Adherence to this protocol will help ensure uniformity among measurement programs and allow valid inter-comparison of results. The investigator should also follow guidance provided by the EPA in *Protocols for Radon and Radon Decay Product Measurements in Homes,* or other appropriate EPA measurement guidance documents.

Scope

This protocol covers, in general terms, the equipment, procedures, and quality control objectives to be used in performing the measurements. It is not meant to replace an instrument manual but instead to present guidelines to be incorporated into standard operating procedures by anyone providing measurement services. Questions about these guidelines should be directed to the EPA.

Method

An AT consists of a small piece of plastic or film enclosed in a container with a filter-covered opening or similar design for excluding radon decay products. Radon diffuses into the container, and alpha particles emitted by the radon and its decay products strike the detector and produce sub-microscopic damage tracks. At the end of the measurement period, the detectors are turned in to a laboratory. Plastic detectors are placed in a caustic solution that accentuates the damage tracks so that they can be counted using a microscope or an automated counting system. The number of tracks per unit area is correlated to the radon concentration in air using a conversion factor derived from data generated at a calibration facility. The number of tracks per unit of analyzed detector area produced per unit of time (minus the background) is proportional to the radon concentration. AT detectors function as true integrators and measure the average concentration over the exposure period.

Many factors contribute to the variability of AT results, including differences in the detector responses within and between batches of plastic, non-uniform plate-out of decay products inside the detector holder, differences in the number of background tracks, and variations in etching conditions. Since the variability in AT results decreases with the number of net tracks counted, counting more tracks over a larger area of the detector, particularly at low exposures, will reduce the uncertainty of the result.

Equipment

ATs are available from commercial suppliers. These suppliers offer contract services in which they provide the detector and subsequent analysis and reporting for a fixed price. Establishing an in-house capability to provide packaged detectors, a calibration program, and an analysis program would probably not be practical or economically advantageous for most users. Therefore, details for establishing the analytical aspects of an AT program are omitted from this protocol. Additional details concerning AT programs have been reviewed elsewhere.

Assuming ATs are obtained from a commercial supplier, the following equipment is needed to initiate a measurement:

- an AT in an individual sealed container (such as an aluminized plastic bag) to prevent extraneous exposure before deployment;

- a means to attach the AT to its measurement location, if it is to be hung from the wall or ceiling;

- an instruction sheet for the occupant, a sample log sheet, and a shipping container (along with a prepaid mailing label, if appropriate);

- manufacturer's instructions for re-sealing the detector at the time of retrieval and prior to returning it to the supplier for analysis; and

- a data collection log, if appropriate.

Pre-Deployment Considerations

The plans of the occupant during the proposed measurement period should be considered before deployment. The AT measurement should not be made if the occupant will be moving during the measurement period. Deployment should be delayed until the new occupant is settled in the house.

The AT should not be deployed if the user's schedule prohibits terminating the measurement at the appropriate time.

Measurement Criteria

General conditions must be met to ensure standardization of measurement conditions.

A 12-month AT measurement provides information about radon concentrations in a building during an entire year, so the closed-building conditions do not have to be satisfied to perform a valid year-long measurement.

DEPLOYMENT

Location Selection

Standard criteria must be considered when choosing a measurement device location.

If the detector is installed during a site visit, the final site selected should be shown to the building occupant to be certain it is acceptable for the duration of the measurement period.

Timely Deployment

A group of ATs should be deployed into houses as soon as possible after delivery from the supplier. In order to minimize chances of high background exposures, users should not order more ATs than they can reasonably expect to install within the following few months. If the storage time exceeds more than a few months, the background exposures from a sample of the stored detectors should be assessed to determine if they are different from the background of detectors that are not stored for long periods. The supplier's instructions regarding storage and background determination should be followed. This background assessment of detectors stored for long periods is not necessary if the analysis laboratory routinely measures the background of stored detectors, and if the stored detectors remain tightly sealed.

The sampling period begins when the protective cover or bag is removed. The edge of the bag must be cut carefully, or the cover removed, so that it can be reused to re-seal the detector at the end of the exposure period. The detector and the radon-proof container should be inspected to make sure that they are intact and have not been physically damaged in shipment or handling.

Retrieval of Detectors

At the end of the measurement period (usually 90 days for short-term tests, and one year for long-term measurements), the detector should be inspected for damage or deviation from the conditions entered in the logbook at the time of deployment. Any changes should be noted in the logbook. The time and date of removal should be entered on the data form for the detector and in the logbook, if used. The detector should then be re-sealed according to the instructions provided by the supplier. After retrieval, the detectors should be stored in a low-radon environment and returned as soon as possible to the analytical laboratory for processing. In many cases, attempts at re-sealing ATs have not been totally successful, resulting in some continued exposure of the detectors beyond the deployment period. This extra exposure could bias the results high if the detectors are held for a significant length of time prior to analysis.

Documentation

Standard information should be documented.

ANALYSIS REQUIREMENTS

Sensitivity

The lower limit of detection (LLD) is dependent upon the stability of the number of background tracks. The background may be less variable if a greater area is analyzed. With today's ATs, routine counting can achieve an LLD of 1 pCi/L-month, and an LLD of 0.2 pCi/L-month may be achieved by counting additional area.

Precision

The precision should be monitored using the results of the duplicate detectors, rather than a precision quoted by the manufacturer. The precision of an AT system is dependent upon the total number of tracks counted on the flank and test detector and, therefore, the area of the detector that is analyzed. If few net tracks are counted, poor precision is obtained. Thus, it is important that the organization performing the measurement with an AT arranges for counting an adequate area or number of net tracks.

Quality Assurance

The quality assurance program for AT measurements involves five separate parts:

1. calibration;
2. known exposure measurements;
3. duplicate (collocated) detectors;
4. control detectors; and
5. routine instrument checks.

The purpose of a quality assurance program is to identify the accuracy and precision of the measurements, and to ensure that the measurements are not influenced by exposure from sources outside the environment to be measured. The quality assurance program should include the maintenance of control charts; general information is also available.

Calibration

Every AT laboratory system should be calibrated in a radon calibration chamber at least once every 12 months. Determination of a calibration factor requires exposure of ATs to a known radon concentration in a radon exposure chamber. These calibration exposures are to be used to obtain or verify the conversion factor between net tracks per unit area and radon concentration. (Participation in the EPA's former National Radon Proficiency Program [RPP] did not satisfy the need for annual calibration, as this program was a proficiency test rather than an internal calibration.)

The following guidance is provided to manufacturers and suppliers of AT services as minimum requirements in determining the calibration factor:

- ATs should be exposed in a radon chamber at several different radon concentrations or exposure levels similar to those found in the tested buildings (a minimum of three different concentrations).

- A minimum of 10 detectors should be exposed at each level.

- A calibration factor should be determined for each batch or sheet of detector material received from the material supplier. Alternatively, calibration factors may be established from several sheets, and these factors extended to detectors from sheets exhibiting similar sensitivities (within pre-established tolerance limits).

Known Exposure Measurements

Anyone providing measurement services with AT devices should submit ATs with known radon exposures (spiked samples) for analysis at a rate of three per 100 measurements, with a minimum of three per year and a maximum required of six per month. Known exposure (spiked) detectors should be labeled in the same manner as field detectors to ensure identical processing. The results of the spiked detector analyses should be monitored and recorded. Any significant deviation from the known concentration to which they were exposed should be investigated.

Duplicate (Collocated) Detectors

Anyone providing measurement services with AT devices should place duplicate detectors in enough houses to test the precision of the measurement. The number of duplicate detectors deployed should be approximately 10% of the number of detectors deployed each month, or 50, whichever is smaller. The pair of detectors should be treated identically in every respect. They should be shipped, stored, opened, installed, removed, and processed together, and not identified as duplicates to the processing laboratory. The samples selected for duplication should be distributed systematically throughout the entire population of measurements. Groups selling measurements to homeowners can accomplish this by providing two detectors instead of one to a random selection of purchasers, with instructions to place the detectors side by side. Consideration should be given to providing some means to ensure that the duplicate devices are not separated during the measurement period. Data from duplicate detectors should be evaluated using the procedures described by Goldin, Taylor, or the EPA. Whatever procedures are used must be documented prior to beginning measurements. Consistent failure in duplicate agreement may indicate a problem in the measurement process and should be investigated.

CONTROL DETECTORS

Laboratory Control Detectors

The laboratory background level for each batch of ATs should be established by each laboratory or supplier. Suppliers should measure the background of a statistically significant number of unexposed ATs that have been processed according to their standard operating procedures. Normally, the analysis laboratory or supplier calculates the net readings (which are used to calculate the reported sample radon concentrations) by subtracting the laboratory blank values from the results obtained from the field detectors.

Field Control Detectors

Field control detectors must be a component of any AT measurement program. Field control ATs (field blanks) should consist of a minimum of 5% of the devices that are deployed every month, or 25, whichever is smaller. Users should set these aside from each shipment, keep them sealed and in a low-radon environment (less than 0.2 pCi/L), label them in the same manner as the field ATs to assure identical processing, and send them back to the supplier with the field ATs for analysis. These control devices are necessary to measure the background exposure that accumulates during shipment and storage. The results should be monitored and recorded. If one or a few field blanks have concentrations significantly greater than the LLD established by the supplier, it may indicate defective packaging or handling. If the average value from the field control devices (field blanks) is significantly greater than the LLD established by the supplier, this average value should be subtracted from the individual values reported for the other devices in the exposure group.

It may be advisable to use three sets of detectors (pre-exposure, field, and post-exposure background) in order to allow the most thorough and complete evaluation of radon levels. For example, one group of detectors (pre-exposure detectors) may be earmarked for background measurement, and returned for processing immediately after the other detectors are deployed. The results from these detectors determine if the number of tracks acquired before deployment is significant and should be subtracted from the gross result. The second set of background detectors (post-exposure background detectors) are obtained just before the field monitors are to be collected, and are opened and kept in the same location as the returning field monitors for the same duration, and returned with them. Finally, this "post-exposure background" is subtracted from the field results, if found to be significant. In general, a value of 1 pCi/L or greater for any blank AT indicates a significant level that should be investigated, and potentially subtracted from the field AT results.

Routine Instrument Checks

Proper functioning of the analysis instruments and proper response by their operators require that the equipment be subject to routine checks. Daily or more frequent monitoring of equipment and operators is vital to ensuring consistently accurate results.

Electret Ion Chamber (EC, ES, EL) Detectors

Protocol for Using Electret Ion Chamber Radon Detectors (EC or ES, EL) to Measure Indoor Radon Concentrations

Purpose

This protocol provides guidance for using electret ion chamber radon detectors (EC) to obtain accurate and reproducible measurements of indoor radon concentrations. Adherence to this protocol will help ensure uniformity among measurement programs and allow valid inter-comparison of results. Measurements made in accordance with this protocol can produce either short-term or long-term measurements, depending on the type of EC employed. The investigator should also follow guidance provided by EPA in Protocols for Radon and Radon Decay Product Measurements in Homes, or other appropriate EPA measurement guidance documents.

Scope

This protocol covers, in general terms, the equipment, procedures and quality control objectives to be used in performing the measurements. It is not meant to replace an instrument manual but, rather, to provide guidelines to be incorporated into standard operating procedures by anyone providing measurement services.

Method

Short-term (ES) and long-term (EL) ECs require no power, and function as true integrating detectors, measuring the average concentration during the measurement period.

The EC contains a charged electret (an electrostatically charged disk of Teflon) which collects ions formed in the chamber by radiation emitted from radon and radon-decay products. When the device is exposed, radon diffuses into the chamber through filtered openings. Ions which are generated continuously by the decay of radon and radon-decay products are drawn to the surface of the electret and reduce its surface voltage. The amount of voltage reduction is related directly to the average radon concentration and the duration of the exposure period. ECs can be deployed for exposure periods of two days (one day for research purposes) to 12 months, depending on the thickness of the electret and the volume of the ion chamber chosen for use. These deployment periods are flexible, and valid measurements can be made with other deployment periods, depending on the application.

The electret must be removed from the EC chamber and the electret voltage measured with a special surface voltmeter both before and after exposure. To determine the average radon concentration during the exposure period, the difference between the initial and final voltages is divided first by a calibration factor, and then by the number of exposure days. A background radon concentration equivalent of ambient gamma radiation is subtracted to compute radon concentration. Electret voltage measurements can be made in a laboratory or in the field.

Equipment

The following equipment is required to measure radon using the EC detection method:

- an EC of the type recommended for the anticipated exposure period and radon concentration (ES or EL);
- an instruction sheet for the user, and a shipping container with a label for returning the

detector(s) to the laboratory, if appropriate;

- a specially-built surface voltmeter for measuring electret voltages before and after exposure; and

- a data collection log.

Pre-Deployment Considerations

The plans of the occupant during the proposed measurement period should be considered before deployment. The ES or EL measurement should not be made if the occupant will be moving during the measurement period. Deployment should be delayed until the new occupant is settled in the house.

The ES or EL should not be deployed if the user's schedule prohibits terminating the measurement at the appropriate time. The ES or EL should be inspected prior to deployment to see that it has not been damaged during handling and shipping.

Measurement Criteria

General conditions must be met to ensure standardization of measurement conditions. A 12-month EL measurement provides information about radon concentrations during an entire year, so the closed-building conditions do not have to be satisfied to perform a valid year-long measurement.

DEPLOYMENT

Location Selection

Standard criteria must be considered when choosing a measurement device location.

Timely Deployment

Both ESs and ELs should be deployed as soon as possible after their initial voltage is measured. Until an ES or EL is deployed, an electret cover should remain in place over the electret to minimize voltage loss due to background radon and gamma radiation.

Retrieval of Detectors

The recommended deployment period for the very short-term ESs is two days (one day for research or special circumstances), two to seven days for the short-term ESs, and one to 12 months for the long-term ELs. If the occupant is terminating the sampling, the instructions should state when and how to terminate the sampling period. EC units integrate the radon (ion) signal permanently, so variations from these recommended measurement periods are acceptable to accommodate special circumstances as long as the final electret voltage for any measurement remains above 150 volts. In addition, the occupant should also be instructed to send the ES or EL to the laboratory as soon as possible—preferably, within a few days following exposure termination.

At the end of the monitoring period, the ES or EL should be inspected for any deviation from the conditions described in the logbook at the time of deployment. Any changes should be noted. The electret should be covered again using the mechanism provided.

Documentation

Standard information must be documented. In addition, the serial number, type, and supplier of the chamber and electret, along with a code number or description that uniquely identifies the customer, building, room and sampling position, must be documented. If the temperature of the room in which the EC is analyzed after exposure is significantly different from the temperature of the room in which the EC was analyzed prior to exposure (more than 10° F), those temperatures need to be recorded.

Analysis Requirements

In general, all ESs or ELs should be analyzed in the field or in the laboratory as soon as possible following removal from buildings. A background correction must be made to the radon concentration value obtained because electret ion chambers have a small response to background gamma radiation. If the temperature at the time of analysis is significantly different than at the time when the pre-exposure voltage was determined (more than 10° F), a temperature correction factor may be necessary (consult the manufacturer). It is therefore advisable to measure voltages after the temperatures of the reader and detector have stabilized to a room temperature in which both pre- and post-exposure voltages have been measured.

Sensitivity

For a seven-day exposure period using an ES, the lower level of detection or LLD as the concentration that can be measured with a 50% error is about 0.2 pCi/L. For an EL, the LLD is about 0.3 pCi/L or less for a three-month measurement. Note that this definition of LLD is different from that for radiation counting instruments, as defined for other methods.

Precision

Precision should be monitored by using the results of duplicate detector analyses. This method can produce duplicate measurements with a coefficient of variation of 10% or less at 4 pCi/L or greater. An alternate measure of precision is a relative percent difference, defined as the difference between two duplicate measurements divided by their mean; note that these two measures of precision are not identical quantities. It is important that precision be monitored continuously over a range of radon concentrations, and that a systematic and documented method for evaluating changes in precision be part of the operating procedures.

Quality Assurance

The quality assurance program for measurements with ES or EL detectors includes five parts:

1. calibration;
2. known exposure detectors;
3. duplicate (collocated) detectors;
4. control detectors; and
5. routine instrument checks.

The purpose of a quality assurance program is to assure and document the accuracy and precision of the measurements, and assure that the measurements are not influenced by exposure from sources outside the environment to be measured.

Calibration

Every ES or EL detector system (detectors plus reader) should be calibrated in a radon calibration chamber at least once every 12 months. Initial calibration for the system is provided by the manufacturer. Determination of calibration factors for ES or EL detectors requires exposure of the detectors to known concentrations of radon-222 in a radon exposure chamber..Since ESs and ELs are also sensitive to exposure to gamma radiation, a gamma exposure-rate measurement in the test chamber is also required.

The following guidance is provided to manufacturers and suppliers of EC services as minimum requirements in determining the calibration factor:

- Detectors should be exposed in a radon chamber at several different radon concentrations or exposure levels similar to those found in the tested buildings (a minimum of three different concentrations).
- A minimum of 10 detectors should be exposed at each level.
- The period of exposure should be sufficient to allow the detector to achieve equilibrium with the chamber atmosphere.

Known Exposure Detectors

Anyone providing measurement services with ES or EL detectors should subject them to known radon exposures (spiked samples) for analysis at a rate of three per 100 measurements, with a minimum of three per year and a maximum required of six per month. Blind calibration detectors should be labeled in the same manner as the field detectors to ensure identical processing. The results of the spiked detector analysis should be monitored and recorded, and any significant deviation from the known concentration to which they were exposed should be investigated.

Duplicate (Collocated) Detectors

Anyone providing measurement services with EC devices should place duplicate detectors in enough houses to test the precision of the measurement. The number of duplicate detectors deployed should be approximately 10% of the number of detectors deployed each month, or 50, whichever is smaller. The duplicate devices should be shipped, stored, exposed and analyzed under the same conditions, and not identified as duplicates to the processing laboratory. The samples selected for duplication should be distributed systematically throughout the entire population of samples. Groups selling measurement services to homeowners can accomplish this by providing two detectors instead of one to a random selection of purchasers, with instructions to place the detectors side by side. Consideration should be given to providing some means to ensure that the duplicate devices are not separated during the measurement period. The analysis of duplicate data should follow the methodology described by Goldin, Taylor, or the EPA. Whatever procedures are used must be documented prior to beginning measurements. Consistent failure in duplicate agreement may indicate a problem in the measurement process and should be investigated.

Control Detectors for Background Gamma Exposure and Electret Stability Monitoring

Electrets should exhibit very little loss in surface voltage due to internal electrical instabilities. Anyone providing measurement services with ES or EL detectors should set aside a minimum of 5% of the electrets or 10 (whichever is smaller) from each shipment and evaluate them for voltage drift. They should be kept covered with protective caps in a low-radon environment and analyzed for voltage drift over a time period similar to the time period used for those deployed in homes. Any voltage loss found in the control electrets of more than 1 volt per week over a three-week test period for ESs, or 1 volt per month over a three-month period for ELs, should be investigated.

ECs are sensitive to background gamma radiation. The equivalent radon signal in picocuries per liter (pCi/L) per unit background radiation in micro roentgens per hour (µR/hr) is determined by the manufacturer for three different types of EC chambers currently available. This is specific to the chamber and not to the electret used in the chamber. These parameters are 0.07, 0.087 and 0.12 for H, S and L chambers, respectively. Depending on the type of chamber employed in the EC, one of these values must be multiplied by the gamma radiation level at the site (in µR/hr) and the product (in equivalent pCi/L) subtracted from the apparent radon concentration. The gamma radiation at the measurement site is usually taken from the EPA list of average background by the state, as provided by the manufacturer. However, it can also be measured with an EC unit that is sealed in a radon-proof bag available from the manufacturer, or measured directly using appropriate radiation detection instruments. The latter step is necessary for accurate radon measurements at very low levels, such as those encountered in the outdoor environment.

Routine Instrument Checks

Proper operation of the surface voltmeter should be monitored following the manufacturer's procedures for zeroing the voltmeter and analyzing a reference electret. These checks should be conducted at least once a week while the voltmeter is in use.

Activated Charcoal (AC) Adsorption Devices

Protocol for Using Activated Charcoal (AC) Adsorption Devices to Measure Indoor Radon Concentrations

Purpose

This protocol provides guidance for using activated charcoal (AC) adsorption devices to obtain accurate and reproducible measurements of indoor radon concentrations. As referred to in this section, ACs are those charcoal adsorption devices that are analyzed by gamma scintillation (including open-faced canisters, diffusion barrier canisters, and diffusion bags). Charcoal detectors analyzed by liquid scintillation are covered under a separate protocol. Adherence to this protocol will help ensure uniformity among measurement programs and allow valid inter-comparison of results. Measurements made in accordance with this protocol will produce results representative of closed-building conditions. Measurements made under closed-building conditions have a smaller variability, and are more reproducible than measurements made when the building conditions are not controlled. The investigator should also follow guidance provided by the EPA in *Protocols for Radon and Radon Decay Product Measurements in Homes*, or other appropriate EPA measurement guidance documents.

Scope

This section covers, in general terms, the sample collection and analysis method, the equipment needed, and the quality control objectives of measurements. It is not meant to replace an instrument manual but, rather, to provide guidelines to be incorporated into standard operating procedures by anyone providing measurement services. Questions about these guidelines should be directed to the U.S. EPA's Office of Radiation and Indoor Air.

Method

ACs are passive devices requiring no power to function. The passive nature of the activated charcoal allows continual adsorption and desorption of radon. During the measurement period (typically two to seven days), the adsorbed radon undergoes radioactive decay. Therefore, the technique does not uniformly integrate radon concentrations during the exposure period. As with all devices that store radon, the average concentration calculated using the mid-exposure time is subject to error if the ambient radon concentration varies substantially during the measurement period.

A device commonly used by several groups consists of a circular, 6- to 10-centimeter-diameter container that is approximately 2.5 cm deep and filled with 25 to 100 grams of activated charcoal. One side of the container is fitted with a screen that keeps the charcoal in but allows air to diffuse into the charcoal.

In some cases, the charcoal container has a diffusion barrier over the opening. For longer exposures, this barrier improves the uniformity of response to variations of radon concentration with time. Desiccant is also incorporated in some containers to reduce interference from moisture adsorption during longer exposures. Another variation of the charcoal container has charcoal packaged inside a sealed bag, allowing the radon to diffuse through the bag. All ACs are sealed with a radon-proof cover or outer container after preparation.

The measurement is initiated by removing the cover to allow radon-laden air to diffuse into the charcoal bed where the radon is adsorbed onto the charcoal. At the end of the measurement period, the device is securely re-sealed and returned to a laboratory for analysis.

At the laboratory, the ACs are analyzed for radon decay products by placing the charcoal, still in its container, directly on a gamma detector. Corrections may be needed to account for the reduced sensitivity of the charcoal due to adsorbed water. This correction may be done by weighing each detector when it is prepared, and then re-weighing it when it is sent to the laboratory for analysis. Any weight increase is attributed to water adsorbed on the charcoal. The weight of water gained is correlated to a correction factor, which is derived empirically by using a method discussed elsewhere. This correction factor is used to correct the analytical results. This correction is not needed if the configuration of the AC is modified to reduce significantly the adsorption of water, and if the user has demonstrated experimentally that, over a wide range of humidity, there is a negligible change in the collection efficiency of the charcoal within the specified exposure period.

AC measurement systems are calibrated by analyzing detectors exposed to known concentrations of radon in a calibration facility.

Equipment

ACs made specifically for ambient radon monitoring can be obtained from suppliers or can be manufactured using readily available components. Some charcoal canisters designed for use in respirators or in active air sampling may be adapted for use in ambient radon monitoring.

The following equipment is required to measure radon using ACs:

- a charcoal container sealed with a protective cover;
- an instruction sheet and sampling data sheet for the occupant, and a shipping container (along with a prepaid mailing label, if appropriate); and
- a data collection log.

Laboratory analysis of the exposed devices is performed using a sodium-iodide gamma scintillation detector to count the gamma rays emitted by the radon decay products on the charcoal. The detector may be used in conjunction with a multi-channel gamma spectrometer, or with a single-channel analyzer with the window set to include the appropriate gamma energy window. The detector system and detector geometry must be the same used to derive the calibration factors for the device.

Pre-Deployment Considerations

The plans of the occupant during the proposed measurement period should be considered before deployment. The AC measurement should not be made if the occupant will be moving during the measurement period. Deployment should be delayed until the new occupant is settled in the house.

The devices should not be deployed if the occupant's schedule prohibits terminating the measurement at the time selected for sealing the device and turning it in to the laboratory.

Measurement Criteria

General conditions must be adhered to in order to ensure standardization of measurement conditions.

DEPLOYMENT

Location Selection

Standard criteria must be used when choosing a measurement device location.

Timely Deployment

ACs should be deployed within the shelf-life specified by the supplier. Until ACs are deployed, they should remain tightly sealed to maintain maximum sensitivity and low background.

For charcoal canisters, the sealing tape and protective cover should be removed from the canister to begin the sampling period. The cover and tape must be saved to re-seal the canister at the end of the measurement. For the diffusion bags, there is a radon-proof mailing container that is sealed at the end of the deployment period. This container may be separate from the radon-proof packaging. The device should be inspected to see that it has not been damaged during handling and shipping. It should be intact, with no charcoal leakage. For canisters, the device should be placed with the open side up toward the air. Apart from the device, nothing should impede air flow around the device.

Retrieval of Detectors

The detectors should be deployed for a two- to seven-day measurement period, as specified in the supplier's instructions. If the occupant is terminating the sampling, the instructions should state when to terminate the sampling period and indicate that a deviation from the schedule may be acceptable if the time of termination is documented on the device. In addition, the occupant should also be instructed to send the device to the laboratory as soon as possible—preferably, the day of termination. The analysis laboratory should be calibrated to permit accurate analysis of devices deployed for some reasonable time beyond the recommended sampling period. For example, a detector deployed for 24 hours beyond the recommended sampling time may not present an analysis problem to the measurement laboratory.

At the end of the monitoring period, the detector should be inspected for any deviation from the conditions described in the logbook at the time of deployment. Any changes should be noted. The detector should be re-sealed using the original protective cover.

After the device is retrieved, it must be turned in to the laboratory as soon as possible for analysis. The detector should be analyzed at least three hours after the end of sampling to allow for ingrowth of decay products.

Documentation

Standard information must be documented so that data interpretation and comparison can be made. In addition, the test location temperature may need to be recorded, depending on the device's configuration.

Analysis Requirements

ACs should be analyzed in the laboratory as soon as possible following removal from the houses. The maximum allowable delay time between the end of sampling and analysis will vary with the radon concentration and background experienced in each laboratory and should be evaluated, especially if sensitivity is of prime consideration. Corrections for the radon-222 decay during sampling, during the interval between sampling and counting, and during counting should be made. If the device does not have a moisture barrier, the detector should be weighed, and, if necessary, a correction should be applied for the increase in weight due to moisture adsorbed. A description of the procedure used to derive the moisture correction factor is provided elsewhere.

Sensitivity

For a two- to seven-day exposure period, the lower level of detection (LLD) should be 0.5 pCi/L or less. This LLD can normally be achieved with a counting time of up to 30 minutes. The LLD should be calculated using the results of the laboratory background determination.

Precision

Precision should be monitored using the results of the duplicate detector analyses described in this protocol. This method can produce measurements with a coefficient of variation of 10% or less at 4 pCi/L or greater. An alternate measure of precision is a relative percent difference, defined as the difference between two duplicate measurements divided by their mean; note that these two measures of precision are not identical quantities. It is important that precision be monitored frequently over a range of radon concentrations, and that a systematic and documented method for evaluating changes in precision be part of the operating procedures.

Quality Assurance

The quality assurance program for ACs includes five parts:

1. calibration;
2. known exposure detectors;
3. duplicate (collocated) detectors;
4. control detectors; and
5. routine instrument checks.

The purpose of this program is to identify the accuracy and precision of the measurements, and to assure that the measurements are not influenced by extraneous exposures. The quality assurance program should include the maintenance of control charts; general information is also available.

Calibration

Every AC system should be calibrated in a radon calibration chamber at least once every 12 months. Determination of calibration factors for ACs requires exposure of the detectors to known concentrations of radon-222 in a radon exposure chamber. The calibration factors depend on the exposure time and may also depend on the amount of water adsorbed by the charcoal container during exposure. These calibration factors should be determined using the procedures described previously. Calibration factors should be determined for each AC measurement system (container type, amount of charcoal, gamma detector type, etc.).

Known Exposure Detectors

Anyone providing measurement services with AC detectors should submit charcoal detectors with known radon exposures (spiked samples) for analysis at a rate of three per 100 measurements, with a minimum of three per year and a maximum required of six per month. Known exposure (spiked) detectors should be labeled in the same manner as the field detectors to assure identical processing. The results of the spiked detector analysis should be monitored and recorded, and any significant deviation from the known concentration to which they were exposed should be investigated.

Duplicate (Collocated) Detectors

Anyone providing measurement services with AC devices should place duplicate detectors in enough houses to test the precision of the measurement. The number of duplicate detectors deployed should be approximately 10% of the number of detectors deployed each month, or 50, whichever is smaller. The duplicate detectors should be shipped, stored, exposed and analyzed under the same conditions, and not identified as duplicates to the processing laboratory. The locations selected to receive duplicates should be distributed systematically throughout the entire population of samples. Groups selling measurement services to homeowners can do this by providing two detectors instead of one to a random selection of purchasers, with instructions to place them side by side. Consideration should be given to providing some means to ensure that the duplicate detectors are not separated during the measurement period. Data from duplicate detectors should be evaluated using the procedures described by Goldin, Taylor, or the EPA. Whatever procedures are used must be documented prior to beginning measurements. Consistent failure in duplicate agreement may indicate a problem in the measurement process and should be investigated.

CONTROL DETECTORS

Laboratory Control Detectors

The laboratory background level for each batch of ACs should be established by each laboratory or supplier. Suppliers should measure the background of a statistically significant number of unexposed detectors that have been processed according to their standard operating procedures (laboratory blanks). Normally, the analysis laboratory or supplier calculates the net readings (which are used to calculate the reported sample radon concentrations) by subtracting the laboratory blank values from the results obtained from the field detectors.

Field Control Detectors

Field control detectors (field blanks) should consist of a minimum of 5% of the devices that are deployed every month, or 25, whichever is smaller. Large users of ACs should set these aside from each shipment, keep them sealed and in a low-radon environment (less than 0.2 pCi/L), label them in the same manner as the field detectors to ensure identical processing, and send them back to the supplier with one shipment each month for analysis. These control devices measure the background exposure that may accumulate during shipment or storage, and the results should be monitored and recorded. If one or a few of the field control detectors have concentrations significantly greater than the LLD established by the supplier, it may indicate defective devices or poor procedures. If most of the controls have concentrations significantly greater than the LLD, the average value of the field controls should be subtracted from the reported field detector concentrations and the supplier notified of a possible problem.

Routine Instrument Checks

Proper operation of all radiation-counting instruments requires that their response to a reference source be constant to within established limits. Therefore, counting equipment should be subject to routine checks to ensure proper operation. This is achieved by counting an instrument check source at least once per day. The characteristics of the check source (i.e., geometry, type of radiation emitted, etc.) should be similar to the samples to be analyzed, if possible. The count rate of the check source should be high enough to yield good counting statistics in a short time (for example, 1,000 to 10,000 counts per minute).

Charcoal Liquid Scintillation (LS)

Protocol for Using Charcoal Liquid Scintillation (LS) Devices to Measure Indoor Radon Concentrations

Purpose

This protocol provides guidance for using charcoal liquid scintillation (LS) devices to obtain accurate and reproducible measurements of indoor radon concentrations. Adherence to this protocol will help ensure uniformity among measurement programs and allow valid inter-comparison of results. Measurements made in accordance with this protocol will produce results representative of closed-building conditions. Measurements made under closed-building conditions have a smaller variability and are more reproducible than measurements made when the building conditions are not controlled. The investigator should also follow guidance provided by the EPA in *Protocols for Radon and Radon Decay Product Measurements in Homes* or other appropriate EPA measurement guidance documents.

Scope

This protocol covers, in general terms, the equipment, procedures, and quality control objectives to be used in performing the measurements. It is not meant to replace an instrument manual but, rather, presents guidelines to be incorporated into standard operating procedures by anyone providing measurement services.

Method

LS devices are passive detectors requiring no power to function. The passive nature of the activated charcoal allows continual adsorption and desorption of radon. The adsorbed radon undergoes radioactive decay during the measurement period. Therefore, the technique does not integrate uniformly radon concentrations during the exposure period. As with all devices that store radon, the calculated average concentration is subject to error if the ambient radon concentration adsorbed during the first half of the sampling period is substantially higher or lower than the average over the period.

Several companies now provide a type of LS device that is a capped, 20-ml liquid scintillation vial that is approximately 25 mm in diameter by 60 mm and contains 1 to 3 grams of charcoal (other designs are also feasible). In some cases, the vial contains a diffusion barrier over the charcoal, which improves the uniformity of response of the device to variations of radon concentration with time, particularly for longer exposures. Some LS devices include a few grams of desiccant, which reduces interference from moisture adsorption by the charcoal. All LS devices are sealed with a radon-proof closure after preparation.

A measurement with the LS device is initiated by removing the radon-proof closure to allow radon-laden air to diffuse into the charcoal where the radon is adsorbed. At the end of the exposure period (typically, two to seven days), the device is securely re-sealed and returned to the laboratory for analysis.

At the laboratory, the devices are prepared for analysis by radon desorption techniques. This technique reproducibly transfers a major fraction of the radon adsorbed on the charcoal into a vial of liquid scintillation fluid. These vials of liquid scintillation fluid containing the dissolved radon are placed in a liquid scintillation counter and counted for a specified number of minutes (e.g., 10 minutes) or until the standard deviation of the count is acceptable (e.g., less than 10%).

Equipment

LS devices made specifically for ambient radon monitoring are supplied and analyzed by several laboratories.

The following equipment is required to measure radon with an LS device:

- LS devices properly sealed by the supplier;
- an instruction sheet for the occupant, and a shipping container (along with a prepaid mailing label, if appropriate); and
- a data collection log.

Pre-Deployment Considerations

The plans of the occupant during the proposed measurement period should be considered before deployment. The LS measurement should not be made if the occupant will be moving during the measurement period. Deployment should be delayed until the new occupant is settled in the house. The LS device should not be deployed if the occupant's schedule prohibits terminating the measurement at the time selected for closing the device and turning it in to the laboratory.

MEASUREMENT CRITERIA

Deployment

LS devices should be deployed in buildings within the shelf life specified by the supplier. Until they are deployed, they should remain tightly sealed to maintain low background. The protective cap should be removed from the device to begin the sampling period. The cap must be saved to re-seal the device at the end of the measurement. The device should be inspected to assure that it has not been damaged during handling and shipping. It should be intact, with no charcoal leakage. The device should also be placed with the open vial's mouth up. Nothing should impede air flow around the device.

Retrieval of Devices

The device should be deployed for the measurement period specified in the instructions supplied by the analytical laboratory (usually, between two days and one week). If the occupant is terminating the sampling, the instructions should state when to terminate the sampling period and indicate that the actual time of termination must be documented on the device. In addition, the occupant also should be instructed to send the device to the laboratory as soon as possible—preferably, the day of sample termination. The analysis laboratory should be calibrated to permit accurate analysis of devices deployed for some reasonable time beyond the recommended sampling period. For example, a detector deployed for 24 hours beyond the recommended sampling time may not present an analysis problem to the measurement laboratory.

At the end of the monitoring period, the device should be inspected for any deviation from the conditions described in the logbook at the time of deployment. Any changes should be noted. The device should be re-sealed using the original protective cap.

DOCUMENTATION

Analysis Requirements

LS devices should be returned to the supplier's analysis laboratory as soon as possible following removal from the houses. The maximum allowable delay time between the end of sampling and analysis should not exceed the time specified by the supplier's instructions, especially if the radon concentration measured is expected to be low. Corrections for radon-222 decay during sampling, during the interval between sampling and counting, and during counting, will be made by the analysis laboratory. The procedures followed by an individual supplier's analysis laboratory may include a correction for moisture as measured by weight gain, if this is significant for their device configuration. Other correction or calibration factors applied by the analysis laboratory must include factors accounting for the transfer of radon from the charcoal to the scintillation fluid under rigorously controlled conditions, and for the counting efficiency achieved with the specified scintillation mixture and liquid scintillation counting system.

Sensitivity

The lower limit of detection (LLD) should be specified by individual suppliers for LS devices exposed and shipped according to their directions. It is estimated that LLDs of a few tenths of a picocurie per liter (pCi/L) are achievable for some LS devices. The LLD should be calculated using the results of the laboratory control devices.

Precision

Precision should be monitored and recorded periodically using the results of the duplicate device analyses. Measurements made with this method can produce duplicate results with a coefficient of variation of 10% or less at 4 pCi/L or greater. An alternate measure of precision is a relative percent difference, defined as the difference between two duplicate measurements divided by their mean; note that these two measures of precision are not identical quantities. It is important that precision be monitored frequently over a range of radon concentrations, and that a systematic and documented method for evaluating changes in precision be part of the operating procedures.

Quality Assurance

The quality assurance program for an LS system includes five parts:

1. calibration;

2. known exposure devices;

3. duplicate (collocated) devices;

4. control devices; and

5. routine instrument checks.

The purpose of a quality assurance program is to identify the accuracy and precision of the measurements, and to ensure that the measurements are not influenced by exposure from sources outside the environment to be measured. The quality assurance program should include the maintenance of control charts.

Calibration

Every LS laboratory system should be calibrated in a radon calibration chamber at least once every 12 months. Determination of calibration factors for LS devices requires exposure of calibration devices to known concentrations of radon-222 in a radon exposure chamber at carefully measured radon concentrations. The calibration factors depend on the exposure time and may also depend on the amount of water adsorbed by the device during exposure. Calibration factors should be determined for a range of different exposure times and, if appropriate, humidities.

Known Exposure Devices

Anyone providing measurement services with LS devices should submit devices with known radon exposures (spiked samples) for analysis at a rate of three per 100 measurements, with a minimum of three per year and a maximum required of six per month. Known exposure (spiked) devices should be labeled in the same manner as the field devices to ensure identical processing. The results of the spiked device analysis should be monitored and recorded, and any significant deviation from the known concentration to which they were exposed should be investigated.

Duplicate (Collocated) Devices

Anyone providing measurement services with LS devices should place duplicate detectors in enough houses to test the precision of the measurement. The number of duplicate detectors deployed should be approximately 10% of the number of detectors deployed each month, or 50, whichever is smaller. Each pair of duplicate devices should be shipped, stored, exposed, and analyzed under the same conditions. The samples for duplication should be distributed systematically throughout the entire population of samples. Groups selling measurement services to homeowners can do this by providing two detectors instead of one to a random selection of purchasers with instructions to place them side by side. Consideration should be given to providing some means to ensure that the duplicate devices are not separated during the measurement period. Data from duplicate devices should be evaluated using procedures described by Goldin, Taylor, or the EPA. Whatever procedures are used must be documented prior to beginning measurements. Consistent failure in duplicate agreement may indicate a problem in the measurement process and should be investigated.

Control Devices

The laboratory background level for each batch of LS devices should be established by each laboratory or supplier. Suppliers should measure the background of a statistically significant number of unexposed LS devices that have been processed according to their standard operating procedures (laboratory blanks). Normally, the analysis laboratory or supplier calculates the net readings (which are used to calculate the reported sample radon concentrations) by subtracting the laboratory blank values from the results obtained from the field detectors.

Field control devices (field blanks) should consist of a minimum of 5% of the devices that are deployed every month, or 25, whichever is smaller. Large users of LS detectors should set these aside from each shipment, keep them sealed and in a low radon environment (less than 0.2 pCi/L), label them in the same manner as the field devices, and send them back to the supplier, with one shipment each month for analysis. These control devices measure the background exposure that may accumulate during shipment or storage, and the results should be monitored and recorded. If one or a few of the field control detectors have concentrations significantly greater than the LLD established by the supplier, it may indicate defective devices or procedures. If most of the controls have concentrations significantly greater than the LLD, the average value at the field controls should be subtracted from the reported field device concentration, and the supplier notified of a possible problem.

Proper operation of all radiation-counting instruments requires that their response to a reference source be constant to within established limits. Therefore, counting equipment should be subject to routine checks to ensure proper operation. This is achieved by counting an instrument check source at least once a day. The characteristics of the check source (i.e., type of radiation emitted) should be similar to the samples to be analyzed, if possible. The count rate of the check source should be high enough to yield good counting statistics in a short time (for example, 1,000 to 10,000 counts per minute).

Protocol for Using Grab Sampling Bag and Three-Day Scintillation Cells

Purpose

This protocol provides guidance for three similar methods that measure indoor radon air concentrations: grab radon sampling techniques (GB, GC, GS), pumps with collapsible bags as devices (PB), and three-day integrating evacuated scintillation cells (SC). Adherence to this protocol will help obtain accurate and reproducible measurements, ensure uniformity among measurement programs, and allow valid comparisons of results. Measurements made in accordance with this protocol will produce results representative of closed-building conditions. Measurements made under closed-building conditions have a smaller variability and are more reproducible than measurements made when the building conditions are not controlled.

Results of grab sampling are influenced greatly by conditions that exist in the building during and for up to 12 hours prior to the measurement. Therefore, it is especially important when making grab measurements to conform to closed-building conditions for 12 hours before the measurement. Grab sampling techniques are not recommended for measurements made to determine the need for remedial action. The reader should also refer to the EPA's guidance document *Protocols for Radon and Radon Decay Product Measurements in Homes* or other appropriate EPA measurement guidance documents.

Scope

This section covers, in general terms, the equipment, procedures, and quality control objectives to be used in performing the measurements. It is not meant to replace an instrument manual but, rather, presents guidelines to be incorporated into standard operating procedures by anyone providing measurement services.

Methods

There are three grab radon sampling methods covered in this section. The first method is known as grab radon scintillation cell (GS). A sample of air is drawn into and sealed in a flask or cell that has a zinc sulfide phosphor coating on its interior surfaces. One surface of the cell is fitted with a clear window that is put in contact with a photomultiplier tube to count light pulses (scintillations) resulting from alpha disintegrations from the air sample interacting with the zinc sulfide coating. The number of pulses is proportional to the radon concentration in the cell. The cell is counted about four hours after filling to allow the short-lived radon decay products to reach equilibrium with the radon. After the cells are placed in the counters, the counting system should be allowed to dark-adapt for two minutes. Correction factors are applied to the counting results to compensate for decay during the time between collection and counting, and for decay during counting if the counting time is long (greater than one hour). Supplementary information on this technique is provided herein. In a variation of this method used in some portable instruments, air is pumped continuously through a flow-through-type scintillation cell for just a few minutes. Alpha particles resulting from the decay of radon gas and decay products are counted as the gas is swept through.

A second grab method covered by this protocol is known as grab radon activated charcoal (GC) and uses air pumped through activated charcoal to collect the sample. A charcoal-filled cartridge is placed into a sampler and air is pumped through the carbon cartridge. The pump with a charcoal cartridge is not flow-dependent, but it must remain operational at the sampling location until the charcoal collects enough radon to be in equilibrium with the radon at the sampling location. A sampling duration of one hour has been found to be optimal for most systems. The cartridge must be weighed prior to and after sampling in order to correct for the reduced sensitivity of the charcoal due to adsorbed water. The cartridges are analyzed by placing them on a sodium iodide gamma scintillation system or a germanium gamma detector. The GC system must be calibrated by analyzing cartridges pumped with known concentrations of radon in a qualified facility.

The third grab method is known as grab radon pump/collapsible bag (GB) and uses the same technology for pump/collapsible bag (PB) devices. The GB method covered in this section differs only in that the bag is filled over a much shorter collection period than in the PB method described below.

Pump/Collapsible Bag (PB) Devices

One of the older and simpler methods of making an integrated measurement of the concentration of radon over a period of time is to collect a sample of ambient air in a radon-proof container over the desired sampling time period and measure the resulting radon concentration in the container.

One practical method is to use a small pump with a very low and uniform flow rate to pump ambient air into an inflatable and collapsible radon-proof bag. After the desired sampling period (typically, 24 hours), the concentration of radon in the bag can be analyzed by any of the standard methods, such as the GS protocol using the appropriate radon decay correction factors. For this method, the counting system should be allowed to dark-adapt for two minutes after the cells are placed in the counters. The main purpose of the collapsible bag is to avoid variation in pump flow rate due to buildup of back-pressure in the container. Bags that have been measured to have a very low loss of radon by diffusion through the bag have been made of laminated Mylar, aluminized laminated Mylar, and Tedlar®. The pump flow rate is not critical as long as it is suitable for the size of the bag and the sample duration, but variation of the flow rate over the collection time period of the sample will affect the accuracy of the measurement. A number of suitable battery- and/or charger-operated pumps with controlled flow rates are available commercially.

Although this PB method accumulates radon over a period of time for subsequent analysis, it should not be considered a true integrating method. Radon peaks occurring early in the sampling period will leave less radon for analysis than the same size peak occurring toward the end of the sampling period.

Three-Day Integrating Evacuated Scintillation Cells (SC)

This method typically uses Lucas-type scintillation cells that have been outfitted with a restrictor valve attached to the main valve. Samples are collected by opening the valve on an evacuated cell. The restrictor valve is set so that the cell fills from a 30-inch mercury (Hg) vacuum to about 80% of its capacity over a three-day period. At the end of the measurement period, the valve is closed and turned in to the analysis laboratory. Since the volume of the cell is known, the exact volume of filtered air collected over the three-day measurement period can be calculated from the vacuum gauge reading at the conclusion of the sampling period.

The sample is analyzed on an alpha scintillation counter. Prior to counting, the pressure in the cell is brought to one atmosphere by adding radon-free (aged) air so that the sample is analyzed under the same conditions that prevailed during calibration of the cell. To allow radon and radon decay products to grow into equilibrium and to allow any radon decay products that may have been collected to decay, the sample should be counted no sooner than four hours after the end of the measurement period. After the cells are placed in the counters, the counting system should be allowed to dark-adapt for two minutes.

During the three-day sampling period, some of the radon that has been collected decays. The midpoint of the sampling period cannot be used for the decay correction factor because the air flow into the cell is greater during the initial time of sampling. Therefore, the fraction of radon that decays must be calculated from the shape of a plot of percent fill versus time. This must be measured for each cell. This factor should be applied as a correction during data reduction.

Since this method accumulates radon over a period of time for subsequent analysis, it is not a true integrating method. Radon peaks occurring early in the sampling period will leave less radon for analysis than the same size peak occurring toward the end of the sampling period.

EQUIPMENT

Grab Radon Scintillation Cell (GS) Method

The equipment needed for this method includes the following:

- a scintillation cell (flask) or cells to be filled at the site;
- a pump to flow air through the cell or to evacuate the cell (depending on the valve arrangement on the cell);
- a clock to measure time from collection to counting;
- a filter and filter holder to attach to the air-inlet valve of the cell; and
- a data collection log.

The equipment required for analyzing the air sample includes the following:

- a photomultiplier tube and high-voltage assembly in a light-tight chamber;
- a scaler-timer for registering pulses from the photomultiplier tube assembly and timing the counting interval;
- a National Institute of Standards and Technology (NIST)-traceable alpha check source and scintillation disc;
- a calibration flask or cell;
- a vacuum pump and cell flushing apparatus; and
- aged air or nitrogen for flushing counting cells.

Grab Radon Activated Charcoal (GC)

The equipment needed for this method includes the following:

- a charcoal cartridge with both apertures sealed with protective metallic or other impermeable covers;
- a pump to pull air through the cartridge;
- a data collection log;
- a sodium iodide gamma scintillation detector and analyzer; and
- an analytic scale capable of weighing small differences in weight (up to several grams) due to water adsorbed by the charcoal.

Laboratory analysis of the saturated charcoal cartridge is performed using a sodium iodide gamma scintillation detector to count the gamma rays emitted by the radon decay products adsorbed on the carbon. The detectors may be used in conjunction with a multi-channel gamma spectrometer or with a single-channel analyzer calibrated to include the appropriate gamma energies.

Grab Radon Pump/Collapsible Bag (GB) Sampling

The equipment requirements for this method are similar to those for the PB method.

The following equipment is required to conduct measurements using the GB method:

- a pump with a suitable uniform flow rate. The materials of the pump should not absorb or off-gas any substantial amount of radon;

- a collapsible bag of tested, low radon-loss material; and
- a data collection log.

Three-Day Integrating Evacuated Scintillation Cells (SC)

The following equipment is required to measure radon with an evacuated cell:

- an evacuated cell with the restrictor valve and vacuum gauge prepared by the supplier;
- an instruction sheet and a shipping container (along with a prepaid mailing label, if appropriate); and
- a data collection log.

Pre-Deployment Considerations

The plans of the occupant during the proposed measurement period should be considered before deployment. The measurement should not be made if the occupant will be moving during the measurement period. Deployment should be delayed until the new occupant is settled in the house.

The measurement devices should not be deployed if the occupant's schedule prohibits terminating the measurement at the time selected.

Prior to collection of the grab radon sample, proper operation of the counting equipment must be verified, and counter efficiency and background must be determined. In addition, a background for each cartridge or cell should be determined prior to sampling. This may be done using the procedures for flask counting.

For highly accurate cell measurements, it is necessary to standardize cell pressure prior to counting because the path lengths of alpha particles are a function of air density. For example, a cell calibrated at sea level and used to count a sample collected at Grand Junction, Colorado (1,370 meters above sea level) would overestimate the radon activity of the sample by about 9%. This error probably approaches the maximum that would be encountered; therefore, it may not be necessary to make this correction if this error can be tolerated. Correction procedures are given elsewhere.

Measurement Criteria

General conditions must be met to ensure standardization of measurement conditions.

Deployment and Location Selection

Standard criteria must be considered when choosing a measurement device location.

Sampling with GB, GC and GS

All air samples drawn into scintillation cells or flasks must be filtered to remove radon decay products and other airborne radioactive particulates. The sampling hose should be short so as to draw room air (not hose air) into the cell. Filters may be reused many times as long as they remain undamaged and functional.

For collection of a sample using a single-valve (Lucas-type) cell, the cell is evacuated to at least 25 inches of mercury, the filter is attached to the cell, and the valve is opened, allowing the cell to fill with air. At least 10 seconds should be allowed for the cell to fill completely. To ensure a good vacuum at the time of sampling, the cell may be evacuated using a small hand-operated pump in the room being sampled. It is good practice to evacuate the cell at least five times, allowing it to fill completely with room air each time. The air to be sampled must flow through the filter each time. If it can be demonstrated that the cells and valves do not leak, it is acceptable to evacuate the cells in the laboratory and simply attach the filter and open the valve in the building to collect a sample.

To sample using the double-valve, flow-through type cell, the filter should be attached to the inlet valve, and a suitable vacuum pump should be attached to the other valve. The pump may be motor-driven or hand-operated. To begin sampling, both valves should be opened and the pump operated to flow at least 10 complete air exchanges through the cell. The pump is then stopped and both valves are closed.

Sampling using the GC or GB method is accomplished by opening and attaching a prepared sealed cartridge or collapsible bag to the sampling pump. For charcoal cartridges, the pump should draw air through the cartridge at approximately the same rate as that used in calibrating the system. Sampling should continue until the charcoal collects enough radon to be in equilibrium with the radon at the sampling site. A one-hour sampling period is typical for most GC systems. For the GB method, the pump should have a known uniform flow rate and the system should be leak-proof.

Timely Deployment of SCs

SC devices should be deployed within the period specified by the supplier. Until they are deployed, they should remain tightly sealed to maintain maximum sensitivity and accuracy. To deploy the SC device, the reading of the attached vacuum gauge must be recorded on the log sheet, along with the start date and start time of the sample. The sample collection is started by opening the main valve according to the supplier's instructions.

RETRIEVAL OF DEVICES

Grab Radon Sampling Techniques

All pertinent sampling information should be recorded after completing the measurement. The detectors should be packaged carefully for return to the counting location so that the samples will not be lost due to breakage, valves being opened, or loss of cartridge integrity.

Three-Day Integrating Evacuated Scintillation Cells (SC)

The SC device should be deployed for the measurement period specified in the instructions supplied by the analytical laboratory (typically, three days). If the occupant is terminating the sampling, the instructions should state when and how to terminate the sampling period and indicate that the actual time of termination must be documented on the data form. In addition, the vacuum gauge reading must be recorded on the data form after the sampling valve is closed. The occupant should also be instructed to send the device to the laboratory as soon as possible—preferably, on the day of sample termination.

At the end of the monitoring period, the device should be inspected for any deviation from the conditions described in the logbook at the time of deployment. Any changes should be noted.

Documentation

Standard information must be documented so that data interpretation and comparison can be made. In addition to this list, the following are method-specific details of documentation requirements.

For GBs, GCs, and GSs, the serial numbers of cells, cartridges, bags, pumps, and counting equipment should also be recorded.

For PBs, the serial numbers of bags, pumps, and equipment used for analysis of the radon concentration should also be recorded.

For SCs, the start time and stop time of the vacuum gauge readings should also be recorded, along with the serial numbers of the cells and counting equipment.

COUNTING AND CALCUATIONS

Grab Radon Scintillation Cell (GS) Sampling

Cells should not be counted for at least four hours following the time of collection. Background and check sources should be counted. The cell to be counted is placed on the photomultiplier tube, the cover placed over the cell, and the system allowed to dark-adapt. The cell may then be counted for a sufficient period to collect an adequate number of counts for good counting statistics in relation to the system background counts.

Grab Radon Activated Charcoal (GC) Sampling

Cartridges should not be analyzed for at least four hours after the end of sampling to allow for ingrowth of the radon decay products. Following removal from the sampling location, cartridges should then be analyzed in a laboratory. The cartridge should be weighed and, if necessary, a correction should be applied for the increase in weight due to moisture adsorption. The maximum allowable delay time between the end of sampling and analysis will vary with the background experienced in each laboratory and should be evaluated, especially if sensitivity is of prime consideration. The cartridge should be analyzed on a calibrated sodium iodide gamma scintillation system or a germanium gamma detector.

Grab Radon Pump/Collapsible Bag (GB) Sampling

After a four-hour waiting period, the concentration of radon in the bag can be analyzed by any of the standard methods, including the GS method.

Cell Flushing and Storage

After the cells have been counted and data are satisfactorily recorded, the cells must be flushed with aged air or nitrogen to remove the sample. Flow-through cells are flushed with at least 10 volume exchanges at a flow of about 2 liters per minute. Cells with single valves are evacuated and refilled with aged air or nitrogen at least five times. The cells are left filled with aged air or nitrogen and allowed to sit overnight before being counted for background. If an acceptable background is obtained, the cell is ready for reuse.

Pump/Collapsible Bag (PB) Devices

If the radon concentration in the collapsible bag is to be analyzed on site, the appropriate grab radon sampling protocol should be followed.

If the radon concentration is to be measured by an analysis laboratory, the bag should be delivered to the laboratory as soon as possible following completion of sampling, especially if low concentrations are being measured.

Three-Day Integrating Evacuated Scintillation Cells (SC)

SC devices should be returned to the supplier's analysis laboratory as soon as possible following removal from the buildings. The maximum allowable delay time between the end of sampling and analysis should not exceed the time specified by the supplier's instructions, especially if sensitivity is an important consideration. Corrections for the radon-222 decay during sampling, during the interval between sampling and counting, and during counting, will be made by the analysis laboratory.

ANALYSIS REQUIREMENTS AND SENSITIVITY

Grab Radon Sampling Techniques

The sensitivity of the GS method is dependent on the volume of the cell being used. However, sensitivities of 0.1 picocuries per liter (pCi/L) are achievable (George 1980, George 1983). For the GC method, the lower limit of detection or LLD (calculated using methods described by Altshuler and Pasternack 1963) should be 1.0 pCi/L or less. This can be achieved normally with a counting time of up to 30 minutes. The sensitivity of the GB method depends on the analysis method used.

Pump/Collapsible Bag (PB) Devices

The LLD for a PB will depend on the method used to analyze the contents of the bag. If a GS method is used, an LLD of a few tenths of a pCi/L should be possible.

Three-Day Integrating Evacuated Scintillation Cells (SC)

The LLD should be specified by individual suppliers for SC devices exposed and shipped according to their directions. It is estimated that LLDs of a few tenths of a pCi/L are achievable with these devices.

Precision

The results of duplicates (collocated measurements) should be monitored and recorded using the results of the duplicate device analyses described in this protocol. These methods can produce duplicate measurements with a coefficient of variation of 10% or less at 4 pCi/L or greater. An alternate measure of precision is a relative percent difference, defined as the difference between two duplicate measurements divided by their mean; note that these two measures of precision are not identical quantities. It is important that precision be monitored frequently over a range of radon concentrations and that a systematic and documented method for evaluating changes in precision be part of the operating procedures.

Quality Assurance

The purpose of a quality assurance program is to identify the accuracy and precision of the measurements and to ensure that the measurements are not influenced by exposure from sources outside the intended structure. The quality assurance program should include the maintenance of control charts.

This section describes five parts of a quality assurance program:

1. calibration of the system;
2. known exposure measurements;
3. duplicate (collocated) devices;
4. background measurements/control devices; and
5. routine instrument checks.

Each type of method (GB, GC, GS, PB and SC) requires some variation of all parts of the program.

Calibration

Every device should be calibrated in a radon calibration chamber before being put into service and after any repairs or modifications. Subsequent recalibrations should be done once every 12 months, with cross-checks to a recently calibrated instrument at least semi-annually.

Calibration Factors

Determination of calibration factors requires exposure of calibration devices to known concentrations of radon-222 in a radon exposure chamber at carefully measured radon concentrations. Since the cells are subject to shipping and handling, they should be recalibrated periodically at radon levels similar to those found in tested buildings. Scintillation counting systems used to count exposed cells should be either the system used to calibrate the cell or one calibrated against that system.

Cell Calibration

If a GS method of measuring the radon concentrations is used in the PB or GB methods, the following procedure on calibration should be followed.

The cell counting system consisting of the scaler, detector, and high-voltage supply must be calibrated. The correct high voltage is determined by increasing the high voltage by increments and plotting the resulting counts. This procedure is described elsewhere. Each counting system should be calibrated in a radon calibration chamber before being put into service and after any repairs or modifications. Subsequent recalibrations should be done once every 12 months, with cross-checks to a recently calibrated instrument at least semi-annually. Also, a check source or calibration cell should be counted in each analysis system each day to demonstrate proper operation prior to counting any samples.

A separate calibration factor must be obtained for each cell in the counting system. This is done by filling each cell with radon of a known concentration and counting the cell to determine the conversion factor (in counts per minute per pCi). The known concentration of radon may be obtained from a radon calibration chamber or estimated from a bubbler tube containing a known concentration of radium.

Grab Radon-Activated Charcoal (GC) Method Calibration

This method must be calibrated in a radon calibration chamber to establish a calibration factor for a specific cartridge model. Samples should be taken at different humidities and temperatures to establish correction factors. Calibration should be carried out at several flow rates and exposure times to verify the acceptable limits. Calibration factors must be established with the identical gamma counting system and counting geometry used in sampling.

Known Exposure Measurements

Anyone providing measurement services using these methods should submit devices with known radon exposures (spiked samples) for analysis at a rate of three per 100 measurements, with a minimum of three per year and a maximum required of six per month. Known exposure (spiked) devices should be labeled in the same manner as the field devices to assure identical processing. The results of the known exposure analyses should be monitored and recorded, and any significant deviation from the known concentration to which they were exposed should be investigated.

Duplicate (Collocated) Devices

Anyone providing measurement services with these methods should place duplicate devices in enough houses to test the precision of the measurement. The number of duplicate detectors deployed should be approximately 10% of the number of detectors deployed each month, or 50, whichever is smaller. To the greatest extent possible, care should be taken to ensure that the samples are duplicates, are taken in close proximity, and are away from drafts. The samples selected for duplication should be distributed systematically throughout the entire population of samples. The duplicate devices should be shipped, stored, exposed, and analyzed under the same conditions, and not identified as duplicates to the processing laboratory. Groups selling measurement services to homeowners can accomplish this by making two side-by-side measurements in a random selection of homes. Data from duplicate devices should be evaluated using the procedures described by Goldin, Taylor, or the EPA. Whatever procedures are used must be documented prior to beginning measurements. Consistent failure in duplicate agreement may indicate a problem in the measurement process and should be investigated.

BACKGROUND MEASUREMENTS AND CONTROL DEVICES

Background Measurements

A background count for each type of system is determined prior to measurement. When the GC method is used, the background of the charcoal should also be assessed routinely.

Laboratory Control Devices

The background level for each device should be established by each supplier. Suppliers should measure the background of each device before each use or periodically, with a frequency based on experience. In order to calculate the radon concentrations of the sample, the background should be subtracted from the field readings taken with that cell.

Field Control Devices

Field control devices (field blanks) should consist of a minimum of 5% of the devices that are deployed every month, or 25, whichever is smaller. Users should set these aside from each shipment, keep them sealed and in a low radon environment (less than 0.2 pCi/L), label them in the same manner as the field devices, and send them back to the supplier with one shipment each month for analyses. It may be clear to the analysis laboratory that these are blanks; however, it is still important to conduct the analysis. For the SC method, careful initial and final readings of the vacuum gauges on the control cells and the cell background counts on analysis will be of some use in detecting an occasional leaking cell, but any background detected in a leaking cell is not relevant to the measured field sample concentrations.

Routine Instrument Checks

Proper operation of all radiation counting instruments requires that their response to a reference source be constant to within established limits. Therefore, counting equipment should be subject to routine checks to ensure proper operation. This is achieved by counting an instrument check source at least once a day. The characteristics of the check source (i.e., geometry, type of radiation emitted, etc.) should be similar to the samples to be analyzed, if possible. The count rate of the check source should be high enough to yield good counting statistics in a short time (for example, 1,000 to 10,000 counts per minute).

Pumps and flow meters should be checked routinely to ensure accuracy of volume measurements. This may be performed using a dry-gas meter or other flow measurement device of traceable accuracy.

Supplementary Information for the Grab Radon Sampling Scintillation Cell (GS) Method

The procedure described below is that used by the EPA's Office of Radiation and Indoor Air Program in its field measurement programs. It is designed for measurements made using specific cell counters and their associated cells. Equipment is available from several suppliers, and it may be necessary to modify the procedure slightly to accommodate these differences. For example, the correct cell volume must be used in calculating the activity in the cell.

The following is a general procedure for equipment used by the EPA:

1. The cells to be used are flushed with aged air or nitrogen to remove traces of the previous sample. It may be necessary to store cells for 24 hours prior to re-use if the cell had contained a high activity sample. Each cell is placed in the counter and allowed two minutes for the system to become dark-adapted. The background of the cell is then counted for 10 minutes. Background data are recorded for each cell.

2. At the survey site, the sample is collected by flowing air into the longer tube in the top of the double-valve cell for a period sufficient to allow 10 air exchanges. For the single-valve cells, it is only necessary to open the valve on the evacuated cells and allow 10 to 15 seconds for complete filling. Cells must be filled with air forced through a filter to prevent entry of airborne particulates.

3. The filled cells must be allowed to equilibrate for four hours prior to counting. The cells should not be exposed to bright light prior to counting.

4. The cells are placed in the counters, and the systems are allowed to dark-adapt for two minutes. The cells are then counted. Counting time will vary based on the activity in the cell; however, at least 1,000 counts are desirable to provide good statistics.

5. The activity in the sample is calculated and corrected for ingrowth and decay, as described below.

Calculation of Results

The radon concentration in pCi/L is determined using the following formula:

pCi/L = cpm(s) - cpm (bkg)/E x C/A x 1/V

where:

cpm(s) = Counts per minute for the sample

cpm(bkg) = Counts per minute for background

E = Efficiency of the system determined for each cell. For the cells used by the EPA, the factor is typically, 4-5 cpm/pCi.

C = Radon correction factor for decay during counting (from Exhibit 2-1)

A = Radon correction factor for decay of radon from time of collection to start of counting (from Exhibit 2-1)

V = Volume of counting cell in liters (L)

Sample Calculation

The following sample calculation demonstrates the procedure for calculating results:

Background count for system = 10 counts in 10 minutes, or 1 cpm

Sample count for two hours (120 minutes) = 1,200 counts, or 10 cpm

System efficiency (E) from cell calibration = 4.62 cpm/pCi

Count time correction (C) for two hours = 1.00757

Delay time correction (A) for four hours = 0.97026

Volume correction (V) for cell = 0.170 L

pCi/L = 10 cpm - 1 cpm/4.62 cpm/pCi x 1.00757/0.97026 x 1/0.170 L = 11.9

Unfiltered Track (UT) Detection

Protocol for Using Unfiltered Track (UT) Detection to Measure Indoor Radon Concentrations

This section provides guidance for using unfiltered track (UT) detection to obtain accurate and reproducible measurements of indoor radon concentrations. As the EPA and others acquire more experience with this interim technique, the guidelines may be revised. Adherence to this protocol will help ensure uniformity among measurement programs and allow valid inter-comparison of results. The investigator should also follow guidance provided by the EPA in *Protocols for Radon and Radon Decay Product Measurements in Homes* or other appropriate EPA measurement guidance documents.

Scope

This protocol covers, in general terms, the equipment, procedures, and quality control objectives to be used in performing the measurements. It is not meant to replace an instrument manual but, rather, presents guidelines to be incorporated into standard operating procedures by anyone providing measurement services.

Method

A UT detector consists of a piece of cellulose nitrate film packaged in a shielded container. Alpha particles emitted by radon and its decay products in air strike the detector and produce submicroscopic damage tracks. Cellulose nitrate is sensitive to alpha energies between about 1.5 MeV and 4.8 MeV. It is not sensitive to radon decay products that plate out on the detector, since their energies are above 5 MeV. Because the device detects (with different sensitivities) both radon and radon decay products, the equilibrium ratio (calculated as WL x 100 per pCi/L of radon) between radon decay products and radon can affect the device's ability to accurately measure the concentration of radon gas. While the effect may not be pronounced at values typically found in homes (estimated in the range of 20 to 60%), the error becomes significant when extreme values are encountered. Based on the EPA's specifications, devices of this type (which are produced by several manufacturers) can be operated over an equilibrium range of about 40%, with the midpoint value available from the manufacturer.

At the end of the measurement period, the detectors are turned in to a laboratory for processing and analysis. Detectors are placed in a caustic solution that accentuates the damage tracks so that they can be counted using a microscope or an automatic spark counter. The detector may be exposed on one or both sides. The number of tracks per unit area is correlated to the radon concentration in air using a conversion factor derived from data generated at a calibration facility. This conversion factor may vary for different ranges of equilibrium ratio because of the contribution from radon or radon decay products. Within a predetermined range, the number of tracks produced per unit of analyzed detector area per unit of time is proportional to the radon concentration.

Several factors contribute to the variability of the UT measurement results, including equilibrium ratio, differences in the detector response within and between batches of film, detector placement, differences in the number of background tracks, variations in etching conditions, and type of readout mechanism. Since the variability in UT measurement results decreases as the number of net tracks counted increases, counting more tracks over a larger area of the detector will reduce the uncertainty of the result. Whereas a counting area of a few square millimeters is typical with the filtered alpha track detector, it is more common to count 1 or more square centimeters with the UT detector.

Equipment

UT detectors are available from commercial suppliers. These suppliers offer contract services in which they provide the detector and subsequent analysis and reporting for a unit price. Establishing an in-house capability to provide packaged detectors, a calibration program, and a readout program would probably not be practical or economically advantageous for most users. Therefore, details for establishing the analytical aspects of a UT program are omitted from this protocol.

Assuming that UT detectors are obtained from a commercial supplier, the following equipment is needed to initiate monitoring in a house:

- the UT detector packaged in an individual shielded container to prevent extraneous exposure before deployment;

- an instruction sheet for the occupant, a sample log sheet, and a shipping container (along with a mailing label, if appropriate);
- some means for sealing the detector at the time of retrieval and prior to returning it to the supplier for analysis; and
- a data collection log, if appropriate.

Pre-Deployment Considerations

The plans of the occupant during the proposed measurement period should be considered before deployment. The UT measurement should not be made if the occupant will be moving during the measurement period. Deployment should be delayed until the new occupant is settled in the house. The UT detector should not be deployed if the user's schedule prohibits terminating the measurement at the appropriate time.

Measurement Criteria

General conditions must be met to ensure standardization of measurement conditions.

Deployment

Standard criteria must be considered when choosing a measurement device location. If the detector is installed during a site visit, the final site selected should be shown to the building occupant to be certain it is acceptable for the duration of the measurement period.

A batch of UT detectors should be deployed in buildings as soon as possible after delivery from the supplier. To minimize chances of high background exposures, testing organizations should not order more detectors than they can reasonably expect to install within the following few months. If the storage time exceeds more than a few months, the background exposures from a sample of the stored detectors should be assessed to determine if they are different from the background of detectors that are not stored for long periods. The supplier's instructions regarding storage and background determination should be followed. This background assessment of detectors stored for long periods is not necessary if the analysis laboratory routinely measures the background of stored detectors, and if the stored detectors remain tightly sealed.

The sampling period is initiated when the cellulose nitrate film is exposed. The detector should be inspected to ensure that it is intact and has not been physically damaged in shipment or handling.

Retrieval of Detectors

The device should be deployed for the measurement period specified in the instructions supplied by the analytical laboratory. If the occupant is terminating the sampling, the instructions should state when to terminate the sampling period and indicate that the actual time of termination must be documented on the device. In addition, the occupant also should be instructed to send the device to the laboratory as soon as possible—preferably, the day of sample termination. The analysis system should be calibrated to permit accurate analysis of devices deployed for some reasonable time beyond the recommended sampling period.

At the end of the measurement period, the detector should be inspected for damage or deviation from the conditions entered in the logbook at the time of deployment. Any changes should be noted in the logbook. The date of removal should be entered on the data form for the detector and in the logbook. The detector is then re-sealed according to instructions supplied by the manufacturer. After retrieval, the detectors should be turned in to the analytical laboratory as soon as possible for processing.

Documentation

Standard information must be documented so that data interpretation and comparison can be made.

Analysis Requirements

The UT method permits analysis of large counting areas and thus can achieve high sensitivity. The lower limit of detection (LLD) and the precision of a UT system are, in part, dependent upon the total number of tracks counted. The number of tracks counted is dependent on the total area analyzed, the number of film emulsion sides exposed (one or two), the length of time of deployment, and the radon concentration being measured.

The precision should be monitored using the results of the duplicate detectors described in this protocol, rather than a precision quoted by the manufacturer. It is important that precision be monitored continuously over a range of radon concentrations and that a systematic and documented method for evaluating changes in precision be part of the operating procedures.

Quality Assurance

The quality assurance program for a UT system includes five parts:

1. calibration;

2. known exposure measurements;

3. duplicate (collocated) detectors;

4. control detectors; and

5. routine instrument checks.

The purpose of a quality assurance program is to identify the accuracy and precision of the measurements and to ensure that the measurements are not influenced by exposure from sources outside the environment to be measured. The quality assurance program should include the maintenance of control charts.

Every UT laboratory system should be calibrated in a radon calibration chamber at least once every 12 months. Determination of a calibration factor requires exposure of UT detectors to a known radon and decay product concentration in a radon exposure chamber. These calibration exposures are to be used to obtain or verify the conversion factor between net tracks per unit area and radon concentration.

The following guidance is provided to manufacturers and suppliers of this device as minimum requirements in determining the calibration factor:

- UT detectors should be exposed in a radon chamber at several different radon and decay product concentrations similar to those expected in the tested buildings (a minimum of three different concentrations). Concentrations of radon decay products must be known in order to be included in the calculation of the calibration factor.

- A minimum of 10 detectors should be exposed at each level.

- A calibration factor should be determined for each batch of detector material received from the material supplier. Alternatively, calibration factors may be established from several sheets, and these factors extended to detectors from sheets exhibiting similar sensitivities (within pre-established tolerance limits).

- Altitude of the radon chamber must be known if located at more than 600 feet (200 meters) above sea level so that a correction can be included in the calculation of the calibration factor.

Known Exposure Measurements

Anyone providing measurement services with UT detectors should submit detectors with known radon and decay product exposures (spiked samples) for analysis at a rate of three per 100 measurements, with a minimum of three per year and a maximum required of six per month. Known exposure (spiked) detectors should be labeled in the same manner as field detectors to ensure identical processing. The results of the spiked detector analyses should be monitored and recorded. Any significant deviation from the known concentrations to which they were exposed should be investigated.

Duplicate (Collocated) Detectors

Anyone providing measurement services with UT devices should place duplicate detectors in enough houses to test the precision of the measurement. The number of duplicate detectors deployed should be approximately 10% of the number of detectors deployed each month, or 50, whichever is smaller. The pair of detectors should be treated identically in every respect. They should be shipped, stored, opened, installed, removed, and processed together, and not identified as duplicates to the processing laboratory. The samples selected for duplication should be distributed systematically throughout the entire population of measurements. Groups selling measurements to homeowners can do this by providing two detectors (instead of one) to a random selection of purchasers, with instructions to place the detectors side by side. Consideration should be given to providing some means to ensure that the duplicate devices are not separated during the measurement period. Data from duplicate detectors should be evaluated using the procedures described by Goldin, Taylor, or the EPA. Whatever procedures are used must be documented prior to beginning measurements. Consistent failure in duplicate agreement may indicate a problem in the measurement process and should be investigated.

Control Detectors

The laboratory background level for each batch of UT detectors should be established by each supplier. Suppliers should measure the background of a statistically significant number of unexposed detectors that have been processed according to their standard operating procedures. Normally, the analysis laboratory or supplier calculates the net readings (which are used to calculate the reported sample radon concentrations) by subtracting the laboratory blank values from the results obtained from the field detectors.

Field control UT detectors (field blanks) should consist of a minimum of 5% of the devices that are deployed every month, or 25, whichever is smaller. Users should set these aside from each shipment, keep them sealed and in a low radon environment (less than 0.2 pCi/L), label them in the same manner as the field UT detectors to assure identical processing, and send them back to the supplier with the field UT detectors for analysis. These control devices are necessary to measure the background exposure that accumulates during shipment and storage. The results should be monitored and recorded. If one or a few field blanks have concentrations significantly greater than the LLD established by the supplier, it may indicate defective packaging or handling. If the average value from the field control devices (field blanks) is significantly greater than the LLD established by the supplier, this average value should be subtracted from the individual values reported for the other devices in the exposure group.

Proper functioning of the analysis instruments and proper response by their operators require that the equipment be subject to routine checks. Daily or more frequent monitoring of equipment and operators is vital to ensuring consistently accurate results.

Quiz #8

1. T/F: Short-term measurements lasting 90 days or less should be made under closed-building conditions.

   ☐ True
   ☐ False

2. To the extent reasonable, all windows, outside vents and external doors should be closed (except for normal entrance and exit) for _____ hours prior to and during the measurement period.

   ☐ two
   ☐ eight
   ☐ 12
   ☐ 48

3. T/F: The CW detector should be programmed to run continuously, recording the periodic integrated WL and, when possible, the total integrated average WL.

   ☐ True
   ☐ False

4. T/F: An alpha track (AT) detector consists of a small piece of plastic or film enclosed in a container with a filter-covered opening or similar design for excluding radon decay products.

   ☐ True
   ☐ False

5. T/F: With the EC test, the amount of voltage reduction is directly related to the average radon concentration and the duration of the exposure period.

   ☐ True
   ☐ False

6. Activated-charcoal adsorption (AC) devices are passive devices requiring _____ to function.

   ☐ no power
   ☐ power

7. A measurement with an LS device typically lasts_____ days.

   ☐ one to two days
   ☐ two to seven days
   ☐ seven to 14 days

8. T/F: A UT detector consists of a piece of cellulose nitrate film packaged in a shielded container.

   ☐ True
   ☐ False

Answer Key is on page 351.

Active Devices

Introduction

Active devices need to be plugged into an electrical outlet to function. In the next three sections, we'll learn about the following:

- the protocol for using continuous working-level (CW) monitors to measure indoor radon-decay product concentrations;
- the protocol for using radon progeny integrating sampling units (RPISU or RP) to measure indoor radon decay product concentrations; and
- the protocol for using grab sampling working level (GW) units to measure indoor radon decay product concentrations.

Radon Progeny Integrating Sampling Units

Protocol for Using Radon Progeny Integrating Sampling Units (RPISU or RP) to Measure Indoor Radon Decay Product Concentrations

This protocol provides guidance for using radon progeny integrating sampling units (RPISU or RP) to produce accurate and reproducible measurements of indoor radon decay product concentrations. Adherence to this procedure will help ensure uniformity in measurement programs and allow valid inter-comparison of results. Measurements made in accordance with this protocol will produce results representative of closed-building conditions. Measurements made under closed-building conditions have a smaller variability, and are more reproducible than measurements made when the building conditions are not controlled. The investigator should also follow guidance provided by the EPA in *Protocols for Radon and Radon Decay Product Measurements in Homes* or other appropriate EPA measurement guidance documents.

Scope

This section covers, in general terms, the equipment, procedures, analysis, and quality control objectives for measurements made with RPs. It is not meant to replace an instrument manual but, rather, presents guidelines to be incorporated into standard operating procedures by anyone providing measurement services.

METHOD

Thermoluminescent Dosimeter (TLD) RP

There are three types of RPs. The TLD type contains an air-sampling pump that draws a continuous, uniform flow of air through a detector assembly. The detector assembly includes a filter and at least two TLDs. One TLD measures the radiation emitted from radon decay products collected on the filter, and the other TLD is used for a background gamma correction. This RP is intended for a sampling period of 48 hours to a few weeks.

Analysis of the detector TLDs is performed in a laboratory using a TLD reader. Interpretation of the results of this measurement requires a calibration for the detector and the analysis system based on exposures to known concentrations of radon decay products.

Alpha Track Detector (ATD) RP

A second type of RP consists of an air-sampling pump and an ATD assembly. The air-sampling pump draws a continuous, uniform flow of air through a filter in the detector assembly where the radon decay products are deposited. Opposite to the side of the filter where the radon decay products are deposited is a cylinder with three collimating cylindrical holes. Alpha particles emitted from the radon decay products on the filter pass through the collimating holes and through different thicknesses of energy-absorbing film before impinging on a disc of alpha track detecting plastic film (LR-115 or CR-39). Analysis of the number of alpha particle tracks in each of the three sectors of the film allows the determination of the number of alpha particles derived from Radium A (Po-218) and Radium C (Po-214). This feature allows the determination of the equilibrium factor for the radon decay products. This type of RP is intended for a sampling period of about 48 hours to a few weeks.

Etching and counting of the alpha track assembly is carried out by mailing the detector film to the analysis laboratory. Interpretation of the results of this measurement requires a calibration for the detector, and the analysis system based on exposure to known concentrations of radon decay products.

Electret RP

The electret RP is similar in operation to the TLD-type RP, except that the TLD is replaced with an electret. The current model of this device contains a one-liter-per-minute constant air flow pump and collects the decay products on an 11.4 cm2 filter. As the radon decay products that are collected on the filter decay, negatively charged ions generated by alpha particle radiation are collected on a positively charged electret, thereby reducing its surface voltage. This reduction has been demonstrated to be proportional to the radon decay product concentration.

RPs are true integrating instruments if the pump flow rate is uniform throughout the sampling period. The electret must be removed from the chamber and the electret voltage measured with a special surface voltmeter both before and after exposure. To determine the average radon concentration during the exposure period, the difference between the initial and final voltages is divided first by a calibration factor, and then by the number of exposure days. A background radon concentration equivalent of ambient gamma radiation is subtracted to compute radon concentration. Electret voltage measurements can be made in a laboratory or in the field.

Equipment

The three types of RP sampling systems include a sampling pump and the detector assembly. Sampling with the TLD-type RP requires either a fresh detector assembly or fresh TLD chips to be inserted in the detector assembly. Using the electret-type RP requires a sufficient charge on the electret. Sampling with the ATD-type RP requires a fresh detector disc (LR-115 or CR-39). An air flow rate meter should be available for checking flow rates with the RP, and spare filters should be available as replacements, as needed.

Pre-Deployment Considerations

The plans of the occupant during the proposed measurement period should be considered before deployment. The RP measurement should not be made if the occupant will be moving during the measurement period. Deployment should be delayed until the new occupant is settled in the house.

The RPISU should not be deployed if the user's schedule prohibits terminating the measurement at the appropriate time.

Prior to installation in the building, the pump should be checked to ensure that it is operable and capable of maintaining a uniform flow through the detector assembly. Extra pump assemblies should be available during deployment in case a problem is encountered. Arrangements should be made with the occupant of the building to ensure that entry into the building is possible at the time of installation, and to determine availability of a suitable electrical outlet near the sampling area in the selected room.

Measurement Criteria

General conditions must be met to ensure standardization of measurement conditions.

Deployment and Operation

Standard criteria must be considered when choosing a measurement device location. In addition, the air intake (sampling head) should be placed at least 20 inches above the floor, and at least 4 inches from surfaces that may obstruct flow.

Operation

The RP should be installed and, if possible, the air flow rate checked with a calibrated flow meter. The location, date, starting time, running time meter reading, and flow rate should be recorded on the detector assembly envelope and in a log. The RP should be observed for a few minutes after initiating measurements to ensure continued operation. The occupants should also be informed about the RP and requested that they report any problems or pump shutdown. The occupants should be aware of the length of time the RP will be operated, and an appointment should be arranged to retrieve the unit. The occupants should also be informed of the criteria for the standardized measurement conditions.

The sampling period should be at least 48 hours, and may need to be longer, depending on the type of RP head. A longer operating time decreases the uncertainty associated with the measurement result.

Retrieval of Devices

Prior to pump shutdown, the flow rate should be measured with a calibrated flow meter (if possible), and the unit should be briefly observed to ensure that it is operating properly. The detector assembly or detector film should be removed for processing, and the date, time, running time meter reading and flow rate should be recorded both on the envelope and in a logbook. The filter should be checked for holes or dust loading, and any other observed conditions that might affect the measurement. If TLDs or film discs are to be removed from the detector assembly, removal should be delayed for at least three hours after sampling is completed to allow for decay and registration of radon decay products on the filter.

Documentation

Standard information that must be documented so that data interpretation and comparison can be made.

In addition, the serial numbers of the RPs, TLDs, film discs or electrets must be recorded.

Analysis Requirements

Analysis of the film from the ATD-type RPs requires an analysis laboratory equipped to etch and count alpha track film.

Analysis of TLD-type RPs requires a TLD reader. The TLD reader is an instrument that heats the TLDs at a uniform and reproducible rate, and simultaneously measures the light emitted by the thermoluminescent material. The readout process is carefully controlled, with the detector purged with nitrogen to prevent spurious emissions. Prior to analyzing the RPISU dosimeters, the TLD reader should be periodically tested using dosimeters exposed to a known level of alpha or gamma radiation. TLDs are prepared for re-use by cleaning and annealing at the prescribed temperature in an oven.

Analysis of the electret-type RPs requires a specially-built surface voltmeter for measuring electret voltages before and after exposure.

Sensitivity

The lower limit of detection (LLD) should be specified by individual suppliers for RP detectors exposed according to their directions. The LLD will depend on the length of the exposure and the background of the detector for materials used. The LLD should be calculated using the results of the laboratory control devices.

Precision

Precision should be monitored and recorded using the results of the duplicate detector analyses. This method may achieve a coefficient of variation of 10% at radon decay product concentrations of 0.02 WL or greater. An alternate measure of precision is a relative percent difference, defined as the difference between two duplicate measurements divided by their mean; note that these two measures of precision are not identical quantities. It is important that precision be monitored continuously over a range of radon concentrations, and that a systematic and documented method for evaluating changes in precision be part of the operating procedures.

Quality Assurance

The quality assurance program for an RP system includes five parts:

1. calibration;

2. known exposure detectors;

3. duplicate (collocated) detectors;

4. control detectors; and

5. routine instrument checks.

The purpose of a quality assurance program is to identify the accuracy and precision of the measurements, and to ensure that the measurements are not influenced by exposure from sources outside the environment to be measured. The quality assurance program should include the maintenance of control charts.

Users of electret-type RPs should follow the quality assurance guidance given for electret ion chamber devices.

Calibration

Every RP should be calibrated in a radon calibration chamber before being put into service and after any repairs or modifications. Subsequent re-calibrations should be done once every 12 months, with cross-checks to a recently calibrated instrument at least semi-annually. Calibration of RPs requires exposure in a controlled radon exposure chamber where the radon decay product concentration is known during the exposure period. The detector must be exposed in the chamber using the normal operating flow rate for the RP sampling pumps. Calibration should include exposure of a minimum of four detectors exposed at different radon decay product concentrations representative of the range found in routine measurements. The relationship of TLD reader units or etched track reader units to working level (WL) for a given sample volume, and the standard error associated with this measurement should be determined. Calibration of the RPs also includes testing to ensure accuracy of the flow rate measurement.

Known Exposure Devices

Anyone providing measurement services with RP devices should submit detectors with known decay product exposures (spiked samples) for analysis at a rate of three per 100 measurements, with a minimum of three per year and a maximum required of six per month. Known exposure detectors should be labeled in the same manner as the field detectors to assure blind processing. The results of the known exposure detector analysis should be monitored and recorded, and any significant deviation from the known concentration to which they were exposed should be investigated.

Duplicate (Collocated) Detectors

Anyone providing measurement services with RP devices should place duplicate detectors in enough houses to test the precision of the measurement. The number of duplicate detectors deployed should be approximately 10% of the number of detectors deployed each month, or 50, whichever is smaller. The duplicate detectors should be shipped, stored, exposed and analyzed under the same conditions. The samples selected for duplication should be distributed systematically throughout the entire population of samples. Groups selling measurement services to homeowners can do this by making two side-by-side measurements in a random selection of homes. Data from duplicate detectors should be evaluated using the procedures described by Goldin, Taylor, or the EPA. Whatever procedures are used must be documented prior to beginning measurements. Consistent failure in duplicate agreement may indicate a problem in the measurement process and should be investigated.

Control Detectors

TLD-type RPs use a TLD that is shielded from the gamma radiation emitted by the material on the filter. This TLD is incorporated in the detector assembly to measure the environmental gamma exposure of the sampling detector. The two TLDs are processed identically and the environmental gamma exposure is subtracted from the sample reading. Electret-type RPs also require an environmental gamma background correction.

Laboratory Control Detectors

The laboratory background level for each batch of assembled TLDs should be established by each supplier. Suppliers should measure the background of a statistically significant number of unexposed thermoluminescent assemblies that have been processed according to their standard operating procedures. To calculate the net readings used to calculate the reported sample radon concentrations, the analysis laboratory subtracts this laboratory blank value from the results obtained from the field detectors.

Similarly, the laboratory background level for each batch of ATD-type RPs should be established by each supplier of these detectors. Suppliers should measure the background of a statistically significant number of unexposed detector films that have been processed according to their standard operating procedures. The analysis laboratory will subtract this laboratory blank value from the results obtained from the field detectors before calculating the final result.

Users of electret-type RPs should follow similar control detector procedures.

Field Control Detectors (Blanks)

Field control detectors (field blanks) should consist of a minimum of 5% of the detectors deployed each month, or 25, whichever is smaller. Users should set these aside from each shipment, keep them sealed, label them in the same manner as the field detectors, and, where applicable, send them back to the analysis laboratory as blind controls with one shipment each month. These field blank detectors measure the background exposure that may accumulate during shipment or storage. The results should be monitored and recorded. If one or a few of the field blanks have concentrations significantly greater than the LLD established by the supplier, it may indicate defective material or procedures. If the average value from the background control detectors (field blanks) is significantly greater than the LLD established by the supplier, this average value should be subtracted from the individual values reported for the other detectors in the exposure group. The cause for the elevated field blank readings should then be investigated.

Routine Instrument Checks

Proper operation of all analysis equipment requires that their response to a reference source be constant to within established limits. Therefore, analysis equipment should be subject to routine checks to ensure proper operation. This is achieved by counting an instrument check source at least once a day during operation.

Pumps and flow meters should be routinely checked to ensure accuracy of volume measurements. This may be performed using a dry-gas meter or other flow measurement device of traceable accuracy.

Grab Sampling Working Level (GW)

Protocol for Using Grab Sampling Working Level (GW) to Measure Indoor Radon Decay Product Concentrations

This section provides guidance for using the grab sampling working-level (GW) technique to provide accurate and reproducible measurements of indoor radon decay product concentrations. Adherence to this protocol will help ensure uniformity among measurement programs and allow valid inter-comparison of results. Measurements made in accordance with this procedure will produce results representative of closed-building conditions. Measurements made under closed-building conditions have a smaller variability and are more reproducible than measurements made when the building conditions are not controlled.

The results of the GW method are influenced greatly by conditions that exist in the building during and for up to 12 hours prior to the measurement. It is, therefore, especially important when making grab measurements to conform to the closed-building conditions for 12 hours before the measurement. Grab sampling techniques are not recommended for measurements made to determine the need for remedial action. The investigator should also follow guidance provided by the EPA in *Protocols for Radon and Radon Decay Product Measurements in Homes* or other appropriate EPA measurement guidance documents.

Scope

This section covers, in general terms, the equipment, procedures and quality control objectives to be used in performing the measurements. It is not meant to replace an instrument manual but, rather, to present guidelines to be incorporated into standard operating procedures by anyone providing measurement services. Questions about these guidelines should be directed to the EPA.

Methods

Grab sampling measurements of radon decay product concentrations in air are performed by collecting the decay products from a known volume of air on a filter, and by counting the activity on the filter during or following collection. Comparable results may be obtained using all these methods. This procedure, however, will describe two methods that have been used most widely with good results. These are the Kusnetz Procedure and the Modified Tsivoglou Procedure.

The Kusnetz Procedure may be used to obtain results in working levels (WL) when the concentration of individual decay products is unimportant. Decay products from up to 100 liters of air are collected on a filter in a five-minute sampling period. The total alpha activity on the filter is counted at any time between 40 and 90 minutes after the end of sampling. Counting can be done using a scintillation-type counter to obtain gross alpha counts for the selected period. Counts from the filter are converted to disintegrations using the appropriate counter efficiency. The disintegrations from the decay products collected from the known volume of air may be converted into WLs using the appropriate Kusnetz factor for the counting time used.

The Tsivoglou Procedure, as modified by Thomas, may be used to determine WL and the concentration of the individual radon decay products. Sampling is the same as that used for the Kusnetz Procedure; however, the filter is counted three separate times following collection. The filter is counted between the interval of two to five minutes, six to 20 minutes, and 21 to 30 minutes, following completion of sampling. Count results are used in a series of equations to calculate concentrations of the three radon decay products and WL.

Equipment

The equipment required for radon decay product concentration determination by GW consists of the following items:

- an air-sampling pump capable of maintaining a flow rate of 2 to 25 liters per minute through the selected filter. The flow rate should not vary significantly during the sampling period;
- a filter holder (with adapters for attachment) to accept a 25- or 47-mm diameter, 0.8-micron membrane or glass fiber filter;

- a calibrated air flow measurement device to determine the air flow through the filter during sampling;

- a stopwatch or timer for accurate timing of sampling and counting;

- a scintillation counter and a zinc sulfide scintillation disc;

- a National Institute of Standards and Technology (NIST)-traceable alpha calibration source to determine counter efficiency; and

- a data collection log.

Pre-Deployment Considerations

The occupant's plans during the proposed measurement period should be considered before deployment. The GW measurement should not be made if the occupant will be moving during the measurement period. Deployment should be delayed until the new occupant is settled in the house.

The GW device should not be deployed if the user's schedule prohibits terminating the measurement at the appropriate time.

Pre-Measurement Testing

Prior to collection of the sample, proper operation of the equipment must be verified, and the counter efficiency and background must be determined. This is especially critical for the Tsivoglou Procedure, in which the sample counting must begin two minutes following the end of sampling.

The air pump, filter assembly, and flow meter must be tested to ensure that there are no leaks in the system. The scintillation counter must be operated with the scintillation tray (where applicable) and scintillation disc in place to determine background for the counting system. Also, the counter must be operated with an NIST-traceable alpha calibration source in place of a filter in the counting location to determine system counting efficiency. Both the system background and system efficiency are used in the calculation of results from the actual sample.

Measurement Criteria

General conditions must be met to ensure standardization of measurement conditions.

Deployment

Standard criteria must be considered when choosing a measurement device location.

Sampling

A new filter should be placed in the filter holder prior to entering the building. Care should be taken to avoid puncturing the filter to prevent leakage. The sampling is initiated by starting the pump and the clock simultaneously. The air flow rate should be noted and recorded in a logbook. The time the sampling is begun should also be recorded. The sampling period should be five minutes, and the time from the beginning of sampling to the time of counting must be recorded precisely.

Documentation

Standard information that must be documented so that data interpretation and comparison can be made.

Analysis Requirements

Analysis may be done using the Kusnetz Procedure, the Modified Tsivoglou Procedure, or other procedures described elsewhere. If the Tsivoglou Procedure is used, the counting must be started two minutes following the end of sampling. Analysis using the Kusnetz Procedure must be performed between 40 and 90 minutes following the end of sampling. A counting time of 10 minutes during this period is usually used.

The filter from the holder must be removed using forceps and carefully placed facing the scintillation phosphor. The side of the filter on which the decay products were collected must face the phosphor disc. The chamber containing the filter and disc should be closed and allowed to dark-adapt prior to starting counting. For the Tsivoglou method, this procedure of placing the filter in the counting position must be done quickly, since the first of the three counts must begin two minutes following the end of sampling. If the counter used has been shown to be slow to dark-adapt, the counting should be done in a darkened environment. Additional details on the procedure and calculations are available.

Sensitivity

For a five-minute sampling period (10 to 20 liters of air) on a 25-mm filter, the lower limit of detection (LLD) using the Kusnetz or modified Tsivoglou counting procedure can be approximately 0.0005 WL.

Precision

Precision should be monitored using the results of duplicate measurements. Sources of error in the procedure may result from inaccuracies in measuring the volume of air sampled, characteristics of the filter used, and measurement of the amount of radioactivity on the filter. The method can produce duplicate measurements with a coefficient of variation of 10% or less at 0.02 WL or greater. An alternate measure of precision is a relative percent difference, defined as the difference between two duplicate measurements divided by their mean; note that these two measures of precision are not identical quantities. It is important that precision be monitored continuously over a range of radon concentrations, and that a systematic and documented method for evaluating changes in precision be part of the operating procedures.

Quality Assurance

The quality assurance program for a GW system includes three parts:

1. calibration of the system;
2. duplicate measurements; and
3. routine instrument checks.

The purpose of a quality assurance program is to identify the accuracy and precision of the measurements, and to ensure that the measurements are not influenced by exposure from sources outside the environment to be measured. The quality assurance program should include the maintenance of control charts.

Calibration

Pumps and flow meters used to sample air must be calibrated routinely to ensure accuracy of volume measurements. This may be performed using a dry-gas meter or other flow measurement device of traceable accuracy.

Every GW device should be calibrated in a radon (decay product) calibration chamber before being put into service and after any repairs or modifications. Subsequent re-calibrations should be done once every 12 months, with cross-checks to a recently calibrated instrument at least semi-annually. Grab measurements should be made in a calibration chamber with known radon decay product concentrations to verify the calibration factor. These measurements should also be used to test the collection efficiency and self-absorption of the filter material being used for sampling. A change in the filter material being used requires that the new material be checked for collection efficiency in a calibration chamber.

Duplicate Measurements

Anyone providing measurement services with GW devices should place duplicate detectors in enough houses to test the precision of the measurement. The number of duplicate detectors deployed should be approximately 10% of the number of detectors deployed each month, or 50, whichever is smaller. To the greatest extent possible, care should be taken to ensure that the samples are duplicates. The filter heads should be relatively close to each other and away from drafts. Care should also be taken to ensure that one filter is not in the discharge air stream of the other sampler. The measurements selected for duplication should be distributed systematically throughout the entire population of measurements. Data from duplicate samples should be evaluated using the procedures described by Goldin, Taylor, or the EPA. Whatever procedures are used must be documented prior to beginning measurements. Consistent failure in duplicate agreement may indicate a problem in the measurement process and should be investigated.

Routine Instrument Checks

Proper operation of all radiation counting instruments requires that their response to a reference source be constant to within established limits. Therefore, counting equipment should be subject to routine checks to ensure proper operation. This is achieved by counting an instrument check source at least once a day. The characteristics of the check source (i.e., geometry, type of radiation emitted, etc.) should be similar to the samples to be analyzed, if possible. The count rate of the check source should be high enough to yield good counting statistics in a short time (for example, 1,000 to 10,000 counts per minute).

The radiological counters should have calibration checks run daily to determine counter efficiency. This is particularly important for portable counters taken into the field that may be subject to rugged use and temperature extremes. These checks are made using an NIST-traceable alpha calibration source, such as Am-241. In addition, the system background count rate should be assessed regularly.

Pumps and flow meters should be checked routinely to ensure accuracy of volume measurements. This may be performed using a dry-gas meter or other flow measurement device of traceable accuracy.

SUPPLEMENTARY INFORMATION FOR THE GRAB SAMPLING WORKING-LEVEL (GW) METHOD

Sample Collection

Two commonly used methods are described below. There are several other methods reported in the industry's literature. Sampling using these methods requires collection of radon decay products on a filter, and measuring the alpha activity of the sample with a calibrated detector at time intervals that are specific for each method.

The filter is installed in the filter-holder assembly and attached to the pump. The pump is then operated for exactly five minutes, pulling air through the filter. The starting time and air flow rate should be recorded. The pump is stopped at the end of the five-minute sampling time. At this time, the stopwatch should be started or reset.

Sample Counting: Modified Tsivoglou Technique

The filter is carefully transferred from the filter-holder assembly to the detector. The collection side of the filter is oriented toward the face of the detector. The counter is operated for the following time intervals (after sampling has stopped): two to five minutes, six to 20 minutes, and 21 to 30 minutes. The total counts for each time period are then recorded.

Sample Counting: Kusnetz Technique

The filter is carefully transferred from the filter-holder assembly to the detector. The collection side of the filter is oriented toward the face of the detector. The counter is operated over any 10-minute time interval between 40 minutes and 90 minutes after sampling starts. The total counts for the sample and the time (in minutes after sampling) at the midpoint of the 10-minute time interval are then recorded.

Data Analysis

Data analysis for the two different techniques is described below.

Modified Tsivoglou Technique

The concentration in picocuries per liter (pCi/L) of each of the radon decay products (Po-218, Pb-214 and Po-214) can be determined by using the following calculations:

$$C_2 = 1/FE \ (0.16921 \ G_1 - 0.08213 \ G_2 + 0.07765 \ G_3 - 0.5608 \ R)$$

$$C_3 = 1/FE \ (0.001108 \ G_1 - 0.02052 \ G_2 + 0.04904 \ G_3 - 0.1577 \ R)$$

$$C_4 = 1/FE \ (-0.02236 \ G_1 + 0.03310 \ G_2 - 0.03765 \ G_3 - 0.05720 \ R)$$

It is important to note that the constants in these equations are based on a 3.04-minute half-life of Po-218. The working level (WL) associated with these concentrations can then be calculated using the following relationship:

Where:

C2 = concentration of Po-218 (RaA) in pCi/L;

C3 = concentration of Pb-214 (RaB) in pCi/L;

C4 = concentration of Po-214 (RaC') in pCi/L;

F = sampling flow rate in liters per minute (Lpm);

E = counter efficiency in counts per minute/disintegrations per minute (cpm/dpm);

G1 = gross alpha counts for the time interval of two to five minutes;

G2 = gross alpha counts for the time interval of six to 20 minutes;

G3 = gross alpha counts for the time interval of 21 to 30 minutes; and

R = background counting rate in cpm.

(Reference: Thomas 1972)

Kusnetz Technique

WL is calculated as follows:

WL = C/Kt VE

Where:

C = sample cpm - background cpm;

Kt = factor determined from Exhibit 3-1 (PHS 1957) for time from end of collection to midpoint of counting;

V = total sample air volume in liters [calculated as flow rate (L/m) x sample time (m)]; and

E = counter efficiency in cpm/dpm.

SAMPLE PROBLEMS

Sample Problem for the Modified Tsivoglou Technique

Given:

F = sampling flow rate = 3.5 Lpm

E = counting efficiency = 0.47 cpm/dpm

G1 = 880

G2 = 2660

G3 = 1460

R = 0.5

Calculate:

$C2 = 1/3.5 \times 0.47\ (0.16921 \times 880 - 0.08213 \times 2660 + 0.07765 \times 1460 - 0.05608 \times 0.5)$

$C2 = 26.8\ pCi/L$

$C3 = 1/3.5 \times 0.47\ (0.001108 \times 880 - 0.02052 \times 2660 + 0.04904 \times 1460 - 0.1577 \times 0.5)$

$C3 = 10.9\ pCi/L$

$C4 = 1/3.5 \times 0.47\ (-0.02236 \times 880 + 0.03310 \times 2660 - 0.03766 \times 1460 - 0.05720 \times 0.5)$

$C4 = 8.1\ pCi/L$

$WL = (1.028 \times 10\text{-}3 \times 26.8 + 5.07 \times 10\text{-}3 \times 10.9 + 3.728 \times 10\text{-}3 \times 8.1)$

$WL = 0.11$

Sample Problem for the Kusnetz Technique

Background count = 3 counts in 5 minutes, or 0.6 cpm

Standard count = 5,985 counts in 5 minutes, or 1,197 cpm

Efficiency = 1197 cpm - 0.6 cpm/2,430 dpm = 0.49 (known source of 2,439 dpm)

Sample volume = 4.4 liter/minute x 5 minutes = 22 liters

Sample count at 45 minutes (time from end of sampling period to start of counting period) = 560 counts in 10 minutes, or 56 cpm

Kt at 50 minutes (from Exhibit 3-1) = 130

WL = 56 cpm - 0.6 cpm/130 x 22 L x 0.49

WL = 0.04

Continuous Radon (CR) Monitors

Protocol for Using Continuous Radon (CR) Monitors to Measure Indoor Radon Concentrations

This section provides guidance for using continuous radon monitors (CR) to measure indoor radon concentrations accurately and to obtain reproducible results. Adherence to this protocol will help ensure uniformity among measurement programs and allow valid comparison of results. Measurements made in accordance with this protocol will produce results representative of closed-building conditions. Measurements made under closed-building conditions have a smaller variability and are more reproducible than measurements made when the building conditions are not controlled. The investigator should also follow guidance provided by the EPA in *Protocols for Radon and Radon Decay Product Measurements in Homes* or other appropriate EPA measurement guidance documents.

Scope

This section covers, in general terms, the sample collection and analysis method, the equipment needed, and the quality control objectives of measurements made with CRs. It is not meant to replace an instrument manual but, rather, to present guidelines to be incorporated into standard operating procedures by anyone providing measurement services.

Method

There are three general types of CR monitors covered by this protocol.

In the first type, ambient air is sampled for radon in a scintillation cell after passing through a filter that removes radon decay products and dust. As the radon in the cell decays, the radon decay products plate out on the interior surface of the scintillation cell. Alpha particles produced by subsequent decays, or by the initial radon decay, strike the zinc sulfide coating on the inside of the scintillation cell, thereby producing scintillations. The scintillations are detected by a photomultiplier tube in the detector, which generates electrical pulses. These pulses are processed by the detector's electronics, and the data are usually stored in the memory of the monitor where results are available for recall or transmission to a data logger or printer.

This type of CR monitor uses either a flow-through cell or a periodic-fill cell. In the flow-through cell, air is drawn continuously through the cell by a small pump. In the periodic-fill cell, air is drawn into the cell once during each pre-selected time interval; then, the scintillations are counted, and the cycle repeated. A third variation operates by radon diffusion through a filter area, with the radon concentration in the cell varying with the radon concentration in the ambient air after a small diffusion time lag. The concentrations measured by all three variations of cells lag the ambient radon concentrations because of the inherent delay in the radon decay product disintegration process.

A second type of CR monitor operates as an ionization chamber. Radon in the ambient air diffuses into the chamber through a filtered area so that the radon concentration in the chamber follows the radon concentration in the ambient air with some small time lag. Within the chamber, alpha particles emitted during the decay of radon atoms produce bursts of ions, which are recorded as individual electrical pulses for each disintegration. These pulses are processed by the monitor electronics; the number of pulses counted is usually displayed on the monitor, and the data are available for processing by an optional data logger/printer.

A third type of CR monitor functions by allowing ambient air to diffuse through a filter into a detection chamber. As the radon decays, the alpha particles are counted using a solid-state silicon detector. The measured radon concentration in the chamber follows the radon concentration in the ambient air by a small time lag.

Equipment

The equipment required depends on the type and model of CR monitor used. Aged air or nitrogen must be available for introduction into the CR monitor to measure the background count rate during calibration. For scintillation cell-type CRs, sealed scintillation cells with a measured low background should be available as spare cells.

Pre-Deployment Considerations

The plans of the occupant during the proposed measurement period should be considered before deployment. The CR measurement should not be made if the occupant will be moving during the measurement period. Deployment should be delayed until the new occupant is settled in the house.

Pre-Sampling Testing

Before and after each measurement, the CR monitor should be carefully tested, according to the manufacturer's directions, to verify that the correct input parameters and the unit's clock or timer are set properly, and to verify the operation of the pump. Flow rates within the range of the manufacturer's specifications are satisfactory.

After every 1,000 hours of operation of scintillation cell-type CRs, the background count rate should be checked by purging the unit with clean, aged air or nitrogen, in accordance with the procedures identified in the operating manual for the instrument. In addition, the background count rate of all CR types should be monitored more frequently by operating the instrument in a low-radon environment.

Participation in a laboratory inter-comparison program should be conducted initially, and at least once every 12 months thereafter, and after equipment repair to verify that the conversion factor used by the CR monitor is accurate. This is done by comparing the unit's response to a known radon concentration. At this time, the correct operation of the pump should be verified. (Participation in the EPA's National Radon Proficiency Program [RPP] did not satisfy the need for annual calibration, as this program was a performance test rather than an internal calibration.)

Measurement Criteria

General conditions must be met to ensure standardization of measurement conditions.

Deployment and Operation

Standard criteria must be considered when choosing a measurement device location.

Operation

The CR monitor should be programmed to run continuously, periodically recording the radon concentration for at least 48 hours. Longer measurements may be required, depending on the CR type and radon level being measured. An increase in operating time decreases the uncertainty associated with using the measurement result to represent a longer-term average concentration.

Care should be taken to account for data that are produced before equilibrium conditions have been established in a flow-through cell. Generally, conditions stabilize after the first four hours. Measurements made prior to this time are low and should either be discarded or used to estimate radon concentrations using pre-established system constants. If the first four hours of data from a 48-hour measurement are discarded, the remaining hours of data can be averaged and are sufficient to represent a two-day measurement.

Retrieval of Monitors

When the measurement is terminated, the operator should document the stop date and stop time, and whether the closed-building conditions are still in effect.

Documentation

The serial numbers of the CR monitor, scintillation cells and other equipment must also be recorded.

RESULTS

Sensitivity

Most CR monitors are capable of a lower limit of detection (LLD) of 1 picocurie per liter (pCi/L) or less.

Precision

Most CR monitors can achieve a coefficient of variation of less than 10% at 4 pCi/L or greater. An alternate measure of precision is a relative percent difference, defined as the difference between two duplicate measurements divided by their mean; note that these two measures of precision are not identical quantities. It is important that precision be monitored continuously over a range of radon concentrations and that a systematic and documented method for evaluating changes in precision be part of the operating procedures.

Quality Assurance

The quality assurance program for CR measurements includes four parts:

1. calibration;
2. background measurements;
3. duplicate measurements; and
4. routine instrument checks.

The purpose of a quality assurance program is to identify the accuracy and precision of the measurements, and to ensure that the measurements are not influenced by exposure from sources outside the environment to be measured. The quality assurance program should include the maintenance of control charts.

Calibration

Every CR monitor should be calibrated in a radon calibration chamber before being put into service and after any repairs or modifications. (Note that an inherent element in the calibration process is a thorough determination of the background count rate using clean, aged air or nitrogen.) Subsequent re-calibrations and background checks should be done at least once every 12 months, with cross-checks to a recently calibrated instrument at least semi-annually. All cells need individual calibration factors.

Background Measurements

After every 1,000 hours of operation of scintillation cell-type CRs (about every twentieth 48-hour measurement), and whenever any type of CR is calibrated, the background should be checked by purging the monitor with clean, aged air or nitrogen. In addition, the background count rate should be monitored more frequently by operating the instrument in a low-radon environment. Cells that develop a high background after prolonged use should be re-conditioned by the manufacturer.

Duplicate Measurements

When two or more CR monitors of the same type are available (e.g., scintillation cell, ionization chamber, or silicon detector-types), the precision of the measurements can be estimated by operating the monitors side by side. The analysis of duplicate results should follow the methodology described by Goldin, Taylor, or the EPA. Whatever procedures are used must be documented prior to beginning measurements. Consistent failure in duplicate agreement may indicate a problem in the measurement process and should be investigated.

Routine Instrument Checks

Proper operation of all radiation counting instruments requires that their response to a reference source be constant to within established limits. Therefore, counting equipment should be subject to routine checks to ensure proper operation. This is achieved by counting an instrument check cell (for scintillation cell-type CRs) prior to beginning each measurement. The count rate of the check source should be high enough to yield good counting statistics in a short time (for example, 1,000 to 10,000 counts per minute).

If a check source is unavailable or incompatible with the type of CR monitor being used, an informal inter-comparison with another measurement method that has proven reliability (for example, in the EPA's National RMP Program) should be conducted at least every tenth measurement. In addition, it is important to regularly check all components of the equipment that affect the result, including battery and electronics, and to document these checks.

Pumps and flow meters should be checked routinely to ensure accuracy of volume measurements. This may be performed using a dry-gas meter or other flow measurement device of traceable accuracy.

Quiz #9

1. T/F: The three types of radon progeny (RP) sampling systems include a sampling pump and the detector assembly.

    ☐ True
    ☐ False

2. The RP measurement _____ if the occupant will be moving during the measurement period.

    ☐ should be made
    ☐ should not be made

3. _____ installation in the building, the pump should be checked to ensure that it is operable and capable of maintaining a uniform flow through the detector assembly.

    ☐ After
    ☐ Prior to

4. When making grab measurements, it is especially important to conform to closed-building conditions for _____ the measurement.

    ☐ two days after
    ☐ 12 hours before
    ☐ 12 hours after

5. T/F: The equipment required for radon decay product concentration determination by GW consists of an air sampling pump capable of maintaining a flow rate of 2 to 25 liters per minute through the selected filter.

    ☐ True
    ☐ False

6. _____ , the continuous radon (CR) monitor should be tested carefully, according to manufacturer's directions, to verify that the correct input parameters and the unit's clock or timer are set properly, and to verify the operation of the pump.

    ☐ Before and after each 10 measurements
    ☐ After 100 measurements
    ☐ Before and after each measurement

Answer Key is on page 351.

Mitigation for Existing Homes

Introduction

In this section, we'll learn about the following topics of the Radon Mitigation Standards (RMS):

- Background
- Purpose
- Participants
- Scope
- Assumption
- Implementation
- Limitations
- Reference Documents
- Description of Terms
- General Practices
- Building Investigation
- Worker Health and Safety
- Systems Design
- Systems Installation
- Materials
- Monitors and Labeling
- Post-Mitigation Testing
- Contracts and Documentation

The EPA ceased operation of its National Radon Proficiency Program (RPP) on September 30, 1998. The EPA-issued Radon Measurement (RMP) and Mitigation (RCP) Program photo identification cards, and any item with the EPA's logo or name listing letters and identification numbers have not been valid since the the EPA closed its proficiency program in October 1998.

Background

The 1988 Indoor Radon Abatement Act (IRAA) required the EPA to develop a voluntary program to evaluate and provide information on contractors who offer radon control services to homeowners. The Radon Contractor Proficiency (RCP) Program was established to fulfill this portion of the IRAA. Individuals meeting the EPA's National Radon Proficiency Program (RPP) requirements are now known as mitigation service providers. In December 1991, the EPA published Interim Radon Mitigation Standards as initial guidelines for evaluating the performance of radon mitigation contractors under the RCP Program. Over the past several years, the effectiveness of the basic radon mitigation techniques set forth in the Interim Standards has been validated in field applications throughout the United States. This experience now serves as the basis for the more detailed and final Radon Mitigation Standards (RMS) set forth in this section.

Purpose

The purpose of the RMS is to provide radon mitigation contractors with uniform standards that will ensure quality and effectiveness in the design, installation, and evaluation of radon mitigation systems in detached and attached residential buildings three stories or fewer in height. The RMS is intended to serve as a model set of requirements that can be adopted or modified by state and local jurisdictions to fulfill objectives of their specific radon contractor certification or licensure programs.

Participants

Minimum requirements are established in the RMS for individuals nationwide who perform radon remediation work and wish to participate in the EPA's RPP as mitigation service providers. To successfully participate in the EPA's RPP, the mitigation contractor shall have completed all training, examination, and other program requirements, and shall agree to follow the provisions of the RMS.

Scope

The requirements addressed in the RMS include the following categories of contractor activity:

- general practices;
- building investigation;
- worker health and safety;
- systems design;
- systems installation;
- materials, monitors and labeling;
- post-mitigation testing; and
- contracts and documentation.

Assumption

Before applying the provisions of the RMS, it is assumed that appropriate radon/radon decay product measurements have been performed within the structure, and that the owner has decided that radon remediation is necessary.

Implementation

The RMS includes requirements for installation of radon remediation systems and provides a basis for evaluating the quality of those installations. It may be adopted by state regulatory agencies for state or local radon mitigation contractor licensure programs. It may also be used as reference during inspection of in-progress or completed radon mitigation work.

Contractors shall personally conduct a follow-up inspection of any radon mitigation systems installed by their firm or by subcontractors to ensure conformance with the requirements of the RMS.

The EPA will evaluate reports of non-compliance with the RMS that are referred to the agency by states and other agencies that monitor radon mitigation services. Based on its evaluation, the EPA may initiate established RCP program de-listing procedures against contractors that the agency or states (with certification programs) find are in violation of the mandatory provisions of the RMS. In addition, the EPA or its agent may conduct inspections of radon mitigation projects. State radon program personnel or their contracted representatives are considered EPA agents for conducting such inspections.

Those provisions of the RMS that are considered to be mandatory are prefaced by the term "shall." Provisions that are considered good practice but that are not mandatory are prefaced by the terms "should" or "recommended."

The RMS will be updated as necessary and in response to technological advances and field experience.

Limitations

Although the provisions of the RMS have been carefully reviewed for potential conflicts with other regulatory requirements, adherence to the RMS does not guarantee compliance with the applicable codes or regulations of any other federal, state or local agency having jurisdiction.

Where discrepancies exist between provisions of the RMS and local codes or regulations, local codes shall take precedence. However, where compliance with local codes necessitates a deviation from the RMS, the EPA recommends that RPP-listed mitigation service providers (mitigation contractors) report the deviation in writing to the appropriate EPA Regional Office and the appropriate state regulatory official within 30 days. It should be noted that the EPA is not requiring the reporting that is recommended in this paragraph. States with radon mitigation contractor certification programs may require that contractors give prior notification of their intent to deviate from the RMS for research or other purposes.

The RMS is not intended to be used as a design manual, and compliance with its provisions will not guarantee reduction of indoor radon concentrations to any specific level.

The RMS does not apply to radon mitigation systems installed prior to its effective date, except when a previously installed system is altered. Altering radon mitigation systems does not include activities such as replacing worn-out equipment or providing new filters, while leaving the remainder of the system unchanged. Mitigation systems installed prior to the effective date of the RMS should be in compliance with the requirements in force at that time (i.e. *EPA Interim Radon Mitigation Standards*, December 15, 1991, as amended by the *Addendum on Backdrafting* of October 1, 1992). If a radon mitigation system is found that does not comply with current standards, contractors should recommend to their clients that the system be upgraded or altered to meet current standards.

Because of the wide variation in building design, size, operation and use, the RMS does not include detailed guidance on how to select the most appropriate mitigation strategy for a given building.

The provisions of the RMS are limited to proven technologies and methods. However, publication of this standard is not intended to inhibit research or evaluation of other innovative radon mitigation techniques. When such research is conducted, a performance standard shall be applied, i.e., post-mitigation radon levels shall be at or below the EPA's current action level (4 pCi/L), and the systems design criteria in paragraph 13.0 shall be applied. Contractors who expect to deviate from proven radon mitigation technologies and methods (as defined in the RMS and other EPA references in Part 8.0) for purposes of research on innovative mitigation techniques shall obtain prior approval from state regulatory offices, document the non-standard techniques, and inform the client of the deviation from standard procedures. In cases where radon mitigation is not regulated by the state, contractors shall obtain prior approval from a regional EPA office.

At this time, the RMS does not include standards for installing systems to mitigate radon in water. However, the EPA is currently developing a standard that will regulate radon levels in domestic water supplies. Following publication of that standard, the RMS may be revised, as appropriate, to include standards for the installation of systems that are effective in reducing radon levels in water.

Reference Documents

The following documents are sources of additional radon mitigation information and are recommended reading for contractors participating in the EPA's RPP program as mitigation service providers:

- EPA Training Manual, "Reducing Radon In Structures (Third Edition)," January 1993.
- "Radon Reduction Techniques for Detached Houses, Technical Guidance (Second Edition)," EPA/625/5-87/019, January 1988.
- "Application of Radon Reduction Methods," EPA/625/5-88/024, August 1988.
- "Indoor Radon and Radon Decay Product Measurement Device Protocols," EPA 402-R-92-004, July 1992.
- "Protocols for Radon and Radon Decay Product Measurements in Homes," EPA 402-R-92-003, June 1993.
- "A Citizen's Guide To Radon (Second Edition)," EPA 402-K92-001, May 1992.
- "Consumer's Guide to Radon Reduction," EPA, 402-K92-003, August 1992.
- "Home Buyer's and Seller's Guide to Radon," EPA 402-R-93-003, March 1993.
- "ASHRAE Standard 62-1989," Appendix B, Positive Combustion Air Supply.
- "National Gas Code," Appendix H (p.2223.1-98), 1988, Recommended Procedure for Safety Inspection of an Existing Appliance Installation.
- "Chimney Safety Tests User's Manual," Second Edition, January 12, 1988, Scanada Shelter Consortium, Inc., for Canada Mortgage and Housing Corp.
- OSHA "Safety and Health Regulations for Construction, Ionizing Radiation," 29 CFR 1926.53.
- OSHA "Occupational Safety and Health Regulations, Ionizing Radiation," 29 CFR 1910.96.
- NIOSH "Guide to Industrial Respiratory Protection," DHHS (NIOSH) Publication No. 87-116, September 1987.
- NCRP "Measurement of Radon and Radon Decay Daughters in Air," NCRP Report No. 97, November 1988.
- EPA Handbook, "Sub-Slab Depressurization for Low Permeability Fill Material," EPA/625/6-91/029, July 1991.
- "Radon Reduction Techniques for Existing Detached Houses, Technical Guidance (Third Edition) for Active Soil Depressurization Systems," EPA/625/R-93-011, October 1993.

Description of Terms

Terms not defined herein should have their ordinary meaning within the context of their use. (Ordinary meaning is as defined in Webster's Ninth New Collegiate Dictionary.)

back-drafting: a condition where the normal movement of combustion products up a flue—resulting from the buoyant forces on the hot gases—is reversed, so that the combustion products can enter the house. Back-drafting of combustion appliances (such as fireplaces and furnaces) can occur when depressurization in the house overwhelms the buoyant force on the hot gases. Back-drafting can also be caused by high air pressures or a blockage at the chimney or flue termination.

backer rod: a semi-rigid foam material resembling a rope of various diameters used to fill around pipes, etc., to assist in making a sealed penetration. For example, where a pipe is inserted through a concrete slab, a length of backer rod is jammed into the opening around the pipe. Caulking is then applied to the space above the backer rod and between the outside of the pipe and the slab opening. The purpose of the backer rod is to hold the semi-fluid caulk in place until it sets or hardens.

block-wall depressurization: a radon mitigation technique that depressurizes the void network within a block-wall foundation by drawing air from inside the wall and venting it to the outside.

certified: a rating applied by some jurisdictions to individuals or firms that are qualified and authorized to provide radon testing or mitigation services within the area of their jurisdiction.

client: the person, persons or company that contracts with a radon mitigation contractor to install a radon-reduction system in a building.

combination foundations: buildings constructed with more than one foundation type, e.g., basement/crawlspace or basement/slab-on-grade.

communication test: a diagnostic test designed to qualitatively measure the ability of a suction field and air flow to extend through the material beneath a concrete slab floor, and thus evaluate the potential effectiveness of a sub-slab depressurization system. This qualitative test is commonly conducted by applying suction on a centrally located hole drilled through the concrete slab, and simultaneously observing the movement of smoke downward into small holes drilled in the slab at locations separated from the central suction hole. (See also **pressure field extension.**)

contractor: an individual listed in the EPA's RPP Program—specifically, one listed as a mitigation service provider, or certified by a state that requires adherence to the RMS.

crawlspace depressurization: a radon control technique designed to achieve lower air pressure in the crawlspace relative to indoor air pressure by use of a fan-powered vent that draws air from within the crawlspace. (See also **mechanically ventilated crawlspace system.**)

diagnostic tests: procedures used to identify or characterize conditions within buildings that may contribute to radon entry or elevated radon levels, or may provide information regarding the performance of a mitigation system.

drain tile loop: a continuous length of drain tile or perforated pipe extending around all or part of the internal or external perimeter of a basement or crawlspace footing.

mitigation system: any system or steps designed to reduce radon concentrations in the indoor air of a building.

mechanically ventilated crawlspace system: a radon control technique designed to increase ventilation within a crawlspace, achieve higher air pressure in the crawlspace relative to the air pressure in the soil beneath the crawlspace, or achieve lower air pressure in the crawlspace relative to the air pressure in the living spaces by use of a fan. (See also **crawlspace depressurization**.)

pCi/L: the abbreviation for picocuries per liter, which is a unit of measure for the amount of radioactivity in a liter of air. The prefix "pico" means a multiplication factor of 1 trillionth. A curie is a commonly used measurement of radioactivity.

perimeter channel drain: a means for collecting water in a basement via a large gap or channel between the concrete floor and the wall. Collected water may flow to aggregate beneath the slot (a French drain) or to a sump where it can be drained or pumped away.

pressure field extension: the distance that a pressure change is induced in the sub-slab area, measured from a single or multiple suction points. (See also communication test.)

radon: a naturally occurring radioactive element (Rn-222) that exists as a gas and is measured in picocuries per liter (pCi/L).

radon decay products (RDPs): the four short-lived radioactive elements (Po-218, Pb-214, Bi-214 and Po-214) that exist as solids and immediately follow Rn-222 in the decay chain. They are measured in working levels (WL).

re-entrainment: the unintended re-entry into a building of radon that is being exhausted from the vent of a radon mitigation system.

soil gas: the gas mixture present in soil that may contain radon.

soil-gas retarder: a continuous membrane or other comparable material used to retard the flow of soil gases into a building.

stack effect: the overall upward movement of air inside a building that results from heated air rising and escaping through openings in the building envelope, thus causing indoor air pressure in the lower portions of the building to be lower than the pressure in the soil beneath or surrounding the building's foundation.

sub-membrane depressurization: a radon control technique designed to achieve lower air pressure in the space under a soil-gas retarder membrane laid on the crawlspace floor, relative to the air pressure in the crawlspace, by use of a fan-powered vent that draws air from beneath the membrane.

sub-slab depressurization (active): a radon control technique designed to achieve lower sub-slab air pressure relative to indoor air pressure by use of a fan-powered vent to draw air from beneath the concrete slab.

sub-slab depressurization (passive): a radon control technique designed to achieve lower sub-slab air pressure relative to indoor air pressure by use of a vent pipe (without a fan) routed through the conditioned space of a building, and connecting the sub-slab area to the outdoor air. This system relies primarily on the convective flow of warmed air upward in the vent to draw air from beneath the concrete slab.

working level (WL): a unit of radon decay product exposure rate; numerically, any combination of short-lived radon decay products in 1 liter of air that will result in the ultimate emission of 130,000 MeV of potential alpha energy. This number was chosen because it is approximately the total alpha energy released from the short-lived decay products in equilibrium with 100 pCi of Rn-222 per liter of air.

working-level month (WLM): a unit of exposure used to express the accumulated human exposure to radon decay products. It is calculated by multiplying the average working level to which a person has been exposed by the number of hours exposed, and dividing the product by 170.

General Practices

The following general practices are required for all contacts between radon mitigation contractors and clients.

In the initial contact with a client, the contractor shall review any available results from previous radon tests to assist in developing an appropriate mitigation strategy.

Based on guidance contained in *A Citizen's Guide to Radon, Second Edition,* or subsequent revisions of that document, the contractor shall refer the client to the discussions of interpreting indoor radon test results and the health risk associated with the radon level found in the building. The Consumer's Guide to Radon Reduction is an appropriate reference for providing advice on actions to take to reduce indoor radon levels. Similar documents developed by states and mandated for dissemination by state regulations may also be used as references.

When delays in the installation of a permanent radon control system are unavoidable due to building conditions or construction activities, and a temporary system is installed, the contractor shall inform the client about the temporary nature of the system. A label that is readable from at least 3 feet shall be placed on the system. The label shall include a statement that the system is temporary and that it will be replaced with a permanent system within 30 days. The label shall also include the date of installation, and the contractor's name, phone number and RPP identification number.

(EXCEPTION: The 30-day limit on use of a temporary mitigation system may be extended in cases where a major renovation or change in building use necessitates a delay in installation of a permanent mitigation system that is optimized to the new building's configuration or use. The appropriate state or local building official or radon program official should be notified when this exception is being applied.)

When the selected mitigation technique requires use of sealants, caulks or bonding chemicals containing volatile solvents, prior to starting work, the contractor shall inform the client of the need to ventilate work areas during and after the use of such materials. Ventilation shall be provided as recommended by the manufacturer of the material.

Building Investigation

The contractor shall conduct a thorough visual inspection of the building prior to initiating any radon mitigation work. The inspection is intended to identify any specific building characteristics and configurations (e.g., large cracks in slabs, exposed earth in crawlspaces, open stairways to basements) and operational conditions (e.g., continuously running HVAC systems or operational windows) that may affect the design, installation and effectiveness of radon mitigation systems. As part of this inspection, clients should be asked to provide any available information on the building (e.g., construction specifications, plans, drawings, etc.) that might be of value in determining the radon mitigation strategy.

To facilitate selection of the most effective radon control system and avoid the costs of installing systems that subsequently prove to be ineffective, it is recommended that the contractor conduct diagnostic tests to assist in identifying and verifying suspected radon sources and entry points. Radon grab sampling, continuous radon monitoring, and use of chemical smoke sticks are examples of the types of diagnostic testing commonly used.

It is recommended that during the building investigation, contractors routinely perform diagnostic tests to evaluate the existence of, or the potential for, back-drafting of natural-draft combustion appliances.

The following checklist of steps has been extracted from material in these references and may be used to test for existing or potential back-drafting conditions:

1. Close all windows and doors, both external and internal.

2. Open all HVAC-supply and return-air duct vents and registers.

3. Close fireplace and wood-stove dampers.

4. Turn on all exhaust and air-distribution fans and combustion appliances except the appliance being tested for back-drafting.

5. Wait five minutes.

6. Test to determine the indoor-outdoor pressure differential in the room where the appliance being tested is located. If the pressure differential is a negative 5 pascals or more, assume that a potential for back-drafting exists.

7. To begin a test for actual spillage of flue gases, turn on the appliance being tested. (If the appliance is a forced-air furnace, ensure that the blower starts to run before proceeding.)

8. Wait five minutes.

9. Using either a smoke tube or a carbon-dioxide gas analyzer, check for flue-gas spillage near the vent hood.

10. Repeat steps 4 through 9 for each natural-draft combustion appliance being tested for back-drafting. Seasonal and extreme weather conditions should be considered when evaluating pressure differentials and the potential for back-drafting.

If spillage is confirmed from any natural-draft combustion appliance, clients shall be advised of the back-drafting condition, and that active (fan-powered) radon mitigation systems cannot be installed until the condition has been corrected. The contractors should advise their clients to contact an HVAC contractor if correcting an existing or potential back-drafting condition is necessary.

If installation of a sub-slab depressurization system is contemplated and characteristics of the sub-slab material are unknown, a communication test is recommended.

As part of the building investigation, a floor plan sketch shall be developed (if not already in existence and readily available) that includes illustrations of the building foundation (slab on grade, basement or crawlspace area). The sketch should include the location of load-bearing walls, drain fixtures, and HVAC systems. It should be annotated to include suspected or confirmed radon entry points, results of any diagnostic testing, the anticipated layout of any radon mitigation system piping, and the anticipated locations of any vent fan and system warning devices for the envisioned mitigation systems. The sketch shall be finalized during installation and shall be included in the documentation.

Worker Health and Safety

Contractors shall comply with all OSHA, state and local standards and regulations relating to worker safety and occupational radon exposure.

In addition to the OSHA and NIOSH standards, the following requirements that are specifically or uniquely applicable for the safety and protection of radon mitigation workers shall be met:

- The contractor shall advise workers of the hazards of exposure to radon and the need to apply protective measures when working in areas of elevated radon concentrations.

- The contractor shall have a worker protection plan on file that is available to all employees and is approved by any state or local regulating agencies that require such a plan. (EXCEPTION: A worker protection plan is not required for a contractor who is a sole proprietor, unless required by state or local regulations.)

- The contractor shall ensure that appropriate safety equipment, such as hard hats, face shields, ear plugs, steel-toe boots and protective gloves, are available on the job site during cutting, drilling, grinding, polishing, demolishing, or other activity associated with radon mitigation projects.

- All electrical equipment used during radon mitigation projects shall be properly grounded. Circuits used as a power source should be protected by ground-fault circuit interrupters (GFCI).

- When work is required at elevations above the ground or floor, the contractor shall ensure that ladders or scaffolding are safely installed and used.

- Work areas shall be ventilated to reduce worker exposure to radon decay products, dust, and other airborne pollutants. In work areas where ventilation is impractical, or where ventilation cannot reduce radon levels to less than 0.3 WL (based on a short-term diagnostic test, such as a grab sample), the contractor shall ensure that respiratory protection conforms with the requirements in the NIOSH Guide to Industrial Respiratory Protection. NOTE: If unable to make working-level measurements, a radon level of 30 pCi/L shall be used.

- Where combustible materials exist in the specific area of the building where radon mitigation work is to be conducted, and the contractor is creating any temperatures high enough to induce a flame, the contractor shall ensure that fire extinguishers suitable for Type A, B and C fires are available in the immediate work area. Pending development of an approved personal radon exposure device and a protocol for its use, contractors shall record employee exposure to radon at each work site, based on:

  1. the highest pre-mitigation indoor radon or working-level measurement available; and

  2. the time employees are exposed (without respirator protection) at that level.

NOTE: This approach is not intended to preclude the alternative use of on-site radon or radon decay product measurements to determine the exact exposure. Consistent with OSHA-permissible exposure limits, contractors shall ensure that employees are exposed to no more than four working-level months (WLM) over a 12-month period. An equilibrium ratio of 50% shall be used to convert radon exposure to WLM.

- In any planned work area where it is suspected that friable asbestos may exist and be disturbed, radon mitigation work shall not be conducted until a determination is made by a properly trained or accredited person that such work will be undertaken in a manner that complies with applicable asbestos regulations.

- When mitigation work requires the use of sealants, adhesives, paints, or other substances that may be hazardous to health, contractors shall provide employees with the applicable Material Safety Data Sheets (MSDS) and explain the required safety procedures.

System Design

All radon mitigation systems shall be designed and installed as permanent, integral additions to the building, except where a temporary system has been installed.

All systems shall be designed to avoid the creation of other health, safety or environmental hazards to the building's occupants, such as back-drafting of natural-draft combustion appliances.

They shall also be designed to:

- maximize radon reduction;
- in consideration of the need to minimize excess energy usage, avoid compromising moisture and temperature controls, and other comfort features; and
- minimize noise.

All radon mitigation systems and their components shall be designed to comply with the laws, ordinances, codes and regulations of relevant jurisdictional authorities, including applicable mechanical, electrical, building, plumbing, energy and fire-prevention codes.

System Installation

General Requirements

- All components of radon mitigation systems installed in compliance with provisions of the RMS shall also be in compliance with the applicable mechanical, electrical, building, plumbing, energy and fire-prevention codes, standards and regulations of the local jurisdiction.
- The contractor shall obtain all required licenses and permits, and display them in the work areas, as required by local ordinances.
- Where portions of structural framing material must be removed to accommodate radon vent pipes, the material removed shall be no greater than that permitted for plumbing installations by applicable building or plumbing codes.
- Where the installation of a radon mitigation system requires pipes or ducts to penetrate a firewall or other fire resistance-rated wall or floor, penetrations shall be protected in accordance with applicable building, mechanical, fire and electrical codes.
- When installing radon mitigation systems that use sump pits as the suction point for active soil depressurization, if sump pumps are needed, it is recommended that submersible sump pumps be used.

Radon Vent Pipe Installation Requirements

- All joints and connections in radon mitigation systems using plastic vent pipes shall be permanently sealed with adhesives, as specified by the manufacturer of the pipe material used. Joints or connections in other vent pipe materials shall be made airtight.
- Attic and external piping runs in areas subject to sub-freezing conditions should be protected to avoid the risk of vent pipe freeze-up.
- Radon vent pipes shall be fastened to the structure of the building with hangers, strapping, or other supports that will adequately secure the vent material. Existing plumbing pipes, ducts or mechanical equipment shall not be used to support or secure a radon vent pipe.
- Supports for radon vent pipes shall be installed at least every 6 feet on horizontal runs. Vertical runs shall be secured either above or below the points of penetration through floors, ceilings and roofs, or at least every 8 feet on runs that do not penetrate floors, ceilings or roofs.
- To prevent blockage of air flow into the bottom of radon vent pipes, these pipes shall be

supported or secured in a permanent manner that prevents their downward movement to the bottom of suction pits or sump pits, or into the soil beneath an aggregate layer under a slab.

- Radon vent pipes shall be installed in a configuration that ensures that any rainwater or condensation within the pipes drains downward into the ground beneath the slab or soil-gas retarder membrane.

- Radon vent pipes shall not block access to any areas requiring maintenance or inspection. Radon vents shall not be installed in front of or interfere with any light, opening, door, window, or equipment access area required by code. If radon vent pipes are installed in sump pits, the system shall be designed with removable or flexible couplings to facilitate removal of the sump pit cover for sump pump maintenance.

- To prevent re-entrainment of radon, the point of discharge from vents of fan-powered soil depressurization and block-wall depressurization systems shall meet all of the following requirements:

    1. be above the eaves of the roof;

    2. be 10 feet or more above ground level;

    3. be 10 feet or more from any window, door or other opening into conditioned spaces of the structure that is less than 2 feet below the exhaust point; and

    4. be 10 feet or more from any opening into an adjacent building.

The total required distance from the point of discharge to openings in the structure (10 feet) may be measured either directly between the two points, or be the sum of measurements made around any intervening obstacles. Whenever possible, the exhaust point should be positioned above the highest eaves of the building and as close as possible to the roof's ridgeline.

- When a radon mitigation system is designed to draw soil gas from a perimeter drain tile loop (internal or external) that discharges water through a drain line to daylight or a soakaway, a one-way flow valve, water trap, or other control device should be installed in or on the discharge line to prevent outside air from entering the system while allowing water to flow out of the system.

Radon Vent Fan Installation Requirements

- Vent fans used in radon mitigation systems shall be designed or otherwise sealed to reduce the potential for leakage of soil gas from the fan housing.

- Radon vent fans shall be sized to provide the pressure difference and air flow characteristics necessary to achieve the radon-reduction goals established for the specific mitigation project.

- Radon vent fans used in active soil depressurization or block-wall depressurization systems shall not be installed below ground, nor in the conditioned (heated/cooled) space of a building, nor in any basement, crawlspace or other interior location directly beneath the conditioned spaces of a building. Acceptable locations for radon vent fans include attics not suitable for occupancy (including attics over living spaces and garages), garages that are not beneath conditioned spaces, and on the exterior of the building.

- Radon vent fans shall be installed in a configuration that avoids condensation buildup in the fan housing. Whenever possible, fans should be installed in vertical runs of the vent pipe.

- Radon vent fans mounted on the exterior of buildings shall be rated for outdoor use, or installed in a watertight protective housing, and they shall be mounted and secured in a manner that minimizes transfer of vibration to the structural framing of the building.

- To facilitate maintenance and future replacement, radon vent fans shall be installed in the vent pipe using removable couplings or flexible connections that can be tightly secured to both the fan and the vent pipe.

- The intakes of fans used in crawlspace pressurization or pressurization of the building itself shall be screened or filtered to prevent ingestion of debris or personal injury. Screens or filters shall be removable to permit cleaning and replacement, and building owners shall be informed of the need to periodically replace or clean such screens and filters. This information shall also be included in the documentation.

Suction Pit Requirement for Sub-Slab Depressurization (SSD) Systems

To provide optimum pressure field extension of the sub-slab communication zone, adequate material shall be excavated from the area immediately below the slab penetration point of the SSD system's vent pipes.

Sealing Requirements

- Sump pits that permit entry of soil gas or that would allow conditioned air to be drawn into a sub-slab depressurization system shall be covered and sealed. The covers on sumps that previously provided protection or relief from surface water collection shall be fitted with a water or mechanically trapped drain. Water traps should be fitted with an automatic supply of priming water.

- Openings around radon vent-pipe penetrations of the slab, the foundation walls, or the crawlspace soil-gas retarder membrane shall be cleaned, prepared and sealed in a permanent, airtight manner using compatible caulks or other sealant materials. Openings around other utility penetrations of the slab, walls or soil-gas retarder shall also be sealed.

- Where a block-wall depressurization (BWD) system is used to mitigate radon, openings in the tops of such walls, and all accessible openings or cracks in the interior surfaces of the walls shall be closed and sealed with polyurethane or equivalent caulks, expandable foams, or other fillers and sealants. Openings or cracks that are determined to be inaccessible or beyond the ability of the contractor to seal shall be disclosed to the client and included in the documentation.

- Openings, perimeter channel drains, or cracks that exist where the slab meets the foundation wall (floor-wall joint) shall be sealed with urethane caulk or equivalent material. When the opening or channel is greater than 1/2-inch in width, a foam backer rod or other comparable filler material shall be inserted in the channel before application of the sealant. This sealing technique shall be done in a manner that retains the channel feature as a water control system. Other openings or cracks in slabs or at expansion or control joints should also be sealed. Openings or cracks that are determined to be inaccessible or beyond the ability of the contractor to seal shall be disclosed to the client and included in the documentation.

- When installing baseboard-type suction systems, all seams and joints in the baseboard material shall be joined and sealed using materials recommended by the manufacturer of the baseboard system. Baseboards shall be secured to walls and floors with adhesives designed and recommended for such installations. If a baseboard system is installed on a block-wall foundation, the tops of the block wall shall be closed and sealed.

- Any seams in soil-gas retarder membranes used in crawlspaces for sub-membrane depressurization systems shall be overlapped at least 12 inches and should be sealed. To enhance the effectiveness of sub-membrane depressurization systems, the membrane should also be sealed around interior piers and to the inside of exterior walls.

- In combination basement-crawlspace foundations where the crawlspace has been confirmed as a source of radon entry, access doors and other openings between the basement and the adjacent crawlspace shall be closed and sealed. Access doors required by code shall be fitted with airtight gaskets and a means of positive closure, but shall not be permanently sealed. In cases where both the basement and the adjacent crawlspace areas are being mitigated with active SSD and SMD systems, sealing of the openings between those areas is not required.

- When crawlspace depressurization is used for radon mitigation, openings and cracks in floors above the crawlspace that would permit conditioned air to pass out of the living spaces of the building shall be identified, closed and sealed. Sealing of openings around hydronic heat or steam-pipe penetrations shall be done using non-combustible materials. Openings or cracks that are determined to be inaccessible or beyond the ability of the contractor to seal shall be disclosed to the client and included in the documentation.

Electrical Requirements

- Wiring for all active radon mitigation systems shall conform to provisions of the National Electric Code (NEC) and any additional local regulations.

- Wiring may not be located in or chased through the mitigation installation ducting, or any other heating or cooling ductwork.

- Any plugged cord used to supply power to a radon vent fan shall be no more than 6 feet in length, and no plugged cord may penetrate a wall or be concealed within a wall.

- Radon mitigation fans installed on the exterior of buildings shall be hard-wired into an electrical circuit. Plugged fans shall not be used outdoors.

- If the rated electricity requirements of a radon mitigation system fan exceeds 50% of the circuit's capacity into which it will be connected, or if the total connected load on the circuit (including the radon vent fan) exceeds 80% of the circuit's rated capacity, a separate dedicated circuit shall be installed to power the fan.

- An electrical disconnect switch or circuit breaker shall be installed in radon mitigation system fan-circuits to permit de-activation of the fan for maintenance or repair by the building's owner or servicing contractor. (Disconnect switches are not required with plugged fans.)

Drain Installation Requirements

- If drains discharge directly into the soil beneath the slab or through solid pipe to a soakaway, the contractor should install a drain that meets the requirements listed above.

- If condensate drains from air-conditioning units terminate beneath the floor slab, the contractor shall install a trap in the drain that provides a minimum 6-inch standing water seal depth and re-route the drain directly into a trapped floor drain, or reconnect the drain to a condensate pump.

- Perimeter (channel or French) drains should be sealed with backer rods and urethane or comparable sealants in a manner that will retain the channel feature as a water control system.

- When a sump pit is the only system in a basement for protection or relief from excess surface water, and a cover is installed on the sump for radon control, the cover shall be recessed and fitted with a trapped drain that meets the requirements listed above.

HVAC Installation Requirements

- Modifications to an existing HVAC system that are proposed to mitigate elevated levels of radon should be reviewed and approved by the original designer of the system (when possible), or by a licensed mechanical contractor.

- Foundation vents installed specifically to reduce indoor radon levels by increasing the natural ventilation of a crawlspace shall be non-closeable. In areas subject to sub-freezing conditions, the existing location of water supply and distribution pipes in the crawlspace, and the need to insulate or apply heat tape to those pipes, should be considered when selecting locations for installing foundation vents.

- Heat-recovery ventilation (HRV) systems shall not be installed in rooms that contain friable asbestos.

- In HRV installations, supply and exhaust ports in the interior shall be located a minimum of 12 feet apart. The exterior supply and exhaust ports shall be positioned to avoid blockage by snow or leaves, and be a minimum of 10 feet apart.

- Contractors installing HRV systems shall verify that the incoming and outgoing air flow is balanced to ensure that the system does not create a negative pressure within the building. Contractors shall inform building owners that periodic filter replacement and inlet grille cleaning are necessary to maintain a balanced air flow. This information shall also be included in the documentation.

- Both internal and external intake and exhaust vents in HRV systems shall be covered with wire mesh or screening to prevent the entry of animals and debris, and injury to occupants.

Materials

- All mitigation system electrical components shall be UL-listed or of equivalent specifications.

- At a minimum, all plastic vent pipes in mitigation systems shall be made of Schedule 20 PVC, ABS or equivalent piping material. Schedule 40 piping or its equivalent should be used in garages and in other internal and external locations subject to weathering or physical damage.

- Vent pipe fittings in a mitigation system shall be of the same material as the vent pipes. (See the previous section for exceptions when installing vent fans, and for exceptions when installing radon vent pipes in sump pit covers.)

- Cleaning solvents and adhesives used to join plastic pipes and fittings shall be as recommended by their manufacturers for use with the type of pipe material used in the mitigation system.

- When sealing cracks in slabs and other small openings around penetrations of the slab and foundation walls, caulks and sealants designed for such application shall be used. Urethane sealants are recommended because of their durability.

- When sealing holes for plumbing rough-in or other large openings in slabs and foundation walls that are below the ground surface, non-shrink mortar, grouts, expanding foam or similar materials designed for such application shall be used.

- Sump pit covers shall be made of durable plastic or other rigid material and designed to permit airtight sealing. To permit easy removal for sump pump servicing, the cover shall be sealed using silicone or other non-permanent-type caulking materials or an airtight gasket.

- Penetrations of sump covers to accommodate electrical wiring, water-ejection pipes, or radon vent pipes shall be designed to permit airtight sealing around penetrations using caulk or grommets. Sump covers that permit observation of conditions in the sump pit are recommended.

- Plastic sheeting installed in crawlspaces as soil-gas retarders shall be a minimum of 6-mil (3-mil cross-laminated) polyethylene, or equivalent flexible material. Heavier gauge sheeting should be used when crawlspaces are used for storage, or when frequent entry is required for maintenance of utilities.

- Any wood used in attaching soil-gas retarder membranes to crawlspace walls or piers shall be pressure-treated or naturally resistant to decay and termites.

Monitors and Labeling

- All active soil depressurization and block-wall depressurization radon mitigation systems shall include a mechanism to monitor system performance and warn of system failure.

  The mechanism shall be:

  1. simple to read or interpret;

  2. located where it is easily seen or heard by building occupants; and

  3. protected from damage or destruction.

- Electrical radon-mitigation system monitors (whether visual or audible) shall be installed on non-switched circuits, and be designed to re-set automatically when power is restored after service or power-supply failure. Battery-operated monitoring devices shall not be used unless they are equipped with a low-power warning feature.

- Mechanical radon mitigation system monitors, such as manometer-type pressure gauges, shall be clearly marked to indicate the range or zone of pressure readings that existed when the system was initially activated.

- A system description label shall be placed on the mitigation system, the electric service entrance panel, or other prominent location. This label shall be legible from a distance of at least 3 feet and include the following information: "Radon Reduction System," the installer's name, phone number and RCP identification number, the date of installation, and an advisory that the building should be tested for radon at least every two years or as required or recommended by state or local agencies. In addition, all exposed and visible interior radon mitigation system vent pipe sections shall be identified with at least one label on each floor level. The label shall read: "Radon Reduction System."

- The circuit breakers controlling the circuits on which the radon vent fan and system-failure warning devices operate shall be labeled "Radon System."

Post-Mitigation Testing

- After installation of an active radon control system (e.g., SSD), the contractor shall re-examine and verify the integrity of the fan-mounting seals and all joints in the interior vent piping.

- After installation of any active radon mitigation system, the contractor shall measure suctions or flows in system piping or ducting to assure that the system is operating as designed. (NOTE: When SSD systems are installed and activated, a test of pressure field extension is a good practice, particularly when there is uncertainty regarding the permeability of materials under all parts of the slab.)

- Immediately after installation and activation of any active (fan-powered) sub-slab depressurization or block-wall depressurization system in buildings containing natural-draft combustion appliances, the building shall be tested for back-drafting of those appliances. Any back-drafting condition that results from installation of the radon mitigation system shall be corrected before the system is placed in operation.

- Upon completion of radon mitigation work, a test of the mitigation system's effectiveness shall be conducted using an EPA RPP Analytical Service Provider-listed test device, and in accordance with EPA testing protocols or state requirements. This test should be conducted no sooner than 24 hours nor later than 30 days following completion and activation of the mitigation system(s). This test may be conducted by the contractor, by the client, or by a third-party testing firm. If this test is conducted by the mitigation contractor and the test results are accepted by the client as satisfactory evidence of the system's effectiveness, further post-mitigation testing is not required. However, to avoid the appearance of a conflict of interest, the contractor shall recommend to the client that a mitigation system-effectiveness test be conducted by an independent EPA RPP-listed Measurement Service Provider, or state-certified testing firm, or by the client. The contractor should request a copy of the report of any post-mitigation testing conducted by the client or by an independent testing firm.

- To ensure continued effectiveness of the radon mitigation system(s) installed, the contractor shall advise the client to re-test the building at least every two years, or as required or recommended by the state or local authority. Re-testing is also recommended if the building undergoes significant alteration.

Contracts and Documentation

- The EPA recommends that contractors provide the following written information to clients prior to the initiation of work:

    1. the contractor's EPA RPP mitigation service provider identification number;

    2. a statement that describes the planned scope of work that includes an estimate of the time needed to complete the work;

    3. a statement describing any known hazards associated with chemicals used in or as part of the installation process;

    4. a statement indicating compliance with and implementation of all EPA standards and those of other agencies having jurisdiction (e.g., code requirements);

    5. a statement describing any system maintenance that the building owner would be required to perform;

    6. an estimate of the installation cost and annual operating costs of the system; and

    7. the conditions of any warranty or guarantee.

- The EPA recommends that RPP-listed mitigation contractors keep records of all radon mitigation work performed, and maintain those records for three years, or for the period of any warranty or guarantee, whichever is longer.

    These records should include:

    1. the Building Investigation Summary and floor plan sketch;

    2. pre- and post-mitigation radon test data;

    3. pre- and post-mitigation diagnostic test data;

    4. copies of contracts and warranties; and

    5. a narrative or pictorial description of the mitigation system(s) installed.

- Other records or bookkeeping required by local, state or federal statutes and regulations shall be maintained for the period(s) prescribed by those requirements.

- The EPA recommends that health and safety records, including worker radon exposure logs, be maintained for a minimum of 20 years.

- Upon completion of the mitigation project, contractors shall provide clients with an information package that includes:

  1. any building permits required by local codes;

  2. copies of the Building Investigation Summary and floor plan sketch;

  3. pre-and post-mitigation radon test data;

  4. copies of contracts and warranties;

  5. a description of the mitigation system installed and its basic operating principles;

  6. a description of any deviations from the RMS or state's requirements;

  7. a description of the proper operating procedures of any mechanical or electrical systems installed, including the manufacturer's operation and maintenance instructions, and warranties;

  8. a list of appropriate actions for clients to take if the system-failure warning device indicates system degradation or failure; and

  9. the name, phone number, and EPA RPP mitigation service provider identification number of the contractor, and the phone number of the state radon office.

Quiz #10

1. The purpose of the Radon Mitigation Standards (RMS) is to provide radon mitigation contractors with uniform standards that will ensure quality and effectiveness in the design, installation and evaluation of radon mitigation systems in detached and attached residential buildings _____ in height.

    ☐ two stories

    ☐ three stories or fewer

    ☐ four stories or fewer

    ☐ one story

2. T/F: Because of the wide variation in building design, size, operation and use, the RMS does not include detailed guidance on how to select the most appropriate mitigation strategy for a given building.

    ☐ True

    ☐ False

3. T/F: Post-mitigation radon levels shall be at or below the EPA's current action level of 4 pCi/L.

    ☐ True

    ☐ False

4. _____ is a condition where the normal movement of combustion products up a flue, resulting from the buoyant forces on the hot gases, is reversed, so that the combustion products can enter the house.

    ☐ Block-wall depressurization

    ☐ Back-drafting

    ☐ Pressure field extension

5. _____ is a radon mitigation technique that depressurizes the void network within a block-wall foundation by drawing air from inside the wall and venting it to the outside.

    ☐ Perimeter channel draining

    ☐ A drain tile loop

    ☐ Block-wall depressurization

6. _____ is the overall upward movement of air inside a building that results from heated air rising and escaping through openings in the building envelope, thus causing indoor air pressure in the lower portions of a building to be lower than the pressure in the soil beneath or surrounding the building foundation.

    ☐ Stack effect

    ☐ Working leveling

    ☐ Re-entrainment

    ☐ Mitigation

7. T/F: It is recommended that during the building investigation, contractors routinely perform diagnostic tests to evaluate the existence of, or the potential for, back-drafting of natural-draft combustion appliances.

    ☐ True
    ☐ False

8. T/F: Contractors shall comply with OSHA, state and local standards and regulations relating to worker safety and occupational radon exposure.

    ☐ True
    ☐ False

9. T/F: All joints and connections in radon mitigation systems using plastic vent pipes are required to be permanently sealed with adhesives.

    ☐ True
    ☐ False

10. T/F: Radon vent pipes shall be fastened to the structure of the building with hangers, strapping or other supports that will adequately secure the vent material.

    ☐ True
    ☐ False

11. To prevent re-entrainment of radon, the point of discharge from vents of fan-powered soil depressurization and block-wall depressurization systems shall be _____ feet or more from any window, door or other opening into conditioned spaces of the structure that is less than 2 feet below the exhaust point.

    ☐ 10
    ☐ 15
    ☐ 20

12. Whenever possible, fans should be installed in _____ runs of the vent pipe.

    ☐ diagonal
    ☐ vertical
    ☐ horizontal

13. T/F: At a minimum, all plastic vent pipes in mitigation systems shall be made of Schedule 40 PVC, ABS or equivalent piping material.

    ☐ True
    ☐ False

14. Plastic sheeting installed in crawlspaces as soil-gas retarders shall be a minimum of ___-mil polyethylene, or equivalent flexible material.

    ☐ 6

    ☐ 8

    ☐ 12

15. Upon completion of radon mitigation work, a test of the mitigation system's effectiveness shall be conducted no sooner than _____ hours nor later than _____ days following completion and activation of the mitigation system.

    ☐ 48... 30

    ☐ 24... 30

    ☐ 24... four

Answer Key is on page 352.

Mitigation for New Homes

EPA Model Standards for New Residences

The EPA closed its National Radon Proficiency Program on September 30, 1998. This section of the book is based on the EPA Publication 402-R-94-009 (March 1994): *Model Standards of Techniques for Control of Radon in New Residential Buildings.*

This information is intended to serve as a model for use by the Model Code Organizations, states and other jurisdictions as they develop and adopt building codes, appendices to codes, and standards specifically applicable to their unique local and regional radon control requirements.

This information is in response to the requirements set forth in Section 304 of Title III of the Toxic Substances Control Act (TSCA), 15 U.S.C. 2664, commonly referred to as the Indoor Radon Abatement Act (IRAA) of 1988. It is anticipated that future editions of this document will be prepared as additional experience is gained in constructing new radon-resistant residential buildings.

This section covers the following topics:

- Scope
- Limitations
- Reference Documents
- Description of Terms
- Principles of Construction of Radon-Resistant Residential Buildings
- Summary of the Model Building Standards and Techniques
- Construction Methods
- Recommended Implementation Procedures
- Model Building Standards and Techniques

Scope

This section contains model building standards and techniques applicable to controlling radon levels in new construction of one- and two-family dwellings and other residential buildings three stories or fewer in height, as defined in model codes promulgated by the respective Model Code Organizations.

The model building standards and techniques are also applicable when additions are made to the foundations of existing one- and two-family dwellings that result in extension of the building footprint.

This section is not intended to be a building code, nor is it required that it be adopted verbatim as a referenced standard.

It is intended that the building standards and techniques, the construction method, and the recommended procedures for applying them serve as a model for use by the Model Code Organizations and authorities within states and other jurisdictions that are responsible for regulating building construction as they develop and adopt building codes, appendices to codes, and standards, and implementing regulations specifically applicable to their unique local or regional radon control requirements.

The preferential grant assistance authorized in Section 306(d) of the Indoor Radon Abatement Act of 1988 apply for states where appropriate authorities who regulate building construction are taking action to adopt radon-resistant standards in their building codes.

The model building standards and techniques described here are not intended to supersede any radon-resistant construction standards, codes or regulations previously adopted by local jurisdictions and authorities. However, jurisdictions and authorities are encouraged to review their current building standards, codes and regulations, and their unique local or regional radon control requirements, and consider modifications, if necessary.

The EPA document will be updated and revised as ongoing and future research programs suggest revisions of standards, identify ways to improve the model construction techniques, or when newly tested products or techniques prove to be equivalent to or more effective in radon control. Updates and revisions to the model building standards and techniques will undergo appropriate peer review.

The EPA is committed to continuing evaluation of the effectiveness of the standards and techniques, and to research programs that may identify other more effective and efficient methods.

Limitations

The Indoor Radon Abatement Act of 1988 establishes a long-term national goal of achieving radon levels inside buildings that are no higher than those found in ambient air outside of buildings. While technological, physical and financial limitations currently preclude attaining this goal, the underlying objective is to move toward reaching the lowest technologically achievable and most cost-effective levels of indoor radon in new residential buildings.

Preliminary research indicates that the building standards and techniques can be applied successfully in mitigating radon problems in some existing non-residential buildings. However, when applied during construction of new non-residential buildings, their effectiveness has not yet been fully demonstrated. Therefore, it is recommended that, pending further research, these building standards and techniques not be used at this time as a basis for changing the specific sections of building codes that cover non-residential construction.

Although radon levels below 4 pCi/L have been achieved in all types of residential buildings by using these model building standards and techniques, specific indoor radon levels for any given building cannot be predicted due to different site and environmental conditions, building design, construction practices, and variations in the operation of buildings.

These model building standards and techniques are not to be construed as the only acceptable methods for controlling radon levels, and are not intended to preempt, preclude or restrict the application of alternative materials, systems and construction practices approved by building officials under procedures prescribed in existing building codes.

Elevated indoor radon levels caused by emanation of radon from water is of potential concern, particularly in areas where there is a history of groundwater with high radon content. This information does not include model construction standards or techniques for reducing elevated levels of indoor radon that may be caused by the presence of high levels of radon in water supplies. The EPA has suggests a certain approach that state or local jurisdictions should consider as they develop regulations concerning private wells. The EPA is continuing to evaluate the issue of radon occurrence in private wells, and the economic impacts of testing and remediation of wells with elevated radon levels.

While it is not currently possible to make a precise prediction of indoor radon potential for a specific building site, a general assessment on a statewide, county or grouping-of-counties basis can be made by referring to the EPA's Map of Radon Zones and other locally available data. It should be noted that some radon potential exists in all areas. However, the EPA recognizes that, based on available data, there is a lower potential for elevated indoor radon levels in some states and portions of some states, and that adoption of building codes for the prevention of radon in new construction may not be justified in these areas at this time. There is language in the section of "Recommended Procedures" suggesting that jurisdictions in these areas review all available data on local indoor radon measurements, geology, soil parameters, and housing characteristics as they consider whether adoption of new codes is appropriate.

Reference Documents

References are made to the following publications throughout this section. Some of the references do not specifically address radon. They are listed here only as relevant sources of additional information on building design, construction techniques, and good building practices that should be considered as part of a general radon reduction strategy.

- "Building Foundation Design Handbook," ORNL/SUB/86-72143/1, May 1988.
- "Building Radon Resistant Foundations—A Design Handbook," NCMA, 1989.
- "Council of American Building Officials (CABO) Model Energy Code," 1992.
- "Design and Construction of Post-Tensioned Slabs on Ground," Post Tensioning Institute Manual.
- "Energy-Efficient Design of New Buildings Except Low-Rise Residential Buildings," ASHRAE Standard 90.1-1989.
- "Energy-Efficient Design of New Low-Rise Residential Buildings," Draft ASHRAE Standard 90.2 (under public review).
- "Home Buyer's and Seller's Guide to Radon," EPA 402-R-93-003, March 1993.
- "Guide to Residential Cast-in-Place Concrete Construction," ACI 332R.
- "Indoor Radon and Radon Decay Product Measurement Device Protocols," EPA 402-R-92-004, July 1992.
- "Protocols For Radon and Radon Decay Product Measurements in Homes," EPA 402-R-92-003, June 1993.
- "Permanent Wood Foundation System—Basic Requirements, NFPA Technical Report No.7."
- "Radon Control Options for the Design and Construction of New Low-Rise Residential Buildings," ASTM Standard Guide, E1465-92.
- "Radon Handbook for the Building Industry," NAHB-NRC, 1989.
- "U.S. EPA Map of Radon Zones," December 1993.
- "Radon Reduction in New Construction: An Interim Guide," OPA-87-009, August 1987.
- "Radon Reduction in Wood Floor and Wood Foundation Systems," NFPA, 1988.
- "Radon-Resistant Construction Techniques for New Residential Construction: Technical Guidance," EPA/625/2-91/032, February 1991.

- "Radon-Resistant Residential New Construction," EPA/600/8-88/087, July 1988.
- "Guide for Concrete Floor and Slab Construction," ACI 302.1R-89.
- "Ventilation for Acceptable Indoor Air Quality," ASHRAE 62-1989.

Description of Terms

Terms not defined herein should have their ordinary meaning within the context of their use. ("Ordinary meaning" is as defined in Webster's Ninth New Collegiate Dictionary.)

- **action level:** a term used to identify the level of indoor radon at which remedial action is recommended. The EPA's current action level is 4 pCi/L.

- **air passages:** openings through or within walls, through floors and ceilings, and around chimney flues and plumbing chases that permit air to move out of the conditioned spaces of the building.

- **combination foundations:** buildings constructed with more than one foundation type, e.g., basement/crawlspace or basement/slab-on-grade.

- **drain tile loop:** a continuous length of drain tile or perforated pipe extending around all or part of the internal or external perimeter of a basement or crawlspace footing.

- **governmental:** state or local organizations and agencies responsible for building code enforcement.

- **Map of Radon Zones:** an EPA publication depicting areas of differing radon potential in both map form and in state-specific booklets.

- **mechanically ventilated crawlspace system:** a system designed to increase ventilation within a crawlspace, achieve higher air pressure in the crawlspace relative to air pressure in the soil beneath the crawlspace, or achieve lower air pressure in the crawlspace relative to air pressure in the living spaces, by use of a fan.

- **Model Building Codes:** the building codes published by the four Model Code Organizations and commonly adopted by state and other jurisdictions to control local construction activity.

- **Model Code Organizations:** includes the following agencies and the model building codes they promulgate:

  1. Building Officials and Code Administrators International, Inc. (BOCA National Building Code/1993 and BOCA National Mechanical Code/1993);

  2. International Conference of Building Officials (Uniform Building Code/1991 and Uniform Mechanical Code/1991);

  3. Southern Building Code Congress, International, Inc. (Standard Building Code/1991 and Standard Mechanical Code/1991); and

  4. Council of American Building Officials (CABO One- and Two-Family Dwelling Code/1992 and CABO Model Energy Code/1993).

- **pCi/L:** the abbreviation for picocuries per liter, which is used as a radiation unit of measure for radon. The prefix "pico" means a multiplication factor of one-trillionth. A curie is a commonly used measurement of radioactivity.

- **soil gas:** the gas present in soil that may contain radon.

- **soil-gas retarder:** a continuous membrane or other comparable material used to retard the flow of soil gases into a building.

- **stack effect:** the overall upward movement of air inside a building that results from heated air rising and escaping through openings in the building's super-structure, thus causing an indoor pressure level lower than that in the soil gas beneath or surrounding the building's foundation.

- **sub-slab depressurization system (active):** a system designed to achieve lower sub-slab air pressure relative to indoor air pressure by use of a fan-powered vent to draw air from beneath the slab.

- **sub-slab depressurization system (passive):** a system designed to achieve lower sub-slab air pressure relative to indoor air pressure by use of a vent pipe routed through the conditioned space of a building, and connecting the sub-slab area with outdoor air, thereby relying solely on the convective flow of air upward in the vent to draw air from beneath the slab.

- **sub-membrane depressurization system:** a system designed to achieve lower sub-membrane air pressure relative to crawlspace air pressure by use of a fan-powered vent to draw air from under the soil-gas retarder's membrane.

Principles for Construction

The following principles for construction of radon-resistant residential buildings underlie the specific model standards and techniques set forth in "Building Standards and Techniques."

Residential buildings should be designed and constructed to minimize the entrance of soil gas into the living space.

Residential buildings should be designed and constructed with features that will facilitate post-construction radon removal, or further reduction of radon entry if installed prevention techniques fail to reduce radon levels below the locally prescribed action level.

As noted in the limitations, construction standards and techniques specifically applicable to new non-residential buildings (including high-rise residential buildings) have not yet been fully demonstrated. Accordingly, the specific standards and techniques set forth in "Building Standards and Techniques" should not, at this time, be considered applicable to such buildings. However, there are several general conclusions that may be drawn from the limited mitigation experience available for large non-residential construction. These conclusions are summarized below to provide some initial factors for consideration by builders of non-residential buildings.

HVAC systems should be carefully designed, installed and operated to avoid depressurization of basements and other areas in contact with the soil.

As a minimum, the use of a coarse gravel or other permeable base material beneath slabs, and effective sealing of expansion joints and penetrations in foundations below the ground surface will facilitate post-construction installation of a sub-slab depressurization system, if necessary.

Limited mitigation experience has shown that some of the same radon-reduction systems and techniques used in residential buildings can be scaled up in size, number or performance to effectively reduce radon in larger buildings.

Summary of Model Building Standards

The model building standards and techniques are designed primarily for control of radon in new one- and two family dwellings and other residential buildings three stories or fewer in height.

Basement and Slab-on-Grade Foundations

The model building standards and techniques for radon control in new residential buildings constructed on basement and slab-on-grade foundations include:

1. a layer of permeable sub-slab material;

2. the sealing of joints, cracks and other penetrations of slabs;

3. floor assemblies and foundation walls below or in contact with the ground surface;

4. providing a soil-gas retarder under floors; and

5. installing either an active or passive sub-slab depressurization system (SSD).

Additional radon-reduction techniques are prescribed to reduce radon entry caused by the heat-induced stack effect. These include the closing of air passages (also called thermal bypasses), providing adequate makeup air for combustion and exhaust devices, and installing energy-conservation features that reduce non-required air flow out of the building's super-structure.

Crawlspace Foundations

The model building standards and techniques for radon control in new residential buildings constructed on crawlspace foundations include those systems that actively or passively vent the crawlspace to outside air, that divert radon before entry into the crawlspace, and that reduce radon entry into normally occupied spaces of the building through floor openings and ductwork.

Combination Foundations

Radon control in new residential buildings constructed on a combination of basement and slab-on-grade or basement and crawlspace foundations is achieved by applying the appropriate construction techniques to the different foundation segments of the building. While each foundation type should be constructed using the relevant portions of these model building standards and techniques, special consideration must be given to the points at which different foundation types join, since additional soil-gas entry routes exist in such locations.

Construction Methods

The model construction standards and techniques have proved to be effective in reducing indoor radon levels when used to mitigate radon problems in existing homes and when applied in the construction of new homes. In most cases, combinations of two or more of these standards and techniques have been applied to achieve desired reductions in radon levels. Because of success achieved in reducing radon levels by applying these multiple, inter-dependent techniques, limited data have been collected on the singular contribution to radon reduction made by any one of the construction standards or techniques. Accordingly, there has been no attempt to classify or prioritize the individual standards and techniques as to their specific contribution to radon reduction. It is believed that the use of all the standards and techniques (both passive and active) will produce the lowest achievable levels of indoor radon in new homes. Levels below 2 pCi/L have been achieved in over 90% of new homes. It is also believed that the use of only selected (passive) standards and techniques will produce indoor radon levels below the current EPA action level of 4 pCi/L in most new homes, even in areas of high radon potential.

It is recommended that all the passive standards and techniques (including a roughed-in passive radon control system) be used in areas of high radon potential, as defined by local jurisdictions or in the EPA's Map of Radon Zones. Based on more detailed analysis of locally available data, jurisdictions may choose to apply more or less restrictive construction requirements within designated portions of their areas of responsibility. To ensure that new homes are below the locally prescribed action level, in those cases where only passive radon control systems have been installed, occupants should have their homes tested to determine if passive radon control systems need to be activated. In addition, it is recommended that periodic re-tests be conducted to confirm continued effectiveness of the radon control system.

Any radon testing referenced in here should be conducted in accordance with the EPA Radon Testing Protocols or current EPA guidance for radon testing in real estate transactions. It is recommended that all testing be conducted by companies listed in the EPA's Radon Measurement Proficiency Program (RMP) or comparable state-certification programs.

The design and installation of radon control systems should be performed or supervised by individuals (i.e., builders, their representatives, or registered design professionals, such as architects or engineers) who have attended an EPA-approved radon training course, or by an individual listed in the EPA Radon Contractor Proficiency Program.

Recommended Procedures

The following procedures are recommended as guidelines for applying the model building standards and techniques and construction methods contained in this book. These procedures are based on the rationale that a passive radon control system and features for facilitating any necessary post-construction radon reduction should be routinely built into new residential buildings in areas having a high radon potential.

State, county and local jurisdictions that use these model building standards and techniques as a basis for developing building codes for radon-resistant construction should classify their area by reference to the zones in the EPA's Map of Radon Zones, or by considering other locally available data. While the EPA believes that the Map of Radon Zones and its accompanying state-specific booklets are useful in setting general boundaries of areas of concern, the EPA recommends that state and local jurisdictions collect and analyze local indoor radon measurements, and assess geology, soil parameters and housing characteristics—in conjunction with referring to the EPA radon maps—to determine the specific areas within their jurisdictions that should be classified as Zone 1.

State, county and local jurisdictions that use these model building standards and techniques as a basis for developing building codes for radon-resistant construction should specify the construction methods applicable to their jurisdictional area.

In areas classified as Zone 1 in the Map of Radon Zones, or by local jurisdiction, application of the construction method detailed previously is recommended.

In areas classified as Zone 2, home builders may apply any of the radon-resistant construction standards and techniques that contribute to reducing the incidence of elevated radon levels in new homes, including those that are appropriate to the unique radon potential that may exist in their local building area.

In those areas where state and local jurisdictions have analyzed local indoor radon measurements, geology, soil parameters, and housing characteristics, and where they have determined that there is a low potential for indoor radon, the application of radon-resistant construction techniques may not be appropriate. In these areas, radon-resistant construction techniques may not be needed, or limited use of selected techniques may be sufficient.

It is recognized that specific rules, regulations and ordinances covering implementation of construction standards and codes are developed and enforced by state and local jurisdictions. While developing the model construction standards and techniques contained in this section, the EPA also developed several approaches to regulation that states and local jurisdictions may find useful and appropriate as they develop rules and regulations that meet their unique requirements.

For example:

- In areas where the recommended construction method or comparable prescriptive methods are mandated by state or local jurisdictions, regulations would need to include, as part of the inspection process, a review of the radon-resistant construction features by inspectors who have received additional training to ensure that the radon-resistant construction features are properly installed during construction. It would also be necessary to establish requirements for those building officials who review and approve construction plans and specifications to become proficient in identifying and approving planned radon-resistant construction features.

- In any area where surveys have shown the existence of high levels of radon in groundwater, or in areas where elevated levels of indoor radon have been found in homes already equipped with active radon control systems, well water may be the source. In such areas, authorities responsible for water regulation should consider establishing well-water testing requirements that include tests for radon.

Building Standards and Techniques

Foundation and Floor Assemblies

The following construction techniques are intended to resist radon entry and prepare the building for post-construction radon mitigation, if necessary.

A layer of gas-permeable material shall be placed under all concrete slabs and other floor systems that are in direct contact with the ground and are within the walls of the living spaces of the building in order to facilitate installation of a sub-slab depressurization system, if needed.

Alternatives for creating the gas-permeable layer include:

- a uniform layer of clean aggregate, a minimum of 4 inches thick. The aggregate shall consist of material that will pass through a 2-inch sieve and be retained by a 1/4-inch sieve;

- a uniform layer of sand, a minimum of 4 inches thick, overlain by a layer or strips of geotextile drainage matting designed to allow the lateral flow of soil gases; or

- other materials, systems, or floor designs with the demonstrated capability to permit depressurization across the entire sub-floor area.

A minimum 6-mil (or 3-mil cross-laminated) polyethylene or equivalent flexible sheeting material shall be placed on top of the gas-permeable layer prior to pouring the slab or placing the floor assembly to serve as a soil-gas retarder by bridging any cracks that develop in the slab or floor assembly, and to prevent concrete from entering the void spaces in aggregate-base material. The sheeting should cover the entire floor area, and separate sections of sheeting should be overlapped at least 12 inches. The sheeting shall fit closely around any pipe, wire, or other penetrations of the material. All punctures or tears in the material shall be sealed or covered with additional sheeting.

To minimize the formation of cracks, all concrete floor slabs shall be designed, mixed, placed, reinforced, consolidated, finished and cured in accordance with standards set forth in the Model Building Codes. The American Concrete Institute publications *Guide for Concrete Floor and Slab Construction, Guide to Residential Cast-in-Place Concrete Construction,* or the *Post Tensioning Institute's Design and Construction of Post-Tensioned Slabs on Ground* are references that provide additional information on construction of concrete floor slabs.

Floor assemblies in contact with the soil and constructed of materials other than concrete shall be sealed to minimize soil-gas transport into the conditioned spaces of the building. A soil-gas retarder shall be installed beneath the entire floor assembly.

To retard soil-gas entry, large openings through concrete slabs, wood, and other floor assemblies in contact with the soil, such as spaces around the bathtub, shower and toilet drains, shall be filled or closed with materials that provide a permanent airtight seal, such as non-shrink mortar, grouts, expanding foam, or similar materials designed for such application.

To retard soil-gas entry, smaller gaps around all pipe, wire, and other objects that penetrate concrete slabs or other floor assemblies shall be made airtight with an elastomeric joint sealant, as defined in ASTM C920-87, and applied in accordance with the manufacturer's recommendations.

To retard soil-gas entry, all control joints, isolation joints, construction joints, and any other joints in concrete slabs or between slabs and foundation walls shall be sealed. A continuous formed gap (for example, a tooled edge) that allows the application of a sealant that will provide a continuous, airtight seal shall be created along all joints. When the slab has cured, the gap shall be cleared of loose material and filled with an elastomeric joint sealant, as defined in ASTM C920-97, and applied in accordance with the manufacturer's recommendations.

Channel-type (or French) drains are not recommended. However, if used, such drains shall be sealed with backer rods and an elastomeric joint sealant in a manner that retains the channel feature and does not interfere with the effectiveness of the drain as a water-control system.

Floor drains and air-conditioning condensate drains that discharge directly into the soil below the slab or into crawlspaces should be avoided. If installed, these drains shall be routed through solid pipe to daylight, or through a trap approved for use in floor drains by local plumbing codes.

Sumps open to soil or serving as the termination point for sub-slab or exterior drain tile loops shall be covered with a gasketed or otherwise sealed lid to retard soil-gas entry. (NOTE: If the sump is to be used as the suction point in an active sub-slab depressurization system, the lid should be designed to accommodate the vent pipe. If also intended as a floor drain, the lid shall also be equipped with a trapped inlet to handle any surface water on the slab.)

Concrete masonry foundation walls below the ground surface shall be constructed to minimize the transport of soil gas from the soil into the building. Hollow-block masonry walls shall be sealed at the top to prevent the passage of air from the interior of the wall into the living space. At least one continuous course of solid masonry, one course of masonry-grouted solid, or a poured concrete beam at or above the finished ground-surface level shall be used for this purpose. Where a brick veneer or other masonry ledge is installed, the course immediately below that ledge shall also be sealed.

Pressure-treated wood foundations shall be constructed and installed as described in the National Forest Products Association (NFPA)'s manual *Permanent Wood Foundation System: Basic*

Requirements, Technical Report No. 7. In addition, the NFPA publication *Radon Reduction in Wood Floor and Wood Foundation Systems* provides more detailed information on construction of radon-resistant wood floors and foundations.

Joints, cracks, and other openings around all penetrations of both exterior and interior surfaces of masonry block or wood foundation walls below the ground surface shall be sealed with an elastomeric sealant that provides an airtight seal. Penetrations of poured concrete walls should also be sealed on the exterior surface. This includes sealing wall-tie penetrations.

To resist soil-gas entry, the exterior surfaces of portions of poured concrete and masonry block walls below the ground surface shall be constructed in accordance with waterproofing procedures outlined in the Model Building Codes.

Placing air-handling ducts in or beneath a concrete slab floor, or in other areas below grade and exposed to earth, is not recommended unless the air-handling system is designed to maintain continuous positive pressure within such ducting. If ductwork does pass through a crawlspace or beneath a slab, it should be of a seamless material. Where joints in such ductwork are unavoidable, they shall be sealed with materials that prevent air leakage.

Placing air-handling units in crawlspaces or in other areas below grade and exposed to soil gas is not recommended. However, if such units are installed in crawlspaces or in other areas below grade and exposed to soil gas, they shall be designed or otherwise sealed in a durable manner that prevents air surrounding the unit from being drawn into the unit.

To retard soil-gas entry, the openings around all penetrations through floors above crawlspaces shall be sealed with materials that prevent air leakage.

To retard soil-gas entry, access doors and other openings and penetrations between basements and adjoining crawlspaces shall be closed, gasketed, or otherwise sealed with materials that prevent air leakage.

Crawlspaces should be ventilated in conformance with locally adopted codes. In addition, vents in passively ventilated crawlspaces shall be open to the exterior and be of a non-closeable design.

In buildings with crawlspace foundations, the following components of a passive sub-membrane depressurization system shall be installed during construction:

- The soil in both vented and unvented crawlspaces shall be covered with a continuous layer of minimum 6-mil polyethylene sheeting or equivalent membrane material. The sheeting shall be sealed at all seams and penetrations, around the perimeter of interior piers, and to the foundation walls. Following installation of underlayment, flooring, plumbing, wiring, and other construction activity in or over the crawlspace, the membrane material shall be inspected for holes, tears and other damage, and for continued adhesion to walls and piers. Repairs shall be made as necessary.

- A length of 3- or 4-inch-diameter perforated pipe or a strip of geotextile drainage matting should be inserted horizontally beneath the sheeting, and connected to a 3- or 4-inch-diameter T-fitting with a vertical standpipe installed through the sheeting. The standpipe shall be extended vertically through the building floors, terminate at least 12 inches above the surface of the roof, and in a location at least 10 feet away from any window or other opening into the conditioned spaces of the building that is less than 2 feet below the exhaust point, and 10 feet away from any adjoining or adjacent buildings.

- All exposed and visible interior radon vent pipes shall be identified with at least one label on each floor level. The label shall read: "Radon Reduction System."

- To facilitate installation of an active sub-membrane depressurization system, electrical junction boxes shall be installed during construction in proximity to the anticipated locations of vent pipe fans and system-failure alarms.

EXCEPTION: Where local codes permit mechanical crawlspace ventilation or other effective ventilation systems, and if such systems are operated or proven to be effective year-round, the sub-membrane depressurization system components are not required.

In basement and slab-on-grade buildings, the following components of a passive sub-slab depressurization system shall be installed during construction:

- A minimum 3-inch-diameter PVC or other gas-tight pipe shall be embedded vertically into the sub-slab aggregate or other permeable material before the slab is poured. A T-fitting or other support on the bottom of the pipe shall be used to ensure that the pipe opening remains within the sub-slab permeable material. This gas-tight pipe shall be extended vertically through the building floors, terminate at least 12 inches above the surface of the roof, and in a location at least 10 feet away from any window or other opening into the conditioned spaces of the building that is less than 2 feet below the exhaust point, and 10 feet away from any adjoining or adjacent buildings. (NOTE: Because of the uniform permeability of the sub-slab layer, the precise positioning of the vent pipe through the slab is not critical to system performance, in most cases. However, a central location shall be used, where feasible. In buildings designed with interior footings [that is, footings located inside the overall perimeter footprint of the building] or other barriers to the lateral flow of sub-slab soil gas, radon vent pipes shall be installed in each isolated, non-connected floor area. If multiple suction points are used in non-connected floor areas, vent pipes are permitted to be manifolded in the basement or attic into a single vent that could be activated using a single fan.)

- Internal sub-slab and external footing drain tile loops that terminate in a covered and sealed sump, or internal drain tile loops that are stubbed up through the slab are also permitted to provide a roughed-in passive sub-slab depressurization capability. The sump or stubbed-up pipe shall be connected to a vent pipe that extends vertically through the building floors, terminate at least 12 inches above the surface of the roof, and in a location at least 10 feet away from any window or other opening into the conditioned spaces of the building that is less than 2 feet below the exhaust point, and 10 feet away from any adjoining or adjacent buildings.

- All exposed and visible interior radon vent pipes shall be identified with at least one label on each floor level. The label shall read: "Radon Reduction System."

- To facilitate installation of an active sub-slab depressurization system, electrical junction boxes shall be installed during construction in proximity to the anticipated locations of vent pipe fans and system-failure alarms.

- In combination basement and crawlspace and slab-on-grade and crawlspace buildings, the sub-membrane vent may be tied into the sub-slab depressurization vent to permit use of a single fan for suction, if activation of the system is necessary.

Stack Effect-Reduction Techniques

The following construction techniques are intended to reduce the stack effect in buildings and, thus, the driving force that contributes to radon entry and migration through buildings. As a basic principle, the driving force decreases as the number and size of air leaks in the upper surface of the building decrease. It should also be noted that, in most cases, exhaust fans contribute to stack effect.

Openings around chimney flues, plumbing chases, pipes and fixtures, ductwork, electrical wires and fixtures, elevator shafts, and other air passages that penetrate the conditioned envelope of the building shall be closed or sealed using sealant or fire-resistant materials approved in local codes for such application.

If located in conditioned spaces, attic access stairs and other openings to the attic from the building shall be closed, gasketed, or otherwise sealed with materials that prevent air leakage.

Recessed ceiling lights that are designed to be sealed and that are Type IC-rated shall be used when installed on top-floor ceilings and in other ceilings that connect to air passages.

Fireplaces, wood stoves, and other combustion or vented appliances, such as furnaces, clothes dryers and water heaters, shall be installed in compliance with locally adopted codes, or other provisions made to ensure an adequate supply of combustion and makeup air.

Windows and exterior doors in the building's super-structure shall be weatherstripped or otherwise designed in conformance with the air-leakage criteria of the CABO Model Energy Code.

HVAC systems shall be designed and installed to avoid depressurization of the building relative to the underlying and surrounding soil. Specifically, joints in air ducts and plenums passing through unconditioned spaces, such as attics, crawlspaces and garages, shall be sealed.

Active Sub-Slab/Sub-Membrane Depressurization System

When necessary, activation of the roughed-in passive sub-membrane and sub-slab depressurization systems shall be completed by adding an exhaust fan in the vent pipe, and a prominently positioned visible or audible warning system installed to alert the building's occupants if there is loss of pressure or air flow in the vent pipe.

The fan in the vent pipe and all positively pressurized portions of the vent pipe shall be located outside the habitable space of the building.

The fan in the vent pipe shall be installed in a vertical run of the vent pipe.

Radon vent pipes shall be installed in a configuration and supported in a manner that ensures that any rainwater or condensation accumulating within the pipes drains downward into the ground beneath the slab or soil-gas retarder.

To avoid re-entry of soil gas into the building, the vent pipe shall exhaust at least 12 inches above the surface of the roof, in a location at least 10 feet away from any window and other opening into the conditioned spaces of the building that is less than 2 feet below the exhaust point, and 10 feet away from any adjoining or adjacent buildings.

To facilitate the future installation of a vent fan, if needed, the radon vent pipe shall be routed through the attic in a location that will allow sufficient room to install and maintain the fan.

The size and air-movement capacity of the vent pipe fan shall be sufficient to create and maintain a pressure field beneath the slab or crawlspace membrane that is lower than the ambient pressure above the slab or membrane.

Under conditions where the soil is highly permeable, reversing the air flow in an active sub-slab depressurization system and forcing air beneath the slab may be effective in reducing indoor radon levels.

NOTE: The long-term effect of active sub-slab depressurization or pressurization on the soil beneath building foundations has not been determined. Until ongoing research produces definitive data, in areas where expansive soils or other unusual soil conditions exist, the local soils engineer shall be consulted during the design and installation of sub-slab depressurization or pressurization systems.

Quiz #11

1. T/F: A layer of gas-permeable material shall be placed under all concrete slabs and other floor systems that directly contact the ground and are within the walls of the living spaces of the building to facilitate installation of a sub-slab depressurization system, if needed.

    ☐ True
    ☐ False

2. A minimum _____-mil (or 3-mil cross-laminated) polyethylene or equivalent flexible sheeting material shall be placed on top of the gas-permeable layer prior to pouring the slab, or placing the floor assembly to serve as a soil-gas retarder by bridging any cracks that develop in the slab or floor assembly, and to prevent concrete from entering the void spaces in aggregate-base material.

    ☐ 6
    ☐ 8
    ☐ 10
    ☐ 12

3. T/F: Channel-type (or French) drains, if used, shall be sealed with backer rods and an elastomeric joint sealant in a manner that retains the channel feature and does not interfere with the effectiveness of the drain as a water-control system.

    ☐ True
    ☐ False

4. T/F: Joints, cracks, and other openings around all penetrations of both exterior and interior surfaces of masonry block or wood foundation walls below the ground surface shall be sealed with an elastomeric sealant that provides an airtight seal.

    ☐ True
    ☐ False

5. Openings around chimney flues, plumbing chases, pipes and fixtures, ductwork, electrical wires and fixtures, elevator shafts, and other air passages that penetrate the conditioned envelope of the building shall be _____.

    ☐ left open
    ☐ closed or sealed using sealant or fire-resistant materials approved in local codes for such application

Answer Key is on page 353.

How to Build Radon-Resistant Homes

NOTE: Although this section based on the EPA publication directly addresses home builders, home inspectors can gain valuable insights into the practices that go into building a radon-resistant home, especially if there are deficiencies that need to be called out during an inspection and noted in the inspection report.

Building Radon Out

This section is based on the U.S. EPA Publication 402-K-01-002 (April 2001): *Building Radon Out: A Step-by-Step Guide on How to Build Radon-Resistant Homes.*

THE EPA's DISCLAIMER

The EPA strives to provide accurate, complete, and useful information. However, neither the EPA nor any person contributing to the preparation of this information makes any warranty, express or implied, with respect to the usefulness or effectiveness of any information, method or process disclosed in this material, nor does the EPA assume any liability for the use of, or for damages arising from the use of, any information, method or process disclosed herein.

The mention of firms, trade names, or commercial products does not constitute endorsement or recommendation for use.

This section covers the following topics:

- Building the Framework: Introduction
- Does it Make Sense to Build Homes Radon-Resistant?
- Digging Deeper: Questions and Answers
- What Is Radon?
- Is Radon a Significant Health Risk?
- Is Radon a Problem in Homes?
- Is There a Safe Level of Radon?
- How Does Radon Enter a House?
- How Does Air Pressure Affect Radon Entry?
- Does Foundation Type Affect Radon Entry?
- What Can You Do to Reduce Radon New Homes?
- What Are the Radon-Resistant Features?
- Is There a Way to Test the Lot Before Building?
- Would I Incur Liability by Installing the Features?
- Should All New Homes Be Built Radon-Resistant?
- EPA Map of Radon Zones
- List of Zone 1 Counties
- Nuts and Bolts: Installation Guide: Planning

- Answer the Question: To Install or Not to Install?
- Determine What Type of System to Install
- Determine Vent Pipe Location and Size
- Installation
- Basement and Slab-on-Grade Construction: Sub-Slab Preparation
- Gravel
- Perforated Pipe
- Soil-Gas Collection Mat
- Plastic Sheeting
- Seal-Off and Label-Riser Stub
- Lay Foundation
- Crawlspace Construction
- Seal Openings
- Install Vent Pipe
- Sealing Ducts and Air-Handling Units
- Install Electrical Junction Box
- Post-Occupancy Testing
- Activate the System
- Sold: Working With Home Buyers
- Get an Edge on the Market
- Make a Name for Yourself
- What to Tell Home Buyers
- Appendix A: Architectural Drawings
- Appendix B: Glossary
- Appendix C: For More Information
- Appendix D: State Radon Contacts

Introduction

Should you be concerned about radon? Yes.

Radon is a colorless, odorless gas that can cause lung cancer. Your customers rely on you to construct a high-quality, safe home. You can easily make a difference in how much radon gets into the homes you build. By using a handful of simple building practices and common materials, you can effectively lower the radon level in the homes that you build, and build most radon problems right out of the house.

Does it make sense to build homes radon-resistant? Absolutely. There are a number of reasons why you should consider installing radon-resistant features.

You can gain a marketing advantage.

Offering homes with radon-resistant features can attract more potential home buyers, which can translate into closing more sales, and greater profits. Consumers are becoming more aware that radon is a health risk, and building a home with radon-resistant features could give buyers one more reason to purchase a home from you. About one in every six homes is being built radon-resistant in the U.S. every year, averaging about 200,000 homes annually, according to annual surveys of home-builder practices conducted by the National Association of Home Builders (NAHB) Research Center over the past decade. In high radon areas, about one in every three homes is built with such features.

Industry surveys continue to demonstrate a rapidly growing market for more energy-efficient, environmentally friendly, comfortable and healthy homes. Radon-reduction techniques are consistent with state-of-the-art, energy-efficient construction. The features can also decrease moisture and other soil gases entering the home, reducing molds, mildews, methane, pesticide gases, volatile organic compounds, and other indoor air-quality problems. When using these techniques, follow the Model Energy Code (or other applicable energy codes) for weatherization, which will result in energy savings and lower utility bills for the homeowner.

It's a good investment for the home buyer.

It's cheaper to install a radon-reduction system during construction than to go back and fix a radon problem identified later. On average, installing radon-resistant features during construction costs about $350 to $500, or even less, if you already use some of the techniques for moisture control and energy efficiency. Many builders who use the techniques have reported actual costs of $100 or less. In contrast, retrofitting an existing home will typically cost between $800 and $2,500.

It's effective.

A basic radon-reduction system, called a passive sub-slab depressurization system, effectively reduces radon levels by an average of about 50% and, in most cases, to levels below the EPA's action level. An upgraded system, called an active sub-slab depressurization system, includes an in-line fan to provide even further reductions.

It's simple to install.

All of the techniques and materials are commonly used in construction. No special skills or materials are required.

Upgrading is easy.

After occupancy, all homes should be tested for radon, even those built with radon-resistant features. The EPA recommends that homes with radon levels at or above 4 picocuries per liter of air (pCi/L) be mitigated. Homes with a passive system can be upgraded to an active system with the simple installation of a special in-line fan to further reduce the radon level. Typically, the passive system includes a junction box in the attic to make the future installation of the fan easy. This upgrade is also used by some builders to control moisture in basements and crawlspaces.

Questions and Answers

What is radon?

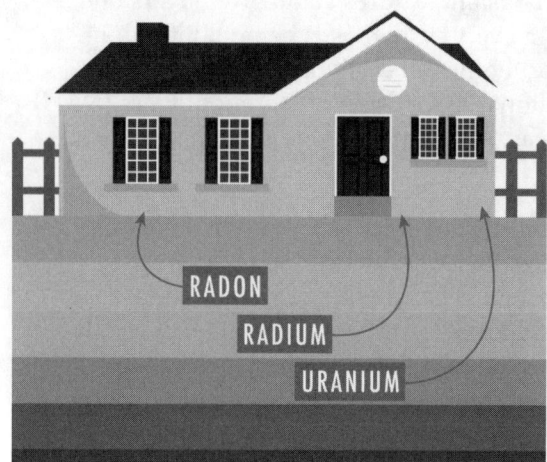

Radon is a radioactive gas. It comes from uranium and radium in soil, which can be found everywhere in the world. Uranium is present in rocks, such as granite, shale, phosphate, and pitchblende. Uranium breaks down into radium, which then decays into radon. This gas can easily move up through the soil into the atmosphere. Natural deposits of uranium and radium—not manufactured sources—produce most of the radon present in the air.

Radon is in the soil and air everywhere in varying amounts. People cannot see, taste, feel or smell radon. There is no way to sense the presence of radon. Radon levels are commonly expressed in picocuries per liter of air (pCi/L), where a picocurie is a measure of radioactivity. The national average of indoor radon levels in homes is about 1.3 pCi/L. Radon levels outdoors, where radon is diluted, average about 0.4 pCi/L.

Radon in the soil can be drawn into a building and can accumulate to high levels. Every building and home has the potential for elevated levels of radon. All homes should be tested for radon, even those built with radon-resistant features. The EPA recommends taking action to reduce indoor radon levels when levels are 4 pCi/L or higher.

Is radon a significant health risk?

When radon enters a home, it decays into radioactive particles that have a static charge, which attracts them to particles in the air. These particles can get trapped in your lungs when you breathe. As the radioactive particles break down further, they release bursts of energy that can damage the DNA in lung tissue. In some cases, if the lung tissue does not repair the DNA correctly, the damage can lead to lung cancer.

Not everyone exposed to elevated levels of radon will develop lung cancer, but your risk of getting radon-induced lung cancer increases as your exposure to radon increases, either because the radon levels are higher or you live in the home longer. Smokers who have high radon levels in their homes are at an especially high risk for getting radon-induced lung cancer.

The evidence that radon causes lung cancer is extensive and based on: human data taken from studies of underground miners carried out over more than 50 years in five countries, including the United States and Canada; human data from studies in homes in many different nations, including the U.S. and Canada; and biological and molecular studies.

Radon is classified as a Class A carcinogen (known to cause cancer in humans). Some other Class A carcinogens include arsenic, asbestos and benzene. Energy released from radon decay products damages DNA. Radon decay particles are breathed into the lungs.

Is radon a health problem in homes?

Radon is the second-leading cause of lung cancer in the United States. Radon causes about 20,000 lung cancer deaths per year.

The following are some organizations that have stated that radon is a health threat in homes:

- the U.S. Surgeon General;
- the American Medical Association;
- the American Lung Association;
- the Centers for Disease Control;
- the National Cancer Institute;
- the National Academy of Sciences; and
- the Environmental Protection Agency.

The risk of developing lung cancer from radon has been clearly demonstrated in underground miners. Did you know that the average lifetime radon exposure for the general population is about the same as the levels of exposure at which increased risk has been demonstrated in underground miners? A study released by the National Academy of Sciences on February 19, 1998 called *The Health Effects of Exposure to Indoor Radon* is the most definitive accumulation of scientific data on indoor radon. The report concludes that radon causes 15,000 to 22,000 deaths per year, making it the second-leading cause of lung cancer in the U.S., and a serious public health concern.

Have you heard of Stanley Watras?

Stanley J. Watras was a construction engineer at the Limerick Nuclear Power Plant in Pottstown, Pennsylvania. One day, on his way to work, he entered the plant and set off the radiation monitor alarms, which help protect workers by detecting exposure to radiation. Safety personnel checked him out but could not find the source of the radiation. Interestingly, because the plant was under construction at the time, there was no nuclear fuel at the plant. They discovered the source of radiation exposure when Watras's home was tested and was measured to have very high radon levels (2,700 pCi/L). After installing a radon-reduction system, radon levels in the home tested below 4 pCi/L.

Is there a safe level of radon?

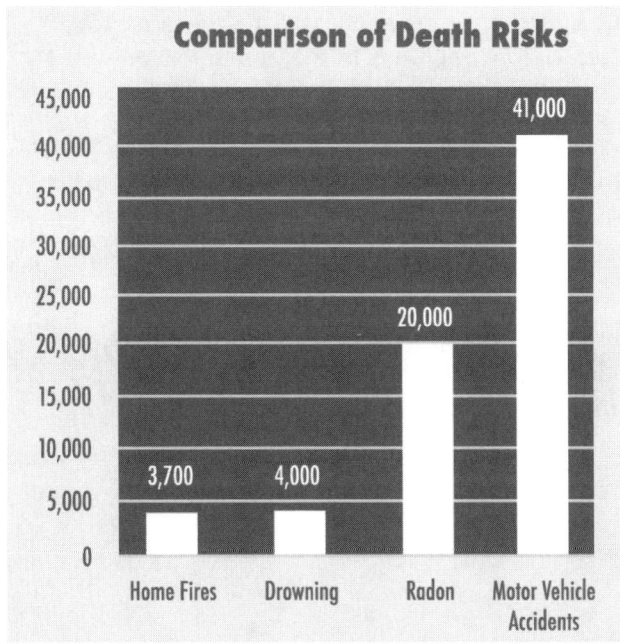

There is no known safe level of radon. As your exposure to radon is increased, so is your risk for developing lung cancer. Even radon levels below 4 pCi/L pose some risk. Homes have been found with radon levels above 20, 100, and, in rare cases, even 2,000 pCi/L. High indoor radon levels have been found in every state.

The EPA, the Surgeon General, the Centers for Disease Control, and many other health organizations recommend that action be taken to reduce indoor radon levels at or above 4 pCi/L, which is a reasonably achievable level of radon in homes using currently available cost-effective techniques. Radon is a significant risk. More people die from lung cancer caused by radon each year than from many other highly publicized causes of death.

How Does Radon Enter a House?

Common Radon Entry Points

There are four main factors that drive radon into homes. All of these factors exist in most homes throughout the country:

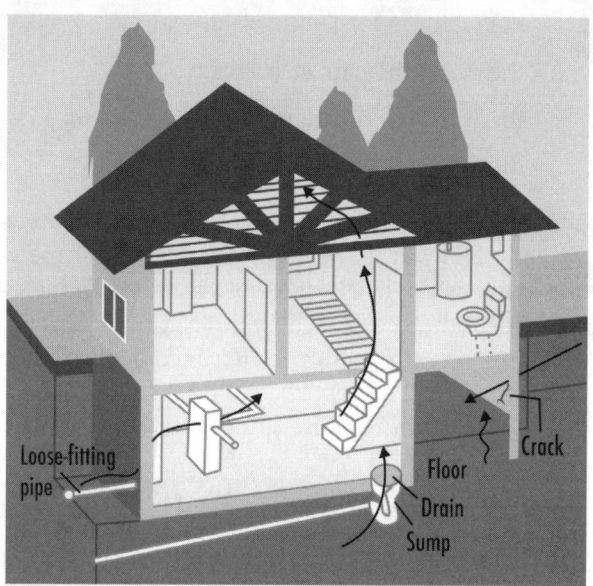

1. Uranium is present in the soil nearly everywhere in the United States.

2. The soil is permeable enough to allow radon to migrate into the home through the slab, basement or crawlspace.

3. There are pathways for the radon to enter the basement, such as small holes, cracks, plumbing penetrations, and sumps. All homes have radon-entry pathways.

4. An air-pressure difference between the basement or crawlspace and the surrounding soil draws radon into the home.

How does air pressure affect radon entry?

The air pressure in a house is generally lower than in the surrounding air and soil, particularly at the basement and foundation levels. This difference in pressure causes a house to act like a vacuum, drawing air containing radon and other soil gases in through foundation's cracks and other openings. Some of the replacement air comes from the underlying soil and can contain radon.

One reason why this pressure difference occurs is because exhaust fans remove air from inside the house. When this air is exhausted, outside air enters the house to replace it. Another cause for a pressure difference is that warm air rises and will leak from openings in the upper portion of the house when temperatures are higher indoors than outdoors. This condition, known as stack effect, causes unconditioned replacement air to enter the lower portion of the house.

Mechanical systems, such as the furnaces and central air conditioners, may also contribute to the difference in air pressure. In areas with very short, mild winters, mechanical systems can be the dominant driving force. Air handlers and leaky return ducts can not only draw in radon, but they can also distribute it throughout a home.

Warm air rises up and out through leaks in the building envelope. Air is also drawn out by mechanical ventilation (e.g., bathroom fans and clothes dryers) and combustion exhaust. Replacement air enters the house by infiltration in lower levels. Soil gases are also drawn into the home where the house contacts the ground.

Does Foundation Type Affect Radon Entry?

Because radon can literally be sucked into a home, any home can potentially have a radon problem. All conventional house construction types have been found to have radon levels exceeding the action level of 4 pCi/L.

Basement

Radon can enter through floor-to-wall joints, control joints and cracks in the slab.

Crawlspace

The vacuums that exist within a home are exerted on the crawlspaces causing radon and other gases to enter the home from the earthen area below. Even with crawlspace vents, a slight vacuum is still exerted on the crawlspace. Measurements in homes with crawlspaces have shown elevated radon levels.

Warm air rises up and out through leaks in the building envelope. Air is also drawn out by mechanical ventilation (e.g., bathroom fans and clothes dryers) and combustion exhaust.

Replacement air enters the house by infiltration in lower levels. Soil gases are also drawn into the home where the house contacts the ground.

Slab-on-Grade

Radon can enter a home regardless of whether or not there is a basement. Slabs built on grade can have just as many openings to allow radon to enter as do basements.

Manufactured Homes

Unless these buildings are set up on piers without any skirting placed around them, interior vacuums can cause radon to enter these types of homes, as well.

What can you do to reduce radon in new homes?

You can easily draw radon away and help prevent radon from entering the home with the following basic steps. You may already be employing many of these techniques in the homes that you build. All of the techniques have additional benefits associated with them, and they are very easy to install.

Install a sub-slab (or sub-membrane) depressurization system.

The objective of these systems is to create a vacuum beneath the foundation which is greater in strength than the vacuum applied to the soil by the house itself. The soil gases that are collected beneath the home are piped to a safe location to be vented directly outside.

Use mechanical barriers to soil-gas entry.

Plastic sheeting, and foundation sealing and caulking can serve as barriers to radon entry, entry of other soil gases, and moisture.

Reduce stack effect.

Sealing and caulking reduce stack effect and, thus, reduce the negative pressure in lower levels of the home.

Install air-distribution systems so that soil air is not "mined."

Air-handling units and all ducts in basements and, especially, in crawlspaces should be sealed to prevent air (and radon) from being drawn into the system. Seamless ducts are preferred for runs through crawlspaces and beneath slabs. Any seams and joints in ducts should be sealed.

Can we keep radon out by sealing the cracks?

Sealing large cracks and openings is important to do, both in the lower portion of the home to reduce radon entry-points, and in the upper portion of the home to reduce stack effect. However, field research has shown that attempting to seal all of the openings in a foundation is both impractical and ineffective as a stand-alone technique. Radon can enter through very small cracks and openings which can often be too small to locate and effectively seal. Even if all cracks could be sealed during construction (which would be costly), building settlement may cause new cracks to occur. Therefore, sealing large cracks and openings is one of the key components of radon-resistant construction, but not the only technique that should be employed.

What pulls the soil gas through pipe?

If pipe is routed through a warm space (such as an interior wall or the furnace flue chase, following local fire codes), the stack effect can create a natural draft in the pipe. Because this method requires no mechanical devices, it is called a passive soil-depressurization system.

If further reduction is necessary to bring radon levels in a home below the action level of 4 pCi/L, or even lower, an in-line fan can be installed in the pipe to activate the system. The system is then called an active soil depressurization system. The future installation of the fan can be made easier with a little planning during construction.

What are the radon-resistant features?

The techniques may vary for different foundations and site requirements, but the basic elements of the passive sub-slab depressurization system follow.

In many parts of the country, the gravel beneath the slab (the gas-permeable layer), plastic sheeting, and sealing

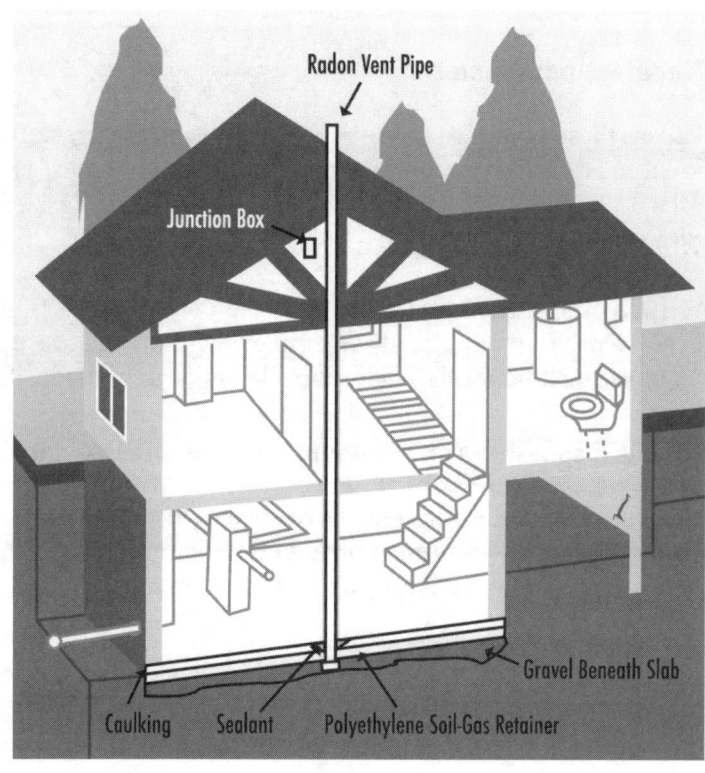

and caulking are already employed for moisture reduction. In these cases, simply adding the vent pipe and junction box is extremely cost-effective for reducing radon, so much so that even the cost-conscious organization Habitat for Humanity, which relies on donations and grants for its funding, has been adding these features in many of its homes.

Popular and Effective Radon-Resistant Features in New Construction

Gas-Permeable Layer

Usually, a 4-inch layer of clean, coarse gravel is used beneath the slab to allow the soil gas to move freely underneath the house. Other options are to install a loop of perforated pipe or a soil-gas collection mat (also known as a drainage mat or soil-gas matting).

Plastic Sheeting

Polyethylene sheeting is placed on top of the gas-permeable layer to help prevent the soil gas from entering the home. The sheeting also keeps concrete from clogging the gas-permeable layer when the slab is poured.

Vent Pipe

A 3- or 4-inch PVC or other gas-tight pipe (commonly used for plumbing) runs from the gas-permeable layer through the house and roof to safely vent radon and other soil gases above the house. Although some builders use 3-inch pipe, field results have indicated that passive systems tend to function better with 4-inch pipe.

Junction Box

An electrical junction box is wired in case an electric venting fan is needed later to activate the system.

Sealing and Caulking

All openings in the concrete foundation floor are sealed to prevent soil gas from entering the home. Also, sealing and caulking the rest of the building envelope reduces stack effect in the home.

Is there a way to test the lot before building?

Soil testing for radon is not recommended for determining whether a house should be built radon-resistant. Although soil testing can be done, it cannot rule out the possibility that radon could be a problem in the house you build on that lot. Even if soil testing reveals low levels of radon gas in the soil, the amount of radon that may enter the finished house cannot be accurately predicted because one cannot predict the impact that the site preparation will have on introducing new radon pathways, or the extent to which a vacuum will be produced by the house. Furthermore, the cost of a single soil test for radon ranges from $70 to $150, and at least four to eight tests could be required to accurately characterize the radon in the soil at a single building site. Therefore, the cost to perform soil testing is very high when compared with installing the passive radon system in high radon-potential areas.

Why not wait to install the features until after the home is completed and a radon test is performed?

It is much easier and far less costly to prepare the sub-grade to improve soil-gas flow before the slab is cast. Also, the pipe itself can be run more easily through the house before it is finished. This significantly improves aesthetics and can reduce subsequent system operating costs by planning to route the pipe through warm space to maximize passive operation of the system.

The best way to determine the radon level in a home is to test the home for radon after occupancy.

Would I incur liability by installing the features?

New homes built in the U.S. are not required to meet a specified radon level. You are not required to test a home, nor to guarantee that a home will meet a specified radon level. By installing radon-resistant features, you are pro-actively offering your home buyers features designed to reduce radon levels. Adopting radon-resistant building techniques should not increase your liability risks in any jurisdiction as long as due care is exercised in following the proper construction techniques. Especially in high radon areas, radon-resistant features may actually help you market and sell the homes you build.

Once you have decided to build radon-resistant, you will want to make sure to install the features properly. If your building code includes provisions for the radon features, follow your code requirements. Otherwise, follow the guidance provided in this document, or in any of the following documents:

Should All New Homes Be Radon-Resistant?

All homes could benefit from having a radon-reduction system. However, it is especially cost-effective to install the features in homes with the greatest potential for high radon levels.

The potential for elevated radon levels is not uniform throughout the U.S. The EPA and the U.S. Geological Survey have identified areas of the country with the greatest potential for high radon levels. The map to follow is based on indoor radon measurements, local geology, and population densities compiled in an effort to rank radon potentials in all counties across the U.S. The map indicates three radon-potential zones defined by the likelihood of finding radon measurements within certain ranges when a short-term closed-building radon test is performed.

The EPA recommends that all homes built in Zone 1 areas (with high radon potential) install radon-reduction systems. The NAHB also recommends using the passive system in homes in high radon potential areas (Zone 1). Zone 1 counties are listed by state.

If you are building in a Zone 2 or 3 area, the homes you build could still have high radon levels, particularly if there is a radon "hot spot" in your county. According to an annual survey by the NAHB Research Center, about 60,000 homes in Zones 2 and 3 are built with radon-resistant techniques each year. You may want to consider applying the techniques in these areas, too. Since the map was developed, many states have acquired additional information on high radon areas. Contact your state radon office for more information.

Consumers have asked for the radon-reduction features in many different parts of the country and in all three radon zones.

Installation Guide

Installation is easy.

As you'll see in this section, installing radon-resistant features is simple because you use common building practices and materials. Proper installation of the radon-resistant features is very important. Improper installation could actually increase indoor radon levels. This section gives you step-by-step instructions—the nuts and bolts—on how to install radon-resistant features. The techniques presented here apply primarily to new one- and two-family dwellings, and other residential buildings three stories or fewer in height.

PLANNING

Step 1: Answer These Questions

To install or not to install?

To help you answer this question, consider the following points: Do you want to reap the benefits of installing the features? The features not only protect your customer's health, but they also affect your bottom line—your profit. A small investment up front on your part may make a big difference in return down the road, particularly as home buyers are increasingly looking for environmentally conscious builders and healthy homes.

Are you building in a Zone 1 area?

Check the radon potential map and the list of Zone 1 counties. Some states and counties have done further research on radon potential, and you can check with your state and county governments to find out whether additional information is available.

If you are building in a Zone 1 area, you should install radon-resistant features in the homes that you build. Some builders also choose to install the features in Zone 2 and 3 areas, particularly if radon-resistant construction is a common practice in those areas.

Are you required by code to use radon-resistant techniques?

Some states and local jurisdictions have adopted Appendix F of the 1995 *CABO One- & Two-Family Dwelling Code*, Appendix D of the 1998 *International One- & Two-Family Dwelling Code*, or a similar code requiring installation of the radon-resistant features. The International Code Council's new International Residential Code, published in 2000, also contains a voluntary appendix for radon-resistant construction requirements that becomes effective if the appendix is adopted with the code. If you don't already know what is required in your area, check with your local code official for more information.

Are other builders in your area installing radon-resistant features?

If so, you may want to find out why they are installing the features, how much it costs to install the features in your area, and what the market response has been.

Are the home buyers in your area interested in features that improve indoor air quality and/or energy efficiency?

A sub-slab depressurization system not only helps to reduce indoor radon levels, but also may help to reduce moisture and other soil gases. The techniques also improve energy efficiency, which can translate into energy savings for the home buyer.

Step 2: Determine What Type of System to Install

There are three general types of radon-reduction systems that builders have installed.

Recommended Option: Passive Sub-Slab or Sub-Membrane Depressurization System

It is cost-effective and recommended to install a complete passive sub-slab or sub-membrane depressurization system, which would be fully functioning as soon as construction is finished. The home should be tested after occupancy, and the passive system should be activated if post-occupancy testing reveals radon levels at or above 4 pCi/L.

Upgraded Option: Active Sub-Slab or Sub-Membrane Depressurization System

Activating a passive system by adding an in-line fan would be an effective upgrade during construction. Virtually all homes with an active system have radon levels below the 4 pCi/L action level.

Not Recommended: Passive System Rough-In

Some builders perform only the sub-slab preparation and stub the vent pipe above the slab. A vent pipe can be connected and routed through the home and roof later if radon levels are high.

It is much more cost-effective to run the vent pipe through the house during construction rather than after the walls have been closed up. However, if you elect to rough in a radon-reduction system, it is important to be clear with the home buyer that the home is not equipped with a functioning system. Be sure to seal off the riser stub so that radon is not being vented into the living space. Also, label the stub so it is not used as a plumbing waste line.

Step 3: Determine Vent Pipe Location and Size

Route the pipe through warm spaces.

The vent pipe exhausts radon collected from beneath the slab or crawlspace. One objective of a radon system in a new home is to install it in such a manner that a natural draft occurs in the pipe to draw the radon from the soil without the use of a fan. To accomplish this, route the pipe up through a warm part of the house and exhaust it through the roof.

Ideally, the vent pipe should be installed in a vertical run with the least number of elbows, which could restrict air flow. A radon vent pipe can also be run through the same chase as the furnace and water-heater flue. Do not tie them together but, rather, allow for enough room to route the radon vent pipe up alongside the flues with proper clearances consistent with local building and fire codes. This means that the riser should be brought up through the slab within the same room as the furnace or water heater. This requires a little planning on your part to identify this location before the slab is poured, and to allow for sufficient room in the chase.

In cold climates, do not route the pipe up through an outside wall. Routing the pipe up an outside wall will reduce the natural thermal stack effect in the vent pipe, reducing its effectiveness. It will also make it difficult to install a fan in the attic if it is needed later on. A better option is to route the pipe up through an interior wall. In hot climates and predominantly air-conditioned houses, the passive stack will depend more on wind, a hot attic, and sun heating the pipe.

Discharge Location

To prevent radon from re-entering the house, or any other nearby buildings, make sure the vent pipe exhausts:

- a minimum of 12 inches above the surface of the roof;
- a minimum of 10 feet away from any windows and other openings in the building; and
- a minimum of 10 feet away from any windows and other openings in adjoining and adjacent buildings.

If you are routing the pipe through the same chase as the furnace flue, the vent pipe needs to exit the roof at least 10 feet away from the furnace flue. Plan to elbow the pipe away from the flue in the attic to maintain this separation above the roof. However, the additional elbows and horizontal pipe length will restrict air flow through the pipe if the system is activated. Use 45-degree joints to reduce friction.

Use 4-inch pipe when possible.

When deciding between 3-inch and 4-inch pipe (PVC or ABS), the 3-inch pipe size is the minimum you should use. However, 4-inch pipe is the preferred choice for a couple of reasons. Field results have indicated that passive systems tend to function better with 4-inch pipe. A 4-inch pipe will also allow for a quieter system, if the system is activated.

Installation: Step 1

The type of system you install also depends on the foundation type. Please refer to the relevant sections in the EPA guides that correspond to the type of foundation you will be using for:

- Basement and Slab-on-Grade Construction
- Crawlspace
- Combination Foundation

Treat each foundation separately and use the appropriate techniques for each foundation segment. Pay special attention to the points at which different foundation types join because soil-gas entry routes exist in such locations.

INSTALLATION: STEP 1A

Basement and Slab-on-Grade Construction

If the house you are building has a slab-on-grade or basement foundation, the radon gas must be able to move laterally beneath the slab to the location where the vent pipe collects the gas. There are three basic methods for improving soil gas collection beneath slabs.

Gravel

This option is generally chosen in regions of the country where gravel is plentiful and economical, and where gravel is required by the building code for water drainage. A continuous 4-inch layer of 1/2-inch to 3/4-inch of clean gravel (no fines) placed beneath a slab provides a largely unrestricted path for radon to be collected. This size of gravel provides a drainage layer and capillary break for moisture control.

SUB-SLAB PREPARATION

Perforated Pipe Alternative

In some regions of the country, gravel is not a feasible option, either because native soils are sufficiently permeable and gravel is not required for water drainage, or because lack of local supply makes gravel very expensive. One alternative is to use the native fills beneath the slab and lay in a loop of perforated pipe to improve soil gas movement. This method is already employed in some homes with the use of a drain tile loop. The loop of perforated pipe works well because the soil gases need only move to the loop rather than all the way across the slab, as in the case of a single collection point.

Soil-Gas Collection Mat Alternative

In some areas, the perforated pipe option may not be feasible if the labor needed to dig a trench for the pipe loop is too expensive, or if sub-grade soils are compacted or frozen. The third option is to install interconnected strips of drainage mats (soil gas mats) on top of the sub-grade and beneath the slab. Drain mats consist of plastic material that resembles an egg crate. Wrapped around the "egg crate" is a geotextile filter fabric that allows for the passage of air but prevents the infiltration of wet concrete. The mat can be laid directly on top of the prepared sub-grade, which should be a uniform layer of sand (native or fill), a minimum of 4 inches thick. The concrete can be poured directly over the soil gas collection mat.

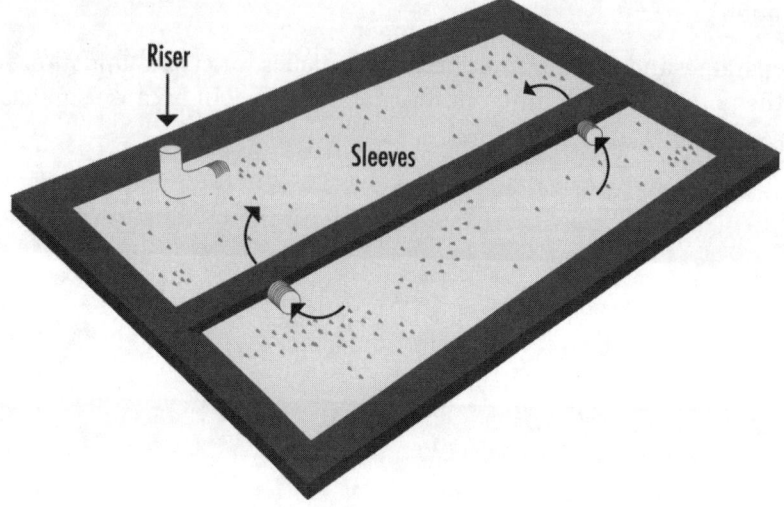

Place a uniform layer of clean aggregate under all concrete slabs or floor systems that directly contact the ground and are within the walls of the living spaces. Use a minimum 4-inch-thick layer. The gravel should be about 1/2- to 3/4-inch in size. Smaller or fine gravel or gravel that is not as uniform in sizewill restrict air movement under the slab.

Grade-Beam Obstructions

A grade beam or intermediate footing is often installed beneath a slab to support a load-bearing wall, presenting a barrier to the lateral flow of air beneath the slab to the soil gas collection point. There are a few options that can be used to avoid grade-beam obstructions to soil gas air flow.

Option 1:

Use post-and-beam construction by setting teleposts that support overhead beams on pads, rather than continuous footings.

Option 2:

Provide a means for air to flow through the grade beam. This is can be done by inserting at least two 4-inch pipe sleeves between the form boards or trench, and pouring the grade beam over them. A minimum of two pipes should be installed at opposite ends of the grade beam. One pipe should be installed every 10 feet. Tape the ends so concrete does not enter the ends of the pipe while pouring the footing. Remove the tape when forms are removed and before connecting to the pipe loop, if a pipe loop is used.

Option 3:

Add a second riser on the other side of the grade beam. Tie the riser into the vertical vent stack, or run a second vent stack.

Inserting Vent Pipe in Gravel

Place a 3- or 4-inch T-fitting at the location where you want the riser to extend through the slab. The size of the T or elbow will depend on the diameter of vent pipe you will be installing.

Connect a short stub (at least 8 inches) of 3- or 4-inch PVC pipe vertically into the T.

Recommended Improvement: Soil gas air flow can be somewhat restricted if the pipe is inserted into the gravel, and the gravel fills the pipe, especially if the system is later activated. To allow for airflow over a larger area, lay 3- or 4-inch perforated and corrugated pipe (recommended minimum length of 10 feet) in the gravel and connect it to the radon vent riser TEE fitting. Depending on the location of the riser, an elbow fitting may be used in place of a TEE fitting when using additional piping in the gravel. Make sure that the concrete does not plug up the pipe during pour.

Pipe Alternative: Perforated Pipe

Lay a 3- or 4-inch-diameter perforated drainpipe in a trench around the foundation perimeter just inside the foundation footing. This could be the same pipe loop used for under-slab drainage. Be sure the pipe is covered by at least 1 inch of fill to keep concrete from filling perforations.

What kind of pipe works best?

Perforated and corrugated pipe is flexible, which makes it easy to lay down in a trench. The perforations also allow for good soil gas collection. It is recommended that the pipe be covered with a geotextile cloth to prevent fines from clogging the holes.

How much pipe do I need?

Based on field work for slab areas less than 2,000 square feet, it is recommended to lay a continuous loop of 3- or 4-inch-diameter perforated pipe in the sub-grade, with the top of the pipe located a nominal 1 inch below the concrete slab. The pipe loop should be located approximately 12 inches from the inside of the exterior perimeter foundation walls. For slab areas greater than 2,000 square feet but less than 4,000 square feet, the same configuration may be used, but the pipe size should be a minimum of 4 inches in diameter. Slab designs in excess of 4,000 square feet should have separate loops for each 2,000 to 4,000 square feet, depending on the size of pipe utilized (3-inch or 4-inch).

Install in loops rather than straight sections.

The reason for laying out the pipe in a loop is to allow for the soil gas to enter the collection pipe from two sides. Also, if the pipe is crushed at one point during the construction, the soil gas will still be drawn to the vent pipe.

Connecting Pipe Loop to Riser

Close the loop by connecting the ends to short pipe stubs and to opposite legs of a 3- or 4-inch PVC T. Connect a short stub of 3- or 4-inch PVC pipe vertically into the T.

Installation Tip: For a more secure connection, when 3-inch corrugated pipe is used for the loop, the corrugated pipe can be inserted into a 4-inch PVC TEE by securing with sheet metal screws. When 4-inch corrugated pipe is used, 4-inch by 4-inch rubber couplings can be used to connect the perforated pipe to the solid PVC pipe stubs.

Crossing Grade Beams

In buildings where interior footings or other barriers separate the sub-grade area, the loop of pipe should penetrate or pass beneath these interior footings and barriers. Lay the loop before the grade beams are poured, or lay a length of non-perforated but corrugated pipe across the trench before pouring a grade beam. If the latter method is used, tape off the ends of the pipe before pouring the beam, remove the tape after pouring, and finish connecting the loop.

Mat Alternative: Soil Gas Collection Mat

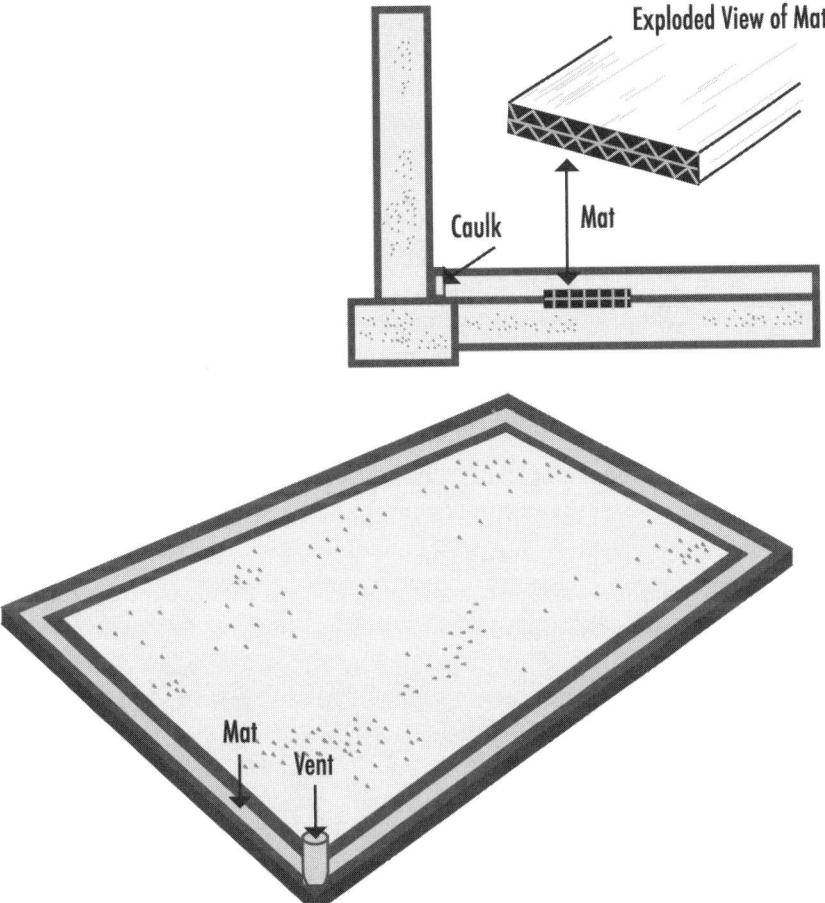

Exploded View of Mat

Caulk   Mat

Mat   Vent

First, install a uniform layer of sand a minimum of 4 inches thick. Next, place a layer of drainage matting over the sand, or lay a loop of matting inside the exterior perimeter foundation walls (no farther than a nominal 12 inches from the perimeter foundation walls).

In buildings where interior footings or other barriers separate the sub-grade area, the matting should penetrate these interior footings or barriers to form a continuous loop around the exterior perimeter.

Slabs larger than 2,000 square feet but less than 4,000 square feet should have an additional strip of matting that bisects the loop, forming two areas equally impacted by the two halves of the rectilinear loop. Slab designs in excess of 4,000 square feet should have successive loops of drain mat, with one riser per 4,000 square feet of area.

Mat Material

Use a soil gas collection mat or drainage mat having minimum dimensions of 1 inch in height by 12 inches wide, and a nominal cross-sectional air flow area of 12 square inches. The mat matrix should allow for the movement of air through it, and yet be capable of supporting the weight of the concrete above it. The matrix should be covered by a geotextile filter cloth on all four sides to prevent dirt and wet concrete from entering the matrix. Repair all breaches and joints in the geotextile cloth prior to pouring the slab.

Some mats that are sold for radon reduction are only 1/2-inch high and have only one side covered with a geotextile cloth. If this material is used, use a minimum width of 24 inches. To keep concrete from entering the matrix, it will need to be covered with geotextile cloth. Do not cover it with plastic strips because differential drying of the concrete can occur and cause a crack in the concrete along the edge of the plastic.

Connecting the Soil Gas Collection Mat to the Vent Pipe

There is a special adaptor fitting that will accept the flat mat and adapt to a round vent pipe (see graphic). This type of adaptor is available from soil gas collection mat and drainage mat suppliers, and from radon mitigation equipment suppliers. The mat is inserted into the flat ends, and the geotextile fabric is taped to the edges to prevent wet concrete from entering the T-fitting. The top of the T is made of molded plastic to keep wet concrete out. After the concrete is poured, the top can be cut with a hacksaw, and a 4-inch riser inserted and glued or cemented into place.

Seal Cloth Tears with Duct Tape

To ensure that wet concrete does not enter the mat interior, cuts and tears should be sealed with duct tape.

Making Splices: When making splices, split the fabric of the two ends to be joined. Lay the core from one end on top of the core from the other end with a three inch overlap. Lay the fabric back over the top of the splice and thoroughly seal with duct tape to keep the wet concrete from seeping in. Drive at least two 8-inch long staples through the mat at this point, being sure to drive them through the point where the two ends overlap.

Making a T in a Mat: If you need to connect a length of mat in the middle of another length of mat, make a T by cutting back the geotextile cloth, overlapping the interior matrix, replacing the cloth, securing with nails or landscape staples, and using duct tape to seal openings in the geotextile cloth.

Securing the Mat: To keep the mat in place while the concrete is being poured, the mat should be nailed down with 8-inch landscape staples, or 60 penny nails, about every 7 feet.

INSTALLATION: STEP 1B

Plastic Sheeting

Laying plastic sheeting between the gas-permeable layer and the concrete slab or floor assembly serves several important purposes. The sheeting can prevent concrete from flowing down and clogging the gas-permeable layer. It can also bridge any cracks that may develop in the slab or floor assembly, thereby reducing soil gas entry. Finally, the plastic sheeting can act as a vapor barrier to reduce moisture and other soil gas entry (besides radon) into the home.

Prior to pouring the slab or placing the floor assembly, lay a minimum 6-mil (or 3-mil cross-laminated) polyethylene or equivalent flexible sheeting material on top of the gas-permeable layer. The sheeting should cover the entire floor area.

Separate sections of sheeting should be overlapped by at least 12 inches. Below a slab, it is not necessary to seal the joint between overlapping sheets of plastic.

The sheeting should fit closely around any pipes, wires and other penetrations.

Repair any punctures and tears in the material. Duct tape may work for small, uniform tears and holes. For larger tears, cover with an additional piece of overlapping sheeting.

INSTALLATION: STEP 1C

Seal Off and Label Riser Stubs

Regardless of the sub-grade collection method used, you will have a short stub of pipe sticking up to which the vent piping system will later be attached. Care should be taken to cover the end of the pipe so that it does not become filled with concrete when the slab is poured.

Label this stub so that someone does not mistakenly think it is tied to the sewer and set a commode on it.

Support the stub, perhaps off a wall, so that it stays vertical as the wet concrete is poured.

Alternative for Combination Foundations

Some builders have found it to be more economical to tie the different foundations together into a single riser. Place a pipe to connect the sub-grade area to the crawlspace in the trench of the intervening footing prior to pouring the foundation walls. This pipe should be 4-inch perforated and corrugated pipe to prevent accumulation of water, which could block air flow. Cover with geotextile cloth. Tape the ends of the crossover to keep from getting debris in it until the pipe can be connected to the slab and crawlspace systems.

INSTALLATION: STEP 1D

Lay Foundation

Foundation walls and slabs should be constructed to reduce potential radon entry routes. In general, openings in walls and slabs should be minimized, and necessary openings and joints should be sealed.

Foundation Walls

In poured concrete walls, all control joints, isolation joints, and any other joints should be caulked with an elastomeric sealant, such as polyurethane caulk.

Hollow-block masonry walls typically have cavities that can allow radon movement. To prevent this, hollow-block walls should be topped with a continuous course of solid block, or be grouted solid on the top. Alternatively, use a solid concrete beam at or above the finished ground level or a full sill plate.

Damp-proof foundation walls, and seal any penetrations through the walls.

Slab

Pour a strong slab, and take steps to control cracking. Although concrete slabs will almost inevitably crack, control joints can help the concrete to crack in planned locations. As with the foundation walls, all control joints or other joints should be sealed with polyurethane caulk to reduce radon entry.

Do not deliberately puncture holes in the plastic sheeting prior to pouring the slab. Some contractors will do this to allow excess water to drain from the wet concrete. Putting holes in the plastic sheeting decreases (but does not eliminate) its effectiveness as a soil-gas retarder. It is preferable to use low-slump concrete, which has a lower water-to-cement ratio.

Similarly, some contractors will put a layer of sand on top of the polyethylene both to protect it and to absorb water from the concrete mix. This practice is not recommended. The sand may become wet from the concrete or rising groundwater and would have to dry to the interior through the concrete. The presence of the polyethylene sheeting during this drying process may cause moisture problems above the slab.

Trap any condensate or floor drains that pass through the slab, or route them through non-perforated pipe to daylight. Mechanical traps should be used rather than "wet" traps, which can dry out.

Sump pits that are open to the soil or fed by drain tile loops should be covered with a gasketed lid.

Installation: Step 2

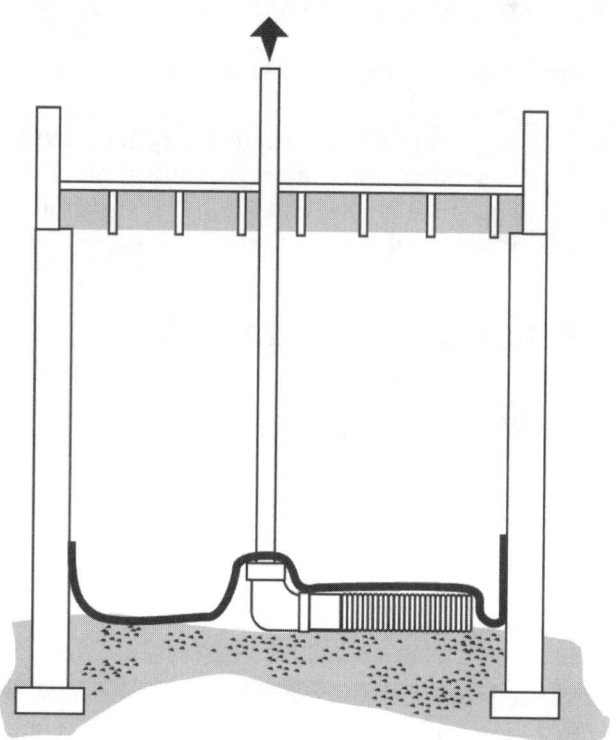

Crawlspace Construction

Crawlspaces are best treated by covering the entire crawlspace floor with plastic sheeting, laying a perforated collection pipe beneath the plastic sheeting, and connecting the pipe to the radon vent riser. Crawlspaces should be constructed consistent with applicable building codes. Access doors and other openings and penetrations between basements and adjoining crawlspaces should be closed, gasketed, or otherwise sealed with materials that prevent air leakage.

Location of Riser

The riser can be located anywhere in the crawlspace. It does not need to be in the center, so plan on placing it anywhere in the crawlspace that will be convenient for crawlspace access and for routing the pipe up through the house.

Install Pipe

Lay a length of 3- or 4-inch-diameter corrugated and perforated pipe, or a strip of geotextile drain matting on the soil at the location where you will run the radon vent pipe up.

Install Plastic Sheeting

Clear the crawlspace area of objects which may puncture the plastic sheeting. Lay a continuous layer of minimum 6-mil (or 3-mil cross-laminated) polyethylene sheeting (or equivalent membrane material) to cover the entire crawlspace area.

Amount of Plastic

Plan on using enough plastic to allow overlap of seams by 12 inches. The edges should also be brought up on the foundation walls about 12 inches to allow for proper adhesion. It is critical to allow for enough excess plastic so that if a vacuum is drawn underneath the plastic, the plastic can conform to the surface of the crawlspace floor (like vacuum packaging). If the amount of excess plastic is insufficient, the plastic may stretch over a depression in the dirt like a trampoline.

Special Precautions

It may be necessary to take special precautions to ensure that the plastic sheeting will not be damaged after occupancy. In high-traffic areas, the polyethylene should be overlain by heavier material along expected traffic routes. Various materials have been used for this purpose, including roofing felt, EPDM rubberized roofing membrane, and drainage mat. Also, if there may be foot traffic over the entire crawlspace floor, or if the crawlspace has very irregular floors, such as sharp, protruding rocks, it may be advisable to use thicker cross-laminated plastic sheeting, or to lay a heavier material underneath the polyethylene between the sheeting and the crawlspace floor.

Cross-Laminated Polyethylene Sheeting

The minimum thickness of plastic sheeting should be 6-mil polyethylene sheeting. However, this material is not very durable if the crawlspace will be accessed frequently, or if the occupants would like to use this area as storage. Regular 8- to 10-mil sheeting would provide better puncture resistance. High-density cross-laminated polyethylene has even greater puncture resistance and is stronger and more durable. Unlike the regular polyethylene sheeting, which can be torn by hand even with a thickness of 10 mil, the high-density cross-laminated material cannot be torn by hand, even though its thickness may be only 4 mil. Due to its significantly increased puncture resistance, the cross-laminated polyethylene sheeting is recommended. The high-density sheeting is also available in white, making the crawlspace brighter and more suitable for use as a storage space.

OPTIONAL IMPROVEMENT: SEALING SEAMS AND EDGES OF PLASTIC SHEETING

Sealing the Sheeting

Although not required in current radon-resistant construction building codes, increasing the air-tightness of the seams in the plastic sheeting may enhance the system's effectiveness and integrity. Sealing should be sufficiently durable to withstand anticipated traffic through the crawlspace. To effectively seal the plastic sheeting, use a 1/2-inch-wide bead of caulk.

Type of Caulk

Polyurethane caulk will provide some adhesion to the polyethylene sheeting. However, acoustical sealant, butyl rubber, or butyl acrylic caulks form a more durable bond with the plastic. Field work suggests that other proprietary sealants are also effective, such as Pro Flex Sealant by Geocel.

Sealing Seams

Seams between adjoining sheets of sheeting are usually sealed by applying a continuous bead of sealant between the sheets in the 12-inch strip where the sheets overlap. Press the overlapping sheets firmly together.

Sealing Edges and Seams

Brush the walls with a wire brush at 6 to 12 inches above the crawlspace floor to remove any dirt and loose deposits.

Make sure the sheeting lays flat on the crawlspace floor, right up to the wall. Leave several inches of slack on the vertical section of the plastic rising up the wall to help prevent the plastic from pulling on the seam due to foot traffic, or by the system itself when it is functioning.

Plan on using one 11-ounce tube of caulk to attach an 8-foot length of plastic to the wall.

Secure the plastic to the wall at 6 to 12 inches above the crawlspace floor with a 1/2-inch-wide bead of acoustical sealant or butyl caulk along the wall.

For a more durable connection, consider using mechanical fasteners (such as strapping) to hold the plastic to the wall. If there is an obstruction to the wall within 6 to 12 inches of the floor (such as a crawlspace access door), trim the sheeting to pass beneath the obstruction, and caulk the sheeting to the wall around the obstruction. At corners, cut and tuck the plastic sheeting neatly, and make sure that the sealing is also airtight.

Keeping the Plastic in Place

While the caulk is curing, use duct tape along the seam to hold the sheets together. The tape can secure the seam to keep the seam from breaking during the cure as workers complete installation. When sealing edges, it is also a good idea to temporarily tape the free edge of the plastic so it will stay in place as the caulk cures. Place weights on the plastic to keep it from being pulled off the walls as you work on the rest of the crawlspace.

Vertical Penetrations

The sheeting needs to be sealed around posts and plumbing lines. It is easier to seal a large sheet to a flat apron section than to try to fit it around the obstacle. You can use scraps of plastic to form an apron to fit around these obstructions. Also, try to plan your seams along rows of piers. When sealing around plumbing risers, make sure that the cleanout is accessible.

Riser Installation

The vent pipe needs to be connected to the perforated pipe beneath the plastic in a manner that prevents air leakage. The plastic sheeting can be wrapped around the vent pipe and securely taped to the pipe.

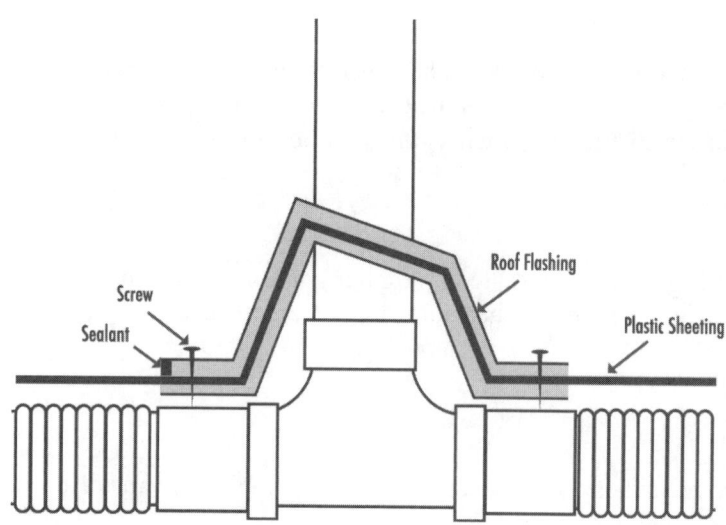

Screw

Sealant

Roof Flashing

Plastic Sheeting

Another way to prevent air leakage around the joint is to use two roof-flashing hoods. One roof flashing goes below the plastic, and one is placed above the plastic to provide a flat area to which the plastic can be sealed. The riser is sealed by the rubber grommet on the roof flashing. The two roof flashings are then secured by sheet-metal screws. Depending on the location of the riser, there may be either a PVC T or an elbow beneath the plastic that has a short 4-inch stub of pipe to which the corrugated and perforated pipe will be connected.

Label the Riser and Plastic

It is a very good idea to label the riser within the crawlspace so it is not confused with any other plumbing. It is also a good idea to label the plastic to state that the plastic should not be removed and, if cut, it should be patched or replaced.

After home construction is completed, inspect the sheeting for damage, and repair as necessary.

Installation: Step 3

Seal openings.

After pouring the slab or placing the floor assembly, seal major openings in the slab to retard soil-gas entry through openings in the slab or floor assembly.

Use materials that provide a permanent, airtight seal, such as non-shrink mortar, grouts, expanding foam, or similar materials. When caulking slab openings, it is best to utilize a polyurethane caulk, which has excellent adhesion characteristics for concrete. The following are some examples of locations to be caulked after the concrete slab has cured and before framing is installed.

Seal floor-to-wall joints.

Floor-to-wall joints are critical places to seal. Brush debris away from the joint before applying caulk. Apply enough caulk so that when smoothed with a piece of cardboard cut in a convex form, the caulk will come out onto the floor and up on the wall about 3/8-inch. For a cold joint-type, an 11-ounce tube of caulk will cover approximately 12 feet. For an expansion-type, the same tube of caulk will cover 8 feet.

Seal control joints.

Control joints in the concrete slab, whether they are saw-cut or made with grooving tools, should be cleaned and filled with caulk. Even if they are not cracked initially, they will likely develop cracks in the future, and caulking them before the floor finishes are in place makes sense. A gun-grade polyurethane or flowable polyurethane can be used. This seal blocks radon entry but does not interfere with expansion of the control joint.

Seal open sumps.

An open sump may allow radon into the house from beneath the entire foundation. Make sure to cover and seal the sump. The sump cover, which must be removable to allow for regular maintenance and inspection of the sump pump, is usually sealed by bolting it directly to the slab or sump liner lip, and made airtight through the use of a gasket or silicone-caulk seal.

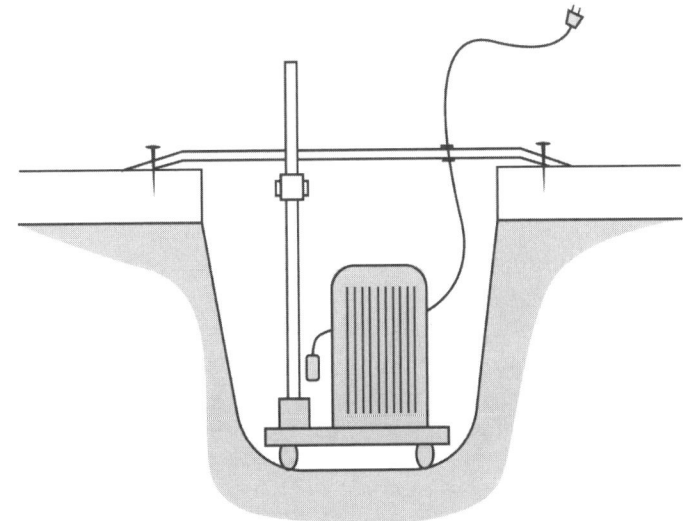

If the sump is intended as a floor drain, make sure the lid is equipped with a trapped drain to handle surface water on the slab.

Alternative: Tie into Sumps

The sump can also be incorporated into the radon system.

If the sump is used without a drain tile loop, install a sump pit cover specifically designed to accommodate a radon vent pipe and run the vent pipe directly from the sump. These sump covers are available from numerous building supply stores, as well as catalog firms dealing in equipment and supplies for radon mitigation contractors.

If the sump pit where the radon vent pipe will be located also includes a pump, a cover can be ordered that includes both an opening for the radon vent pipe and holes for the pump's water discharge line and electrical connection.

Because sump cover removal and re-sealing is required every time maintenance is performed, consider using a sump cover with a transparent door or see-through viewing window. These doors, which are usually screwed into the cover and sealed with a gasket, are generally large enough to permit limited access to the pump switch without removing the sump cover and breaking the seal. Window sump covers are fairly inexpensive.

If the sump is connected to a drain tile loop, the radon vent pipe could be inserted directly into the sump or into any convenient section of the drain tile loop (then cover and seal the open sump). Although installing the radon vent pipe in a remote section of the drain tile loop is slightly more difficult than directly into the sump, it may offer a better exhaust route through the home's interior spaces, and it also may offer the homeowner easier access to the sump.

Other Places to Seal the Slab and Foundation

Use a polyurethane caulk around locations where plumbing and other utility service lines pass through slab and below-grade walls. Use a full sill plate over the upper row of block walls in basements, or make the upper row solid block.

Seal hollow-block foundation walls at the top. Use at least one continuous course of solid masonry, one course of masonry-grouted solid, or a poured concrete beam at or above the finished ground surface. Where a brick veneer or other masonry ledge is installed, the course immediately below that ledge should be sealed.

Caulk joints, cracks, and other openings around all penetrations of both exterior and interior surfaces of masonry block or wood foundation walls below the ground surface. Penetrations of poured concrete walls should also be sealed on the exterior surface. This includes sealing wall-tie penetrations.

Other Considerations

Placing air-handling ducts in or beneath a concrete slab floor or in other areas below grade is not recommended unless the air-handling system is designed to maintain continuous positive pressure within the ductwork. This is to prevent radon from being drawn into the ductwork and then distributed throughout the house.

If ductwork does pass through a crawlspace or beneath a slab, it should be of seamless material or sealed tightly. Where joints in the ductwork are unavoidable, seal them to prevent air leakage.

Placing air-handling units in crawlspaces or in other areas below grade and exposed to soil gas is not recommended. However, if they are installed in these areas, make sure that they are designed or sealed in a durable manner to prevent air surrounding the unit from being drawn into the unit.

Avoid using floor drains and air-conditioning condensate drains that discharge directly into the soil below the slab or into the crawlspace. If installed, these drains should be routed through solid pipe to daylight, or through a trap approved for use in floor drains. Mechanical traps should be used rather than wet traps, which can dry out.

The bottom of channel-type (French) drains should be sealed with backer rod and caulking. Water drainage should be directed to a suitable drain.

Installation: Step 4

Install Vent Pipe

Be sure to run the pipe up through the roof before the roofer installs the roof system. This will allow the roofer to properly flash around the pipe. If possible, avoid angles in the pipe to maximize air flow and reduce radon.

Type of Pipe

Use Schedule 40 PVC or ABS pipe. Do not use both. These two types of pipe require different cleaners and cements.

The pipe does not need to be pressure-rated, so a pipe rated for drain, waste and vent (DWV) applications will be the most cost-effective. Do not use a pipe thinner than Schedule 40. Do not use sheet-metal ductwork because of the likelihood of breakage or leaks at joints.

All joints should be primed and glued in a manner similar to indoor plumbing.

Do Not Trap the Pipe

Plan your pipe routing to minimize the length of pipe and fittings and to contain no traps.

Do not install traps, intentional or accidental, in the pipe that will collect water and restrict or stop air movement. Air from the soil will have some moisture in it. As this air moves through sections of the vent pipe located in cold spaces, such as an attic, some moisture can condense. It is important that this water can drain back down to the soil. Insulating the pipe in the attic will reduce moisture condensation and maintain upward thermal draft in the pipe as it passes through unconditioned space.

Piping should also slope back to the suction pipe at a minimum angle of 1/8-inch per foot.

Allow for Future Installation of Fan

Although passive radon systems are effective for reducing radon levels by an average of about 50%, it is always a good idea to plan ahead in case adding an in-line fan is needed for further radon reduction to bring indoor levels below 4 pCi/L, or in case the future occupant wants to lower the radon levels as much as possible.

During installation of the vent pipe, consider these criteria for locating a fan in the future:

- it cannot be inside the living space of the house;
- it cannot be in the crawlspace beneath the home;

- it is most often located in the attic or attached garage (unless there is living space above the garage);
- it requires a 30-inch vertical run of pipe for installation; and
- it requires an unswitched electrical junction box.

Maintain the Fire-Resistance Ratings of Walls and Ceilings

If you route your vent pipe through the wall between the house and the garage, you will need to put a fire barrier around the pipe (on the inside of the garage) to maintain the integrity of the wall. Install a fire barrier with a rating equal to the wall.

Note that some ceilings are also fire-rated ceilings and will require fire barriers, as well.

Label the Radon Vent Pipe

Label the exposed portions of the pipe so that during construction, other people will be aware that the pipe is not part of the sewer system. It is recommended that the radon vent system be labeled in a conspicuous location on each floor level. Also, occupants and future occupants will know that it is part of a radon vent system.

Places to label include:

- where the riser exits the slab;
- where the pipe is seen in closets; and
- at pipe run through the attic.

Recommended Improvement: Screen on Discharge

It is a good idea to put a 1/4-inch mesh screen on the discharge to keep birds from nesting in the pipe. Rain caps can reduce radon flow and can force radon (if the system is activated) back down toward the openings into the living spaces. In most areas, they are not needed. For very high rainfall areas, use alternative special devices that prevent large amounts of rain from entering the system while still allowing the air to vent up and away from the building. These devices are available through radon mitigation supply distributors. Another design option, which is more commonly used with commercial applications than with residential installations, is an annular rain cap, pictured here.

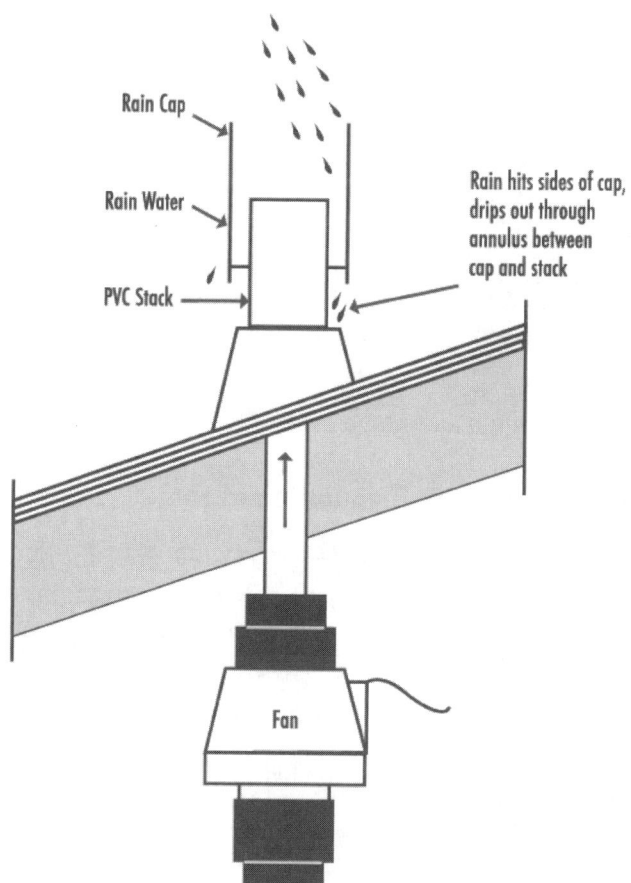

Installation Tip: Support the Pipe

Support the pipe using plumber's straps at least one every 6 feet in horizontal runs, and one every 8 feet in vertical runs.

Installation Tip: Insulate the Pipe

In cold climates, insulate the pipe where it is routed through unheated spaces, such as an unoccupied attic.

Installation: Step 5

Seal Ducts and Air-Handling Units

HVAC systems should be carefully designed, installed, and operated to avoid depressurization of basements and other areas in contact with the soil. Ideally, ductwork should remain in the conditioned space of the home. It is very important to seal joints in air ducts and plenums passing through unconditioned spaces, such as attics, crawlspaces, and attached garages.

In addition to avoiding problems with unwanted air distribution, sealing ducts can save energy, make the home more comfortable, and lower heating and cooling costs.

Installation: Step 6

Install an Electrical Junction Box for Future Installation of a Fan

Although a passive system alone is enough to keep radon levels below 4 pCi/L, occasionally, the homeowner will want or need to activate the system by adding a fan to further lower radon levels in the home. To prepare for this possibility, pre-wire the attic when installing a passive system. An unswitched electrical junction box should be installed in the attic or attached garage within 6 feet of the vent pipe.

For an attic with interior access, many building codes require a light to be installed. In this case, if the junction box for the light is located at an appropriate location for the fan, another junction box will not be necessary, and wiring the additional outlet will be simple. The fan outlet does not require a dedicated circuit; it may branch off the existing circuit for the light.

Installation: Step 7

Post-Occupancy Testing

The figure above illustrates one example of a radon-testing device. There are many other types of devices available. After the home is completed and occupied, it should be tested to determine whether the passive system needs to be activated. You should recommend to the home buyer that they test the home after they move in, and activate the system if the radon level is at or above 4 pCi/L.

Some builders who install passive systems test the homes they build and activate the passive radon systems if the radon levels are at or above 4 pCi/L. In all cases, you should advise the homeowners to re-test sometime in the future to confirm that radon levels remain low.

Obtaining a Test Kit

There are many kinds of low-cost, do-it-yourself radon test kits that you can buy online, at the local hardware store, and at other retail outlets. Coupons for short-term and long-term radon test kits are available from the National Safety Council.

TYPES OF RADON TESTS

Short-Term Tests

The quickest way to test is with a short-term test. Short-term test kits remain in the home for two days to 90 days, depending on the device. Because radon levels tend to vary from day to day and season to season, a short-term test is less likely than a long-term test to give the home's year-round average radon level. If you or the homeowner need results quickly, a short-term test followed by a second short-term test may be used, or two short-term tests may be performed simultaneously.

Long-Term Tests

Long-term tests remain in the home for more than 90 days. A long-term test will give a reading that is more likely than a short-term test to give the home's year-round average radon level.

How to Use a Test Kit

Follow the test kit's instructions. For short-term tests, close all windows and outside doors, and keep them closed throughout the test, except for normal entry and exit. If you are doing a short-term test lasting just two or three days, be sure to also close windows and outside doors at least 12 hours before beginning the test. (This testing protocol is called closed-building conditions.) Do not conduct short-term tests lasting just two or three days during unusually severe storms or periods of unusually high winds because such conditions can affect the test results.

The test kit should be placed in the lowest lived-in level of the home (for example, the basement, if it is to be used frequently). Otherwise, place the kit on the first floor. It should be put in a room that is used regularly, such as a living room, play room, den or bedroom, but not the kitchen or bathroom. Place the kit at least 20 inches above the floor in a location where it won't be disturbed, and away from drafts, high heat, high humidity, and exterior walls. Leave the kit in place for as long as specified in the device's instructions. Once the test is completed, re-seal the package and send it to the lab specified on the package right away for analysis. You should receive test results within a few weeks.

Steps for Testing

If you are conducting the radon test prior to the sale of the home, you will likely want to get results as quickly as possible by following these testing steps.

Step 1:

Conduct a short-term test for at least 48 hours. After the first test has been completed, conduct a follow-up short-term test for at least 48 hours.

Alternatively, take two short-term tests at the same time in the same location for at least 48 hours.

Step 2:

If the average of the two tests is 4 pCi/L or more, activate the passive radon reduction system.

Step 8: Activating the System (Optional)

This section provides basic guidelines if you decide to install an in-line fan to activate the system. Some states require that in-line fans for radon reduction be installed by a certified radon mitigation contractor. Call your state radon contact for a list of certified contractors (see Appendix D for a list of phone numbers).

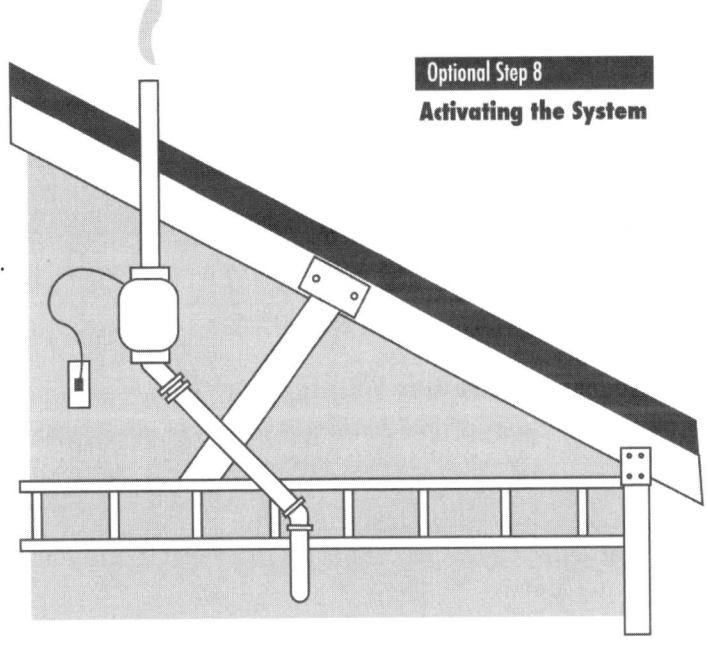

Optional Step 8

Activating the System

Location

The fan and all positively pressurized portions of the vent pipe should be located outside the habitable space in the building.

The ideal location is in the attic or in an attached garage, where the fan housing and vent pipe can be sheltered from the elements, yet be outside the building's conditioned spaces. Sheltering the fan maximizes its efficiency and life expectancy by minimizing exposure to extreme temperatures and moisture. Placement in a non-conditioned space prevents the accidental pumping of radon directly into the home, should a leak occur in the fan housing or at the vent-pipe joints.

Building designs that call for a flat roof or cathedral ceiling (or some other design feature that makes the attic installation unworkable) may necessitate placing the fan on the roof or in an exterior venting pipe.

Appropriate fan locations include:

- unoccupied attic;
- outside the house; or
- in the attached garage.

Inappropriate fan locations include:

- in the crawlspace;
- in the basement; and
- in an occupied attic.

Type of Fan

Although various types of fans are suitable for this purpose, the most commonly used fans are centrifugal fans, often referred to as in-line, tubular or tube fans.

The size and air-movement capacity of the vent pipe fan should be sufficient to maintain a pressure field beneath the slab or crawlspace membrane that is lower than the ambient pressure above the slab or membrane. Most contractors have found 90-watt in-line fans to be adequate for most home styles, locations and sizes. You can also look for a fan capable of moving 100 cubic feet of air per minute at 1 inch of water column, which should be sufficient for most applications.

How to Install

Install the fan in a vertical run of the vent pipe. This will prevent outdoor precipitation from accumulating in the fan and fan's housing. Do not use an angled portion of the pipe. To reduce vibrations and noise transmission, use flexible airtight couplings instead of rigid couplings. Secure the couplings tightly to the fan using circular hose clamps.

In regions with prolonged or extreme cold, both fans and attic vent pipes should be insulated to reduce condensation and the possibility of vent exhaust freeze-up. Freeze-up is most often found in regions with extremely cold winters and in systems having high air-flow rates, as well as high moisture levels in the sub-slab soil.

Install a System-Failure Warning Device

A system-failure warning device should be used to alert occupants to any malfunction of the system or drop in its suction flows. The types of warning devices include pressure gauges, manometers, and visual or audible alarms. Unless the indicator is integral to the fan's power supply, the audible or visual alarm should be connected to a separate circuit so that it will activate if the power to the fan is interrupted.

Working with Home Buyers

All home buyers want to know that they're buying a quality home. There are a few simple things you can do to educate your customers that radon-resistant features make sense both from a health standpoint and an investment standpoint. The activities suggested here are inexpensive and easy to implement. They will make your company stand apart from the other builders in your area by demonstrating your commitment to customer satisfaction and healthy homes.

Make the Radon System a Custom Feature

Prominently list the availability of a radon system as a custom feature in all your sales, promotional and advertising materials. Emphasize the desirability of a radon system in the same way you would hardwood floors, 9-foot ceilings, upgraded appliances, master bedroom suites, etc. These are all features that enhance the value of the house and make it more enjoyable to live in. Stress the economic advantage of adding a radon system while the home is being built, thereby avoiding a more expensive, retrofit installation.

Include a Brochure on Radon Systems in All Your Sales Information

Provide a pamphlet on the basics of radon systems in all your sales literature. You might include radon maps for your specific geographical area, as well as easy-to-understand information on why a radon system is important, how it operates, the costs involved, and other questions that home buyers might ask when considering a radon system. A number of useful consumer-oriented publications are available and can be ordered in bulk, such as the brochure *Buying a New*

Home? How to Protect Your Family from Radon, as well as radon maps. See Appendix C for more information.

Educate Your Sales Team

All sales associates should be as knowledgeable and positive about the value of a radon system as they are about every other feature you offer. Have them stress not only the amenities you provide, but also the solid construction techniques you offer, including a radon system. Help your sales staff understand the radon system and how it works so that they can explain its benefits to sales prospects. An on-site review of the system by a construction supervisor is an excellent way to start. In addition, have your sales personnel become familiar with your radon informational materials, and ask them to go over these materials with prospective home buyers.

Use Your Model Home as a Promotional Tool

Install a radon system in your model home. Advertise it as another "must-have" feature that is desired by many new home buyers. Consumers expect a builder to include the "latest and greatest" product offerings in the model home; make a radon system one of those special elements, and promote it accordingly.

Post Signs

Highlight the value of a radon system by placing an explanatory sign in the basement or near the crawlspace area of your model home. This will make prospective home buyers aware of the system's availability, function and benefits. As you prepare to install radon systems in your new homes, increase the interest of drive-by prospects by placing a "Radon System Being Installed" placard on the site.

MARKETING STRATEGIES THAT PROMOTE RADON AWARENESS

To increase home buyers' awareness of radon, consider the following promotional and marketing activities, which are simple ways to build your reputation in the community as a knowledgeable builder of quality, radon-resistant homes.

Print Media

Prepare a news release on the availability of your new homes. This can include a complete discussion of features, size, location, floor plans, etc. Prominently mention that you are the "only builder in your area" to offer radon systems (if this is appropriate and accurate). Explain why you have chosen to provide this important feature to members of your community.

Website Promotion

More consumers are relying on the Internet for information about buying a new home. Develop a special web page on radon systems to integrate with your existing website.

Make a Name for Yourself

One of the most effective ways of marketing radon systems is to promote yourself as a knowledgeable builder concerned about radon and equipped to do something about it. By providing consumers with general information about radon and radon systems, you will establish yourself as a socially responsible builder who is attentive to the health and well-being of the community's families. This reputation is likely to give you an edge over your competitors by making your homes more desirable to today's health-conscious consumers.

Alert Local Realtors

Many Realtors are familiar with the radon issue as it relates to existing homes. Consider holding a seminar of local realtors to discuss the importance of including radon systems in new construction. Let them know that you are a builder who offers such systems in your houses, and that you are willing to work with any client they may have who is concerned about the possibility of radon in their home.

Consider Doing a Public Service Announcement

A radio public service announcement about radon's health effects and the value of a radon system in protecting people is a relatively inexpensive but highly effective means of increasing community awareness about radon and expanding the demand for radon systems. Your 30-second announcement can conclude by identifying your company as the sponsor of the information and a builder who is interested in protecting people from radon.

Offer Community Educational Materials

Brief informational brochures and fact sheets on radon and radon systems can be developed for free distribution in grocery stores, schools, libraries, banks, community centers, etc. These materials can help increase awareness of radon's impact on the community and the value of radon systems in reducing radon exposure. Display your company's name and logo on all educational materials you distribute.

Become a Television or YouTube Star

Community television programs on "moving up" or "buying your dream home" are always of interest to consumers. Use these programs to promote radon systems. Arrange to appear on a community-based television program and use the opportunity to talk about why you offer radon systems in your homes. Local cable stations are especially good outlets for this type of activity.

You can also record and upload your own YouTube video. When you upload it, take advantage of tagging it with relevant terms, such as "radon," "new home construction," and others that will help consumers conducting Google and YouTube searches find your video easily.

WHAT TO TELL HOME BUYERS

Once you have sold the house, there are a few key items to tell your home buyer about the radon features that you have installed in their new home.

What Features Have Been Installed?

Let your home buyer know whether you have installed a passive radon system, an active radon system, or a rough-in for a sub-slab depressurization system. Explain what the features are designed to do.

Passive System

If you have installed a passive system, let the home buyer know that they should test their home for radon. Tell the homeowner that if the tests indicate a radon level at or above the action level of 4 pCi/L, it is recommended that they hire a radon mitigation contractor to activate the system, or you could offer to activate the system.

Active System

If you have installed an active system, recommend to the home buyer that they conduct a radon test after they have occupied the home. Let them know where the system-failure warning device is located, and inform them that if the device indicates a system failure, the fan is no longer working to vent radon out of the home. The homeowner should then contact a radon mitigation contractor to check the system.

Rough-In for Sub-Slab Depressurization

If you have installed a rough-in for sub-slab depressurization, it is very important for the home buyer to be aware that the house has not been equipped with a functioning radon system. Explain that the home would need to be tested for radon. If the tests indicate a radon level at or above the action level of 4 pCi/L, it is highly recommended that the homeowner hire a radon mitigation contractor to install the rest of the radon system.

Does This Mean That the House Has High Radon?

Some home buyers may be concerned that you have installed the radon system because the house has high radon levels. Simply explain that there is no way of knowing whether a home has high radon levels until the home is completed and a radon test is performed. Tell them that a passive system will reduce radon levels by about 50%, on average. Also tell them that the home should be tested, and that the system should be activated if further reductions are desired, or if radon levels are at or above 4 pCi/L. If the radon features had not been installed, it could cost $800 to $2,500 to fix a radon problem after construction has been completed.

How Does the Home Buyer Test for Radon?

The following are recommended steps for the home buyer to test for radon once they have moved into the home. These steps are slightly different from the steps outlined for builders because the homeowner has more time to perform long-term tests.

Step 1:

Conduct a short-term test for at least 48 hours. If the result is 4 pCi/L or higher, perform a follow-up test (Step 2) to be sure.

Step 2:

Follow up with either a long-term test or a second short-term test. For a better understanding of the year-round average radon level, conduct a long-term test. For faster results, perform a second short-term test.

Step 3:

If you followed up with a long-term test and the result is 4 pCi/L or higher, activate the passive system. If you followed up with a second short-term test and the average of the two short-term tests is 4 pCi/L or higher, consider activating the system. The higher the short-term results, the more certain you can be that you should activate the passive radon system. Once the system has been activated, the radon testing should be repeated with a short-term test (preferably between 24 hours and 30 days after activation).

Hopefully, you now see the benefits of building homes with radon-resistant features, and you are familiar with the techniques for installing the features. To follow is additional information that you may find useful, including architectural drawings, and information about how to order a video by the National Home Builders Association to view the features being installed.

Appendix A: Architectural Drawings

The following are three architectural drawings of the passive, active, and crawlspace radon-reduction systems to help you visualize the complete radon features as they should be installed.

These drawing are available for free in a larger format through the National Service Center for Environmental Publications as EPA Document 402-F-95-012. They are also available electronically on the EPA's website as PDF files and as CAD drawings. For more information, see Appendix C.

Passive Sub-Slab Depressurization System

Used for basement and slab-on-grade construction:

Architectural Drawing

Passive Sub-Slab Depressurization System
Used for basement and slab-on-grade construction

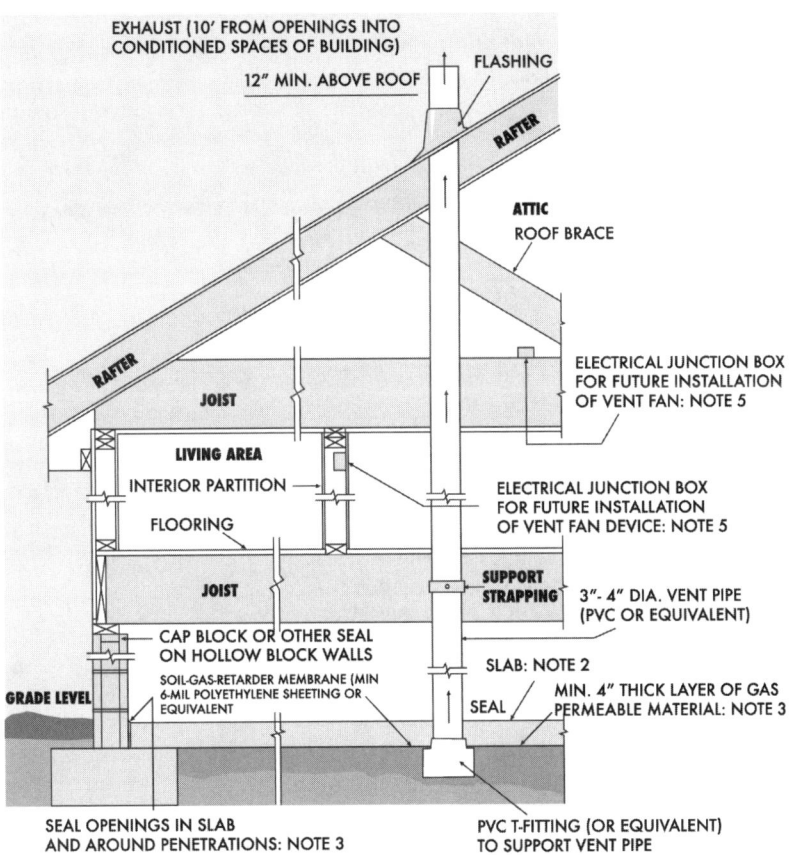

EXHAUST (10' FROM OPENINGS INTO CONDITIONED SPACES OF BUILDING)

FLASHING

12" MIN. ABOVE ROOF

RAFTER

RAFTER

ATTIC
ROOF BRACE

JOIST

ELECTRICAL JUNCTION BOX FOR FUTURE INSTALLATION OF VENT FAN: NOTE 5

LIVING AREA

INTERIOR PARTITION

ELECTRICAL JUNCTION BOX FOR FUTURE INSTALLATION OF VENT FAN DEVICE: NOTE 5

FLOORING

JOIST

SUPPORT STRAPPING

3"- 4" DIA. VENT PIPE (PVC OR EQUIVALENT)

CAP BLOCK OR OTHER SEAL ON HOLLOW BLOCK WALLS

SLAB: NOTE 2

SOIL-GAS-RETARDER MEMBRANE (MIN 6-MIL POLYETHYLENE SHEETING OR EQUIVALENT)

MIN. 4" THICK LAYER OF GAS PERMEABLE MATERIAL: NOTE 3

GRADE LEVEL

SEAL

SEAL OPENINGS IN SLAB AND AROUND PENETRATIONS: NOTE 3

PVC T-FITTING (OR EQUIVALENT) TO SUPPORT VENT PIPE

PASSIVE SUB-SLAB DEPRESSURIZATION RADON CONTROL SYSTEM FOR NEW CONSTRUCTION

NOTES:
1. ALL CONCRETE SLABS THAT COME IN CONTACT WITH THE GROUND SHALL BE LAID OVER A GAS PERMEABLE MATERIAL MADE UP OF EITHER A MINIMUM 4"-THICK UNIFORM LAYER OF CLEAN AGGREGATE OR A MINIMUM 4"-THICK UNIFORM LAYER OF SAND, OVERLAIN BY A LAYER OR STRIPS OF MANUFACTURED MATTING DESIGNED TO ALLOW THE LATERAL FLOW OF SOIL GASES.

2. ALL CONCRETE FLOOR SLABS SHALL BE DESIGNED AND CONSTRUCTED IN ACCORDANCE WITH LOCAL BUILDING CODES. ADDITIONAL REFS: AMERICAN CONCRETE INSTITUTE PUBLICATIONS. AC1302.1R- & AC1332R OR THE POST-TENSIONING INSTITUTE MANUAL, "DESIGN AND CONSTRUCTION OF POST-TENSIONED SLABS ON GROUND."

3. ALL OPENINGS, GAPS AND JOINTS IN FLOOR AND WALL ASSEMBLIES IN CONTACT SOIL OR GAPS AROUND PIPES, TOILETS, BATHTUBS OR DRAINS PENETRATING THESE ASSEMBLIES SHALL BE FILLED OR CLOSED WITH MATERIALS THAT PROVIDE A PERMANENT AIR-TIGHT SEAL. SEAL LARGE OPENINGS WITH NON-SHRINK MORTAR, GROUTS OR EXPANDING FOAM MATERIALS AND SMALLER GAPS WITH AN ELASTOMERIC JOINT SEALANT, AS DEFINED IN ASTM C920-87.

4. VENT PIPES SHALL BE INSTALLED SO THAT ANY RAINWATER OR CONDENSATION DRAINS DOWNWARD INTO THE GROUND BENEATH THE SLAB OR SOIL-GAS-RETARDER MEMBRANE.

5. CIRCUITS SHOULD BE A MINIMUM 15 AMP, 115 VOLT.

Passive Sub-Membrane Depressurization System

Used for crawlspace construction:

Architectural Drawing

Passive Sub-Membrane Depressurization System

Used for crawlspace construction

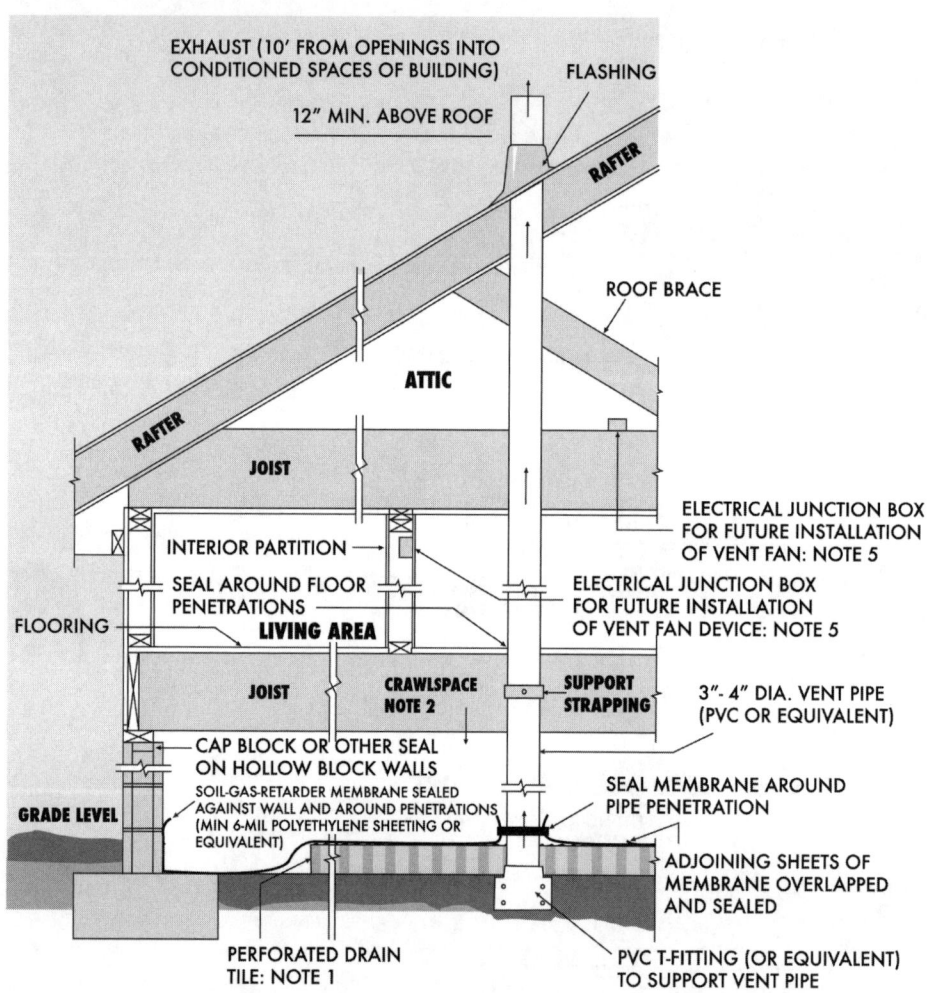

PASSIVE RADON CONTROL SYSTEM FOR NEW CONSTRUCTION

NOTES:

1. INSTALL A LENGTH OF 3"- OR 4"-DIAMETER PERFORATED DRAIN
    TILE HORIZONTALLY BENEATH THE SHEETING AND CONNECT TO
    "T" FITTING WITH THE VERTICAL STANDPIPE THROUGH THE
    SOIL GAS-RETARDER MEMBRANE. THIS HORIZONTAL PIPE SHOULD
    NORMALLY BE PLACED PARALLEL TO THE LONG DIMENSION OF THE
    HOUSE AND SHOULD EXTEND NO CLOSER THAN 6 FEET
    TO THE FOUNDATION WALL.

2. VENTILATE CRAWLSPACE IN CONFORMANCE WITH LOCAL CODES;
    VENTS SHALL BE OPEN TO THE EXTERIOR AND BE OF NONCLOSEABLE
    DESIGN.

3. CIRCUITS SHOULD BE A MINIMUM OF 15 AMP, 115 VOLT.

Active Sub-Slab Depressurization System

Uses a fan to mechanically draw air from beneath the slab (or membrane) through the vent pipe:

Architectural Drawing

Active Sub-Slab Depressurization System

Uses fan to mechanically draw air from beneath the slab (or membrane) through the vent pipe

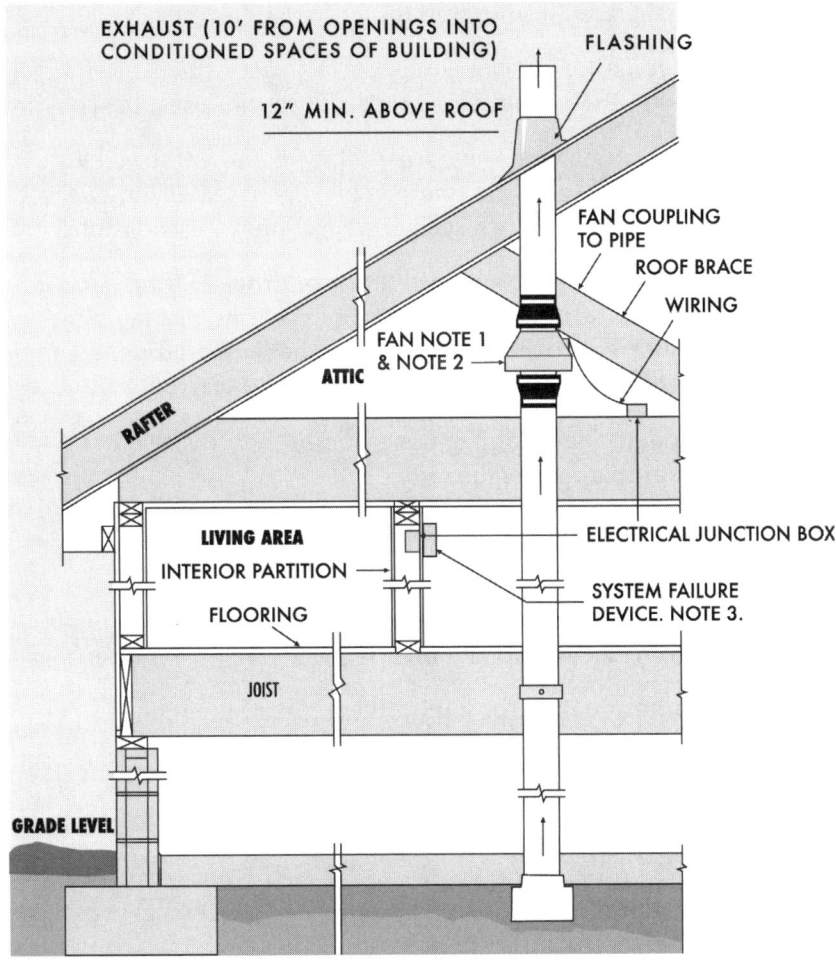

ADDITIONAL COMPONENTS REQUIRED FOR ACTIVATION OF PASSIVE SUB-SLAB DEPRESSURIZATION OR CRAWLSPACE RADON CONTROL SYSTEM

NOTES:

1. INSTALL THE VENT FAN IN THE VERTICAL RUN OF THE VENT PIPE. THE SIZE AND AIR-MOVEMENT CAPACITY OF THE VENT FAN SHALL BE SUFFICIENT TO CREATE AND MAINTAIN A PRESSURE FIELD BENEATH THE SLAB OR CRAWLSPACE MEMBRANE THAT IS LOWER THAN THE PRESSURE ABOVE THE SLAB OR MEMBRANE.

2. ALL POSITIVELY PRESSURED PORTIONS OF THE VENT PIPE AND FAN SHALL BE LOCATED OUTSIDE THE HABITABLE SPACE OF THE BUILDING.

3. PROVIDE A VISIBLE OR AUDIBLE WARNING SYSTEM TO ALERT BUILDING OCCUPANTS IF THERE IS A LOSS OF PRESSURE OR AIR FLOW IN THE VENT PIPE.

Appendix B: Glossary

- **active system:** passive system with the addition of a fan to more actively draw radon from the soil into the stack where it dissipates into the atmosphere. A system-failure warning device or alarm is also installed to alert the occupant if the system is not working.

- **action level:** homeowners should take action to lower radon levels indoors when levels are at or above 4 pCi/L.

- **aggregate:** a coarse material, such as gravel, placed below the slab.

- **ASTM Standard Guide 1465-92:** a radon guidance booklet published in 1992 by the American Society for Testing and Materials according to their consensus process for deciding on the content.

- **building code:** criteria or requirements (i.e., minimum standards) set forth and enforced by a state or local agency for the protection of public health and safety; is usually based on a model code (see below) and/or model standards published by acknowledged organizations or associations.

- **condensation:** Vapor in the air turns into water on cold surfaces. Beads or drops of water (and frost in extremely cold weather) accumulate on the inside of the exterior covering of a building when warm, moisture-laden air from the interior reaches a point where the temperature no longer permits the air to sustain the moisture it holds.

- **condensate drains:** drains that remove condensation from air-conditioning systems or other equipment, frequently emptying into the sump or below the slab.

- **damp-proofing:** sealing the foundation walls to prevent outside moisture from entering the basement, although not as tightly as in waterproofing.

- **drain tile loop:** refers to a length of perforated pipe extending around all or part of the footing perimeter for draining water away from the foundation of a home.

- **flashing:** material for reinforcing and weatherproofing the joints and angles of the roof and the penetrations through the roof.

- **footing:** the supporting base for the foundation walls of a house.

- **gas-permeable:** a material through which gas passes easily.

- **International Codes:** model codes published by the International Code Council (ICC) to combine all four Model Building Codes into one. The International Residential Code was published in early 2000.

- **junction box:** an enclosed box used to connect or branch electrical wiring.

- **Map of Radon Zones:** The EPA's Map of Radon Zones assigns each of the 3,141 counties in the United States to one of three zones based on radon potential:

    - Zone 1 counties have a predicted average indoor screening level greater than 4 pCi/L;

    - Zone 2 counties have a predicted average indoor screening level between 2 and 4 pCi/L; and

    - Zone 3 counties have a predicted average indoor screening level less than 2 pCi/L.

  Note that elevated radon levels have been found in all counties across the U.S.

- **Model Codes:** documents specifying requirements for building, mechanical, plumbing and fire-prevention installations, and often the basis for state and local building codes.

- **Model Standard:** a document that has been developed and established to connote specified consensus and approval of certain techniques and standards; a prescribed level of acceptability or an approved model used as a basis for comparison; voluntary technical guidance until adopted into a building code. The EPA has published one for radon-resistant new construction called Model Standards and Techniques for Control of Radon in New Residential Buildings.

- **passive system:** short for "passive sub-slab depressurization system," and includes features to reduce radon levels by utilizing barriers to radon entry and stack effect-reduction techniques, and the installation of a PVC pipe running from beneath the slab to the roof; works by using natural pressure differentials between the air in the pipe, and the rest of the home and the outside air.

- **picocuries per liter (pCi/L):** a unit of measure for radon levels.

- **polyethylene sheeting(used as soil-gas-retarder):** plastic sheeting, about drop-cloth weight, used over gravel and under the concrete slab to prevent soil gases from entering the home. The sheeting also prevents the concrete from flowing into the gravel and blocking air flow beneath the slab; also used as a moisture barrier.

- **PVC pipe:** a hollow plastic pipe generally used for plumbing in home construction.

- **slab:** the concrete floor poured over the ground between the foundation walls, either at the ground floor or basement level.

- **soil gas:** any gas emanating from the soil, including radon, methane, and water vapor.

- **stack effect-reduction techniques:** features that prevent or reduce the flow of warm conditioned air upward and out of the building's super-structure. If not reduced, stack effect can actually draw soil gas containing radon into the lower levels of the house. Most of these techniques are part of the International Code Council's Model Energy Code.

- **sub-membrane depressurization:** a system designed to achieve lower sub-membrane air pressure relative to crawlspace air pressure by use of a vent that draws air from beneath the soil-gas retarder membrane; may be a passive system (without a fan) or an active system (with a fan).

- **sub-slab depressurization:** a system designed to achieve lower sub-slab air pressure relative to indoor air pressure; may be a passive system (without a fan) or an active system (with a fan).

- **sump/sump pit:** a hole going below the slab into which water is drained in order to be pumped out; should be sealed to prevent radon from entering the home.

Appendix C: For More Information

Hotlines

- National Safety Council
  1-800-55-RADON
  Hotline answers consumers' specific questions dealing with radon.

- Consumer Federation of America Foundation's Radon Fix-It Program
  1-800-644-6999
  Hotline answers questions for homeowners with high radon levels about how to fix the problem.

- IAQ Info
  1-800-438-4318
  Hotline answers specific indoor air-quality questions.

Literature Referrals

- National Hispanic Indoor Air Quality Hotline
1-800-SALUD-12
Bilingual health information specialists provide answers about radon and provide test kits that include bilingual instructions.

- U.S. EPA
Check out the Indoor Environments Division's homepage for information and online publications about radon and indoor air quality at **www.epa.gov/iaq**

Publications

- *Protecting Your Home from Radon*
Second edition, 1997 (Kladder, D.L., Burkhart, J.F., Jelinek, S.R.). This document details many radon-resistant construction techniques, and includes many useful photos and illustrations. It is available in many public libraries and from the National Environmental Health Association at 1-800-513-8332 or **www.neha.org**

- *Radon-Resistant Construction and Building Codes*
This document provides general information on radon, and an explanation on each section in Appendix D of the1998 International One- and Two-Family Dwelling Code. To download the zipped PDF file, visit the International Code Council's website at **www.iccsafe.org**

- *ASTM E1465-92 Standard Guide for Radon Control Option for the Design and Construction of New Low-Rise Residential Buildings*
This guide covers design and construction methods for reducing radon entry into new low-rise residential buildings, and is intended to assist designers, builders, building officials and others involved in the construction of low-rise residential buildings. Available from the American Society for Testing and Materials (ASTM) at 100 Barr Harbor Drive, West Conshohocken, PA 19428-2959, or by calling (610) 832-9585, or by visiting their website at **www.astm.org**

EPA Publications

Order copies in singles or in bulk from the National Service Center for Environmental Publications (NSCEP) by calling 1-800-490-9198.

Here are some of the available publications:

- *Building a New Home: Have You Considered Radon?*
EPA/402-F-98-001
This colorful brochure discusses the basics of radon-resistant features.

- *Buying a New Home? How to Protect Your Family from Radon*
EPA/402-F-98-008
This brochure provides a quick summary and diagram of the major components of the radon-reduction system—great for educating home buyers about radon.

- *Model Standards and Techniques for Control of Radon in New Residential Buildings*
EPA/402-R-94-009

- *EPA Map of Radon Zones (in color)*
EPA/402-F-93-013

- *Radon Doesn't Have to Be a Problem*
EPA/402-V-95-015
This 12-minute video by the National Association of Home Builders (NAHB) explains radon-

resistant features.

- *Radon Resistant New Homes: A Public Official's Guide to Reducing Radon Risk*
EPA/402-V-95-014
This is a short video by the National Conference of States on Building Codes and Standards (NCSBCS) on radon-resistant features.

Other Sources of Information

International Code Council (ICC)
5203 Leesburg Pike, Suite 708
Falls Church, VA 22041
phone: (703) 931-4533; fax: (703) 379-1546
www.iccsafe.org

The ICC publishes model codes, including the International Residential Code (IRC). The IRC contains an appendix on radon-resistant construction. They also publish a separate guide to radon-resistant construction.

Appendix D: State Radon Contacts

For a complete, up-to-date listing, visit the EPA's website at: **www.epa.gov**

Alabama: (800) 582-1866	**Missouri:** (800) 669-7236
Alaska: (800) 478-8324	**Montana:** (800) 546-0483
Arizona: (602) 255-4845 x244	**Nebraska:** (800) 334-9491
Arkansas: (800) 482-5400	**Nevada:** (775) 687-5394 x275
California: (800) 745-7236	**New Hampshire:** (800) 852-3345 x4674
Colorado: (800) 846-3986	**New Jersey:** (800) 648-0394
Connecticut: (860) 509-7367	**New Mexico:** (505) 476-8531
Delaware: (800) 464-4357	**New York:** (800) 458-1158
District of Columbia: (202) 535-2999	**North Carolina:** (919) 571-4141
Florida: (800) 543-8279	**North Dakota:** (800) 252-6325
Georgia: (800) 745-0037	**Ohio:** (800) 523-4439
Hawaii: (808) 586-4700	**Oklahoma:** (405) 702-5100
Idaho: (800) 445-8647	**Oregon:** (503) 731-4014 x664
Illinois: (800) 325-1245	**Pennsylvania:** (800) 237-2366
Indiana: (800) 272-9723	**Rhode Island:** (401) 222-2438
Iowa: (800) 383-5992	**South Carolina:** (800) 768-0362
Kansas: (800) 693-5343	**South Dakota:** (800) 438-3367
Kentucky: (502) 564-4856	**Tennessee:** (800) 232-1139

Louisiana: (800) 256-2494

Maine: (800) 232-0842

Maryland: (800) 438-2472 x2086

Massachusetts: (800) RADON-95

Michigan: (800) 723-6642

Minnesota: (800) 798-9050

Mississippi: (800) 626-7739

Texas: (800) 572-5548

Utah: (800) 458-0145

Vermont: (800) 439-8550

Virginia: (800) 468-0138

Washington: (360) 236-3253

West Virginia: (800) 922-1255

Wisconsin: (888) 569-7236

Wyoming: (800) 458-5847

U.S. Territories:

Guam: (671) 475-1611

Puerto Rico: (787) 274-7815

Virgin Islands: (212) 637-4013

Tribal Radon Program Offices:

Hopi Tribe in Arizona: (520) 734-2442 x635

Navajo Nation: (520) 871-7863

Inter-Tribal Council of Arizona: (602) 307-1527

Duckwater Shoshone-Paiute Tribe in Nevada: (702) 863-0222

As of September 30, 1998, the EPA no longer runs a National Radon Proficiency Program. Some states regulate providers of radon measurement, mitigation service providers, and measurement devices by requiring registration, certification or licensing. Some of these states issue identification cards. Call your state to learn more. You can also contact the National Environmental Health Association's (NEHA) National Radon Proficiency Program at (800) 269-4174, or contact them at: radonprog@aol.com. Contact the National Radon Safety Board (NRSB) at (303) 423-2674 or by emailing them at info@nrsb.org for more information on radon proficiency.

Radon in Water

Where and how does radon get into drinking water?

Radon in drinking water is a significant health hazard, though a lesser hazard than radon in indoor air. Homes supplied with drinking water from a private well, and community water systems that use wells as water sources have a greater risk of exposure to radon in water.

Radon in water is found in nearly all sources of surface water and groundwater. It is created by the radioactive decay of radium, a naturally occurring radioactive element found in underground rock formations, particularly granite and quartz. Water that flows through or over radium-rich rock formations accumulates radium and, thus, radon resulting from the decay process.

Groundwater typically has much higher levels of radon than surface water. This is because radon in groundwater is trapped by being submerged underground and it cannot easily escape. Because of this, water supplies from underground wells have a much higher probability of having significant levels of radon. Drinking water originating from a surface-water source is probably not a significant health hazard for radon in water. Large, pre-treated municipal water supplies typically have negligible levels of radon in water because this type of water supply is usually drawn from surface-water sources, and because water treatment tends to reduce radon levels even further.

Property owners with wells who have confirmed elevated radon levels in the indoor air should also test their well water for radon. Radon in the water supply can increase the indoor radon levels, although radon entering the home through water will be a small source of risk compared to the levels of radon entering through the soil. The EPA estimates that indoor radon levels will increase by about 1 pCi/L for every 10,000 pCi/L of radon in the water. (The EPA's Office of Ground Water and Drinking Water has developed publications related to radon in drinking water that can be found online at **www.epa.gov/radon/rnwater.html**

What are the risks of radon exposure?

Radon's primary public health risk is by breathing in the indoor air of homes. This contributes to about 20,000 lung cancer deaths each year in the United States, according to the 1999 landmark BEIR VI Report by the NAS on radon in indoor air. Radon is the second leading cause of lung cancer in the U.S. Based on a second NAS report on radon in drinking water, the EPA estimates that it causes about 168 cancer deaths per year: 89% from lung cancer caused by breathing radon released from water; and 11% from stomach cancer caused by drinking radon-contaminated water.

Drinking water that has high levels of radon may be a health risk, but breathing air high in radon concentration is more harmful. Breathing in radon gas over a long period of time can increase the risk of lung cancer. Drinking water contaminated by radon may increase the chances of developing stomach cancer.

While most radon-related deaths are due to radon gas accumulated in houses from seepage through cracks in the foundation, up to 1,800 deaths per year are attributed to radon from household water. Showering, washing dishes, and doing laundry can disturb the water and release radon gas into the breathable air.

As with radon in the indoor air, the only way to be certain of whether there is radon at actionable levels in the home's water supply is to test it.

How is radon in water tested?

Before testing for radon in the residential water supply, test the air. If the indoor air's radon level is high and the home uses groundwater, test the water. If the radon level in the air is low, there is no need to test the water.

For waterborne radon, a simple step to ensure reduced radon levels is to make sure that the bathroom, laundry room, and kitchen are well ventilated. If the well water has only moderate levels of radon, this may adequately reduce exposure to waterborne radon. However, if the well has high levels of radon, consider using water-treatment devices, such as granular activated carbon (GAC) units and home aerators.

What do the results of a water test mean?

Test results are expressed in picocuries of radon per liter of water (pCi/L). In general, 10,000 pCi/L of radon in water contributes roughly 1 pCi/L of airborne radon throughout the house. The EPA advises consumers to take action if the total household air level is above 4 pCi/L.

It is possible to estimate how much the radon in the water supply is affecting the indoor radon level. The formula to gauge whether indoor air levels are elevated is to subtract 1 pCi/L from the indoor air radon level for every 10,000 pCi/L of radon that was found in the water. For example, if there are 30,000 pCi/L of radon in the water, then 3 pCi/L of the indoor measurement may have come from radon in the water.

If most of the radon is not coming from the water, mitigate the indoor levels and then re-test the indoor air to make sure that the source of elevated radon was not coming from the property's well. If a large contribution of the radon in the house is coming from the water supply, the homeowner should consider installing a special water treatment system to remove the radon. The EPA recommends installing a water treatment system only when there is a radon problem found in the water supply.

What should I do if I have concerns about radon exposure?

The 1996 Safe Drinking Water Act Amendments required the EPA to establish several new health-based drinking water regulations, including a multimedia approach to address the public health risks of radon exposure.

Consult a healthcare provider to discuss your concerns, and consider using one of the two methods for removing radon from water: aeration treatment or GAC treatment. These methods are discussed in the next section.

Removal of Radon in Water

Remember:

Before testing water for radon, the air should be tested. If the indoor radon level is high and the homeowners use groundwater, test the water. If the radon level is low in the air, there is no need to test the water. Test results are expressed in picocuries of radon per liter of water (pCi/L). In general, 10,000 pCi/L of radon in water contributes roughly 1 pCi/L of airborne radon throughout the house. EPA currently advises consumers to take action if the total household air level is above 4 pCi/L.

For waterborne radon, a simple step to ensure reduced radon levels is to make sure the bathroom, laundry room, and kitchen are well ventilated. If the well water has only moderate levels of radon, this may adequately reduce the exposure to waterborne radon.

How is radon removed from water?

If the well has high levels of radon, it may be necessary to remove it using one of two water-treatment devices/methods, including aeration treatment or granular activated carbon (GAC) treatment.

- Aeration treatment involves spraying water or mixing it with air, and then venting the air from the water before use.
- Granular activated carbon (GAC) treatment filters water through carbon. Radon attaches to the carbon and leaves the water free of radon. The carbon may need special handling for disposal if it is used at a high radon level, or if it has been used for a long time.

In either method, it is important to treat the water where it enters the home (at the point of entry) so that all the water will be treated. Point-of-use devices, such as those installed on a tap or under the sink, will treat only a small portion of the water and are not entirely effective in reducing radon in the household water supply. It is important to maintain home water-treatment units properly. Failure to do so can lead to other water contamination problems. Some homeowners opt for a service contract from the installer to provide for carbon replacement and general system maintenance.

Aeration

Removing radon from water by aeration takes advantage of the fact that radon is readily given off (or volatile) from water to air. Radon in water is removed by passing as much air through the water as efficiently as possible. By venting the now radon-rich air to the outdoors, aeration can remove up to 99.9% of radon from the water. Aeration is practical for central treatment of radon in water (i.e., at a water treatment plant, etc.), but it's expensive for individual households and small public water systems. A household aeration system suitable for high-efficiency radon removal typically costs between $3,000 and $5,000. Special maintenance is required to ensure that waterborne minerals, such as iron and manganese, do not accumulate and foul the aeration system, which may reduce its radon removal efficiency.

Granular Activated Carbon (GAC) Absorption

A second method for treating radon in water is granular activated carbon (GAC) absorption. Water is filtered through granulated carbon (usually in the form of activated charcoal), and radon is attracted onto the surface of the carbon. Maximizing the carbon's surface area and the length of filtration time is crucial to peak radon-removal efficiency. GAC absorption can remove up to 99.9% of radon from water if large amounts of carbon and long contact times are used. Typical removal efficiencies for GAC vary from 50 to 99%. GAC can be used for central treatment schemes for small systems (several hundred users or fewer), but it becomes more expensive for larger systems. GAC is also fairly cost-effective for individual residential wells. If high levels of radon are present, disposing of spent carbon filters may be difficult due to the significant amount of radioactive material present in the filter. Small carbon filters attached to kitchen faucets or under sinks are inadequate for removing radon from the home's drinking water.

Alternatives

An alternative to these active mitigation systems is simple storage. Because radon is a radioactive element that decays over time (Radon-222 has a half-life of 3.8 days), radon levels in water storage tanks will decrease over time. This strategy would probably be most effective for small systems with average radon levels just a bit above the EPA's maximum concentration level.

Another alternative for some private well owners is to connect to an existing community water system having low radon levels. Drinking bottled water alone will not completely eliminate exposure to radon in water, since this strategy does not prevent radon gas from escaping from well water into the indoor air.

More Information

For a more in-depth discussion of these technologies and their associated costs, read the EPA's Health Risk Reduction and Cost Analysis for Radon in Drinking Water. Section 5 of the Federal Register Notice, Costs of Radon Treatment Measures, is particularly helpful in understanding the different technologies.

Quiz #12

1. Before testing for radon in the residential water supply, test the _____.

☐ water
☐ mold
☐ soil
☐ air

2. If the indoor radon level is ____ and the home uses groundwater, test the water.

☐ low
☐ very low
☐ high

3. If the radon level in the air is _____, there is no need to test the water.

☐ high
☐ low

4. T/F: Test results for radon in water are expressed in picocuries of radon per liter of water (pCi/L).

☐ True
☐ False

5. In general, _____ pCi/L of radon in water contributes roughly 1 pCi/L of airborne radon throughout the house.

☐ 10
☐ 10,000
☐ 100,000
☐ 1,000,000

6. If there are 30,000 pCi/L of radon in the water, then _____ pCi/L of the indoor measurement may have come from radon in the water.

☐ 0.30
☐ 3
☐ 30
☐ 10.000

Answer Key is on page 353.

Standards for Inspecting Radon Mitigation Systems

InterNACHI SOP for Inspecting Radon Systems

About Radon and Standards for Inspecting Radon Mitigation Systems

Radon is a radioactive gas that has been found in homes, schools and other buildings around the world. Radon comes from the natural breakdown of uranium in soil and rock, and moves up into the indoor air that people breathe. Radon is the leading cause of lung cancer in non-smokers. Radon mitigation systems reduce radon levels in homes and buildings. Inspection of these systems helps assure that they were installed properly and are performing as designed.

Although this Standard applies to both commercial and residential radon mitigation systems, this standard exceeds the requirements of both InterNACHI's Commercial and Residential Standards of Practices.

Purpose

The purpose of this section is to establish international standards for the inspection of radon mitigation systems. It also provides universal radon mitigation inspection reporting language.

Radon Mitigation System-Specific Definitions

- **active soil-depressurization system:** one or more of the following types of radon mitigation system types involving mechanically driven soil depressurization: sub-slab depressurization; sump (pit) depressurization; drain-tile depressurization; sub-membrane depressurization; hollow-block wall depressurization; and crawlspace depressurization.

- **crawlspace depressurization:** an active radon-mitigation system that lowers the air pressure inside a crawlspace in relation to the rooms adjacent to or above the crawlspace. A fan draws air directly from the air space of the crawlspace and discharges it outside. This type of system is not the best choice because of the great potential for appliance back-drafting and energy loss.

- **defect:** a condition of a radon mitigation system that may have an adverse impact on its performance.

- **depressurization:** a negative pressure created in one area compared to an adjacent area.

- **discharge:** the end of a vent stack pipe open to outside air.

- **drain-tile depressurization:** an active soil-depressurization system whereby a suction point is located at a drain tile.

- **heat-recovery ventilation (HRV) system:** a system that lowers radon levels by using outside air to dilute and pressurize the indoor air. HRV systems are considered active radon mitigation systems.

- **hollow-block wall depressurization:** an active radon mitigation system that depressurizes the open spaces within concrete block foundation walls.

- **inspection:** a non-invasive, visual examination of a radon mitigation system.

- **manifold pipe:** a pipe between a vent stack pipe and suction-point pipe with two or more suction points.

- **radon mitigation system:** any system designed to reduce the radon concentrations of indoor air.

- **radon system piping:** the piping of a passive or active radon mitigation system that is composed of a suction-point pipe, manifold pipe, and vent stack pipe.

- **readily accessible:** a system or component that is, in the judgment of the inspector, capable of being safely observed without the removal of obstacles, detachment, or disengagement of connecting or securing devices, or other unsafe or difficult procedures in order to gain access.

- **sub-membrane depressurization:** an active radon mitigation system that creates low air pressure under a vapor retarder. A common example is when a vapor retarder (polyethylene plastic sheet) is installed over the exposed dirt floor of a crawlspace. The radon fan draws air from below the vapor retarder and sends it outside.

- **sub-slab depressurization (active):** a radon mitigation system that creates low air pressure under a concrete floor using a fan.

- **sub-slab depressurization (passive):** a radon mitigation system that creates low air pressure under a concrete floor without the use of a fan.

- **suction point:** the end of a radon mitigation system that penetrates the slab, wall, vapor barrier, sump cover, or drain tile.

- **sump (pit) depressurization system (active):** a radon mitigation system that has a suction point installed in the sump (pit).

- **vent stack pipe:** a pipe leading from the suction point (in a system with a single suction point) or the manifold pipe (in a system with more than one suction point) to the outside air. In active radon mitigation systems, the radon fan is installed vertically in the vent stack pipe.

For more terminology commonly found in commercial property inspection reports, visit **www.nachi.org/comsop.htm#101**

Goal of Inspection

The goal of the inspection is to provide observations that may indicate that a radon mitigation system was installed improperly, is not performing as designed, or is in need of repair.

Limitations

The inspection is limited to readily accessible and visible portions of the radon mitigation system. The inspection should not be considered all-inclusive or technically exhaustive. It is not a substitute for a radon level measurement.

This standard does not require the inspector to:

- inspect any portion of the system that is not readily accessible and visible.

- activate a system that has been turned off, unplugged, or deactivated.

- measure the radon level.

Optional Add-On Inspection Service

Although InterNACHI's Standards of Practice for Inspecting Commercial Properties and InterNACHI's Standards of Practice for Performing a General Home Inspection do not require the inspector to perform radon mitigation system inspections, one may be offered in conjunction with a complete commercial or residential property inspection, or as a separate, stand-alone inspection service.

VISUAL INSPECTION

Radon Mitigation System Type

The inspector shall describe the radon mitigation system as one of the following types:

- active sub-slab depressurization;
- passive sub-slab depressurization;
- sump (pit) depressurization;
- drain-tile depressurization;
- sub-membrane depressurization;
- hollow-block wall depressurization;
- crawlspace depressurization; or
- heat-recovery ventilation.

Drain-Tile Depressurization Systems

The inspector should inspect drainpipes that extend to daylight for missing devices, such as one-way flow valves, or water traps that prevent outdoor air from entering the sub-slab area.

Sub-Membrane Depressurization Systems

The inspector should inspect the vapor retarder used for sub-membrane depressurization systems (passive or active) for seams that are lapped less than 12 inches, and edges that are not sealed to the walls, posts, or other penetrations.

Hollow-Block Wall Depressurization Systems

The inspector should inspect hollow-block walls for cracks, openings, and open top-courses.

Crawlspace Depressurization Systems

The inspector should inspect the crawlspace for the presence of asbestos-like material and combustible fuel-served appliances located within the crawlspace or in spaces adjacent to the crawlspace.

Heat-Recovery Ventilation (HRV) Systems

The inspector should inspect the area around the HRV system for the presence of asbestos-like material.

Piping and Fittings

The inspector should inspect for:

- penetrations of pipes or ducts that penetrate a firewall or other fire resistance-rated wall or floor not protected in accordance with applicable building, mechanical, fire, or electrical codes;

- submersible pumps not used in systems that use sump pits as the suction point for active soil depressurization if sump pumps are needed;
- joints and connections that are not permanently sealed with adhesives;
- joints and connections that are not airtight;
- attic and external runs subject to sub-freezing that are not protected to prevent the risk of vent pipe freeze-up;
- piping that is not PVC, ABS, or downspout (outside);
- piping subjected to weather or physical damage that is not Schedule 40;
- pipe and fitting connections of different materials;
- piping that isn't solid and rigid;
- reducers that are installed in the direction of air flow;
- radon vent pipes blocking access to any areas requiring maintenance or inspection;
- radon vent pipes not designed with removable or flexible couplings to facilitate removal of the sump pit cover for sump pump maintenance;
- radon vent pipes not installed in a configuration that ensures that any rain water or condensation within the pipes drains downward into the ground beneath the slab or soil-gas retarder membrane; and
- a missing one-way flow valve, water trap, or other control device installed in or on the discharge line to prevent outside air from entering the system while allowing water to flow out of the system when a radon mitigation system is designed to draw soil gas from a perimeter drain tile loop that discharges water through a drain line to daylight or to a soak-away.

Piping Supports

The inspector shall inspect for:

- hangers, strapping, or other supports that inadequately secure the vent material;
- existing plumbing pipes, ducts, or mechanical equipment used to support or secure a radon vent pipe;
- supports installed more than 6 feet apart on horizontal runs;
- supports installed more than 8 feet apart on vertical runs; and
- pipes not supported or not secured in a permanent manner so as to prevent their downward movement to the bottom of suction pits or sump pits, or into the soil beneath an aggregate layer under a slab to prevent blockage of air flow into the bottom of the radon vent pipes.

Materials

The inspector shall inspect for:

- vent pipes not made of Schedule 20 PVC, ABS, or equivalent;
- vent pipes used in garages and in other internal and external locations subject to weathering or physical damage not made of Schedule 40 piping or its equivalent;
- vent pipe fittings in a mitigation system that are not of the same material as the vent pipes;
- cleaning solvents and adhesives to join plastic pipes and fittings that are not recommended by the manufacturers of the pipe material;

- improperly used caulks and sealants at any cracks in slabs or other openings around penetrations of the slab and foundation walls;

- non-shrink mortar, grout, or expanding foam not being used when sealing holes for plumbing rough-in or other large openings in slabs and foundation walls that are below the ground surface;

- sump pit covers not made of durable plastic;

- sump pit covers not providing an airtight seal;

- penetrations of sump covers that are not airtight;

- plastic sheeting installed in crawlspaces as soil-gas retarders that are not a minimum of 6-mil polyethylene or equivalent material; and

- any wood used in attaching soil-gas retarder membranes to walls or piers not pressure-treated or naturally resistant to decay and termites.

Point of Discharge for Fan-Powered Soil Depressurization and Block-Wall Depressurization Systems

The inspector should inspect for:

- the point of discharge being below the eaves of the roof;

- the point of discharge being less than 10 feet above ground level;

- the point of discharge being less than 10 feet away from any window, door, or other opening into conditioned spaces of the structure that is less than 2 feet below the exhaust point; and

- the point of discharge being less than 10 feet away from any opening into an adjacent building.

Radon Fan

The inspector should inspect for:

- radon fans not designed or not sealed to reduce the potential for leakage of soil gas from the fan housing;

- radon fans not sized to provide the pressure difference and air flow characteristics necessary to achieve the radon reduction goals established;

- radon fans installed in the conditioned space of a building, in any basement, crawlspace, or other interior location directly beneath the conditioned spaces of a building;

- radon fans installed in attics that are suitable for occupancy;

- radon fans installed in attached garages beneath conditioned spaces;

- radon fans installed underground;

- radon fans installed in a configuration that allows condensation to build up in the fan housing;

- radon fans that are not mounted vertically;

- radon fans mounted on the exterior of buildings that are not rated for outdoor use or not installed in a watertight protective housing;

- radon fans that are not mounted and secured in a manner that minimizes transfer of vibration to the structural framing of the building;

- radon fans that are not installed using removable couplings or flexible connections to facilitate maintenance and future replacement; and

• radon fans used in crawlspace pressurization or building pressurization that do not have removable screens or filters on the fan intakes to prevent ingestion of debris or personal injury.

Suction Pit for Sub-Slab Depressurization Systems

The inspector should inspect for:

• an inadequate amount of excavated material from the area immediately below the slab penetration point of the system's vent pipes.

Sealing

The inspector should inspect for:

• uncovered or unsealed sump pits that permit entry of soil gas or that would allow conditioned air to be drawn into a sub-slab depressurization system;

• openings around radon vent pipe penetrations of the slab, foundation wall, or crawlspace soil-gas retarder membrane that are not cleaned, prepared and sealed in a permanent, airtight manner;

• open or unsealed openings in the tops of walls and all accessible openings or cracks in the interior surfaces of the walls, where a block-wall depressurization system is used to mitigate radon;

• openings, perimeter channel drains, or cracks where the slab meets the foundation wall that are not sealed;

• seams and joints in the baseboard of baseboard-type suction systems that are not joined and not sealed;

• seams in soil-gas retarder membranes used in sub-membrane depressurization system that are not overlapped at least 12 inches and not sealed;

• open and unsealed access doors and other openings between the basement and the adjacent crawlspace where the crawlspace has been confirmed as a source of radon entry; and

• open and unsealed openings and cracks in floors above the crawlspace that would permit conditioned air to pass out of the living spaces when crawlspace depressurization is used.

Electrical

The inspector should inspect for:

• wiring that does not conform to provisions of the National Electrical Code (NEC) and local building codes;

• wiring located in or chased through ducting;

• cord and plug assemblies supplying power to radon fans that are more than 6 feet in length;

• cord and plug assemblies supplying power to radon fans that pass through walls, floors or ceilings, or that are concealed within building components;

• radon fans installed on the exterior of the building that are not hard-wired into an electrical circuit;

• radon fans used outdoors that are plugged;

• a missing electrical disconnect switch or a missing circuit breaker for radon mitigation system fan circuits;

- a means of disconnect not in sight of its radon fan;

- missing grounded receptacles (required within 6 feet of radon fans installed under roofs);

- missing GFCI receptacles (required within 6 feet of radon fans installed above roofs); and

- missing electrical junction boxes (required within 6 feet of radon fan locations of both active and passive systems).

Drain

The inspector should inspect for:

- condensate drainpipes that are not directed into condensate pumps, not directed into trapped floor drains, or do not have 6-inch or greater standing water-trap seals;

- unsealed perimeter (channel or French) drains; and

- a sump pit (used for protection or relief from excess surface water) that has a cover not recessed and not fitted with a trapped drain.

HVAC

The inspector should inspect for:

- modifications to an existing HVAC system proposed to mitigate elevated levels of radon that are reviewed and approved by a qualified contractor;

- foundation vents (used to reduce indoor radon levels by increasing natural ventilation) that are closable;

- heat-recovery ventilation (HRV) systems that are installed in rooms that contain friable asbestos;

- supply and exhaust ports of heat-recovery ventilation systems installed less than 12 feet apart; and

- confirmation by the contractor that the incoming and outgoing flow from heat-recovery ventilation systems are balanced.

Monitoring and Labeling

The inspector should inspect for:

- a missing mechanism to monitor performance of an active soil depressurization system and block-wall depressurization system and to warn of system failure;

- electrical radon mitigation system monitors installed on switched circuits;

- electrical radon mitigation system monitors not designed to re-set automatically when power is restored after failure;

- manometer-type pressure gauges not clearly marked to indicate the range of pressure readings that existed when the system was initially activated;

- a missing system description label placed on the mitigation system;

- a missing system description label placed on the electric service entrance panel;

- a system description label that is not legible from at least 3 feet away;

- a system description label that does not include all of the following information:

  ◦ "Radon Reduction System";

  ◦ the installer's name and contact information;

  ◦ the date of the installation; and

  ◦ an advisory that the building should be tested for radon at least every two years;

- a missing system description label on each floor level of all exposed and visible interior radon mitigation system vent-pipe sections reading "Radon Reduction System";

- missing identification of the circuit breaker controlling the circuit on which the radon vent fan and system-failure warning devices operate; and

- missing labels on the plastic vapor barrier (if installed).

Sample Reporting Language

Radon Mitigation System Inspection Report

Client: _____

Location of radon-mitigation system: _____

This inspection was performed in substantial compliance with InterNACHI's *International Standards of Practice for Inspecting Radon Mitigation Systems.* It is designed to provide an indication as to whether or not the radon mitigation system was installed improperly, is not performing as designed, or is in need of repair. It is not a substitute for a radon level measurement.

Radon is a radioactive gas that has been found in homes, schools and buildings around the world. Radon comes from the natural breakdown of uranium in soil and rock, and moves up into the indoor air that people breathe. Radon is the leading cause of lung cancer in non-smokers. Radon-mitigation systems reduce radon levels in homes and buildings.

The inspector noted that the radon-mitigation system type was:

____ active sub-slab depressurization;

____ passive sub-slab depressurization;

____ sump (pit) depressurization (active);

____ drain-tile depressurization;

____ sub-membrane depressurization;

____ hollow-block wall depressurization;

____ crawlspace depressurization; or

____ heat-recovery ventilation.

Drain-Tile Depressurization System

____ The inspector noted that the drain pipes that extend to daylight were missing devices, such as one-way flow valves or water traps, that prevent outdoor air from entering the sub-slab area.

Sub-Membrane Depressurization System

____ The inspector noted that the vapor retarder used for the sub-membrane depressurization system (passive or active) had seams that were lapped less than 12 inches, or edges that were not sealed to the walls, posts or other penetrations.

Hollow-Block Wall Depressurization System

____ The inspector noted that the hollow-block walls had cracks, openings or open top-courses.

Crawlspace Depressurization System

___ The inspector noted that the crawlspace had the presence of asbestos-like material, or combustible fuel-served appliances located within the crawlspace or spaces adjacent to the crawlspace.

Heat-Recovery Ventilation (HRV) System

___ The inspector noted the area around the HRV system had the presence of asbestos-like material.

Piping and Fittings

___ The inspector noted piping that is not PVC, ABS or downspout (outside).

___ The inspector noted piping subjected to weather or physical damage that was not Schedule 40.

___ The inspector noted pipe and fitting connections of different materials.

___ The inspector noted piping that wasn't solid or rigid.

___ The inspector noted reducers that were installed in the direction of air flow.

___ The inspector noted piping that was not continually sloped toward the suction point(s).

Piping Supports

___ The inspector noted supports installed more than 6 feet apart on horizontal runs.

___ The inspector noted supports installed more than 8 feet apart on vertical runs.

Discharges

___ The inspector noted discharges less than 10 feet above ground level.

___ The inspector noted discharges less than 6 inches above a roof edge, rake or gable that its stack passed by.

___ The inspector noted discharges that exhausted less than 12 inches above a roof surface through which its stack pipe passed.

___ The inspector noted discharges that exhausted below the roof surface of the highest roof of the building.

___ The inspector noted discharges within 2 feet directly above or less than 10 feet from a window, door or opening.

Radon Fan

___ The inspector noted interior radon fans installed in occupied or conditioned spaces.

___ The inspector noted exterior radon fans installed underground.

___ The inspector noted radon fans that were not connected to the piping with removable couplings or flexible connections.

___ The inspector noted radon fans that were not mounted vertically.

Condensate Bypass

___ The inspector noted missing condensate bypass mechanisms on a system in a cold climate.

Electrical

___ The inspector noted cord and plug assemblies supplying power to radon fans that were more than 6 feet in length.

___ The inspector noted cord and plug assemblies supplying power to radon fans that passed through walls, floors or ceilings, or were concealed within building components.

___ The inspector noted missing means of disconnect, such as a dedicated, labeled electrical breaker or switch, or an electrical plug cord.

___ The inspector noted means of disconnects not in sight of their radon fans.

___ The inspector noted missing grounded receptacles (required within 6 feet of radon fans installed under roofs).

___ The inspector noted missing GFCI receptacles (required within 6 feet of radon fans installed above roofs).

___ The inspector noted missing electrical junction boxes (required within 6 feet of radon fan locations of both active and passive systems).

Condensate Drainpipes

___ The inspector noted condensate drainpipes that were not directed into condensate pumps, not directed into trapped floor drains, or did not have 6-inch or greater standing water-trap seals.

Monitoring Device

___ The inspector noted missing air-flow or pressure-monitoring devices, which are required to provide easily visible or audible indication of system failure or performance in active systems.

Labeling

___ The inspector noted missing piping labels (required on each floor to identify piping as part of a radon system).

___ The inspector noted missing labels on the plastic vapor barrier (if installed).

___ The inspector noted labels that are illegible from a distance of 3 feet.

___ The inspector noted piping or vapor barrier labels that failed to display one the following: "Radon-Mitigation System," "Radon-Reduction System," "Radon System" or "Radon-Removal System."

___ The inspector noted a missing main label that contains the mitigator's name and contact information, date of installation, and a recommendation to test the building for radon every two years.

___ The inspector noted a missing "Radon," "Radon Fan" or "Radon System" label at the disconnect breaker controlling the electrical circuit to the radon fan.

This inspection was performed by: _____

Signature: _____

Code of Ethics

The International Association of Certified Home Inspectors (InterNACHI) promotes a high standard of professionalism, business ethics, and inspection procedures. InterNACHI members subscribe to the following Code of Ethics in the course of their business.

I. Duty to the Public

1. The InterNACHI member shall abide by the Code of Ethics and substantially follow the InterNACHI Standards of Practice.

2. The InterNACHI member shall not engage in any practices that could be damaging to the public or bring discredit to the home inspection industry.

3. The InterNACHI member shall be fair, honest, impartial, and act in good faith in dealing with the public.

4. The InterNACHI member shall not discriminate in any business activities on the basis of race, color, religion, sex, national origin, familial status, sexual orientation, or handicap, and shall comply with all federal, state and local laws concerning discrimination.

5. The InterNACHI member shall be truthful regarding their services and qualifications.

6. The InterNACHI member shall not:

    a. have any disclosed or undisclosed conflict of interest with the client;

    b. accept or offer any disclosed or undisclosed commissions, rebates, profits, or other benefit from real estate agents, brokers, or any third parties having financial interest in the sale of the property; or

    c. offer or provide any disclosed or undisclosed financial compensation directly or indirectly to any real estate agent, real estate broker, or real estate company for referrals or for inclusion on lists of preferred and/or affiliated inspectors or inspection companies.

7. The InterNACHI member shall not release any information about the inspection or the client to a third party unless doing so is necessary to protect the safety of others, to comply with a law or statute, or both of the following conditions are met:

    a. the client has been made explicitly aware of what information will be released, to whom, and for what purpose, and;

    b. the client has provided explicit, prior written consent for the release of his/her information.

8. The InterNACHI member shall always act in the interests of the client unless doing so violates a law, statute, or this Code of Ethics.

9. The InterNACHI member shall use a written contract that specifies the services to be performed, limitations of services, and fees.

10. The InterNACHI member shall comply with all government rules and licensing requirements of the jurisdiction where s/he conducts business.

11. The InterNACHI member shall not perform or offer to perform, for an additional fee, any repairs or associated services to the structure for which the member or member's company has prepared a home inspection report for a period of 12 months. This provision shall not include services to components and/or systems that are not included in the InterNACHI

Standards of Practice.

II. Duty to Continue Education

1. The InterNACHI member shall comply with InterNACHI's current Continuing Education requirements.

2. The InterNACHI member shall pass InterNACHI's Online Inspector Exam once every three years.

III. Duty to the Profession and to InterNACHI

1. The InterNACHI member shall strive to improve the home inspection industry by sharing his/her lessons and/or experiences for the benefit of all. This does not preclude the member from copyrighting or marketing his/her expertise to other Inspectors or the public in any manner permitted by law.

2. The InterNACHI member shall assist the InterNACHI leadership in disseminating and publicizing the benefits of InterNACHI membership.

3. The InterNACHI member shall not engage in any act or practice that could be deemed damaging, seditious or destructive to InterNACHI, fellow InterNACHI members, InterNACHI employees, leadership or directors. Accusations of a member acting or deemed in violation of such rules shall trigger a review by the Ethics Committee for possible sanctions and/or expulsion from InterNACHI.

4. The InterNACHI member shall abide by InterNACHI's current membership requirements.

5. The InterNACHI member shall abide by InterNACHI's current message board rules.

Members of other associations are welcome to join InterNACHI, but a requirement of membership is that InterNACHI must be given equal or greater prominence in their marketing materials (brochures and websites) compared to other associations of membership.

Quiz #13

1. T/F: The InterNACHI member shall not engage in any practices that could be damaging to the public or bring discredit to the home inspection industry.

    ☐ True
    ☐ False

2. T/F: The InterNACHI member shall not discriminate in any business activities on the basis of race, color, religion, sex, national origin, familial status, sexual orientation, or handicap, and shall comply with all federal, state and local laws concerning discrimination.

    ☐ True
    ☐ False

3. T/F: The InterNACHI member shall not have any disclosed or undisclosed conflicts of interest with the client.

    ☐ True
    ☐ False

4. T/F: The InterNACHI member shall not accept or offer any disclosed or undisclosed commissions, rebates, profits, or other benefit from real estate agents, brokers, or any third parties having financial interest in the sale of the property.

    ☐ True
    ☐ False

5. T/F: The InterNACHI member shall not release any information about the inspection or the client to a third party unless doing so is necessary to protect the safety of others, to comply with a law or statute, or for other specific conditions as specified in the Code of Ethics.

    ☐ True
    ☐ False

6. The InterNACHI member shall not perform or offer to perform, for an additional fee, any repairs or associated services to the structure for which the member or member's company has prepared a home inspection report for a period of _____.

    ☐ six months
    ☐ two years
    ☐ 12 months

Answer Key is on page 354.

Appendix I: Answer Keys

Answer Key for Quiz #1

1. **Atoms** are the extremely small particles of which we and everything around us are made.

2. If one atom were the size of the Houston Astrodome, its nucleus would be roughly the size of a **pea**.

3. T/F: The balance of the forces in the nucleus of an atom determines whether a nucleus is stable or unstable (radioactive).
Answer: **True**

4. As an unstable nucleus emits radiation as it disintegrates, the radionuclide transforms to different nuclides, and this process is called **radioactive decay**.

5. A **decay chain** refers to the series of transformations that a given radionuclide will undergo, as well as the kind of radiation it emits, which are characteristic of the radionuclide.

6. Radioactive half-life is the time required for the disintegration of **one-half** of the radioactive atoms that are present when measurement starts.

7. **Radiation** is the energy that is released as particles or rays during radioactive decay.

8. **Radioactivity** is the property of an atom that describes spontaneous changes in its nucleus that create a different nuclide, and these changes usually happen as emissions of alpha or beta particles, and often gamma rays.

9. Radiation that falls within the "**ionizing radiation**" range has enough energy to remove tightly bound electrons from atoms, thus creating ions, and this is the type of radiation that people usually think of as 'radiation.'

10. **Alpha** particles include two protons and two neutrons.

11. We're really concerned with the **alpha** particles, because they can be stopped by a sheet of paper where they release their energy.

12. T/F: Radon is a light gas and tends to collect in high areas of houses such as attics.
Answer: **False**

13. Some decay products of radon emit beta particles, but its alpha-emitting decay products pose a much **greater** health risk.

14. **Gamma** photons can pass through many kinds of materials, including human tissue.

15. Most naturally occurring radioactive materials and many fission products undergo radioactive decay through a series of **transformations** (loss of particles or electromagnetic energy from an unstable nucleus) rather than in a single step.

16. **RDPs** are the source of cell damage in the lungs.

17. T/F: Radon gas tastes like sulphur.
Answer: **False**

18. T/F: If RDPs plate out on a wall, they are a hazard.
    Answer: <u>**False**</u>

19. If the radon concentration is 75 pCi/L, and the decay-product concentration is 0.3 WL, the equilibrium ratio would be calculated as follows: ER = (0.3) x (100) ÷ 75 = <u>**0.4**</u>.

20. T/F: The action-level limit of 0.02 WL corresponds to the derived radon concentration of 4 pCi/L when the equilibrium ratio is 50%.
    Answer: <u>**True**</u>

21. The average indoor radon level is <u>**1.3**</u> pCi/L.

22. If a gallon container held air with 4 pCi/L, there would be about 4 (quarts per gallon) multiplied by 4 (pCi/L) multiplied by 2.22 disintegrations per minutes, or about <u>**35.2**</u> disintegrations per minutes of radon atoms in the container.

23. If there are 100 atoms of a radionuclide that has a half-life of one minute, there will be one-half that number, or <u>**50**</u> atoms of the original radionuclide left one minute later.

24. T/F: If you have an amount of radon with a half-life of 3.8 days, by the end of 3.8 days, you will have half as much.
    Answer: <u>**True**</u>

Answer Key for Quiz #2

1. T/F: Radon is a worldwide health risk in homes.
   Answer: <u>**True**</u>

2. Radon is the <u>**second**</u> leading cause of lung cancer after smoking in many countries.

3. T/F: The World Health Organization (WHO) says radon causes up to 15% of lung cancers worldwide.
   Answer: <u>**True**</u>

4. T/F: There exists a known threshold concentration below which radon exposure presents no risk.
   Answer: <u>**False**</u>

5. Most of the radon ingested in water is excreted within <u>**hours**</u>.

6. T/F: Since alpha particles are more massive and more highly charged than other types of ionizing radiation, they are more damaging to living tissue.
   Answer: <u>**True**</u>

7. T/F: By breaking the electron bonds that hold molecules together, radiation can damage human DNA, the inherited compound that controls the structure and function of cells.
   Answer: <u>**True**</u>

8. T/F: Evidence exists that shows a threshold of exposure below which radon levels are harmless.
   Answer: <u>**False**</u>

9. T/F: Radon is a known human lung carcinogen and is the largest source of radiation exposure and risk to the general public.
   Answer: <u>**True**</u>

Answer Key for Quiz #3

1. T/F: Radon-222 is the radioactive decay product of radium-226, which is found at low concentrations in almost all rock and soil.
Answer: **True**

2. T/F: All homes have some type of radon-entry pathway.
Answer: **True**

3. A difference in **air pressure** between the basement or crawlspace and the surrounding soil draws radon into the home.

4. T/F: Field research has shown that attempting to seal all of the openings in a foundation is both impractical and ineffective as a stand-alone technique.
Answer: **True**

5. The objective of a sub-slab or sub-membrane depressurization system is to create a **vacuum** beneath the foundation, which is greater in strength than the vacuum imposed on the soil by the house itself.

6. T/F: Radon gas is approximately seven times heavier than air.
Answer: **True**

7. Because radon is a chemically inert (unreactive) gas, it can move **easily** through rock and soil and arrive at the surface.

8. We also estimate that about 1 in **15** homes nationwide have levels at or above the level of 4 pCi/L, the level at which EPA recommends taking action to reduce concentrations.

9. T/F: You can see, feel, smell, and taste radon.
Answer: **False**

Answer Key for Quiz #4

1. T/F: The United States Environmental Protection Agency (EPA) recommends that all homes be tested for radon.
Answer: **True**

2. T/F: Even though the biological effects of radon are caused by RDPs, radon gas is usually measured, rather than RDPs.
Answer: **True**

3. The most common measurement method is **time-integrated sampling**, where a device is exposed to the radon gas for a measured amount of time.

4. For short-term testing devices, **closed**-house conditions must be maintained during the testing period.

5. Short-term testing devices should be placed at least **20** inches off the floor, 4 inches from other objects, 12 inches from walls, and 12 inches from the ceiling.

6. The **charcoal liquid scintillation** method is very similar to the activated charcoal detector in that it employs a small vial of activated charcoal for sampling the radon.

7. T/F: Organizations that provide consultant services, or place or retrieve devices, should review the protocol options and the client's needs, and inform the client of the building's and test period conditions necessary for conducting valid measurements.
   Answer: **True**

8. All organizations providing measurement services with passive devices should conduct spiked measurements at a rate of **3** per 100 measurements, with a minimum of three per year, and a maximum required of six per month.

9. **Duplicate** measurements for both active and passive detectors should be side-by-side measurements made in at least 10% of the total number of measurement locations, or 50 each month, whichever is smaller.

10. **Accuracy** is the degree of closeness of a measured or calculated quantity to its actual or true value.

11. T/F: If the occupants' living patterns change and they begin occupying a lower level of their home (such as a basement), the home should be re-tested on that level.
    Answer: **True**

Answer Key for Quiz #5

1. T/F: InterNACHI recommends that initial measurements for non-real estate testing be short-term tests performed under closed-building conditions.
   Answer: **True**

2. InterNACHI recommends testing devices for initial measurements be placed in the **lowest** lived-in level of the home.

3. If the short-term measurement result is equal to or greater than **4** picocuries per liter (pCi/L), or 0.02 working levels (WL), a follow-up measurement is recommended.

4. T/F: Circulating fans should be operating in the test area.
   Answer: **False**

5. If there are no doors or windows to the outdoors in the immediate testing area, the measurement should not be taken within **1 foot** of the exterior wall of the building.

6. Closed-building conditions should be maintained for **12** hours prior to the initiation of measurements lasting less than four days, as well as recommended prior to measurements lasting up to a week.

7. Follow-up testing should be conducted in **the same** location as the first measurement.

8. T/F: If the average of the initial and second short-term results is equal to or greater than 4 pCi/L, radon mitigation is recommended.
   Answer: **True**

Answer Key for Quiz #6

1. T/F: During a real estate test, sequential tests should be conducted under conditions that are as similar as possible, in the same location, and using similar devices and durations.
   Answer: **True**

2. T/F: The results of both measurements of a sequential test should be reported, and the average of the two results should be used to determine the need for mitigation.
Answer: **True**

3. When one measurement result is greater than 4 pCi/L and one measurement result is less than 4 pCi/L, then if the higher result is **twice (or more)** the lower result, then the two results are not within a factor of two, and a re-test should be conducted.

4. Before starting a short-term test lasting less than four days, make sure the active system has been operating for at least **24 hours** before beginning the test.

5. For a real estate test, conduct the radon test for minimum of **48** hours.

6. False **low** results have been primarily associated with testing during a real estate transaction, although they also happen when the occupants of the dwelling are not properly informed about the necessary test conditions.

7. T/F: Prevention interference can be best accomplished by informing the client that the tester is using interference-detecting techniques.
Answer: **True**

Answer Key for Quiz #7

1. **QA or quality assurance** is defined as all activities required to provide the evidence needed to establish confidence that data provided are of the required precision and accuracy.

2. The EPA defines **QA** as an integrated system or program of activities involving planning, quality control, quality assessment, reporting and quality improvement to ensure that a product or service meets defined standards of quality.

3. T/F: There are many quality-control measurements that are performed to assess the quality of procured material and equipment, the continued performance of instruments and procedures, estimated errors of imprecision and bias, and contributions of field and laboratory background.
Answer: **True**

4. The establishment of a QA program **requires** a QA officer within the organization to supervise and, as appropriate, carry out the monitoring, recordkeeping, statistical techniques, and other functions required to maintain high-quality data.

5. Organizations should assure that all work affecting quality of results (such as handling, storing, and analyzing devices) be prescribed in clear and complete written instructions, which are known as **SOPs or standard operating procedures**.

6. The term **calibration** refers to the process of determining the response of an instrument (or measurement system) to a series of known values over the range of the instrument (or measurement system).

7. **Systematic errors** refer to errors that occur consistently and cause a consistently high or low bias in the result.

8. **Accuracy** is the closeness of agreement between a measurement result (or the average of more than one result) and an accepted reference value.

Answer Key for Quiz #8

1. T/F: Short-term measurements lasting 90 days or less should be made under closed-building conditions.
Answer: **True**

2. To the extent reasonable, all windows, outside vents and external doors should be closed (except for normal entrance and exit) for **12** hours prior to and during the measurement period.

3. T/F: The CW detector should be programmed to run continuously, recording the periodic integrated WL and, when possible, the total integrated average WL.
Answer: **True**

4. T/F: An alpha track (AT) detector consists of a small piece of plastic or film enclosed in a container with a filter-covered opening or similar design for excluding radon decay products.
Answer: **True**

5. T/F: With the EC test, the amount of voltage reduction is directly related to the average radon concentration and the duration of the exposure period.
Answer: **True**

6. Activated-charcoal adsorption (AC) devices are passive devices requiring **no power** to function.

7. A measurement with an LS device typically lasts **two to seven days** days.

8. T/F: A UT detector consists of a piece of cellulose nitrate film packaged in a shielded container.
Answer: **True**

Answer Key for Quiz #9

1. T/F: The three types of radon progeny (RP) sampling systems include a sampling pump and the detector assembly.
Answer: **True**

2. The RP measurement **should not be made** if the occupant will be moving during the measurement period.

3. **Prior to** installation in the building, the pump should be checked to ensure that it is operable and capable of maintaining a uniform flow through the detector assembly.

4. When making grab measurements, it is especially important to conform to closed-building conditions for **12 hours before** the measurement.

5. T/F: The equipment required for radon decay product concentration determination by GW consists of an air sampling pump capable of maintaining a flow rate of 2 to 25 liters per minute through the selected filter.
Answer: **True**

6. **Before and after each measurement**, the continuous radon (CR) monitor should be tested carefully, according to manufacturer's directions, to verify that the correct input parameters and the unit's clock or timer are set properly, and to verify the operation of the pump.

Answer Key for Quiz #10

1. The purpose of the Radon Mitigation Standards (RMS) is to provide radon mitigation contractors with uniform standards that will ensure quality and effectiveness in the design, installation and evaluation of radon mitigation systems in detached and attached residential buildings **three stories or fewer** in height.

2. T/F: Because of the wide variation in building design, size, operation and use, the RMS does not include detailed guidance on how to select the most appropriate mitigation strategy for a given building.
Answer: **True**

3. T/F: Post-mitigation radon levels shall be at or below the EPA's current action level of 4 pCi/L.
Answer: **True**

4. **Back-drafting** is a condition where the normal movement of combustion products up a flue, resulting from the buoyant forces on the hot gases, is reversed, so that the combustion products can enter the house.

5. **Block-wall depressurization** is a radon mitigation technique that depressurizes the void network within a block-wall foundation by drawing air from inside the wall and venting it to the outside.

6. **Stack effect** is the overall upward movement of air inside a building that results from heated air rising and escaping through openings in the building envelope, thus causing indoor air pressure in the lower portions of a building to be lower than the pressure in the soil beneath or surrounding the building foundation.

7. T/F: It is recommended that during the building investigation, contractors routinely perform diagnostic tests to evaluate the existence of, or the potential for, back-drafting of natural-draft combustion appliances.
Answer: **True**

8. T/F: Contractors shall comply with OSHA, state and local standards and regulations relating to worker safety and occupational radon exposure.
Answer: **True**

9. T/F: All joints and connections in radon mitigation systems using plastic vent pipes are required to be permanently sealed with adhesives.
Answer: **True**

10. T/F: Radon vent pipes shall be fastened to the structure of the building with hangers, strapping / or other supports that will adequately secure the vent material.
Answer: **True**

11. To prevent re-entrainment of radon, the point of discharge from vents of fan-powered soil depressurization and block-wall depressurization systems shall be **10** feet or more from any window, door or other opening into conditioned spaces of the structure that is less than 2 feet below the exhaust point.

12. Whenever possible, fans should be installed in **vertical** runs of the vent pipe.

13. T/F: At a minimum, all plastic vent pipes in mitigation systems shall be made of Schedule 40 PVC, ABS or equivalent piping material.
Answer: **False**

14. Plastic sheeting installed in crawlspaces as soil-gas retarders shall be a minimum of <u>6</u>-mil polyethylene, or equivalent flexible material.

15. Upon completion of radon mitigation work, a test of the mitigation system's effectiveness shall be conducted no sooner than <u>24</u> hours nor later than <u>30</u> days following completion and activation of the mitigation system.

Answer Key for Quiz #11

1. T/F: A layer of gas-permeable material shall be placed under all concrete slabs and other floor systems that directly contact the ground and are within the walls of the living spaces of the building to facilitate installation of a sub-slab depressurization system, if needed.
Answer: **True**

2. A minimum <u>6</u>-mil (or 3-mil cross-laminated) polyethylene or equivalent flexible sheeting material shall be placed on top of the gas-permeable layer prior to pouring the slab, or placing the floor assembly to serve as a soil-gas retarder by bridging any cracks that develop in the slab or floor assembly, and to prevent concrete from entering the void spaces in aggregate-base material.

3. T/F: Channel-type (or French) drains, if used, shall be sealed with backer rods and an elastomeric joint sealant in a manner that retains the channel feature and does not interfere with the effectiveness of the drain as a water-control system.
Answer: **True**

4. T/F: Joints, cracks, and other openings around all penetrations of both exterior and interior surfaces of masonry block or wood foundation walls below the ground surface shall be sealed with an elastomeric sealant that provides an airtight seal.
Answer: **True**

5. Openings around chimney flues, plumbing chases, pipes and fixtures, ductwork, electrical wires and fixtures, elevator shafts, and other air passages that penetrate the conditioned envelope of the building shall be **closed or sealed using sealant or fire-resistant materials approved in local codes for such application** .

Answer Key for Quiz #12

1. Before testing for radon in the residential water supply, test the **air**.

2. If the indoor radon level is **high** and the home uses groundwater, test the water.

3. If the radon level in the air is **low**, there is no need to test the water.

4. T/F: Test results for radon in water are expressed in picocuries of radon per liter of water (pCi/L).
Answer: **True**

5. In general, **10,000** pCi/L of radon in water contributes roughly 1 pCi/L of airborne radon throughout the house.

6. If there are 30,000 pCi/L of radon in the water, then **3** pCi/L of the indoor measurement may have come from radon in the water.

Answer Key for Quiz #13

1. T/F: The InterNACHI member shall not engage in any practices that could be damaging to the public or bring discredit to the home inspection industry.
Answer: **True**

2. T/F: The InterNACHI member shall not discriminate in any business activities on the basis of race, color, religion, sex, national origin, familial status, sexual orientation, or handicap, and shall comply with all federal, state and local laws concerning discrimination.
Answer: **True**

3. T/F: The InterNACHI member shall not have any disclosed or undisclosed conflicts of interest with the client.
Answer: **True**

4. T/F: The InterNACHI member shall not accept or offer any disclosed or undisclosed commissions, rebates, profits, or other benefit from real estate agents, brokers, or any third parties having financial interest in the sale of the property.
Answer: **True**

5. T/F: The InterNACHI member shall not release any information about the inspection or the client to a third party unless doing so is necessary to protect the safety of others, to comply with a law or statute, or for other specific conditions as specified in the Code of Ethics.
Answer: **True**

6. The InterNACHI member shall not perform or offer to perform, for an additional fee, any repairs or associated services to the structure for which the member or member's company has prepared a home inspection report for a period of **12 months**.

Notes

Notes

Notes

Notes

EDUCATION & TRAINING BOOKS

Whether you're new to the business, an inspector seeking more information, or a veteran of the industry looking to expand your knowledge, these official InterNACHI publications will help you become the best inspector you can be.

We Offer the Following Education & Training Books:

- **How to Inspect the Exterior**
  Item Number: 0094

- **How to Perform Deck Inspections**
  Item Number: 0029

- **Residential Plumbing Overview**
  Item Number: 0064

- **Inspecting HVAC Systems**
  Item Number: 0061

- **Safe Practices for the Home Inspector**
  Item Number: 0038

- **Inspecting the Attic, Insulation, Ventilation & Interior**
  Item Number: 0109

- **How to Perform Electrical Inspections**
  Item Number: 0023

- **How to Inspect Pools & Spas**
  Item Number: 0076

- **How to Perform Roof Inspections**
  Item Number: 0042

- **How to Perform a Mold Inspection**
  Item Number: 0022

- **How to Perform Radon Inspections**
  Item Number: 0028

- **Inspecting Foundation Walls and Piers**
  Item Number: 0065

- **25 Standards Every Inspector Should Know**
  Item Number: 0037

- **How to Inspect for Moisture Intrusion**
  Item Number: 0073

- **International Standards of Practice for Inspecting Commercial Properties**
  Item Number: 0016

- **Structural Issues for Home Inspectors**
  Item Number: 0059

The purpose of these publications is to provide accurate and useful information for home inspectors in order to perform an inspection of the various systems at a residential property. They also serve as study aids for InterNACHI's online courses, as well as reference manuals for on the job.

Find these books plus more tools to grow your inspection business at www.InspectorOutlet.com

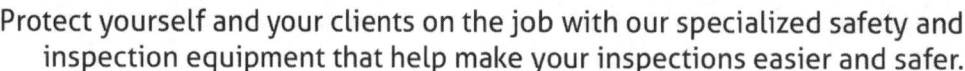